AWAKENING THE WILD WITCH

IRIS BEAGLEHOLE

Published by Te Ra Aroha Press

Cuba St, Wellington, New Zealand

CONTENTS

WELCOME

"The doors to the world of the wild Self are few but precious. If you have a deep scar, that is a door, if you have an old, old story, that is a door. If you love the sky and the water so much you almost cannot bear it, that is a door. If you yearn for a deeper life, a full life, a sane life, that is a door." — Clarissa Pinkola Estés, *Women Who Run With the Wolves*

Welcome to a new step in your journey. I believe it's no accident that you are here, right now. Perhaps you are feeling stuck or ready for something new in your life; perhaps you are already in the midst of chaotic change and looking for tools to help you navigate. In my own life, I've always found books at the right time – just when I absolutely needed to read them.

This book is an invitation to go deeper into your own wild magic – to awaken to your power. My reason for writing this book is for it to find you, in exactly the right time – to share what I've spent decades learning about in my own wild magic.

This book is for you if you're ready for change, ready to go deeper, ready to delve into your own alchemy and transform the inner and outer levels of your life.

If you're like me, and have been seeking out magic and deeper understandings all your life, my wish is that you find echoes of your own wisdom reflected here, and open up to new layers of awareness within – because there are always new depths to explore.

If you're at the beginning or early stages of your magical journey, this book is also written with you in mind. At times you may feel stuck, like nothing is working, or you may have doubts or fears about what lies ahead. Know that these feelings are natural and that you are not alone.

You may not always agree with me, and I wouldn't want it any other way. My philosophy is to always question, because you never know how true something is, until you fully consider the possibility that it isn't true at all. However, if you find aspects challenging, if they snag against you like twigs and branches on a winding forest path, then I do suggest you make the most out of the dissonant feeling. I've always found that if something is offending or challenging me emotionally, I will get far more from the situation if I delve deeply within to find the source of that emotion. Often there are hidden jewels for me to find, old emotions to release, and new healing to experience beneath all the resistance.

As you turn these pages, you may find yourself drawn into a world where the veil between the seen and unseen grows thin, where the wisdom of ancestors mingles with the rustling of leaves in the wind. Like an ancient tree, with its roots reaching deep into the earth and its branches stretching towards the wide open sky, this book aims to help you bridge the realms of the mundane and the magical, to find the extraordinary in the ordinary.

If you're reading this, chances are you've already had some inkling that there's more to reality than meets the eye. Maybe you've experienced synchronicities that seemed too beautiful to be mere coincidence. Maybe you've had vivid dreams that later came true. Or perhaps you've always felt a little bit different, more attuned to the magic of the universe.

My dear friend and druid Modron, Pamela Meekings-Stewart, has four rules for the ritual spaces she holds:

"Come with an open heart. Come with an open mind. Leave your prejudices at the door. Along with your shoes."

I would like to extend the same welcome to you.

WHO ISN'T THIS BOOK FOR?

At the core of what I call "the magical worldview" is a deep sense of meaning that was absent from my own family upbringing yet which I always craved and sought out for myself. **It's the idea that we didn't come here purely by some cruel accident, that our lives mean something.** If you're not on board with this, and you're not interested in deep transformation this is not the book for you.

I've created this book for people who are interested in exploring magic as I understand it, based on my many years of learning and practice. Of course, this book will not be everyone's cup of tea. I'm a very odd person in some ways, and I'm okay with that. My rather random magical and spiritual journey has always been my core driving force. It's part of my "why" – my sense of purpose in life.

If you associate witchcraft with the satanic, I'm afraid I have some bad news for you: most witches do not in fact believe in Satan, who belongs to Abrahamic religions and is primarily a Christian deity. Therefore, it makes sense that most witches, being Pagan rather than Christian do not spare the Christian Devil a second thought.

If this book doesn't feel right for you right now in your life, feel free to put it down and find something that resonates better. You may find you come back to it in later years, or not. Either way, I wish you nothing but wonderful blessings on your path.

There is no one right way when it comes to magic and there is always more to learn.

My approach to magic is rooted in understanding it as a deeply personal and intuitive practice, interconnected with nature, one that requires us to trust our inner wisdom and embrace our unique strengths and challenges. Throughout this book, I'll share the techniques and insights that have been most transformative in my own journey. I encourage you to adapt them to your own needs and experiences.

BECOMING MORE FULLY YOURSELF.

You do not have to identify as a witch to enjoy this book, but you absolutely can if you want to – you don't need anyone's permission! Being a witch is not about becoming someone else, it's about becoming more fully yourself.

This journey of magical awakening is not about escaping reality, but about embracing it and learning to see the world through eyes of wonder and enchantment. It's about realising more and more that we are all connected, that we are all part of the great web of life, and that our thoughts, words and actions echo out into the cosmos, creating change on both seen and unseen levels. Consciously connecting with our intuition and stepping deeper into our magic has wider effects which ripple out into the collective, creating a world that is more compassionate and beautiful. As we each awaken to our own magic and begin to live in alignment with our deeper meaning, we contribute to this broader healing.

I'm here to learn and to share, and to transform through the many layers of experience. There's nothing I love more than writing. If you've read my novels, you may have noticed that they share real magical and healing work beneath the fantastical adventures. With each one, I go through a process of deep transformation myself and share that process with others.

In my understanding, almost all magic happens by accident. That is: we are already wildly magical beings, we just aren't usually fully aware of this. Our ancient ancestors understood the often subtle and mysterious magic happening all around us and within us. They knew that a song is enchantment, transforming our emotions or bringing up memories, that everything we eat and drink has a subtle effect on our energy, that any new connection can transform us. The stories we tell ourselves about our lives are shaping our perception at every single moment. When you read a book, your mind is imagining all kinds of things that didn't previously exist; you're engaging your own unique perspective with the imagination of the author. Because of this, your experience of a book will be different from anyone else's. You'll relate to different things, laugh at different parts. **Your experience in every moment is utterly unique.**

WHERE DOES MAGIC COME FROM?

Many magical and spiritual traditions teach that we came from the divine spark of the universe, born into this realm of forgetting. When we come into this world as innocent babies, we forget everything we knew before.

Why would we do this? This is part of the great mystery of life; however, many sages teach that it is a part of the journey into deeper wisdom, so that we could have an experience of being separate, experience the paradox of this aching disconnection, and deepen our awareness in order to learn and eventually to remember who we truly are and reconnect with the divine.

The path of magic has not always been an easy one. Throughout history, those who dared to walk the edge between worlds, to challenge the status quo and tap into the power within, have often faced persecution. Yet, the flame of magic can never be extinguished; it burns eternal in the hearts of those who are called towards the murky and beguiling depths of existence.

There will be times when you may feel lost, confused, or discouraged in your practice. But the rewards of this journey are beyond measure. As we learn to trust our intuition, embrace both our light and our shadows, and step further into our power with integrity, we discover a deeper joy and connection to the magical.

In the pages that follow, you'll find a wide array of magical tools, including ritual and spellcasting techniques, working with the four elements, connecting deeply with your will, kitchen witchery, astrological wisdom, meditations, exercises for bringing the light of your awareness into shadow work and much more. Each of these practices is designed to help you tap into your own inner wisdom and power, and to create a life that is more full of wonder, meaning, and enchantment.

People often have a misguided view of magic, reflected in dominant culture – the idea the power lies in an outward action, a Latin phrase, a chant, a wave of a wand, that creates an unlikely and miraculous reaction. But in my understanding, it is always in the inner work that the magic happens, and then is reflected into the outer world.

As you journey through this book, remember that magic is not just something you do, but something you are. It is your birthright, your natural state of being. Like a golden thread of light, it weaves through you, connecting you to the stars above and the earth below. All you need to do is remember, to awaken to the truth of who you are.

WHAT DOES IT MEAN TO BE MAGIC? WHAT DOES IT MEAN TO BE A WITCH?

The definition of "witch" is as varied as there are people who choose to use the word. Though not all people who use magic are witches, most people who are witches do deliberately work with magic in one way or another. So what does that mean?

To me, magic is a weaving of the inner and outer, the deeper, the transformative potential of ourselves as active participants in the world. We can shape our world with inner work, with our will and with what we share. The process of engaging with magic is often about how we direct our attention. We can use ritual and spell to do this, or we can do it purely internally.

There is no right way to practice magic, but there are many traps that people can fall into around what is good or bad, what is right or wrong, what should or should not happen. The best advice I can give you is not to believe in anything unless it resonates with you. Don't believe something just because you're afraid. If somebody tells you that you absolutely must or must not do something otherwise bad things will happen to you, that's rubbish. I don't put stock in superstition. For instance, black cats are lovely (not bad luck at all) and chain letters that tell you everything is going to go wrong if you don't follow their rules are ridiculous. I choose not to make that kind of superstition part of my reality.

Now, although I've already made it clear that there's no one right way of being a witch or of living a magical life, I will tell you about my personal understanding of both. To be a witch is to consciously walk a magical path, to understand that we need not be afraid of the shadows of the unconscious. Just as the night time is not bad, there is much delight to be found in both light and darkness. I do not believe in good and bad witches, per se. Of course there's a very small minority of people who call themselves witches but who may be traumatised, twisted, or delusional, who either seek out only the light or only the darkness, but these approaches do not seem complete to me, or particularly effective. To be only love and light and fluffy bunnies is spiritual bypassing or toxic positivity. To be too attached to the darkness can be even more destructive. Both of these approaches are incomplete and get in the way of a deeper transformation, a deeper understanding, and deeper magic.

In my view, being a witch is taking on the ability to weave together the light and the darkness, not just to shy away from our fears, but to open up to the transformational potential of all experience. Being a witch is about stepping into our power and connecting with nature, connecting with our deep self, soul and will. It is about being in the magic and mystery of life as it unfolds.

Of course, without darkness we would not appreciate the light because we would not know any other possibility, just as if we'd only ever known happiness we would not understand it at all. We would not see it. The contrast of the dark ink against light paper bring the detail of a book to life, just as the changing shadows on the film are what creates a movie rather than just watching bright light.

In this work, we must learn to sit with the discomfort rather than bypass it. If we don't have the courage to face our own resistance and feel our difficult emotions we will never be able to liberate ourselves or help anyone else either.

Power must be wielded with care. The shadow of power reflects the uncomfortable unconsciousness – corruption, abuse, and neglect of others' needs. When power is not acknowledged or integrated consciously, it can lead to harmful behaviours driven by fear, greed, or a desire to maintain control.

There are many shadows to be found in magic and power. We've seen them play out in every film and fairy tale, every book and campfire story.

What I have learned in terms of navigating the paradox of power is this: where there's power of any kind that isn't tethered by **integrity, empathy, and responsibility**, it is vulnerable to becoming exploitative. We can draw upon these three things and many others in order to wield our power well, noticing that in areas where we are privileged with power, there's an opportunity to be of service to balance and wellbeing.

In awakening deeper into our wild and witchy magic we can embrace the strong foundations of guiding values like touchstones in our pockets, gathered from rivers and beaches. Our integrity, empathy, responsibility, and reverence for nature and the interconnectedness of all things can shelter us like tall trees growing around a sacred grove.

Being a witch is about connecting with nature, including our own senses as natural beings, appreciating all of the sensations of life, opening up to the vastness and beautiful complexity of experience, and stepping into our power so that we can affect change and transformation both internally and externally in the world around us.

This work requires courage, support, gentle openness, and plenty of rest. Looking after ourselves is key. I suggest that you keep a list of the best ways you can take care of yourself in order to bring these things more closely into your daily life – taking a bath, going for a walk, eating fresh foods, relaxing in a hammock, reading your tarot cards, listening to relaxing music, whatever it is that helps you to rest and restore. This will help in the journey ahead, in my experience, and is just a good idea in general.

HOW DID I BECOME A WITCH?

The first time I encountered the possibility that I could be a witch, my body tingled with recognition. It was a powerful moment of realisation, a thrilling experience of homecoming. I went from feeling dissatisfied and painfully limited by the world, to opening up to a deeper and more magical existence that nourished my soul, supported my healing, and fuelled my creativity.

My magical journey has been a long and winding one. As a child, I yearned for magic and my imagination ran wild in envisioning all kinds of possible worlds. Something within me always took offence at the apparent limitations of the material world, yet I was raised in an academi-cally-minded family with no apparent religion to cling onto.

I began delving into spirituality through my own intuition as a child, but I didn't yet know I could *really* be a witch. I was taken in by charismatic Christianity at the tender age of eleven but the rigid rules, harsh judgement and circular reasoning had left me frustrated. I was fourteen years old when it just so happened that a new friend suggested we study witchcraft. It was a liberating moment where everything clicked into place for me. We spent hours in the library learning about mythology and devouring any magical books we could get our hands on (which were few and far between at the time) and seeking out other information online in the early days of the internet (Netscape navigator anyone?). With a few close friends, we formed a coven and created our own rituals, drawing on what we'd learned. Around this time, I also began practicing magic on my own.

Magic and spirituality became a lifeline to me. I had suffered with depression and anxiety since childhood, and applying what I learned about witchcraft, the psyche, and the divine, in a practical way, has helped me immeasurably over the years.

In this journey, I have been supported and aided by good friends and a few guides. Most notably, in my teens I sought out a therapist who would understand my spiritual pursuits and found an amazing wise woman called Fiona who was experienced in Celtic shamanic practices. She guided me on many meditative journeys and first introduced me to the concept of "the shadow", which we will delve into many times in this book.

When I was eighteen I spent time with family in California who were steeped in the Goddess movement, fell in love with Motherpeace tarot cards and attended a full moon ritual on a beach with a wonderful group of crones. When I returned to New Zealand, I became involved with the pagan community (a broad term for all kinds of magical folk). I started a pagan club at my university in order to connect with interesting people, and organised weekly meetings focused on learning about different magical modalities. I held rituals at my home and attended pagan festivals. In those years I lived and breathed witchcraft, but there were some predatory personalities in the community. I eventually began to put up boundaries and focus instead on my inner work, called by my intuition.

Over the years, I've studied many subjects, formally and informally, which have contributed to my magical knowledge, as well as personal exploration into magic, astrology, and tarot. I studied social sciences at university and completed a PhD, drawn by the magic of society and culture. I undertook a diploma in hypnotherapy because I was fascinated by the power of our minds. I spent a year studying herbal medicine, and I've learned several other modalities in healing. I'm happy to say I'm a big geek when it comes to magic. Though I've taught workshops on many elements of magic over the years, I've never "formally" studied witchcraft or joined a particular tradition, preferring to be guided by my own intuition. There is a strong rebellious streak within me that would prefer to forge my own path than be told what to do.

For years my path focused primarily on my inner work, which helped me to overcome significant internal and external challenges. I often describe myself as an intuitive witch. In my thirties I also became involved in a local magical group which celebrates the full moons, and a connected Druidry group.

Druidry, in the tradition of the Order of Bards, Ovates, and Druids, appealed to me because it is very open-minded – based on the notion that we are all walking our own magical paths. The main focus is a connection with nature, a celebration of creativity, and valuing peace – all things I can get behind! In recent years I've enjoyed many seasonal celebrations with my druid grove, including helping to design and lead rituals myself.

As a novelist, I have wound many of my insights into fiction, but this is the first magical nonfiction book I've written to completion! In fact, I suspect I've been working on this book ever since I began my magical journey and its roots are reflected in my teenage journals. I have wanted, many times, to write openly about the power magic and spirituality can have in our lives.

Now, in my fortieth year, I'm finally ready to share what I've learned so far and what I continue to learn in my magical journey.

It is my wish and intention that this book be inspiring and uplifting, as well as grounded and practical, that it is helpful for you, guiding you to go deeper into who you really are and live a more magical life. I believe that there is no one right way to do anything, and I don't prescribe any particular dogma or doctrine. What I present here are things that I find useful, things that have helped me, and ways of understanding the world that have deepened my understanding over time.

This is the book that I wish I had access to when I first started learning about spirituality, the mind, emotions, healing, and magic. At the time, I wanted magic to happen with sparks and colourful powders, and to be dramatic. But as I've developed maturity, I've come to prefer a subtler kind of magic – magic that's deeply intuitive and attuned to the cycles of nature; magic that allows me to be truly in my power, and which has brought me more success than I ever would have dared to dream when I was younger; magic that pulls me to go within, into the deep wells of the wisdom of the soul, to emerge renewed time and time again. Allow the magic that has developed and moved in my life to do the same in yours, if you want it to.

As Alice Tarbuck says in her gorgeous book, *A Spell in the Wild*:

"The magic is in the wild, and it is also inside us. We are the wilds, and we are the hearth. Come along, won't you? All the world is waiting, and you are waiting too, and there is so much joy, and power, and there is so much work to be done. Let's get to work."

So, my dearest ones, are you ready to embark on this journey of connection, of awakening, of coming home to yourself? Grab your cloak or a cosy blanket, snuggle up with your trusty familiar, and perhaps a steaming mug of your favourite enchanted brew. Take a deep breath, trust in the magic that lies within you, and let's begin.

I am honoured to walk with you on this journey.

With love and magic,
Blessed be.
Iris xx

I
ACCIDENTAL MAGIC

"As above, so below, as within, so without, as the universe, so the soul..."
— an interpretation of the Emerald Tablet, Hermes Trismegistus, 200BCE

*W*e are standing here, in a lush, vibrant forest. The trees are pulsing with life.

You begin to walk, each step an act of surrender to the wild call within you. The forest recognises you, to welcome you home. The earth beneath your feet is soft and yielding, cradling your every footfall in a gentle embrace.

As you go deeper, you feel the layers of your civilised-self falling away. The masks you wear, the roles you play, the fears that bind you – they all seem to dissolve in the face of this wild untamed power. You feel raw, vulnerable, utterly alive.

You approach a clearing. In the centre is a shimmering pool, its surface so still it mirrors the sky. You approach the edge, drawn by a force that seems to emanate from the very depths of your being.

As you gaze into the water, you see your own reflection. But it's not the face you see in the mirror every day. This face is wild, luminous, alive with a fire in your eyes. You realise that this is your true face, the face of your soul.

The longer you look, the more you see. Images begin to swirl in the depths of the pool – memories long forgotten, dreams not yet dreamed, aspects of yourself you've never dared to acknowledge. You see your passions, your desires, your deepest longings. You see the ways in which you've held yourself back, the ways in which you've tamed your own wildness.

You give yourself permission to be who you really are...

And then, in a moment of clarity, you understand. This wildness, this untamed power, this radiance, this is the essence of who you are. It's the source of your power, your creativity, your joy. It's the part of you that knows no bounds.

You feel a rush of energy coursing through your veins, a surge of life force. You feel the wild within you awakening, stirring from a long slumber, power uncoiling in your belly, a fire igniting in your heart.

You stand up, feeling the power of your own wildness moving through you. The forest around you seems shimmers, responding to the call of your awakened soul. You understand that you are not separate from this wildness – you are part of it, woven into the very fabric of the being.

The wildness is not something outside of you, not something to be sought or tamed. It is the very core of your soul, the source of your deepest magic.

In this awakening, you are never the same. You are wilder, truer, more fully alive. You know now that the path to your deepest joy, your greatest fulfilment, is not one that can be reached merely through restraint and control, but must come at least in part through surrender and flow. It is the path of the wild soul.

And now you may live from this place, to let the intuition of your wild soul guide you. You are a force of nature, a child of the wild divine.

AWAKENING TO OUR ACCIDENTAL MAGIC

We're all doing magic, all the time. Every thought we think, every word we speak, every action we take ripples out into the world, creating change on both the seen and unseen levels. This is not something to worry about unnecessarily. We are creatures of habit, shaping our usual worlds the way a spider shapes her web. There is not much to concern ourselves about in continuing our same thought patterns, other than getting the same kinds of results. The question is, how can we do magic more consciously?

For most of us, the vast majority of our magic is accidental and unconscious. This is not to say that you are to blame for things happening in your life or in the world that you're not happy about. How could you possibly be to blame for things you're not aware of? Yet, in the grand unfolding of life, we are all creators, our thoughts and actions the threads that form part of the intricate patterns of our reality. Usually this weaving happens unconsciously, our magic working behind the scenes, shaping our world in ways we may not even realise. This is accidental magic – the power we wield without intention or awareness.

Across cultures, magical traditions recognise that we are not separate from nature, but part of it. The microcosm reflects the macrocosm; nature is alive and responsive.

Walking the witch's path means aligning with these rhythms – honouring the sacred, working with the elements, and connecting with unseen realms and guiding spirits.

How does it feel to you when I tell you that we're always doing magic, it's just that most of the time, this magic happens accidentally? It's a concept that may seem foreign at first, perhaps even a little unsettling. After all, we're taught from a young age that magic is the stuff of fairy tales and fantasy, not a tangible force in our everyday lives.

What if I told you that this notion of magic is a fundamental principle of the universe? This is sometimes called "the magical worldview" – the understanding that reality is reflective. It is the principle of "as above, so below," inscribed on the Emerald Tablet almost two thousand years ago, recording the foundation of alchemy which profoundly influenced Western magical traditions. Most people think of Alchemy as the futile pursuit of turning lead into gold, but it goes much deeper. Alchemy was once synonymous with both science and magic. Alchemy is about actively participating in the art of transformation. The quote above sheds light on this depth and understanding: that we live in a reflective universe, and within it, we are all interconnected – with ourselves, with each other, with the wild magic of the cosmos.

When we begin to awaken to this truth, it's as if a veil is lifted from our eyes. Suddenly, the world around us takes on a new sheen, a luminous quality that was always there but had gone unnoticed. We start to see the magic in the everyday – in the way a smile from a stranger can brighten our mood, in the way a song on the radio seems to speak directly to our soul, in the way a chance encounter can change the course of our lives.

For many years I've marvelled at how people's limiting beliefs about themselves and their lives tend to be so terribly true for them, myself included. This is the power of accidental magic – the way our thoughts, emotions, and beliefs can shape our reality without us even trying. It's the reason why someone who constantly worries about getting sick may find themselves falling ill more often, or why a person who believes they are lucky may seem to attract good fortune wherever they go.

When we're not aware of the magic we're weaving, we can find ourselves stuck in patterns and cycles that don't serve us, creating a reality that feels like it's happening to us rather than one we're actively shaping.

This is where the power of deliberate magic comes in. As we begin to awaken to the magic within us, we start to realise that we have the power to consciously create our reality. We learn to harness the energy of our thoughts and emotions, to use ritual and intention to manifest our desires.

This is not always an easy path. It requires us to confront our shadows, to face the parts of ourselves we may have kept hidden away. It asks us to step into our power. It challenges us to live in integrity, to align our actions with our values, to be true to ourselves and our path.

But as we do this work, as we learn to wield our magic with intention and awareness, something miraculous begins to happen. We start to see our lives transform in ways we never thought possible. We attract people and opportunities that align with our highest good. We find ourselves living in flow, in harmony with a life rich with meaning.

This is deliberate magic: shaping reality through our thoughts, emotions, and actions. We're not victims of fate – we're powerful creators, weaving the threads of our lives with every choice we make.

As we awaken to this truth, we begin to see magic everywhere. In the synchronicities that guide us, in the intuitive nudges that lead us in the right direction, in the moments of serendipity that feel like the world is conspiring in our favour. We gain trust in the unfolding of our lives, knowing that even the challenges and obstacles are part of a greater pattern, a sacred design.

As we deepen our practice, we realise the magic we sought outside was always within. We are the magic – divine sparks shaping the world.

This is the journey of the wild witch – the path of awakening to our deeper nature, of remembering the magic that runs through our veins. It's a journey of self-discovery and self-creation, of aligning with the wisdom of the earth and the cosmos, of claiming our birthright as magical beings. It is a journey of opening up to the healing, insights, and many gifts that wild intuitive magic can bring into our lives.

Stories of magical awakening are so powerful in fiction because we're always doing magic, all the time. We're co-creating reality, interpreting it through our own lenses, making judgements and getting attached to those judgements. This is why stories discovering hidden magical powers are so impactful in fantasy books and films. They resonate with something within us and speak to the process of remembering our own power, of making the unconscious conscious, as Jung would say. In my writing, I'm drawing on my own understanding, imperfect as it may be. I'm not an expert on everything, but writing allows me to explore the magic that I believe in.

So as we begin down this path, dear reader, know that you are not alone. Know that the magic you seek is not some distant, unattainable force; it is a power that resides within you, and always has. Every step, every breath, is an act of magic, and as you learn to work with it deliberately, as you align your will, transformation will unfold, one magical moment at a time.

YOU ARE THE CAULDRON

Think of your life, or your psyche, as a bubbling cauldron. Inside it, there's a potion constantly simmering away, made up of all the ingredients you've gathered – things from your childhood, your family, your upbringing, the lessons you've learned, the people you've been around, and all the other experiences you've had. It's a mix of flavours, some sweet, some bitter, pungent, salty, and sour. These flavours can combine in delicious ways. After all, what is the flavour of chocolate without a little bitterness?

Take a moment to savour your life, as if dipping a spoon into the cauldron and tasting all the flavours. If you have a journal or a notebook you'd like to use for reflection, which I highly recommend, take a moment to write on the following prompts:

What do you notice in the flavours?

What aspects in your life don't quite seem to fit – with jarring flavours that stand out?

What murky feelings might need to be scooped out and examined?

Often we're not fully aware of what's gone into our inner potion, or why it tastes the way it does, why it isn't working as we want it to, or has unintended side effects. Have a look at what's bubbling away in your cauldron. Are there things in there that feel heavy or bitter? Would a little more sweetness or the refreshing tang of something new help to improve the flavour? Are there patterns that you've outgrown but still find yourself stuck with? Magic isn't about pretending everything is fine when it's not – it's about recognising what's there, facing it, and working with it.

The good news is that this cauldron is always refreshing itself. Sure, there might be some old ingredients still swirling in there – past guilt, anger, shame, or patterns you've picked up along the way – but the potion is never finished. There's always more deliberate magic to brew. You can choose to skim off what's no longer serving you, like unhelpful habits, old judgements and beliefs about your limitations, and old pain. Forgive life, forgive yourself, release the past, let it go, and make room for new things.

You can start stirring in the ingredients you do want, rather than just letting the old ones dominate. This is an opportunity to reflect on what inspires you; what colours, textures, foods and beverages, people, animals, movement, books, and experiences light you up? What kinds of deliberate magic are you drawn to? Do you want to spend more time in nature? Make space to celebrate the seasons and moon cycles? Write or draw or paint or sing or dance?

You may need to clear a bit of space, perhaps ladling out your old worries and self-doubt. In trusting that you can take up more deliberate space in your life, you have room for more good things. You can start adding ingredients that feel good. If you know how to taste a soup to see what flavours it needs, you'll know what I mean – maybe you want to bring in more sweetness, so you add honey. Or perhaps you're craving richness, so you add cream. A handful of herbs might bring freshness, or a pinch of spice might wake everything up. What life ingredients are you craving to enhance the experience of your magic? You don't have to get it perfect. In fact, there is no perfect. Just pause now and then to taste what's there, see how it feels, and adjust as you go.

This process isn't just about what's in your cauldron – it's also about what you do with the things you take out. The old guilt, resentment, and pain often need to be experienced and grieved and emotionally composted; they cannot simply be thrown. Sometimes they need to be felt and experienced fully in order to be released. There are many techniques for this processing presented here in this book, and often a simple approach works best. For instance, if you find an old emotion lingering that's ready to come up, take ten to twenty minutes to sit with it, feeling it with openness and acceptance. This is the best way I know to heal and release old emotions. Journalling about them can also help you focus. You may wish to create sacred space (as described later in this chapter) and sit within the safety of this space in order to allow yourself to feel and release emotions. In this way, you can compost the old energy, let the old feelings break down like the autumn leaves return to the earth, where they'll feed new growth.

When we clear out the clutter in our lives – whether it's physical things we no longer need or emotional baggage we've been carrying for too long – we create space for new things to come in. New people, new opportunities, new ideas. It's the same with our inner worlds. When we let go of what's weighing us down, we create room for fresh magic to take root and grow.

This work creates a strong foundation to do magic deliberately. Maybe for now it means spending more time on things that nourish you – reading instead of scrolling social media, spending time in nature, or connecting with someone you care about. Maybe it means bringing more ritual into your life, whether that's lighting a candle for the full moon, writing down your intentions at the new moon, or even just stirring magic into your cup of tea.

You get to decide what magic looks like in your life. It might be making an altar with things that feel special to you (also described later in this chapter), or cooking meals with care and intention. It might be meditating, making talismans (see chapter two), or connecting with water – whether that's at the beach, in a lake, or even in your bathtub. There's no right or wrong way to do this. The point is to take a good look at your life as it is. What do you want to keep and do more of? What do you want to let go of?

Sometimes this process isn't easy. There might be things in your life that feel stuck or heavy, things you can't just get rid of. That's where the real magic often is – in leaning into those challenges, accepting the resistance, and working with it instead of against it. We'll explore more of these challenging things later in the book.

Magic isn't about pretending everything is fine or plastering over reality with pretty words. It's about working with what's real, weeds and all, in order to embrace life and make our realities much, much more satisfying. If you want new growth, you've got to clear some room in the soil first. That means facing the hard things, making space, and being open to what comes next.

More reflective questions:
What's currently brewing in your cauldron?
What do you value and want to keep?
What are you ready to release?
What would you like to start adding more of?

EVERYTHING IS INTERCONNECTED, EVERYTHING IS REFLECTIVE

From the tiniest blade of grass to the farthest star, from your next-door neighbour to a stranger on the other side of the globe, we are all part of one vast, intricate web of being.

The patterns and cycles we observe in nature – the turning of the seasons, the waxing and waning of the moon, the ebb and flow of the tides – are mirrored in the rhythms of our own bodies and lives. By attuning ourselves to these natural rhythms, we can tap into a deep well of wisdom and power that is our birthright as creatures of the Earth.

This extends into the realm of symbol and archetype. The ancient art of astrology, for example, is based on the idea that the movements of celestial bodies reflect and influence the unfolding of human destiny. The tarot, with its images and archetypes, is a tool for gaining insight into the patterns and possibilities of our lives.

In a magical world, there is no such thing as empty matter or blind chance. Everything, from the stones beneath our feet to the wind in the trees, is imbued with spirit, with consciousness, with story.

Growing up in an atheist household, I had no framework for this kind of enchanted worldview. The universe, I was told, was a vast, cold, indifferent place, devoid of inherent meaning or purpose. I took this to mean that we were mere specks of cosmic dust, adrift in an ocean of chaos, our joys and sorrows ultimately signifying nothing. This felt wrong to me on an intuitive level.

I also grew up in a bi-cultural family and my early schooling was in total immersion within the Māori culture and language, indigenous to New Zealand, including mythology, traditional rituals, and the understanding that nature is alive. I knew that the materialist scientific worldview of my family wasn't right for me, but as a child of Cornish, Irish, Scottish, and Lithuanian Jewish heritage, the indigenous tradition I grew up with wasn't mine to claim either, even though it was beautifully inclusive.

It wasn't until I began to study magic, spirituality, and mysticism that I discovered my own path, to connect with the roots of my own ancestry, with older wisdom from before religious colonisation separated us so much from nature. I recognised in various teachings, something I'd intuitively felt all along. I could always sense the presence of unseen forces and deeper levels of meaning.

Cultures across the world and throughout history have understood the world as a living, breathing, sacred whole. Many traditions have a deep reverence for the natural world, and a recognition of the interdependence of all life. They teach that by aligning with the cycles and elements of nature, we can tap into a source of wisdom and power that is greater than our individual selves.

If you feel the call of magic stirring in your blood, know that you are not alone. Know that you are part of an ancient and eternal lineage of those who have dared to peek behind the veil of what we are told to believe, discovering a world of wonder, mystery, and enchantment.

The path of the wild witch is not an easy one. It requires courage, authenticity, and a willingness to confront the shadows of our own inner demons – the fears and limitations that sabotage our lives. It is also a path of joy, connection, and empowerment. By claiming our magic, we reclaim our rightful place as deliberate and powerful creators in this world, shaping our lives into beautiful, magical, inspiring journeys for ourselves and others.

A NOTE ON THE SHADOW

Much of our accidental magic comes from our shadow – from unconsciousness. "The shadow," is a term coined Jung, to name the parts of ourselves we often dare not face which are often buried deep in our unconscious minds.

The shadow represents the repressed, denied, and hidden aspects of our personality – those traits and impulses we deem unacceptable or unworthy. Like the moon's dark side, these facets tend to remain obscured from our conscious awareness, influencing our thoughts, feelings, and behaviours in ways we barely comprehend. Yet, within this darkness lies immense potential for growth and self-discovery.

By beginning the process of gently embracing our shadow, we uncover powerful raw, untamed energy and creativity. We may even learn to find joy in what we previously shunned, transforming our deepest fears and darkest desires into sources of empowerment and liberation. Later in this book we will journey further into this shadowy realm, not to banish the darkness, but to understand and integrate it, and ultimately, to become more whole.

Many spiritual teachings grapple with the question of why there is unfairness in the world. From many esoteric, spiritual, and magical teachings, including Buddhist, Tantric, and alchemical perspectives, it has to do with the unconsciousness that pervades humanity.

We all have shadows – those parts of ourselves we deny or resist. And magic is, in many ways, the process of making the unconscious conscious, of getting to a deeper level of awareness. Like the dark of the moon, our shadows hold the key to our wholeness, the hidden potential waiting to be unveiled.

Reflection questions: Think about your own life.

What accidental magic have you experienced?

What does magic mean to you?

What would it feel like to live a truly magical life?

MYTHOLOGY AND CREATION FROM THE CHAOS OF THE VOID

"A myth is something that has never happened, but is happening all the time."

—Joseph Campbell

We are all magical story-telling creatures, making sense of our lives through our narratives – the stories we tell ourselves in our heads that shape our inner and outer lives. As such, our personal mythos and our collective social mythology are both incredibly important. Our mythos shapes our story, our societies, our ethics, and our imaginings that lead us towards new future possibilities. Many of the myths we grew up with were broken stories – tales of weak princesses who were mere victims of fate, reliant on waiting for a prince to rescue them, of evil witches who wanted nothing more than to curse and manipulate for their own personal gain. I was fortunate to be raised predominantly by a strong woman who was aware of this social pathology and who plied me with bedtime stories where witches could be good and wise, whimsical and charming, which is perhaps why I write empowering witchy stories now.

Campbell, who I quote above, has been criticised for being too universalist in his work, too centred on patriarchal Western traditions and missing complexity. While that is a fair criticism, he has also made some important points. Myth and storytelling is both how we reflect and create culture. It is magic. In this book, I'm focusing on Western traditions deliberately, because I feel there is an urgent need to bring back the older wisdom which has been stripped from dominant culture in the West through centuries of ideological colonisation. When we go back to our roots, embedded within nature, we find depth and wisdom that we desperately need to re-claim at this point in history.

Story is vital to us as human beings, be it the dominant mythos of our culture or the day-to-day stories we tell ourselves about our lives. Stories are powerful magic. They can be transformative and powerful medicine, as Dr Clarissa Pinkola Estes said:

"The story is not told to lift you up, to make you feel better, or to entertain you, although all those things can be true. The story is meant to take the spirit into a descent to find something that is lost or missing and to bring it back to consciousness again."

Many creation myths begin with a void and with chaos. The word "chaos" comes from the Greek word "χάος" (khaos), which originally meant "gap" or "chasm." It referred to the primordial void or the state of the universe before order and creation. The term "chaos" in ancient Greek does not imply disorder as it does in modern usage, but rather an empty, unformed, and indefinite space. Over time, the word evolved to encompass the concept of a disordered or confused state in both ancient and modern contexts.

This is not so different from modern scientific theories about what came before the big bang which seem to circle around a great cosmic vacuum of chaotic pre-matter energy particles popping in and out of existence. Perhaps then, ancestors were intuitively gleaning knowledge that is still only on the periphery of science when they told stories of what came before the gods, the earth, sea, and sky. Through this void and chaos, all things eventually come into being.

In the Māori creation myths I grew up with, Te Kore (roughly translated as the void) came before many stages of Te Pō (the night). Interestingly, Kore was also an early name for the goddess Persephone, associated with the underworld. Greek mythology was influenced by earlier Sumerian mythos in which the goddesses Inanna and Ereshkigal were associated with the underworld and changes of seasons.

In Celtic and Gaelic mythology, creation myths frequently start with a world that is inhospitable or unformed, which then requires the deities or forces to get things into shape. God-like figures or powerful mythical heroes often play crucial roles in shaping the world out of chaos. For example, in Irish mythology, the Tuatha Dé Danann arrive in Ireland to confront existing dark and chaotic forces represented by earlier settlers like the Fomorians, who are often depicted as monstrous and chaotic. The battles between these groups can be seen as metaphoric representations of imposing order on chaos, with the Tuatha Dé Danann bringing skills, knowledge, and social structures that transformed Ireland into a flourishing land.

Another element that hints at the theme of creation from chaos in Celtic myth is the motif of the cauldron, often associated with rebirth and regeneration. Cerridwen's cauldron symbolises a mystical source from which new life can emerge, suggesting a cycle of destruction and creation that rejuvenates the world and maintains balance.

The physical geography in the myths also reflects the transformation from chaos to order. The shaping of the landscape itself—mountains, rivers, and sacred groves—through the actions of mythical beings symbolises the structuring and shaping of the world. This includes tales of giants who throw rocks to form hills or gods who command rivers to flow, carving the land into a more recognisable and habitable state.

Celtic art, similar to Māori art, with its intricate knots and spirals, may also symbolise the complex interaction of chaotic elements moving towards a harmonious and infinite order. These designs reflect a world-view where chaos and order are not opposites but interdependent forces that drive the universe's dynamics. These stories underscore the ability of life to renew and regenerate, continually emerging from chaos into the structure of being.

The mythos of society is deeply magical. It shapes our worldview, even if we don't realise it. The changes in our collective stories over time reflect social changes. Many scholars have noticed that before the rise of patriarchy, in many early cultures, there was more gender balance and in some cases goddess worship was originally more important than for masculine deities. This is reflected in how the earlier Abyssinian mythos centring powerful and generous goddesses like Inanna were gradually eroded and replaced with more focus on hierarchical gods. As more hier-archical traditions, like those of the Roman Empire, began to dominate the mythology of other cultures, with offshoots that colonised much of the world, the focus shifted away from the deep mystical understandings of the void and the underworld. The Roman focus on the Sun King, replaced with the Christian pantheon, cast long shadows that obscured the power of the goddesses of the void, and this imbalance has shaped the stories we tell ourselves and our children.

Many of the fairy tales we grew up with presented women as either innocent naïve princesses or evil step mother witches. There was no room for empowered benevolent witchcraft, or indeed, for witches being another gender. This is beginning to shift as princesses in mainstream children's films can now save themselves or each other, rather than always waiting for a prince, and the stories of "evil witches" can be re-told from their perspective, encouraging empathy and understanding.

Reflections

What stories did you grow up with as a child? In what ways did you wish they were different?

What would your own personal creation myth look like?

What stories most appeal to you now in books and film, and how does this relate to your personal narrative, the stories you tell yourself about your own life?

A BRIEF HISTORY OF WITCHCRAFT

"Magic is not a path for those who desire neatness, sweetness and light, unless they see their true colours clearly. Magic isn't sunlight on a well-mown lawn; it's the shadows at the bottom of a well, the spiders in the corners of the ceiling, the tracking of a black cat under a moonless sky."
  - Silver RavenWolf

The history of witchcraft is both an oddly complex and rather incomplete subject, rich with misunderstood lore, lost records, and hidden secrets.

Witchcraft and magical practice could indeed be as old as humanity itself, emerging from the mists of prehistory where the natural world was both revered and feared. Its roots could be traced back to the Paleolithic era, where cave paintings suggest a belief in magic and the supernatural, depicting shamans dressed in animal skins, dancing amidst the spirits of the hunt. But is that witchcraft? Who is to say?

One thing is fairly clear: the further you go back in history, the harder it is to separate magic from any other type of knowledge. Up until the enlightenment, astrology and astronomy were one combined subject. Dante's great work *Inferno - Purgatorio – Paradiso*, completed in 1321, included planetary realms within the nine levels of heaven, as astrology was deeply connected with medieval philosophy.

Alchemy, believed to be the root of Western magical traditions, was once inseparable from science. In the classical world of Greece and Rome, witchcraft could be seen as a mix of folklore, herbal lore, and the remnants of pre-Olympian religions. The Greek pharmakeia (φαρμακεία) refers to both medicine and magic, underscoring the thin line between healing and hexing. Pliny the Elder, in his *Natural History* (circa 77 AD), speaks of magic's widespread acceptance and its incorporation into daily life, from love potions to protective amulets.

Later in the mediaeval period, the perception of magic and witchcraft took a darker turn, intertwined with the colonisation of Christianity across Europe. The infamous *Malleus Maleficarum*, published in 1487, arguably marked the peak of witch hysteria, providing a guide to the identification, trial, and execution of witches. Heinrich Kramer, one of its authors, stated, "All witchcraft comes from carnal lust, which is in women insatiable." Such texts fuelled centuries of fear, leading to the persecution and execution of thousands, many of whom were women.

Witchcraft is a complex and multifaceted concept that has evolved over centuries, adapting to the cultural, social, and religious contexts in which it finds itself. It is not a religion, but a practice, as denoted by the "craft" part of the word. Witches, in my experience, rarely need the dogma of religion, preferring to be guided by nature and their own intuition. This is not to say that religion is bad or incompatible with witchcraft. Indeed, I've encountered witches of many religions, including Christianity, Judaism, or even those treating Wicca as a religion. Religion is not necessary for witchcraft, but there's no reason why you cannot have both if that works for you (though you may find that many religions are not so open about including witches within their belief systems).

Witchcraft can encompass practices, beliefs, and rituals intended to harness and connect with the natural and supernatural forces of the world, but there are as many "types" of witch as there are witches. The term "witchcraft" itself has its roots in the Old English word "wiccecræft," the meaning of which reflects the early understanding of witchcraft as a craft or skill practiced by individuals with knowledge of magic, herbs, and the supernatural.

The term "witch" has a myriad of meanings. In the Basque tradition, the word for witch is Sorginak, someone who crafts their own fate. This interpretation offers a glimpse into the essence of witchcraft: it is not just a practice but a way of being, a deep, intuitive understanding of the natural world, including ourselves as part of nature, and the forces that can be perceived to run through us all.

The connection between contemporary witchcraft and paganism is strong. Pagan traditions, with their reverence for the natural world and its cycles, offer beliefs and practices that celebrate the earth, the seasons, and so on. Witchcraft, in many of its forms, draws from this wellspring, embracing the cycles of nature as a reflection of the cycles of human existence.

To connect with witchcraft is to open oneself to nature, including our own wild nature. It is to acknowledge the power within and around us, the magic that suffuses every leaf and stone, every drop of water, and every flicker of flame. In embracing the essence of witchcraft, we open ourselves to the mystery and majesty of the universe, crafting our fates with intention, guided by the stars and the rhythms of nature.

Magic has been a universal aspect of human experience, transcending borders, cultures, and epochs. From the ancient shamanistic practices of the indigenous peoples, who connected with the spirits of the land, sea, and sky, to the sophisticated rituals of the Egyptian magicians, who sought to communicate with the gods and guide the souls of the dead through the Duat.

This is not to say that every magical culture is the same – not at all – or even to put that label onto peoples who may have had vastly different understandings. However, we can appreciate and acknowledge that many traditions and cultures over the centuries have drawn wisdom and insight from communion with the natural world. Indeed, there was once no artificial notion of a separation between humans and nature.

In ancient Mesopotamia, for instance, magic was integrated into daily life and state affairs, with incantations and rituals designed to protect against fears and misfortune. The Assyrian and Babylonian magicians, or ashipu, wielded considerable influence, employing amulets, potions, and exorcisms in their work.

The history of magic is merged with the development of alchemy, from the ancient world and into medieval Europe and interconnecting lands. Alchemists sought not only to transform base metals into gold but also to discover the elixir of life, a quest that was as much spiritual as it was material. This pursuit bridged the worlds of science and magic, leading to discoveries that laid the groundwork for modern chemistry.

These examples barely scratch the surface of the global history of magic, yet they underscore the diversity and richness of magical practices across the world. They remind us that magic is a deeply natural endeavour, a way of engaging with the mysteries of the world and beyond, seeking understanding, power, and connection.

The history of witchcraft is also a history of resilience and revival. The 20th century (and earlier in some places) witnessed a renaissance of pagan beliefs and practices, with figures such as Gerald Gardner piecing together and reviving practices based on what was known of ancient paths of the craft. Gardner's claims of belonging to an ancient witch cult have been largely debunked by scholars, but regardless, he played a pivotal role in the revival movement, asserting witchcraft's reverence for nature, its celebration of the divine feminine, and its rich ritualistic practice.

In our modern era, witchcraft has (in many places, at least) transformed from a hostile accusation, or a nasty insult bearing the stigma of evil, warty, fairy tale villains, into something remarkably different: a badge of empowerment for many, embodying a reconnection with the natural world and ancient wisdom. It serves as a reminder of the enduring human need to find magic, to seek knowledge in the shadows, and to embrace the mysteries that lie just beyond the veil of the everyday.

Doreen Valiente, often hailed as the "Mother of Modern Witchcraft," played a pivotal role in shaping contemporary Wiccan and witchcraft practices. Working closely with Gerald Gardner, Valiente contributed significantly to the development of Wiccan rituals and beliefs, authoring much of what has become the foundational text for many practitioners. Her poetic talent and understanding of magic and folklore helped to transform Gardnerian Wicca into a rich and spiritual path. Her works, such as *Witchcraft for Tomorrow* and *The Rebirth of Witchcraft*, continue to inspire and guide those on the witch's path.

While Gardner may have been the public face of the witchcraft revival, it was Valiente who was the true power behind the revival. She was the one who took Gardner's rather scattered ideas and shaped them into a coherent system, writing many of the rituals and invocations that are still used by many today.

As Valiente herself put it, "Gerald was a dear, but he couldn't write a ritual to save his life. That's where I came in." (Okay, okay, she didn't really say that. But I like to imagine she thought it very loudly.)

From these early seeds, the many branches of modern witchcraft began to grow and flourish. In the United States, the 1960s and 70s saw the rise of feminist witchcraft, led by trailblazers like Z Budapest and Starhawk. These badass witches saw the craft as a way to reclaim the power and autonomy that had been stripped by patriarchal religion and society.

Zsuzsanna (Zee) Budapest is known for her role in the development of Dianic Wicca, a feminist form of the craft that places a strong emphasis on the divine feminine and women's spirituality. This movement emerged as an expression of the feminist movement within the sphere of spirituality, offering a space for women to explore and reclaim their power, autonomy, and connection to the Goddess. Budapest's book *The Holy Book of Women's Mysteries* serves as a seminal work in this tradition, embodying the spirit of sisterhood and empowerment.

Starhawk, an activist, eco-feminist, and author, has also been a key figure in the modern witchcraft movement, particularly through her work in reclaiming traditions. This path of witchcraft emphasises the interconnectedness of spirituality and activism, combining the threads of magic, environmentalism, and social justice. Starhawk's book *The Spiral Dance* is a foundational text within the Reclaiming tradition and beyond, offering insights into the rituals, philosophy, and community-building aspects of contemporary witchcraft. Her work invites practitioners to engage with the craft not only as a personal spiritual path but as a means of enacting change in the world.

In the nineties, Silver RavenWolf played a significant role in popularising the craft among a new generation of seekers. Her books offered accessible and engaging introductions to the practice of witchcraft, inviting readers to integrate witchcraft into their daily lives as a means of empowerment and personal transformation. RavenWolf more recently faced backlash over encouraging teens to practice magic outdoors and not tell their parents about their craft. This criticism seems a little odd to me as someone who (even with relatively open minded parents) did exactly those things as a teenager. Sneaking out with my friends to create rituals was actually among the more benign and tame activities that occupied my time as a wily teenager, and was certainly far less dangerous than other things I got up to in my youth. If I'd grown up in a conservative place or with a family with extreme fears of magic influenced by the "Satanic Panic" of the 80s and 90s, it would have likely been far more dangerous to practise witchcraft openly. RavenWolf is also criticised for her resistance to organised and hierarchical religions, just like many people who've been subjected to controlling experiences.

Many others too have contributed to the modern revivals of witchcraft which continue to evolve, embracing diversity, inclusivity, and a deep commitment to the Earth and all its inhabitants. Scott Cunningham's book for the solitary practitioner opened many doors for people seeking to develop their own practice outside of a group setting. Similarly, Margot

Adler's writing has inspired self-initiates far and wide to practise their own craft.

While not without its share of challenges, the modern witchcraft movement is characterised by its fluidity, its openness to reinterpretation and innovation, and its capacity to empower us, drawing on the wisdom of the past while forging new paths into the future. In this vibrant landscape, witchcraft emerges as a myriad of living traditions, that speaks to the soul's yearnings for connection, understanding, and harmony with the great web of life.

And let's not forget that pagan revival practices have not solely been in the US and UK. For instance, the revival of traditional pre-Christian practices in Lithuania began earlier on in the 1800s with a resurgence in folklore leading to Baltic paganism, with rituals and other ancestral traditions of herbal healing, fortune-telling, and spell-casting. Meanwhile, on the flipside of the planet where I live, the Southern Hemisphere has different magical correspondences and different seasons, and indigenous traditions based around these seasons.

You do not need to be born into a particular magical legacy to be a witch. If you feel a connection to magic, a hunger for the mystical, and a willingness to wander in the darkness, then witchcraft is yours to claim.

WHICH WITCH IS WHICH?

Why don't I use the word Wiccan, Wicca, or spell magic with a k? The words we use are important, and they're most significant in how they make us feel. As someone who was involved with the pagan community in my youth, I must admit I have a certain resistance to the term Wicca, associating it with particular revivalist traditions. I don't subscribe to any specific witchcraft tradition except my own, which I create as I go along. So, while for more than twenty years, I've called myself a witch, for most of that time, I haven't identified as Wiccan.

As for magick with a "k", I believe it has served its purpose and is no longer required. It was a useful spelling when Western paganism had its modern revivals, starting in the early 1900s and becoming more large-scale in the later half of the 20th century. At that time, there was a genuine need to differentiate between the mainstream magic based on illusion and magic shows, and the kind of "real magic" that people were practicing. I no longer believe that this need exists. I don't mind people using magic with a "k", but it's not something I particularly feel called to do.

Now that magical practice has come out of the broom closet, been differentiated, and is much more widely known, there's less need to use special spellings. When I use the word magic, I know that people aren't interpreting it as me pulling a rabbit out of a hat, and so I'm happy to use the ordinary spelling because sometimes reclaiming the spelling of a word has a power of its own.

When we use words that have a particular stigma or judgement attached to them, they can create resistance. And so we can either disperse that resistance, use different words, or come up with our own words. That's really up to us. Part of stepping into our power as witches is using our words wisely with clear intention because all our words are spells, even if they're simply spells to make tea or to share that we care about a loved one. As I mentioned before, we are always accidentally doing magic, and now we are stepping more and more consciously into deliberately doing magic.

WHAT IS MAGIC?

Living in this physical world which we often perceive as hard and heavy with limitations, we are faced with a choice: do we surrender to those limitations, or do we work with them? Magic, to me, is about how we work (deliberately or accidentally) to shape our lives and the world around us.

In this wild, intuitive approach to magic it is important to consider the difference between instinct and intuition. It can be our instinct to flinch in fear, but our intuition may beckon us deeper into questioning our fear. Our instinct is wrapped up in our survival, whereas our intuition lies closer to the soul. It may guide us into some strange places, but there will always be opportunities to learn and heal when we listen to our intuition, if only we are open to it. If you aren't sure how to connect with the wild magic of your intuition, here are some suggestions:

- Take some time to close your eyes and feel into your body each day. Your body, as part of nature, is deeply connected with intuitive wisdom when it isn't distracted by survival instincts.
- Spend relaxed time in or near the water. Water, as an element, is deeply intuitive. Notice the patterns the water makes, notice how it feels, allow your mind to quiet as you take it in. Allow yourself to quietly feel.
- Notice the plants around you, whether they are houseplants, local trees, the gardens in the neighbourhoods nearby, or wild forests. Notice their natural wisdom.

Can magic change anything? Can it change everything?

In my experience, there are some things in life that seem to be predetermined, some things that are rather chaotic, and some things that we influence by our will. For instance, you could choose to make yourself a cup of tea, craft a spell, or perform a ritual. All of that is within your control. The outcomes depend on many factors including your attention, focus, and how aligned you are with your intuition and the outcome you seek. There are also other "weather conditions" – other factors and forces – working all around you, including the will of other people, the shadowy machinations of the collective unconscious and your own shadow-self, among other things. We will be working with these unseen forces later in this book.

Yes, even something as simple as making a cup of tea can be magic, and there are many ways it can go wrong. We don't normally think about it because it's so ordinary. If you're in the habit of doing something, it's so much a part of your everyday accidental magic that you might not even realise what you're doing is a form of potion making.

The stories we tell about our lives are a kind of word magic, and that is one of the most powerful kinds of magic we have. Because as human beings, we are narrative creatures. We tell stories all the time. We can tell a story about our lives as one of misery and failure or one of satisfaction and joy – indeed most of us pivot like this depending on our moods. When everything is going wrong, we might tell a woeful tale about how terrible it all is, but the next day after a good night's rest, our story might look far more easeful. The exact words we use matter less than the feeling and meaning attached to them.

The reason the stories we tell ourselves are so very important is because they shape our entire experience of reality. While this book will go more in-depth into different magical practices, symbols, and ways to work with magic that are more obviously witchy on the surface, the most important work we will do is our inner work. This includes journalling answers to the questions presented here and deliberately re-shaping our stories into ones that serve us better – stories that empower us and support our healing and growth.

It's important to start doing this work because it's a good foundation. This is how we find our own power and step into it. It's through connecting deeply with our sense of being – that is the most important thing because it's where our power is – in the present moment.

So take a moment now to let the thoughts slide out of your mind. Let them drift away like clouds in the sky and just connect with the sense of self. Not your thoughts on who you are, but your feeling of the "I" that you are, the "I Am," the being, the *beingness* of you.

You may already be quite familiar with this sensation, or it may be something you're not especially used to. Taking the time to connect with your sense of being is important for the journey ahead and for bringing magic into your life.

A NOTE ON MAGICAL ITEMS AND SPELLCRAFT

While the paraphernalia associated witchcraft – the candles, the caul-drons, the herbs and crystals – can be useful tools for focusing intention and raising energy, they are not necessary to capture the essence of magic itself.

One of the most powerful tools in the witch's basket is the art of spell-craft. A spell is a ritualised intention, a way of focusing and directing energy towards a specific goal. Spells can be as simple as lighting a candle and setting an intention, or as complex as a multi-day undertaking involving multiple participants and elaborate props.

Effective spellcraft is not about the external trappings, but the clarity and potency of working with your intention. Before you begin any spell, take the time to get clear on what it is you desire. What is the essence stripped of all the superficial details? What would it feel like to have this in your life?

This book will go into greater depth on working with the elements, with crystals and herbs, astrology and kitchen witchery, among other things, but perhaps the most important magical tool of all is the one that is always with us: our own body and breath. By learning to cultivate our presence and awareness we can tap into a well of wisdom within.

You do not need to buy any particular magical tools – in your spells and rituals you can work with what you have, or what you can find. Any colour of candle will do, and if you don't have a candle to hand, you can always imagine one.

The path of the wild witch is about reclaiming our own innate power. By aligning ourselves with the rhythms of nature, working with the elements and energies around us, and cultivating a deep sense of presence and purpose, we can move beyond simply doing magic; we can, ourselves, become magic.

AWAKENING TO THE WHEEL OF THE YEAR

In the turning of the wheel, we find the rhythms and cycles of our own magic. As the earth spins and the sun rises and sets, as the moon waxes and wanes, we too realise that we are part of this eternal unfolding.

The Wheel of the Year, as celebrated by various revivalist Celtic and Gaelic traditions, begins after the winter solstice and ends at Samhain. This makes it different from New Year's traditions, where the year begins within a day, for there is a full six weeks between Samhain and Winter Solstice.

There is no one right way to celebrate the seasons and work with their magic, but we can always look to the seasons for guidance, to the cycles of nature, to our family lines, and anything else that provides a web of deep connectedness into the nature of all things. Just as the river flows adapt to the contours of the land yet remain steadfast in course, so too can we navigate the currents of our own magic, responsive to the ebbs and flows of the seasons yet true to our own inner compass.

Imbolc, being the first of the spring festivals or perhaps the last of the winter festivals, provides an opening of new light, new life, new hope coming out of the cold of winter. Many of our ancestors struggled through harsh winters where the food of the harvest would have to be stored and rationed so that people would survive all through the dormancy, the icy snow and storms, until food could be grown again and harvested and stored, and so the cycle continued. Many of the festivals that we celebrate today were themed around the harvest in various ways. So at the time of early spring or late winter, people were looking towards the year, the hope of bringing in the new, and certain seeds would be planted at this time.

As you read this, some metaphorical seeds may be planted within your psyche too. Just as spring opens the doorway for summer and the eventual harvest to come, what you are open to and the seeds that you plant in your mind as you begin will pave the way for you to step deeper and deeper into the totality of your being. These seeds, warmed by the light of intention and nourished by intuition, can sprout into the verdant landscape of your magical life.

May you be blessed, may you find peace, may you find happiness in this journey. May the rush of the wind bring you clarity, may the soft glow of the moon illuminate your path, and may the strength of your own intuitive wild magic support you.

As the wheel turns towards the Spring Equinox, we find the balance of light and dark. In springtime, there is much new growth and there is much experimentation. As we turn towards Beltane fires, we celebrate the abundant potency of nature. As we continue on into the midsummer solstice, the sun is at its peak and we celebrate it in its full glory, and while we can enjoy this, the harvest is yet to come.

As the wheel turns to Lughnasa, the first of the harvest festivals, we delight in the first fruits. Then at the autumn equinox, the light and the dark are balanced again. We have the opportunity here to go deeper into the shadow and integrate the parts of ourselves that are holding us back from connecting with our deeper magic. As we walk the shadowy path towards Samhain, we connect with our ancestors, with the past, and we let go further of that which we no longer need, just as the trees let go of their final leaves.

The crisp autumn wind, the rustling of dry leaves, the earthy scent of mushrooms... As the natural world sheds what it is ready to let go, so too can we shed the layers of our being that no longer serve us, creating space for new magic to take root. And the wheel turns to Yule, the winter solstice, a time of rest, a time of deep stillness and repose for the Earth.

These cycles too happen in our own lives; many happen all at the same time at different levels. There may be a new cycle of growth in terms of your wellness, you may be ending an old cycle in terms of a social circle you no longer want to be part of, you may be feeling energised on this particular day compared to the low ebb that you're finding in bigger cycles, all at the same time. These cycles are happening moment to moment, as well as daily, weekly, seasonally. Some cycles take many years to complete, and we often see these reflected in the longer-term transits of the outer planets.

In the quiet of winter, we can listen for the wisdom of our own souls. This is a time for journeying inward, for tending to the hearth fires of our spirit, for incubating the seeds that will sprout in the spring to come.

You do not have to celebrate each seasonal festival in any formal way, yet stepping deeper into your own wild magic will likely lead you on a journey of noticing, understanding, working with the cycles of nature and of our own being. In our connection to the powerful forces of nature, the force of all creation and inspiration, we open up to directing this force into our lives in ways that are increasingly deliberate rather than accidental.

KEY QUESTIONS FOR NAVIGATING THE UNKNOWN

"Is it true? Is it necessary? Is it kind?" – Rumi

On a beautiful retreat with my dear friend Chantal, who is a wonderful naturopath and writer, we spoke in much depth about how to distinguish intuitive magical truth from the delusions that are rife in our world. In this discussion, we came up with some useful questions, inspired by the poet Rumi's pondering from a thousand years ago.

1.Does this make sense?

2.Is it useful?

3.Does it feel good?

Venturing into the unknown and mysterious realms can be a daunting and exhilarating experience. These realms, whether they exist in the spiritual, intellectual, or emotional planes, are places where conventional maps and guides fail. To navigate these spaces effectively, we can rely on our inner compass, and use guiding principles that help filter, sort, and discern the path ahead. Does this make sense? Is it useful? Does it feel good?

"Does this make sense?" is a useful question to ask when exploring the unknown. Sense-making involves applying the powers of air – rational thinking and reason – to understand new experiences and information. It requires a balance between scepticism and openness, ensuring that while we remain curious, we do not abandon critical thinking. In many traditions, sense-making is reflected in mythology and folklore. These stories often convey complex truths through allegory and metaphor, providing frameworks to understand the world. For example, the labyrinth in Greek mythology is not just a physical maze, it's a symbol of life's intricate and often perplexing journeys. By asking if something makes sense, we align our exploration with a broader understanding that resonates with ancient wisdom.

"Is it useful?" helps us focus our energy on what genuinely benefits us. This criterion filters out distractions and ensures that our actions and decisions contribute to our growth and well-being. In various traditions, usefulness is a key principle. Many indigenous traditions emphasise practical knowledge passed down through generations, ensuring survival and harmony with nature. By assessing the usefulness of our experiences and insights, we honour these traditions of pragmatic wisdom. In the current world, where information overload is a constant challenge, this question helps us prioritise what truly matters.

"Does it feel good?" taps into our intuition. This is not about seeking immediate pleasure but about aligning with a deeper sense of well-being and authenticity. Intuition is a powerful guide, often reflecting truths that are not immediately apparent to the rational mind.

If something doesn't feel good we can follow this by asking "why?"

Are we simply resistant to it because of past pain or fear? Does this new idea create cognitive dissonance (that strange uncomfortable disconnected feeling when new information tests us) because it challenges our previously held views? If either of these is the case, and we know we have some grieving to do of past experiences before we revisit the question of whether the new idea feels good intuitively to us. If it does not feel good, then we can continue to ask why. Is there a disconnection or devaluing of something important within the idea or philosophy? Is it reductionist or dismissive? It's helpful to understand what our intuition is sparking for or against. Many mystical traditions speak of a still, small voice that guides the seeker. Trusting this inner voice can lead to deep insights and a sense of alignment with ourselves.

THE ALCHEMY OF AWARENESS

As we awaken to the magic within and around us, we begin to see the world with new eyes. Suddenly, the most mundane moments and encounters take on a striking significance, a sense of hidden meaning.

This is the alchemy of awareness – the ability to transmute the ordinary into the extraordinary, the mundane lead of everyday life into the gold of spiritual awakening.

One of the most powerful ways to cultivate this kind of awareness is through the practice of presence. By learning to bring our full attention to the present moment, we begin to notice the subtle energies and interconnections that are always at play, just beneath the surface of our normal perception.

As we deepen our awareness we are likely to connect with and work with the natural cycles and rhythms of the Earth. We may find ourselves attuning to the turning of the seasons, the waxing and waning of the moon, and the rising and setting of the sun. In this deepening awareness we see ourselves, more and more, as part of a larger cosmic web of interconnection that links us to all of life.

As we cultivate this sense of connection and attunement, we may begin to notice synchronicities and serendipities showing up in our lives with increasing frequency. These meaningful coincidences remind us that we are on the right track, that our magic is working.

In our deepening wild awareness we begin to engage in co-creation – understanding that we are not passive recipients of reality, but active participants in shaping it. Every thought we think, every word we speak, every action we take ripples out into the world, creating change on both the seen and unseen levels. As we learn to step into our power with intention and integrity, we become wild witch alchemists, transforming our own lives and the world around us. We become channels for divine creativity, birthing new potentials into being.

The path of magic is not always easy. There will be challenges, obstacles, and times of doubt and darkness. But it is in these moments that new strength is forged, that we are called to dig deep and access the inner resources that we may not have even known we had.

The journey of magic is a journey of remembering – remembering who we really are, remembering the power and potential that lies within us, remembering our sacred connection to all of life. It is a journey of coming home to ourselves, and to the world around us.

As we navigate this path, it is important to stay grounded, centred, and connected to our own inner wisdom. This may mean developing a daily practice of meditation, journalling, ritual, and perhaps finding a community of like-minded seekers to support and inspire us on our way.

It may also mean learning to trust the unfolding of our own unique journey, even when it takes us in unexpected or challenging directions. The path of magic is not a straight line, but a winding, spiralling route, full of twists and turns and surprises.

It is in surrendering to this process, in learning to dance with the mystery and the unknown, that we find our greatest power and our deepest joy. It is in embracing the full spectrum of human experience – the light and the dark, the joy and the sorrow, the transcendent and the mundane – that we become truly whole.

As you journey, know that you are supported, guided, and protected by your own soul's power. Know that your magic is a gift, not just to yourself, but to the world.

AWAKENING TO THE DEEPER MYSTERIES AND THE PATTERNS OF MAGIC IN THE UNIVERSE

Awakening is not a once-off kind of thing. Like the rings within a tree, each layer of awareness reveals new understanding. Whether you're new to magical awakening or you've experienced awakening many times over many years, there is always more to wake up to, to understand. There are always deeper and deeper layers of magic in this world and in our experiences.

I invite you to notice more and more, deeper and deeper, as we traverse this journey, this path together. Allow your awakening to deepen because this is one of the greatest gifts and adventures that you can experience in your life. It will bring you deeper and deeper into your knowing and into the adventure of your life. It's an arrival at a deeper level of awareness, bringing more fullness and richness to your life.

Notice the sky, the breeze, the seasons and the cycles where you live.

Notice what the plants are doing – the trees, the flowers, the animals, and the insects. Notice the elements as you find them in your daily life. The outer world is a mirror, reflecting back to you the patterns and the magic that exist within you.

You do not have to go on a retreat or meditate for hours at a time to awaken to the mysteries of life. You can find shimmers in any moment, in any experience. Imagine an apple, its shape, its intense flavour as you bite into it. Let this experience wash over you just like you experience other the sensations of life. Just like apples, life can sometimes be disappointing. As I talk about an apple, be it a tart Granny Smith or a floury Royal Gala past its best, a reflection occurs in your mind as you experience something akin to your memory of your previous encounters with apples – of pleasure, disappointment, discomfort. Be it the apple slices that have browned after sitting around in your lunchbox for hours, or that soothing flavour of cinnamon apple pie or crumble. Tuning into experience like this is powerful magic, even those that seem humble, unsatisfying, or even unpleasant. When we open to experience, we allow ourselves to deepen our awareness, moment by moment.

The outer world is constantly going through cycles, spiralling in and spiralling out. And as we live in a reflective universe, you can see the patterns and cycles if you look closely enough at anything – the seasons, the cycle of birth and death, the fronds of a fern. All these things are evidence of the reflective universe. In fact, almost anything, if you look at it closely enough, can serve as evidence. The magic is everywhere, woven into the fabric of existence, waiting for you to perceive it, to align with it, to work with it.

The ancient maxim "As above, so below" serves as compass to navigate within the Western esoteric tradition. This phrase encapsulates the wisdom that the macrocosm and microcosm reflect each other. This concept is not at all unique to Western traditions and is echoed across the mystical depths of Taoism, Shintoism, and tantra in Hindu and Buddhist traditions and many indigenous cultures, including the one I grew up immersed in.

It is not surprising to find these similarities reflected in the intricate patterns of nature. I cannot, and do not, speak as an expert on any particular tradition, and I do not wish to over generalise, because traditions are complex, varied, and historically are bound intimately to specific places and times. However, it would be rude not to acknowledge that recognising these patterns is manifold, and though there are many differences across traditions and cultures, their many similarities may indeed come from observing the patterns of nature within which they originally evolved.

This principle of a reflective universe suggests that the heavens mirror the earth, and the outer world reflects the inner realms of the human soul. It invites the seeker to understand the universe not as a series of disconnected parts, but as a unified whole, where patterns of stars and planets in the sky, the flight of birds and hum of insects can all reflect insights to us. The body is a microcosm of society, and also of the cosmos; nothing exists in isolation, but everything arises in connection. A holistic approach can honour this deep connectedness.

Fractals are intricate patterns that repeat at different scales, showing an astonishing level of self-similarity whether viewed from afar or up close. They are found in the branching of trees, the formation of coastlines, and even in the structure of human lungs, illustrating the recursive patterns that nature employs. Fractals remind us that the complexity of the cosmos is built from simple repeating patterns, the seen and the unseen, the vast and the minute.

Life speaks to us in the language of patterns, from the fractals in a fern leaf to the spiral arms of a galaxy, echoing the patterns of pinecones, sunflowers, and seashells. These patterns are the fingerprints of the cosmos in which we are included, revealing the inherent symmetry and harmony that underlies the evolution of creation. They remind us that the same mathematical principles that guide the growth of plants and the formation of galaxies also resonate within us.

I find it an astonishing parallel that our galaxy contains approximately a hundred billion stars, just as the human brain is composed of roughly a hundred billion neurons. This suggests that the vastness of the cosmos is reflected in the intricate complexity of our minds. It invites us to wonder at the possibility that our thoughts and dreams are not just fleeting electrical impulses, but are in fact a reflection of the conscious life force of the universe contemplating itself through us.

Human beings seek out meaning and patterns in whatever we see.

This pattern-seeking is sometimes called Apophenia. Our minds can weave all kinds of stories around the patterns we seek including many that are unhelpful. Once we recognise the patterns we have more ability to respond to them and alter them to suit the new stories we want to tell about ourselves and our lives, and this deliberate weaving is a kind of magic. Magic is not only found in the extraordinary. It is woven into the everyday, in the symmetry of a snowflake, the rhythm of the tides, and the vibrant life of the forest.

Reflections

What patterns do you most notice in nature?

Can you find similar patterns in other areas of your life, your work, your family etc?

What story do these patterns tell for you?

AWAKENING TO OUR SELF-WORTH

You are already worthy. You are already infinitely worthy. And how do I know this? Because you are an amazing, magnificent part of this magnificent cosmos. The world would be less without you in it.

The discovery about worthiness is not a seeking of something outside ourselves or even within ourselves. It's an uncovering of what we already are – an awareness, a deepening. You could not be any more worthy than you already are. It's not possible. And yet, many of us go about our days feeling like we're not enough. We are, at our essence, like the sun: always shining, always radiant, yet sometimes obscured by clouds of doubt, pain, fear, and self-judgement.

Of course, it doesn't help that we live in worlds full of other people's judgement of how we should be better or faster or stronger or that we should have accomplished more. We're bombarded by advertisements designed deliberately to make us feel worse so that we spend money on the very products people are trying to sell us.

Loving yourself and connecting with your innate worthiness is a radical act. It is a reclaiming of your power, a casting off of the spells of inadequacy and unworthiness that have been cast upon you.

You do not need the latest lipstick, shampoo, the fanciest new car, or the most desirable cologne. You don't need to buy fancy witchy equipment either! You do not need to purchase or consume or even exercise in order to be worthy. You simply are. So if you choose to have that cologne or that lipstick or to exercise, that is a choice. Your worthiness does not depend on it, not at all.

Just as a tree in the forest is worthy to be there, so too do you deserve completely to be of this living world. And the closer you get to owning that worthiness, to stepping into your power, the more magical your life will become. Enter the world and enter your life. Step into your magic, your radiance, your innate power. For you belong here, as a child of the earth and the stars, as a magical being, a force of nature. The world is waiting for you to bloom.

CREATING AN ALTAR

An altar can serve as a place to commune with your inner self, honour the changing seasons, and connect with the deeper currents of your magic. This does not need to be big or complicated; a windowsill or a shoebox will do, or perhaps you have a table or shelf just waiting to be adorned with witchy seasonal items. Somewhere in your life, there is probably a space waiting to be transformed into a sacred altar. This altar is a reflection of your unique journey, a mosaic collection, a reflection of your inner world, and a portal to the realms of magic and self-discovery.

Begin by selecting a space that calls to you, a place where you feel a sense of peace and possibility. This could be a table, a shelf, or even a humble box. Trust your intuition in selecting a space that suits you.

Once you have chosen your space, it is time to gather items that resonate with your spirit. Look to nature for inspiration and consider the season. In autumn, you might collect vibrant leaves, acorns, or small pumpkins. In spring, fresh flowers, budding branches, or delicate shells may call to your soul.

Consider also the four elements and how you can represent them on your altar. For earth, gather stones, crystals, or a small bowl of soil. For water, include a vessel of water or seashells. For fire, a candle or a piece of charcoal. And for air, feathers, incense, or a bell. Each element brings its own unique energy, adding balance and harmony to your sacred space.

Your altar can also be a place to honour your family heritage and your creative passions. Include photographs, heirlooms, or objects that hold sentimental value, connecting you to your roots and the rich history of your ancestry. If you have a creative practice, add symbols of your craft – paintbrushes, notebooks, or musical instruments – to nurture and inspire your creative spirit.

Before arranging your altar, take a moment to set a clear intention. Is there a specific purpose of this sacred space, or is it more general? Is it for healing, creativity, protection, or something else that resonates deeply with you? You may wish to write your intention on a piece of paper and place it on your altar as a focal point, a reminder of the magic you are invoking.

Now it is time to clear your altar space, both physically and energetically. Clean the surface and remove any clutter, creating a blank canvas for your sacred creation. Then, using a bundle of dried herbs or incense and salt water, cleanse the energetic field of your altar. Visualise any stagnant or negative energy dissipating, leaving behind a pure, vibrant space. As you cleanse, hold your intention in your heart, infusing your altar with your purpose and desires.

With your space cleared and your intention set, begin arranging your items on your altar. Let your intuition be your guide, and trust that each item will find its perfect place. You might create a symmetrical arrangement or opt for an organic, free-flowing design. There is no right or wrong way – this is your personal expression, a reflection of your inner landscape.

As you place each item, take a moment to connect with its energy and significance. You may want to include personal symbols or talismans that hold deep meaning for you, such as a piece of jewellery or a small figurine. These personal touches add a layer of intimacy and power to your altar.

Consider also incorporating elements of light and sound. Some people even add fairy lights. It really is up to you. A small bell, chimes, or a music box can introduce a soothing auditory element, creating a multi-sensory experience.

With your altar complete, it is time to breathe life into it through regular engagement. Spend time with your altar each day, even if only for a few moments. Light a candle, sit in meditation, or simply pause and take a few deep breaths. Use this time to connect with your inner self, to reflect on your journey, and to reaffirm your intentions.

You might also incorporate rituals into your altar practice. This could be as simple as lighting a candle each morning or as elaborate as a full moon ceremony. Let your altar be a living, dynamic part of your daily life, evolving and changing as you grow and transform.

An altar requires regular maintenance and refreshment. Dust and clean your altar often, both physically and energetically. As you do so, take note of any items that no longer resonate with you or your intention. Remove these items and replace them with new ones that reflect your current path.

In this way, your altar remains a mirror of your inner world, a sacred space that evolves and changes with you. It is a constant reminder of your own magic, your own power to create and transform your reality.

SACRED SPACE

Magical traditions have long recognised the importance of preparing a sacred space before ritual. Creating a sacred space often begins with cleansing the area, such as using a broom to sweep away physical and energetic debris then blessing with the smoke of herbs and by sprinkling salt water around. In ritual, this cleansing and blessing happens before a circle is cast, marking a transition from the ordinary world into encountering the sacred and divine. The concept of sacred space does not only apply to ritual, it can be a helpful part of our everyday magical practice and no tools or herbs are even required.

While preparing the physical space is important in many witchcraft practices, creating a sacred space also involves an inner process, turning our attention inward, quieting the mind, and connecting in. Meditation can be a useful tool here. By focusing on our breath and visualising a peaceful place, we create an inner sanctuary where we can connect with our intentions and the divine.

In our inner lives, sacred space is about presence, a gentle awareness, a safety that allows for a level of openness rare in most ordinary life. This begs the question: why would we bother to go to the trouble of burning herbs and sprinkling salt water if we can simply imagine ourselves into sacred space? The answer to this lies most simply in *practice*. When we create sacred space symbolically, using external aids, we open up, more and more, to noticing it, to understanding it, and more easily arriving into it within ourselves.

This inner work helps us to align our thoughts and emotions with the energy of the sacred. It's about finding a place of calm and focus within ourselves, which mirrors the calm and focus we are projecting out into our lives.

Similarly, outer preparations are mirrored by an inner journey. To create sacred space is to open a doorway to the liminal and the divine, to tend to our presence, to draw near to the soul which lies deep beneath ordinary consciousness. It is there, in the depths of the psyche, that sacred space is found.

The word *liminal* means "in between," derived from the Latin word "limen," meaning threshold. It is used to describe a state or space that is transitional or in between, where the usual limits or boundaries are blurred. Liminal spaces can refer to physical areas like doorways, hallways, or transitions that evoke a sense of being between worlds. This can include moments between waking and sleeping or the rites of passage that lead from one phase of life to another. When we invoke sacred space, we deliberately call forth liminality, a space in between the business of the outside world and the churn of our inner thoughts. We set aside out mundane concerns so that we can make space for stillness, so that we can hold space for magic, so that we can invite in the divine.

In sacred space, we enter a state of subtle meditation, connecting with our breath, the rhythm of life that flows like the ebb and tide of the ocean. Visualisation can support this process for those who are so inclined. With our mind's eye we can construct an inner sanctuary, a place of peace and power. This may be an inner temple, a peaceful grove surrounded by forest, a lush blooming garden, a serene beach with open horizons, or a majestic mountain peak.

For those who are not so enthusiastic about visualisation, entering sacred space may simply be via a feeling, a word, or even a sound or scent. It may be holding your hand to your heart just for a moment in order to connect with your presence, letting a song into your mind that draws you into inner-peace, or using subtle items such as a crystal in your pocket.

Whatever works for you is far more important than what anyone's prescribed instructions could tell you, though be aware that what works for you today may change tomorrow, or next year. We, in life, are all changing at every moment, and magic provides us an opportunity to be present with that change and to channel it towards the most wonderful outcomes.

At times, focusing outward, on the outcomes you desire can de-centre you, casting you out of your inner sacred space. When you notice this happening, take slow deep breaths and allow yourself to be aware. Notice how the tensions you are carrying are dispersing your energy and presence. The situation may be highly important, and it may cause stress in your body, but even then, you will be blessed by your own presence in sacred space if only you can allow yourself to come back to it.

Pulling back energy and attention is a powerful magical act. Taking your power back, letting it seep out of your fears, clawing it back from external situations that enrage you, setting it free from old resentments and grudges you may be holding, is some of the most powerful work you can do, gently and subtly freeing you from the tangled web of tensions that many people live their lives stuck between.

For this reason, sacred space and presence is an important starting point in a magical journey, for it is only when you can return to centre and cultivate presence, that you can be free and energised to step into your power with deliberate intent.

Now, I'm not going to pretend this is easy, and as a highly distractable person with an absurdly overactive mind I've found things like sitting still for meditation to be extremely boring! However, I do not need to sit still to cultivate my inner sacred space. Sometimes all I need to do is breathe and connect with my senses, my body, my being. Other times, I need to go for a walk, preferably by the sea, and allow myself to open up to the beauty of nature. At times I simply need a nap, or to lie down and listen to gentle music, or to reach out to a dear friend for a chat. All of these things can help me cultivate my relationship with my inner sacred space which is also my relationship with my deeper psyche and soul.

In this state, the boundaries of the self dissolve, and we become one with the sacred. This is not a thing that can be fully learned or completed. It is a practice and it is ongoing, for in life nothing truly ends, there is always more to unfold. And this is part of what keeps us humble. Surrendering to the soil of our limited existences here.

We cannot win at sacred space, and so the parts of ourselves that long to compete, that want to attain glory, that strive for perfection (the part sometimes called the ego) has no use within sacred space and can simply rest. Within sacred space normal linear time dissolves, and we simply are *as we are* – eternal and ever changing with the humility of knowing that long after our time on this planet, long after the sun has exploded and our galaxy has been consumed by a black hole life will still continue to unfold.

Initially, the concept of sacred space might seem confined to specific rituals or locations. However, as you continue to practice, you realise that sacred space is not limited by physical boundaries. It becomes a state of mind, an awareness that you carry with you. This state of mind allows you to find and create sacredness wherever you are, in whatever you are doing.

Gradually, you start to perceive the sacred in everyday moments – a morning sunrise, the sound of rain, or the simple act of breathing. These moments become touchstones, reminders of the sacredness that permeates all of existence. So it is that we return to sacred space, time and time again, whether it is within ritual, meditation, or even in brief moments during a busy day. Sometimes all it takes is one fleeting moment where you can close your eyes for just a few seconds and connect with your inner presence.

Sacred space also teaches us about boundaries and protection. By marking the edges of our circle, we create a safe and contained area for our work. This concept can be applied to our everyday lives, reminding us to create healthy boundaries and protect our own energy.

BLURRING THE LINES BETWEEN SACRED AND MUNDANE

As you deepen your practice, you may begin to see that every moment, every action, can be infused with sacredness. There is no clear boundary where the sacred ends and the mundane begins. This realisation may shift your perspective, allowing you to approach life with a sense of reverence and wonder.

This shift is not about denying the challenges and difficulties of life but about recognising the inherent sacredness in every experience. By bringing a magical mindset to mundane tasks, you transform them. Cooking, cleaning, and even commuting become opportunities for subtle bliss, reverence, and connection to the divine. Every act becomes a ritual, every moment a chance to commune with the sacred.

As your practice evolves, the sacred space you create begins to expand beyond the confines of your rituals. It becomes a presence that envelops your entire life. The boundaries between your spiritual practice and daily life dissolve, and you find yourself living in a state of continuous sacred awareness.

This process is deeply transformative. The illusions and distractions that once clouded your perception begin to fade away. You see through the superficial layers of reality to the underlying truths. This clarity allows you to step deeper into your power, to act with intention and purpose. You become more aligned with your self and your path, and your power.

This power is not about control, but rather, it is empowerment, authenticity and alignment with your deeper self. With this comes the power to create change in your life and the world around you.

I will say it again, because sometimes these things need to be heard over and over to be understood and remembered: cultivating sacred space, both internally and externally, is an ongoing practice. It involves continually returning to the present moment, reconnecting with your inner self, and honouring the sacredness of nature and all that is. As you do so, you will find that your life becomes richer and more glorious.

The practice of creating sacred space is a gateway to a deeper, more connected way of living. It may start with specific rituals and physical preparations but gradually it can expand to encompass your entire life.

In many spiritual traditions, there is no necessary boundary where the sacred ends and the profane or mundane begins, however in others, the sacred and profane must be kept separate at all costs.

In my experience of witchcraft, our awareness of the sacred expands to encompass all things, eventually. While it can be important to have boundaries – with good reason – it is possible to live a life where all previously disparate parts become woven into the divinity of being.

I do suggest that if you're drawing on traditions in your practice, including ancient deities or cultures that your ancestors belonged to, take the initiative and learn about how the sacred and profane were understood and respected within those cultures. Many cultures and customs separate the sacred and profane for reasons specific to their particular society, often relating to safety and wellbeing. For instance, eating is separated from other activities that might be unsanitary.

It's important to be open to learning rather than getting defensive. To disrespect others whether in wilful arrogance or ignorance, in this reflective universe, is also to disrespect a part of yourself, and that only adds to the burdens of shadow.

I do not wish to "take" from cultures that have had so much taken from them already, unless it is something they are especially open to sharing. You can research the difference between open and closed traditions, or let your intuition guide you, but do pay attention and do your best to take responsibility for your practice and treat other traditions with the respect they deserve. Such an approach creates the space for you to stand more strongly within your own integrity. This does not mean you have to observe any particular ancient custom, but only that you are open to paying respect to the related ancestors and deities.

THE LIMINALITY OF TIME WITHIN SACRED SPACE

This is sacred time, this is sacred space, I am fully present, here and now

The concept of the liminal is central to the creation and experience of sacred space. As I said earlier, liminality refers to the threshold, the in-between state where transformation and change are possible. In sacred space, we step into this liminal realm, a place where the boundaries between the physical and spiritual, the mundane and the magical, blur and dissolve.

Throughout time, in stories and legends, witches have occupied a liminal space, often dwelling on the margins, on the outskirts of society or cast out into the shadows. Sometimes more kindly, they are portrayed as mediators between the mundane and the mystical. They are the wise ones, the healers, the seers, and the protectors, sharing their knowledge of the natural world and its hidden forces to heal, to guide, and sometimes, to exact justice. Their power comes not from dominion over the world but from a deep communion with it, a relationship built on respect, understanding, and the reciprocal exchange of energy.

One of the most fascinating aspects of sacred space is how time behaves differently within it. Liminal time can stretch and compress in ways that defy our usual perceptions. Mere moments within sacred space can feel profoundly extended, rich with meaning and depth, while at other times, entire hours might pass in what seems like the blink of an eye. This fluidity of time is part of the liminal nature of sacred space.

When you enter sacred space, you step out of ordinary time and into what can be thought of as "sacred time." This is a time that exists outside of the usual constraints and flows of daily life. In this state, time becomes a vessel, holding the energy and intention of your practice. It allows for deep immersion and connection, facilitating powerful transformation.

By creating sacred space, you also create a container for sacred time. This container holds the potential for magic and change, allowing you to work within a time that is not bound by the usual rules. Here, you can dive deeply into your rituals and meditations, experiencing a sense of time-lessness that enhances your practice.

In this liminal state, the past, present, and future can converge. You might find yourself gaining insights into past experiences, seeing the present with greater clarity, and receiving glimpses of possible futures. This space is both liberating and transformative. It provides a space where you can explore, experiment, and expand your awareness.

In this state, you may find that your senses are heightened, your intuition sharpened. You become more attuned to the subtle energies around you and within you. This heightened awareness allows you to perceive the sacredness in all things, deepening your connection to the world and to your own inner self.

Allow yourself to let go of the usual constraints and expectations of time. Be present in the moment. Trust that the time you spend in sacred space is exactly what you need, whether it feels like a fleeting moment of communion or a long sojourn with the mystical.

EXERCISE FOR CREATING SACRED SPACE

Sacred space is not just a physical location but a liminal realm where time behaves differently, allowing for deep transformation and connection. By creating this space, you step into sacred time, a vessel that holds the potential for magic and change. Embrace the fluidity of time within this space, and let it enhance your practice and your being.

Materials
A small bowl of water with a little sea salt added
A candle
Incense or a bundle of dried herbs
A lighter or matches

A favourite crystal or talisman (optional)

Steps

Find a quiet spot: Choose a place where you won't be disturbed. This could be a corner of a room, a spot in your garden, or any place that feels comfortable and safe.

Set up your space: Arrange your materials in front of you. Place the bowl of water, the candle, the incense or dried herb bundle, and the dish of salt within easy reach. If you have a crystal or talisman, place it in the centre of your space.

Light the candle: Light the candle and take a moment to focus on the flame. Let its light and warmth fill your mind with a sense of peace.

Cleanse with water: Dip your fingers into the bowl of salted water and lightly sprinkle it around your space. As you do, you may wish to say something like:

"With the powers of water and earth, I cleanse this space."

Cleanse with smoke: Light the incense or dried herb bundle. Waft the smoke around your space, letting it drift into every corner. As you do, you may wish to say something like:

"With the powers of fire and air, I bless this space."

Place your crystal: If you have a crystal or talisman, hold it in your hands and close your eyes. Focus on its energy and let it resonate with your intention to create a sacred space. Place it in the centre of your space.

Chant and Meditate: Sit comfortably and take a few deep breaths. When you are ready you may wish to say:

"This is sacred time, this is sacred space, I am fully present, here and now."

Allow yourself to fully immerse in this moment, letting go of all distractions.

Sit in silence for a few moments. Feel the energy of the sacred space you have created. Notice any changes in your thoughts, feelings, or the atmosphere around you.

Close the Space: When you are ready, take a deep breath. Gently extinguish the candle and incense, and know that you can return to this sacred space whenever you choose.

Reflections

Take a moment to reflect on the experience.

How did it feel to create sacred space?

Did you notice any changes in your energy or mood?

This simple exercise can be performed regularly to maintain a sense of peace and focus in your life. As you become more familiar with the practice, you may wish to personalise it, adding elements that resonate deeply with you.

CIRCLE CASTING

Circle casting tends to begin with creating sacred space, where the mundane world is set aside, and the focus shifts to the magical. This clears the mind and prepares the environment for the work to come.

Once the sacred space is created, it's time to cast the circle. Begin in the east and move deosil or sunwise. The direction which the sun travels appears differently here in the Southern Hemisphere, so we walk from east to north, then west, and finally south, completing the circle back at the east. In the Northern Hemisphere, the sun's path leads us from east to south, then west, and north, returning to the east. By aligning our movements with the sun's journey, we honour the natural rhythms and energies of our environment.

Circle casting is can be done by marking out the perimeter of your sacred space. You can do this physically, with a cord or chalk, or more frequently, the circle is cast with your focused intention as you walk around the boundary of your circle, drawing an energetic line with your hand or sometimes with a wand or staff. As you move, visualise a barrier forming, glowing with protection and peace, enclosing the space in a sphere of clear, sacred energy.

If you are working in a group, usually one person will cast the circle, walking around the inside of the gathered group, pointing with their hand, a wooden wand or staff, drawing it in the air behind people.

When you've completed the circle and returned to the east, take a moment to feel the energy you've raised and the protective barrier you've created. You might envision the circle glowing with light or feel a change in the air. This is your sacred space, a place outside of time, a space for magic.

Within this circle, allow your mind to clear. Feel the energy of the space itself, now cleansed and sealed, ready to support you. Here, in this sacred container, you're free to explore and to connect with the deeper parts of yourself, and to work your magic with clarity and focus. This circle is your container, a bubble set apart from the everyday world, where you can meditate, perform rituals, or engage in magical work without outside interference. It's a place where the energy can build, focused and potent, a sanctuary for your spiritual practice.

When your work is complete, take a moment to acknowledge the peace and protection the circle has provided. Then, gently dissolve the boundary, visualising it fading, as you thank the space for its support. This step is as important as the casting, for it signifies the return to the everyday world, carrying with you the insights and energies of your practice.

To cast a circle is to create a container. You may wish to think about what you'd like to call into this container beforehand, and have a temporary altar set up in the centre before you start. If the circle is being cast for a particular purpose, like a seasonal ritual, your altar will likely be adorned with items representing that reason or season.

Within this space, you can perform your magical work, whether it's a spell, a ritual to honour the season, a moment of meditation, or any other spiritual practice. When you're finished, thank the elements and any deities or spirits you've invited. Walk around the circle in the opposite direction from which it was cast, imagining the circle's energy dissipating or returning to the earth.

The power of the circle lies in the intention and energy you bring to it. Each time you cast a circle, you weave together the seen and unseen, stepping into the role of creator within your own sacred realm.

Now that we have cast the circle, it's time to get experimental with our magic.

2

EXPERIMENTAL MAGIC

"Magic isn't somewhere else...Magic is turning to the world, and seeing it, and knowing we are indistinguishable from it, in all our embodied, strange, soft and edgeless form. We are in the world and it is in us." - Alice Tarbuck

THE FOUR ELEMENTS

In Western magical traditions the four elements – Earth, Air, Fire, and Water – are good friends and companions that guide us. Their presence can be felt in the subtleties of the natural world and within ourselves. Engage with these elements intuitively, allowing them to reveal their mysteries to you.

Earth: Pick up a stone or handful of soil. Notice its weight, its texture. Feel the stability beneath your feet. Spend time in a forest or garden, absorbing the stillness and strength of the land around you. Let Earth show you its secrets.

Air: Close your eyes and breathe deeply. Feel the air fill your lungs and the breeze on your skin. Listen to the rustle of leaves, the songs of the wind. Light incense or hang wind chimes and let their movement guide your thoughts. Let Air share its messages to you.

Fire: Light a candle and watch the flame dance. Sit by a fire and feel its warmth. Allow the sunlight to touch your face. Pay attention to how these experiences make you feel – how they stir your inner fire and awaken your passions. Let Fire reveal its energy to you.

Water: Dip your fingers into a bowl of water or sit by a stream. Listen to the gentle lap of waves or the rush of a river. Gaze into a reflective surface, watching how it mirrors and distorts. Allow yourself to flow with these sensations and discover what Water has to offer.

Spend time with each element, letting them guide you in their own way. Notice how they interact with you, how they ground, inspire, transform, and heal. There is no need for definitions – let your senses and intuition lead you. This chapter goes into more detail on the elements. I have also created a short online course to go deeper into the elements which can be accessed for free if you have this book. Check the "extra goodies" page at the end of the book for details.

SUMMONING THE ELEMENTS IN RITUAL

Summoning the directions and their corresponding elements in ritual practice is a way to honour the energies of the earth and to invite balance and harmony into your sacred space. The process can vary slightly depending on whether you're in the Northern or Southern Hemisphere, due to the different paths the sun takes across the sky in each.

In both hemispheres, East corresponds with the element of Air and West with Water, but in the other two the elements and directions have reversed correspondences (South is Fire in the Northern Hemisphere and Earth in the Southern Hemisphere) because of the reversed polarities and also the reversed directions.

When I call upon the elements, I do so using whatever words naturally come to me, however sometimes it helps to have some prompts or even a script – especially in large planned rituals if a particular style is desired.

Air: Begin by facing the east, the direction of dawn and new beginnings. Invoke the element of air, which represents thoughts, knowledge, and the breath of life. You might say, "Welcome to the powers of Air, keepers of wisdom and clarity, I call upon you to bless this circle with your presence."

Fire: Turn to the south (or north if you're in the Southern Hemisphere), the direction of the noonday sun and the element of fire. This element symbolises energy, passion, and transformation. A summoning might be, "I greet and honour the powers of Fire, spark of life and passion, bringers of change, I invite you to warm this circle with your flames."

Water: Move to face the west, the direction of the setting sun and the element of water. Water represents emotion, intuition, and the mysteries of the deep. You could call upon it with words like, "Spirits of Water, of empathy and compassion, guardians of the depths, I summon you to flow through this circle with your wisdom."

Earth: Finally, turn to the north (or south), the direction of the night and the element of earth. Earth embodies stability, growth, and physical abundance. To summon it, you might say, "I welcome the powers of Earth, grounding, stability, and protectors of the land, I call upon you to hold this circle in your strength."

After calling upon the elements and directions, you stand in the centre of your circle, a place of balance and power, where you are connected to all things.

WORKING WITH THE ENERGY OF DEITIES (OR NOT)

Engaging with gods or deities is one *potential* aspect of witchcraft. Not all witches work with deities. If you do not feel called to work with the energy of any gods or goddesses, some witches find their path leads them more towards an inner connection with their own divine essence or with the spirit of the universe and nature itself. This approach can be equally powerful and fulfilling, focusing on the interconnectedness of all things and the personal empowerment that comes from within. Connecting with your inner divine involves introspection and self-awareness. It's about recognising the spark of divinity within yourself and nurturing that connection through meditation, self-care, and personal rituals that resonate with your soul.

If you do feel called to work with gods, goddesses, and other deities you will likely find that it is a deeply personal and powerful aspect of spiritual work. It requires respect, not only for the rich cultures these deities come from (even if this is your own heritage) but also for the deities themselves, each embodying complex characteristics and energies. When you invite a deity into your ritual space, you're opening a dialogue with ancient energies and wisdom, so it's essential to approach this with mindfulness and preparation.

First, if you feel drawn to work with a specific deity, take time to learn about their origins and stories. Understanding the historical and mythological context of a deity can deepen your connection and respect for both the deity and the culture. It's also a way to ensure your practice is respectful and informed.

Consider their associations and domains. Many deities have elements they are closely tied to, such as love, war, wisdom, or the underworld. These associations can guide how you might invite their presence, whether through offering specific symbols, colours, foods, or incense related to them.

Be open to the lessons and insights that working with a deity can bring into your life, especially if they are associated with more shadowy aspects. Engaging with these deities can be transformative, prompting you to confront and integrate shadow elements within yourself. This work isn't always easy, and must be treated with care and with appropriate respect.

INVOKING DEITIES WITH RESPECT

Preparation: Before the ritual, spend time meditating on the deity's stories and teachings. Create a space that welcomes their energy, perhaps setting up an altar with items that represent them.

Invocation: With clear intention and respect, call to the deity, using names and titles that honour them. Your call can be a simple invitation, expressing your desire for their presence, guidance, or assistance. For example, "Great [Deity's Name], who guides and protects, I invite you into this space. I seek your wisdom and strength."

Engagement: Once you've invited the deity into your space, share your thoughts, questions, or offerings with them. This can be a silent meditation, spoken words, or a physical offering left on your altar.

Appreciation: Always conclude your work with a deity by offering thanks for their presence and any insights or assistance they've provided. Acknowledge their continued guidance and express your appreciation for the connection.

Release: Bid the deity farewell, acknowledging their return to their realm but keeping the door open for future communication and guidance.

Remember, the relationship with a deity is built over time, with respect and mutual understanding. Stay open to their messages and teachings, and always approach this work with appreciation and reverence.

THE ELEMENT OF EARTH

The element of Earth connects us most deeply with nature at its physical, tangible level. This includes our bodies and the entire material world. In the past several hundred years of dominant society, and much further back in some places, there has been a painful disconnection with nature. If you look at scientific, philosophical, and spiritual texts, especially those written before the 1970s, nature was something to be conquered and tamed, not something to be loved or communed with.

This was not the reality for many indigenous societies. There was no "us and them" disconnection from nature. Nature in its many forms is interconnected so deeply with pre-colonised human customs, practices, and beliefs that it's hard to make any kinds of separations. The ethics and values of a society based within nature are interconnected with other kinds of ethics and values, as well as with mythology and the key stories told to the children and elders alike.

You see, mythology can tell us a lot about ourselves. Many traditional societies have myths and stories that involve protecting nature, stories that are told to encourage people not to overfish the rivers or warnings against other destructive behaviours. The element of Earth often needs to be guarded and protected in one way or another within societies. The abundance of the harvest needs to be carefully preserved and rationed in the colder months.

There's something about the material world that has hard limits to it. Earth is a limiting material by nature. This does not make it bad. It is merely how it behaves. And this material world that we live in, though it has many other layers in it, can be seen as the world of limitation. But the challenges and limitations that we face can also lead to new advancements and insights, new strengths, and all kinds of development.

As I write this, I'm sitting on the grass, twigs scratching my legs a little. I can feel the hum of the earth beneath me on this beautiful planet, filled with all its many complex challenges. I can connect with the abundance of nature, the beautiful, ever-changing, ever-transforming reflection that it has mirrored in our own souls.

When we watch the forest, we see that the leaves must fall, even for the evergreens, and that eventually, the trees let go, light a sigh, and fall too, surrendering back to the earth. When they do so, they make room for something new to grow. Life and death are always present with us in the material world and in nature, which may be one reason why in our egoic quests for immortality, human beings have shunned nature to such an extreme, have sought to conquer it, and do not like to look too closely, especially at the shadowy parts. Nature is messy. The leaves fall and they mulch the ground, and new life grows from that rich compost.

Earth is the slowest-moving element. It is steady, it is supportive. Metaphorically, it is structure; it is the skeletons in our bodies. It is also our greatest, deepest joy. The element of earth is associated with pleasure. It is sensual. It is abundant, overflowing with riches beyond measure.

THE PARADOX OF EARTH

The paradox of Earth is that as it relates to the material, it is sometimes considered to be shallow. People who seek money are seen as one-dimensional. To value money and wealth is seen as something that spiritual people wouldn't do. How can we not value all parts of nature? How can we not celebrate, rejoice, and appreciate all of the bounty of this world when it's simply so magnificent?

I'm not sure exactly why there is a trend for spiritual people to be broke a lot of the time. I suspect that there are multiple factors. Perhaps a trauma has occurred in the psyche, which makes people distrust the material world, including their bodies, and therefore seek out the spiritual to compensate. Or they've judged in other people a certain materialistic greed and a poverty in terms of the soul, and they are trying as best they can not to fall into that trap by doing the opposite, by shunning the material world and devaluing it in order to value the spiritual, and so on.

If this sounds like you, I have some slightly challenging news: **this is ALL the spiritual world**. At least from my perspective, there is no separation between material and spiritual, ultimately. All is connected. Nature as we see it reflects all the many patterns of spirituality. Nature is also the material – the material is nature. This includes money, that even includes private jets and fancy cars and plastic mansions, all bizarre parts of nature.

But how can plastic and credit cards and expensive yachts be part of nature? There is no point at which nature ends and the artificial begins. From this perspective, all things are natural and all things are spiritual at their core. This doesn't mean that we can't have good ethics, because we most certainly can, especially when it comes to protecting vulnerable people and natural ecosystems.

Of course, we can have ethics and values, and it's important to consider what feels right and wrong for you, and what values those ethics are based on. But when you burst the bubble of the false dichotomy between what is created by humans and what is nature, you see that human beings *are* nature. There is no point at which nature stops and not-nature begins. We are all simply part of the same continuum of evolving, devolving, messed up, complicated, sometimes incredibly frustrating, absurd and ridiculous nature.

Nature has a way of playing tricks upon itself because it is part of a universe that is continually delving deeper, separating further, and creating all sorts of strange, unusual, and interesting experiences, including the very real, very intense, very limiting experience of being human.

Connecting with the Earth can be a humbling experience and, like I will elaborate on further, to be humbled literally means to be brought down to earth, to the humus of soil. That's where the word comes from. And that's what happens when we connect deeply to the earth. We no longer are deluded into the illusions of separation and disconnection. We begin to see that we are part of the beautiful, complex symmetry of the natural world, and as we lean deeper and deeper into that mystery, synchronicities of magic and joy show up in our lives.

EARTHLY SENSATIONS

Everything we experience in this life is navigated through the physical, material manifestation of our bodies. When you taste a raspberry, the sensory receptors in your tongue transmit complex information through to your brain, which you would interpret as the tangy, sweet, fragrant sensation of the berry, its texture, its scent. All are navigated through the body, in this material manifestation. Of course, the body contains water as well. It breathes air and generates heat which can be related to the element of fire. We experience all these things through the material reality of our bodies, through our senses. Our bodies, alongside almost all of the other objects and beings we interact with in the outer world, are within the domain of the element of Earth.

There is something imminently reductionist about material things. They can be reduced to a pile of atoms, none of which has ever been alive itself individually. Our atoms are being recycled into other things all the time. Our body is cycling through cells, clearing out the old and welcoming in the new all the time. The physical matter that makes up our body is moving and changing, replenishing and relinquishing. Atoms are popping in and out of existence, moving into other forms. As Bill Bryson says in his brilliant *A Short History of Nearly Everything*, at one point some of the atoms inside you probably belonged to Shakespeare. That's how interconnected we all are at that deep, material level.

Many exceptionally rational people similarly want to reduce all the vast, many-layered experiences of existence down to simply things that can be physically measured and documented. The only problem with this convenient take on reality is that it does not fully reflect the very complex, very multi-layered experiences of being a human being. We experience all kinds of irrational things that cannot accurately be measured: our emotions, our spiritual insights, our inspirations and passions often make no sense when viewed entirely through a material lens and neither does consciousness itself. This is the problem that I always had with the kind of scholarly-influenced upbringing that I had. I've always had an intuitively deep sense of being that could not be explained.

My grandfather was a psychologist, and he believed that children entered this world as blank slates, that is, having no personal characteristics of their own, and that they learned their personalities, behaviours, beliefs, and so on from the world around them. This never quite made sense to me, because I have four younger brothers who all have very different personalities despite being raised in the same family. And I witnessed these personalities from a very, very young age. In fact, I am fairly certain that newborns do indeed have personalities. Even with babies, some of them I don't get on with; some of them I get along with famously, just like with people of other ages. There are certain humans that I connect with, and there are some who I don't. With babies, of course, I'm always open to giving them a cuddle.

But the blank slate theory also didn't make any sense to me, because I had many ideas that had never been taught to me, especially not by my family. In fact, many of the things that I've experienced personally, that I've written about in my notebooks since I was a child, I came to see later on reflected in various philosophies and teachings that I encountered at university. Now, these were not the same kinds of philosophies that my family necessarily espoused, and I wouldn't have been exposed to these theories in particular when I was younger, but sometimes truth shines through. And so, as a teenager, I was absolutely sure that the physical material world was only one level of reality. I would even draw diagrams. Sometimes they looked cone-shaped, like a witch's hat, with the physical presented as one layer, and emotional, psychological, and spiritual presented as other layers.

The physical world is not something that needs to be denied. Many spiritual teachings try to disconnect from the pleasures of the body and the excesses of the physical world, such as wealth, and if that is something that you are personally really called to, that makes your heart very, very happy, then by all means, become a hermit, an itinerant monk, whatever it is that really sparks joy for you.

For a long time, I did hold negative views about money. Money was evil. The corporates were the enemies, and maybe they totally are. And yet, on a certain level, they too are part of nature. Just because something's part of nature, it doesn't necessarily make it good. I cannot stress this enough. Cancer is part of nature, and big dodgy corporations function a lot like tumours. However, we can hold multitudes within us, including the very real physical manifestations of nature in all its forms. We can hold these contradictions, hold these complexities, in total grace, still with optimism for a better world, and yet not allow these power structures and systems to take power away from us.

In simply shunning money and powerful corporates – we disconnect further from the shadow of humanity and we allow the spectre of the broken system to take some of our power away from us. We may feel deliciously self-righteous in how that power has been stripped from us, and we may even wish to martyr ourselves to a cause. This can absolutely be worthwhile if that's the experience we are seeking, however there are other options for facing this shadow and for connecting with the earth more fully.

GROUNDING AND CENTRING PRACTICES

Grounding and centring ourselves is important in practices of magic. You don't necessarily need to touch the earth, but this can be a great way to do it. Bringing oneself down to earth: dropping all pretences, letting go of the erratic thoughts in our minds, letting the emotions that confuse or confound us subside just for a moment so that we can connect with this deep and important part of us.

Connecting with the element of Earth can be deeply grounding and centring. These exercises will help you establish a stronger bond with the Earth, bringing stability, calmness, and a sense of rootedness to your magical practice.

. . .

Barefoot Grounding:
  - Find a safe, natural spot such as a garden, forest, or park.
  - Remove your shoes and socks, allowing your bare feet to touch the ground.
  - Stand still, close your eyes, and take several deep breaths.
  - Visualise roots growing from the soles of your feet, extending deep into the Earth.
  - Feel the energy of the Earth rising up through your roots, grounding and centring you.

Earth Meditation:
  - Sit comfortably on the ground, preferably outside on grass, soil, or sand.
  - Place your hands on the Earth, palms down.
  - Close your eyes and take deep, slow breaths.
  - Visualise yourself merging with the Earth, feeling its stability and support.
  - Focus on the sensations of the Earth beneath you and let any worries or stress melt away into the ground.

Tree Connection:
  - Find a tree that you feel drawn to. Trees are powerful symbols of the Earth element and offer grounding and wisdom.
  - Stand or sit next to the tree, placing your hands or back against its trunk.
  - Close your eyes and take deep breaths, feeling the tree's energy.
  - Visualise your energy merging with the tree's energy, feeling grounded and connected.
  - Spend a few moments in silent communion with the tree, listening to any messages it may have for you.

Nature Walks:
  - Take a walk in a natural setting such as a forest, park, or beach.

•As you walk, focus on your senses. Notice the sights, sounds, smells, and textures around you.

•Take deep breaths and feel the Earth beneath your feet with each step.

•Collect small natural objects that catch your eye, such as stones, leaves, or feathers, to use in your magical practice.

Gardening:

•If you have access to a garden or even a few potted plants, spend time tending to them.

•Feel the soil with your hands, plant seeds, and nurture your plants as they grow.

•Gardening is a hands-on way to connect with the Earth and its cycles of growth and decay.

•As you care for your plants, set intentions for growth, abundance, and grounding in your life.

Earthy Crafting:

•Create something with natural materials such as clay, wood, or stone.

•Engage in a hands-on project like pottery, carving, or making natural jewellery.

•As you work with these materials, focus on your connection to the Earth and the grounding energy it provides.

The element of Earth embodies both abundance and limitation. It is the foundation of all life and the structure that supports us. Embrace the paradox presented by the element of Earth by acknowledging the material aspects of existence while also honouring the spiritual connections they represent. Through these grounded exercises, you can deepen your relationship with the Earth, finding stability, balance, and a sense of belonging in the natural world.

THE ELEMENT OF WATER

Most of us have had the experience of stepping into warm water and feeling a deep sense of relaxation. Water is much more highly conductive than air; energy travels through it quickly and directly making more connection. So too are our feelings connected and shared through the element of water. Many people associate water with emotions. Some emotions are more fiery or stoic like fire and earth elements, but even so, the element of water helps us to sink into our feelings; it helps us to be receptive and connected to our emotional nature.

Going into the water is like going into a meditation on the level of the body. In our relationship with this higher level of receptivity we often allow ourselves to be open and to receive insights. We open ourselves up to communion with the deep soul, the part of ourselves that is often considered to be the unconscious. I suggest that this is a misunderstanding. Rather than the "unconscious," what we are communing with in meditation is actually a deeper level of conscious that we are often unaware of in our ordinary "conscious" minds. When I drop down into the unconscious, more and more, I realise I'm connecting with what I sometimes call *the deep soul* or *deeper self*. What is normally called the unconscious, in my understanding, is actually far more aware – far more conscious – than our ordinary everyday awareness. From this perspective, the soul is very deeply conscious, and just like the depths of the ocean, there is much about our soul which is unknown.

The element of water helps us to delve into the intimacy of communion with the soul. It invites us to plunge beneath the surface, to explore the hidden caves and crevices of our innermost being. In the stillness of the deep, we can hear the call of our intuition, the songs of our ancestors, the echoes of our own divine essence.

WATER AS HEALING

The element of water invites us into an intimacy and connectedness with our family, within our home, within the nest of ourselves and our lives. Not all of us feel safe and comfortable within our families. Indeed, there are often sharp challenges and trauma when it comes to our families and our ancestors.

We do not need to keep destructive people close in order to heal our pasts, but this work can be part of going into a deeper intimacy with the self. If we are brave enough to heal trauma from ancestors, from family, within ourselves, we embark on a journey of reclamation. And this doesn't have to have anything to do with how we communicate with living members of our family either. It can be an entirely internal process if we choose it to be, an opening up to healing the wounds of the past. This is one step towards becoming more whole, becoming more deeply connected with our soul, even if the journey can be challenging and confronting at times.

THE DEPTHS OF WATER

Like the depths of the ocean, delving into the depths of the psyche can be terrifying and confronting but it can also be immensely empowering, revealing layers and layers of deeper truth, penetrating down to the deepest levels of reality and stripping away what is false.

This is another element of water that is often lost to the more "love and light" variety of spiritual practitioner. In its depths, water is often associated with the underworld like Mag Mel under the sea in Celtic mythos. The underworld and the ocean are often connected with gods of transformation, with life, death and rebirth, annihilation and renewal.

This is deep magic, and the deepest magic always comes through connection, surrender, transformation, and the annihilation of the former self. In the alchemical waters, we are transmuted, the husks of the seed dissolve so that new life can sprout.

It is in these depths that we often encounter our shadows, those disowned and rejected parts of ourselves that we have cast into the darkness. But it is only by facing and integrating our shadows that we can become truly whole. As Jung said, "One does not become enlightened by imagining figures of light, but by making the darkness conscious."

In these depths, water contains all that is. Here is the unconscious which is actually the deep, deep, deep consciousness, containing everything – all our dreams, all our hopes, all our despair, all our deep longing, all that is mystical, spellbinding, beautiful, and mesmerising.

Water is connection, even to loneliness and isolation, to powerlessness. For all these things are connected within one of the great paradoxes of the universe. We are the universe experiencing itself subjectively; the universe as a whole is one and alone. To be everything, to be connected to every single thing, to be singular, is a strange paradox indeed.

There is both the expanding undying beauty of love that connects all things, contrasted with the expanding and undying loneliness of only being one. If we can coexist within these paradoxes, we bring ourselves deeper into the mysteries of being, into our power as magicians.

Water is life. Without water, there would be no life as far as we know. Take a glass of drinking water, preferably not too cold, and as you drink it, allow yourself to be exquisitely present as you feel the sensation of the water rushing through you, rejuvenating your body. Take some long gulps of water and allow the connectivity to enter into your experience.

Feel the water as it touches your lips, as it flows over your tongue, as it slides down your throat. Can you feel it entering your stomach, imagine it spreading out into your bloodstream, reaching every cell of your being? You are not separate from this water; you are this water. Your body is about 60% water, your brain and heart are 73% water, your lungs are about 83% water. You are a walking, talking, miracle of watery life.

When creating rituals around water in your life, they can be as simple or as complex as you want them to be. You could have a relaxing bath, perhaps with scented bath salts or oils. This can be an entirely satisfying solo ritual. You could simply consume an entire glass of water in heightened awareness, and that could be a water ritual.

You could walk by the ocean, or by a river, or by a lake, or any natural body of water that's in your vicinity, and that could be your water ritual. Sit by the water's edge and allow yourself to just be. Watch the play of light on the surface, the ripples and waves, the dancing reflections. Listen to the sounds – the lapping, the rushing, the gurgling. Smell the scent of the water, of the life within and around it.

Maybe you'll feel called to wade in, to immerse a hand or foot, or your whole body. Maybe you'll gather some of the water to take home with you as a sacred talisman. Or maybe you'll simply sit in quiet communion, allowing the water to speak to your soul.

You might choose to work with water in your magical practice in a more structured way. You could take a bowl of water, charge it with the energy of the full moon by placing it out under the moonlight, and then place it on your altar. You can use water as a scrying medium, gazing into a dark bowl and allowing images and insights to arise from the depths. You can incorporate sacred water into your spellwork, using it to cleanse and consecrate your tools, your space, and yourself.

Water does not need offerings of gold, fruits, or wine. Water needs offerings of connection and your deeply felt emotions. So if you're working with the element of water, know that part of this is a surrendering feeling. When you feel emotions most deeply, when they overwhelm you, this is a good time to go to the sea if you're able to, or to a river, lake, or stream, or even to just have a meditative shower or bath. Allow yourself to commune with the water, offer the overwhelming sensations of the emotion to the element of water and allow it to soothe you in return.

Allow yourself to feel it all – the joy, the sorrow, the fear, the love, the rage, the ecstasy. Sometimes it might feel like you are being pulled under by the emotions, drowning in them. Let go and feel. Just as letting go and floating can save people in the ocean, whereas fighting the current leaves us exhausted and helpless. Let the feelings flow through you like a river, carving out new landscapes within your heart. Let yourself cry, surrender to it, and eventually you will surface with a new lightness, a new freedom.

Sometimes you may want to let yourself laugh until you cry, let yourself be moved and changed by the currents of your being.

Emotions are magical, for it is in feeling that we heal. It is in allowing ourselves to be vulnerable, to be seen in our wholeness, that we find our strength. It is in diving deep into the waters of our soul that we discover the pearls of our deeper self.

This element holds so many entry points, so many opportunities for awakening deeper into the mysteries of being. The path of water is the path of the mystic, the dreamer, the poet. It is the path of flow and surrender, of intuition and imagination, of healing and transformation.

The element of water has innate healing potential. Just as the rain that nourishes the earth, so too can reconnecting with the reservoir of compassion in this deep soul replenish our minds, hearts, and bodies.

Water follows the path of least resistance, and there are many teachings that reflect this, such as the Zen proverb of being like water, surrendering to the flow of life. And in doing so, by dropping resistance, we open ourselves up to so much more. It may not seem like a lot at the time, but much in the same way a stream can carve huge canyons into the earth over millennia, reshaping the entire landscape over time, so too can the gentle flow of this life force and the element of water in your life shape and change the entire landscape of your life.

PRACTICAL EXERCISES FOR CONNECTING WITH THE ELEMENT OF WATER

Water, with its fluidity and depth, offers numerous ways to connect with our emotions and the deeper aspects of our being. Here are some practical exercises to enhance your relationship with this powerful element.

Water Meditation:

•Find a quiet place where you can sit comfortably. If possible, sit near a natural body of water like a river, lake, or the ocean. If not, you can do this with a bowl of water, while running a bath, or even filling the kitchen sink before doing the dishes! It's also lovely to do this when you can hear the sound of rain.

•Close your eyes and take deep breaths, focusing on the sound of the water if you can hear it. If you have a bowl of water, gently swirl it and listen to the sound.

•Visualise yourself connecting with the water, feeling its flow, and its depth. Allow your mind to drift, like a leaf on the surface of a stream.

•Spend at a few moments in this meditative state, letting go of any tension or worries, and allowing the water to refresh your spirit.

Bath Ritual:

•Run a bath. If you like you can add some sea salt, Epsom salt, or skin safe essential oils that resonate with you (like lavender for relaxation).

•You may wish to light some candles around the bath or play soft, calming music.

•As you soak in the bath, visualise the water washing away any negativity or stress. Imagine the water surrounding you with regenerating healing energy.

•Spend as long as you need in the bath, allowing the element of water to nurture and rejuvenate you.

Scrying with Water:

•Before you begin, you may wish to create sacred space as described in the first part of this book. You don't need to do a whole ritual unless you want to, you can simply intend or visualise the sacred space in your mind. You may also wish to call upon the insight, protection, or guidance of one or more deities if that feels right for you.

•Fill a dark bowl or cauldron with water and place it on your altar or a dedicated space.

•Light a candle and place it so that its light reflects on the surface of the water. You may also wish to light incense nearby for added reflections.

•Sit comfortably and gaze into the water, allowing your mind to relax and open to any images or impressions that arise. The trick to this is to relax your mind enough that you're no longer in the dominant "thinking mind" but are in a more dream-like state.

•Do not try to analyse or over-think, merely allow the images and impressions to arise. When they do, acknowledge them, staying open for any further sensations or meanings or echoes of wisdom at the back of your mind.

•You may wish to send a whispered or silent message of thanks when any insights come through.

•If you're not really sure what you're looking at, that's a normal part of the process. Acknowledge your feelings of confusion and allow them to be as they are, then allow yourself to go deeper into relaxation.

•You may find that as you relax your mind further while staring at the water, unusual patterns emerge. Let them. Do not try to make sense of them, rather, allow any meaning to come through in its own way and in its own good time.

•Remember that scrying can help you access deeper insights and messages from deeper and more shadowy levels of consciousness. If any fears arise, know that you are safe. Acknowledge them and breathe slowly and gently, remembering that you can stop this at any time. You are also allowed to put up any boundaries against your fears that you need right now, because this is your magic – you get to decide.

•If you are ready to, allow yourself to go deeper and see what else emerges.

•When you feel like it's time to draw the scrying to an end, thank any deities that you might have called upon or sensed during the scrying. Put out the candle, empty the water slowly (you may wish to use it to water plants). And take some time to reflect on what you've just experienced. If you didn't see much, that is perfectly fine. You may find that something comes through later, through a dream, or occurs to you at an unexpected moment.

Moon-blessed water:

•The moon is deeply connected with the element of water, influencing its tides and other cycles. You can create water blessed with the light of the full moon to physically and symbolically connect with both the compassionate energy of the moon and the element of water.

•On the night of a full moon, fill a glass container with fresh water.

•Place the container outside or on a windowsill where it can absorb the moon's light.

•You may wish to add herbs and crystals to the water, depending on what feels right for you.

•Leave it overnight, and in the morning, collect your moon-blessed water.

•This water is now charged with lunar energy and can be used in spells, rituals, or as a cleansing spray for your space.

Emotional Release with Water:

•When feeling overwhelmed by emotions, find a private space where you can cry freely, ideally near water or in the shower.

•Allow your tears to flow or visualise them – as a release of emotion.

•Imagine the water releasing your pain, sadness, or anger, leaving you feeling lighter and more at peace.

Creative Flow:

•Engage in a creative activity that involves water, such as painting with watercolours, making a collage with images of water, or writing poetry inspired by the sea or rain.

•Allow yourself to enter a state of flow, where your creativity can move freely like water, unimpeded by judgement or expectations.

Water invites us to delve into our depths, to explore the unknown territories of our soul. Through these exercises, you can develop a deeper connection with this element, enhancing your magical practice and bringing a sense of fluidity and intuition into your daily life. Water is not just about softness and surrender; it is also about the power of transformation and the strength found in adaptability and flow.

THE ELEMENT OF AIR

As we explore the elements, we begin in the East, where the sun rises. This direction is generally associated with the element of air. Air is such a necessity in every moment, as we breathe in and breathe out. Attention to this is a simple process and is an excellent way to deepen our awareness. Notice the oxygen as it flows into your lungs and out again, as it caresses your skin in a light breeze, or as it almost bowls you over in a gale. Allow the element of air to rush right through you energetically.

When we pay attention to the element of air, we notice the level of our being below our everyday thinking – our deeper awareness. We notice our mind and its constant chatter, and we allow that chatter to drift away as we deepen our focus.

Air is the element of clarity, the element of quick-wittedness, yet it is also associated with the mind in general and all the circular problems we find ourselves in, mentally. Too often we sink our energy into thought patterns that do not serve us well. In noticing our recurring mental patterns, we have an opportunity to see them from a broader perspective, allowing us more choices in what we continue to give energy to in our minds. We can ask ourselves if our limiting beliefs are really absolutely true and we can let go of the thoughts that are no longer helpful. You may wish to let go of particular mental traps, and instead, ground yourself in something that really does serve you and fulfil you.

WORD MAGIC

"We are creatures of words. We are creatures of imagination. We live on the edges of dreams and the margins of thought. We live in the whisper of the page." – Whiti Hereaka, *Pūrākau*

The stories we tell ourselves and the words we speak are all spells. This includes the stories you tell yourself about your identity, your personality, your limitations. These spells can be woven from childhood;

indeed they often are. As young children we are so susceptible to the judgements of others, and we collect them into our understandings of who we are. For instance, when I was a young child, I was told over and over again by an adult in my life that I was lazy, useless, and selfish. I was only a child, but I believed that these things were indeed wrong with me, and it wasn't until I was an adult that I managed to shed a lot of these limiting beliefs and discovered that none of them were true!

Yes, words are spells, but do not fret and definitely don't let this make you overly anxious about everything you say or think, for this is a powerful thing to know. For instance, if you often have a thought that you're not enough in some way, could you write down ten times, a hundred times, that you are enough? Can you tell yourself, face to face in the mirror, "I am enough." What other things would you like to tell yourself? What other word spells would you like to create? Perhaps you could whisper to yourself that you are wise and wild and powerful.

SPELL FOR RELEASING OTHER PEOPLE'S JUDGEMENTS

Understanding that the stories and words we absorb in childhood can shape our self-perception is crucial for personal growth. The following spell is designed to help you shed those limiting labels and reclaim your power. By consciously acknowledging and letting go of limiting, hurtful, and unnecessary judgements, you can transform your personal story, replacing old, harmful beliefs with empowering ones. This spell guides you through a process of release and renewal, enabling you to embrace your inherent worth and your deeper potential.

You will need:
- Two pieces of paper
- A pen or pencil

Step one:
On the first piece of paper, write down all the negative labels and judgements that you were labelled with, especially during your childhood. Allow yourself to reflect on any shaming, blaming, or otherwise limiting judgements you faced. If overwhelming emotions come up during thing process, it's perfectly fine to pause or stop. You may wish to

soothe yourself by wrapping your arms around yourself, wrapping yourself in a blanket, going for a walk, or even having a bath or shower – whatever works to calm you. As emotions arise, breathe through them, slowly and gently, allowing yourself to experience them as safely as you can because opening up to the feelings will help them to release. Know that you are safe to stop this anytime, or even to complete the spell with a support person or therapist present. It's important to keep your mind in a safe space in order to process and heal, so feel free to adapt this in whichever ways feel right for you.

If, on the other hand, you are not sure what judgements might be buried deep, you may be able to excavate old memories by talking to someone who was there during your childhood like a friend of family member. You can also excavate by thinking back to old painful memories – many of these come with harsh and limiting judgements from others, or even by looking at the patterns in your life. What tends to upset you? What are you afraid that these things mean about you? Where in your childhood could this come from? For instance, if you have a pattern of other people disempowering you, could this hint to a judgement you faced of "being weak"? Are you afraid people will think you're "lazy," "selfish," "useless," "stupid," "unworthy," or "unlovable"?

I put the above words in quotation marks because they are absolutely not true. Do you know how I know? Because I've looked into the eyes of many newborn babies and I've seen their awareness, their goodness, and their grace. That is also the same for you. You were that baby. Not only that, somewhere, beneath all the layers, you still are that baby. That is your being – you are pure, and possess an old magical awareness. Nothing you did as a child or teenager could change that. Nothing you do as an adult can change that either, so allow all the judgements to come up, like splinters you're removing from your body. Put them down on the paper, and see them for the falsehoods that they are.

Once you have written them all down, touch each judgement one by one and say:

I release you, I release myself, I am whole, I am free.

Repeat this as many times as necessary, allowing all the feelings and buried emotions to pour out. You may also wish to say additional things to release these old judgements. You can yell and cry and swear if that helps, or you can simply acknowledge that these things are no longer your burdens to bear – they never belonged to you in the first place, they were simply companions who came with you on your journey, shaping you and perhaps protecting you from falling into more dangerous situations. You may even wish to thank them if that helps you to let them go. "Hello, judgement of ... thank you for trying to protect me by encouraging me to try harder or to steer clear of situations and people that might have caused me more harm. I don't need you anymore. I release you."

You may find that some of these judgements are hard to shake because they've become deeply embedded beliefs. If so, it may help to picture yourself as a newborn baby – innocent and present and whole. This is who you are, underneath all the layers of sediment you've picked up over your life. Yet, none of the limiting judgements you've been carrying with you make sense for this babe that you are. Connect more deeply with that innocent presence within you. Does this help you to release them? If not, what else would help? Is there something else you need to say or do? Are there any extra words you need to add to the paper? Keep going until the process feels complete to you.

Step two:

Take a moment to bask in the new space you've opened up in your psyche now that you've released those old judgements. You may wish to close your eyes for a few moments and meditate on the feelings of release and expansion.

Now, on a new piece of paper, write down all the positive labels you wish to reclaim and give yourself. These could include words like:

Strong
Courageous
Powerful
Inspired
Wise
Worthy
Brilliant
Successful
Wonderful
Enough
Brave
Capable
Confident

Vibrant
Creative
Graceful
Joyful

Note, that the word "successful" here doesn't have to mean anything external. You can simply allow yourself to recognise that you are successful exactly as you are – successfully being you.

Envision yourself at your best. What qualities do you see there? What qualities do you admire in others that you are now ready to claim for yourself? Write them all down!

Now, touch each of your words and say, "I am [word]," as in, "I am strong, I am courageous, I am powerful."

Notice the resonance with the statement. If you are not quite feeling it, you may wish to look beneath the surface to see if there's another limiting judgement holding you back. If you like, you can go back to the first sheet of paper and see if there is more that you need to release. For example, if you're struggling to feel strong, ask yourself if you still have more releasing to do around judgements of being weak.

Step Three

Once you have done all the releasing and reclaiming, you may wish to tear up or burn the releasing sheet of paper (taking care to burn it in a safe fire-proof vessel of course). As you do so, appreciate that those past judgements and labels you were given not only limited you but also gave you a unique experience of the world, enabling you to relate to others who have similarly suffered. Allow yourself to appreciate all you have learned on this journey of selfhood so far, and let go of all you no longer need.

Fold up the new words you've given yourself and put them in a special place. This is your new spell, your new story. You may wish to take a few moments to savour and process the experience of the spell as you might savour a complex meal or process a movie that has imprinted on you. Writing about a spell also helps to imprint it in your mind, helping the magic to set and settle. What was the experience like for you? Did you feel a release? Is there more releasing to do? What is the difference between your old story about yourself and the new story you're now writing?

As you process, in the coming days and weeks, you may find subtle changes occurring around you, in the way you treat yourself and reflected in the way other people treat you. Notice these changes and make notes about them in your magical journal. Be gentle with yourself, especially for the next few days. Drink lots of water and try eating only the foods your body most craves. Notice any additional limitations that come up, because this is bound to happen once the excavation work begins – and don't worry – this is a good thing. When additional limiting judgements come to the surface, you do not have to repeat the whole spell unless you wish to. You can simply acknowledge them in your journal and repeat releasing words like:

I release you, I release myself, I am whole, I am free.

You can journal deeper into where these limiting judgements came from, and explore how they are not in fact true at a deeper level. You can breathe slowly, gently, through the feelings that arise and when you feel the release and the completion of the process, you can revel in the new spaciousness you've created and anchor in your new story in the ways that resonate most for you.

I am strong
I am confident
I am brave
I am powerful

THE EXHILARATION OF WIND AND THE WILD CIRCUS OF THE MIND

I live in one of the windiest cities in the world. Wellington is known for few other things besides being the incredibly windy and somewhat creative capital of New Zealand. When a gale is blowing, we say, "Oh, it must be Tuesday." I don't know exactly what climate you're in, but I do encourage you in your magical journey to spend time in the wind. Not everyone enjoys the sensation of wind. It can be agitating and frustrating, but it can blow out the cobwebs of your mind and clear the energy.

The Element of Air can be a clearing and clarifying force, although it can also be cloudy at times. Many spiritual teachings have a rather negative view of the mind, seeing it as something which must be conquered or defeated, something that distracts one from broader spiritual pursuits. Our monkey minds are active. They run circles around us. They plague us with illusions and delusions, with stress and fears and frustrating mental loops.

However, I have found it much more productive, magically speaking, to work with the mind rather than against it. I don't have the energy or the inclination to make my mind an enemy anymore. The same is true for all aspects of self. If you resist and try to cut off a part of your being, you're limiting, suppressing, and rejecting aspects of self which therefore tend to become shadow. As you might know by now, my philosophy is to connect with and embrace these things, including the shadow. And if possible, to do so in a way that's enjoyable. Because why not? There's no evidence of a universal law that says becoming spiritually or magically awakened must be a gruelling and unpleasant process.

The mind is brilliant and not entirely explained. In fact, there's no clear scientific theory of consciousness despite the fact that it's the only thing we can ultimately experience life through. It's often said that there are two sides to the brain, presenting a paradox. One side is considered rational and reasonable and the other side is creative and illogical. When both of these hemispheres of the brain are more connected, it's considered a good thing. As babies, an important stage of development is crawling. If babies miss the crawling stage, they miss valuable left-right brain connections. When you crawl, you put your right hand and left knee forward, and then vice versa with the left hand and the right knee, thereby integrating both sides of the body and mind. If babies don't learn to crawl, they sometimes are unable to do so as adults. One of my cousins worked in dance therapy where she taught adults how to crawl as part of the therapy. When you can do things with both sides of your body or swap things around that you would normally do with one or the other, you're activating your brain in different ways and stretching the connections in your mind.

AFFIRMATIONS

Affirmations can be powerful tools for personal transformation and self-improvement. They are positive statements repeated to help reprogramme the subconscious mind, encouraging us to believe in the positive words we are saying. However, research has shown that affirmations don't work if we don't genuinely connect with them. In such cases, repeating affirmations can increase our internal discord, as the subconscious mind rejects statements that feel fundamentally untrue. This dissonance can lead to frustration and a sense of failure rather than the intended positive reinforcement.

Affirmations work best when they are connected with our values and when we can fully support them. When affirmations resonate with our core beliefs and self-worth, they have the potential to create significant positive changes. For example, I have spent years saying the affirmation "I love myself" every single day, sometimes over and over, because self-love was something I dearly needed to cultivate. This daily practice helped me gradually embrace and internalise the affirmation, fostering a genuine sense of self-love and acceptance. Here are some affirmations to consider:

I am open to creativity and inspiration.
I value myself.
I trust in my path and enjoy life's journey.
I align with my goals and dreams.
I let my inner light shine.
I am open to deep magical transformation.
I am always growing and evolving.
I trust my intuition.
I am worthy of love and happiness.
I nurture my inner child.
I accept and celebrate who I am.
I align with my dreams.
I am open to wisdom and guidance.
I cultivate love and compassion.
I appreciate the beauty in my life.
I embrace my beautiful imperfections.

These exercises and affirmations can help you connect with the element of air, bringing clarity and a sense of freedom to your mind and spirit.

With each of these affirmations, notice how they feel. Try saying each one out loud and see how it resonates. Is there anything about it that you'd change? If something isn't resonating it could be that the words don't have good connotations for you, or it could be that there's a negative self-belief underneath the surface that's getting in the way of you feeling good, like a splinter that you might want to examine and release before you return to the positive statement. I encourage experimenting with affirmations because they are tremendously powerful magical tools – deliberately using words as spells – which can be greatly empowering. Simple things like this, over time, are like paving stones in the structures you're building in your life. Each one may seem simple and small, but together they can be mighty.

Be aware that big flashy instant transformational experiences might feel amazing but they are often fleeting as we've just experienced a bump of dopamine, adrenalin, endorphins, or oxytocin. These states can be highly enjoyable, but just like any peak experience, it pays to stay grounded and prepare for things to keep changing.

THE ELEMENT OF FIRE

The element of fire has long been associated with passion, devotion, motivation, inspiration, rage, and fury. Fire quite obviously burns. Unlike the other elements, fire is hot and bright. It roars through us and bends with our will, with our desires, and yet we often block its path.

In experimenting with the element of fire, you may wish to light a candle or experiment in some other way, as it is mesmerising and is often considered romantic. Fire is uniquely destructive; obviously water, earth, and wind can also do a lot of damage, but it doesn't take a natural disaster for fire to be devastating, just as our rage, if not worked with appropriately, can harm others or ourselves.

We must take great care with our fiery passions, including our anger. Fire dances. It is contagious, much like rage can be. When we tell someone about the injustice that is causing us pain and anger and they relate to our plight, they too will likely feel that burning emotion. In polite society, suppressing rage and anger is often seen as the appropriate thing to do. However, quashing our feelings only hurts us in other more subtle or passive-aggressive ways. The energy of fire needs to be released; it needs to be active and to have an outlet; to be channelled into something useful the way that the flames in a fireplace provide warmth or the cooking flame has, for millennia, allowed us to consume food in more comfortable and nourishing ways.

At times, rage can be so powerful that it can consume us, but in those moments, the more aware we are, the more choices we have. When a loved one doesn't meet our expectations, instead of snapping at them or trying to punish them, retaliating with our words and actions, we can be aware, pause for a moment, and just experience our rage. We can trace it to its roots, and here we might find other realisations that were previously unconscious.

- Is the reason a partner, parent, or child angers us so much because we, as children, experienced powerlessness from something similar?
- Are we trying to fight them now, when we really want to fight for our own power when we were young and defenceless?
- How can we reclaim our own power in ways that we don't regret later (which only disempowers us further), and instead use our rage for constructive action?

I come from a family who values pacifism; fighting and violence of any sort was considered vulgar and inappropriate in much of my childhood and yet everyone in my family experienced rage. Some cultures are better at being peaceful than others, but across all of humanity there is the fight, there is the struggle, and there is rage. If we can channel it into things that are helpful, that drive us forward, that help us to change situations in beneficial ways, then we are channelling this force in an empowering way.

In working with the element of fire, frustration in our lives, even over boring matters, can also be a reflection point. Where is our fire caught up? Perhaps we don't want to do some tedious admin task. Perhaps we are furious at the courier for not delivering our mail. Even these dreary, tiresome, frustrating things can reveal a deeper lesson about our own power and powerlessness. When we trace the sensations back to their roots, we have the option to plant a new seed there and clear the way for a different pathway to grow forth.

WHERE DO YOU NEED TO TAKE ACTION IN YOUR LIFE?

Anger can be a brilliant motivating force capable of spurring us. We can harness our anger in order to send that email that we really should send but felt resistant over, in order to book that dentist appointment, or even to do the dishes. Yes, these things often do sound mundane, don't they? But sometimes it's in the most mundane of tasks that our fire is misspent.

We waste a lot of our energy on things that we haven't done. Tasks which could probably be accomplished in a matter of minutes can haunt us for weeks and weeks on end, and we think of them, we moan about how we haven't done them yet, we put off till tomorrow what could have been done today. How many of us consider ourselves "procrastinators?"

I stopped believing in procrastination over ten years ago when I explored the concept and experience more deeply and discovered it was actually just some kind of resistance getting in my way. Either I didn't really want to do a task, or I was somehow afraid or confused about it. Addressing that resistance was far more constructive than to continue to drape myself in the blanket of the label of procrastination and then feel both guilty and sorry for myself in equal measure while I made no progress. Instead, I'd identify the resistance – was I stuck in progress on my thesis because I was a procrastinator? Or was it that I was afraid of writing the next chapter? Did I need to do more research? In this process, I'd find the opportunities for progress. When writing novels, I sometimes find that a project needs to rest for a while so that the seeds have time and peace to germinate and grow into the next stage. At other times, I need to take action and I'm just afraid of doing so. In recognising this, I have the option to take a deep breath and let my passion drive me through that fear into action.

If you feel stuck on taking action or moving forward with a project and you find yourself limited by beliefs about being too lazy or being a procrastinator, you may wish to go back to the releasing spell in the Air section. After releasing this limiting belief and burning it with the element of fire in order to transform it, ask yourself:

- Is this the right time to take action?
- Does the project need to rest for a bit?
- Is there something else I need to do first?
- Is there *really* something else I'm waiting on, or am I just saying this because I'm afraid?
- What action makes the most sense?
- What else is standing in my way?

How can you tell if you're holding yourself back out of fear, or if there really is waiting that needs to happen? For me, when I need to wait, I feel a burning impatience and frustration. The sensation is hot and irritated. Whereas when I'm holding myself back out of fear, the sensation is cold and more reserved. Often there is a subconscious anxiety at play. For instance, I might feel resistant about publishing this book because it is deeply personal and because it makes me feel vulnerable to be so open about my deeply held understandings and experiences. In this case, I know that in the past I've held back from writing this kind of book. I've tried quite a few times, and stopped. I've found it far easier to tell my truth through the imaginative veil of fiction (because all my novels tell these kinds of truths in their own way – because this is the story I'm here to tell, this is my life's work), but to be so open in a non-fiction format is scary. I also know that I'm ready.

I still had a lot of deep work to do. I had to get far more comfortable with vulnerability and even with humiliation because revealing our truths and taking risks is humiliating (humbling to the ego which always likes to be in control).

Now, when I feel the fear, I know I am ready to work with it. I know that some people won't like this book. Some people will hate it! That is the case with practically all things. No matter how you might try to water yourself down to be appealing or non-threatening to other people, you can't completely avoid nasty judgements because they're often not really about you. Just like our judgements of other people are reflections of our own inner pain and fear. This is not to say our judgements are wrong, but simply that they are subjective and distorted. Strong emotions like fear and pain and anger distort things, but to deny them only distorts our perception further. However, we can open up to the feelings, embrace them and release old distortions.

We can even channel the emotion into action. This is particularly true for anger which is a powerful driving force. If we could only channel all of our anger into positive action, as a species, we could all complete those pesky menial tasks so they don't clutter up our psyches anymore, clearing the way for us to be more deeply connected with our passion, our inspiration, our power. We could also put more energy into creating than destroying – something our world clearly needs!

ANGER AS A GUARDIAN – ANGER REDIRECTED

Anger usually arises within us when our boundaries have been crossed, when our expectations are not being met, when we feel there has been an injustice or unfairness, small or large, against us or others. Anger is a guardian of the psyche, connected to the warrior planet Mars. When we are living in our power with the element of fire, we are able to defend ourselves when needed in ways that serve us and avoid unnecessary destruction.

We've all probably had times when our anger and rage has gotten out of control, when we've said cruel things or done destructive things that we later wished we hadn't. Many of us fear the fire within us for this reason and try to douse our anger instead. However, avoiding it, suppressing it, turning away from it will only make it worse. People who suppress their anger often either have it surge up in violent and destructive ways or they take it out on themselves in the form of self-destructive thoughts and behaviours, or simply depression; none of these are helpful.

So instead of suppressing and turning away from anger, it makes sense to connect with that fiery energy, to understand it, to learn to handle it in a way where it does not burn us. Playing with fire is considered a dangerous thing. However, if done with care, safety, and awareness, it can be quite fun and rather magical. Many people begin their magical journey with simple spells involving writing something down on a piece of paper and burning it over a candle, for instance. Fire's transformation is just as the phoenix burns to ashes and is born anew, so too does the fire within us burn us to cinder and then rebirth us into the world. Fire drives deep transformation if we work with it rather than let it unconsciously burn us.

You may wish to experiment with fire internally by contemplating your passions and the things that you absolutely cannot stand. Try writing a list of the things you're absolutely passionate about and the things you detest. You may find interesting correspondences between both lists. Sometimes, when we are young, our passions get buried by people who seek to snuff out our spark, by people who are afraid of their own passions and certainly afraid of ours, by people who want to protect us from disappointment. Many of us have a history of this happening, a whole burial ground inside us of dreams that have been covered over and suppressed. The good news is that these dreams do not have to stay buried. If we leave them to fester, they will leave us bitter and more likely to take out our toxicity on other people. We have a choice. Instead of continuing to suppress them, we can excavate our buried dreams and passions and give them life.

FIRE AS PASSION AND INSPIRATION

What did you want to be as a child? I wanted to be an artist, but then at school, teachers told me I wasn't creative because I didn't colour in between the lines, because I didn't use the right colours either. One teacher even told me to throw a picture I had drawn of myself into the bin because he didn't like the way that I'd coloured the skin. Many of these small traumas caused me to lose confidence in drawing and painting, and even though I possessed some basic skills in these areas as a teenager, I never had the confidence to develop them further. However, in my early adulthood, I decided to take up painting in a very intuitive way, allowing myself to freely spill along the canvas in different shades and colours instead of trying to paint something in particular, which seemed too arduous to me at the time. I wanted to merely see what happened when my intuition led my hand. So instead of *trying* to do something, I did the opposite. Bizarrely, people saw all sorts of images in the paintings that I produced: a dolphin, a snake, even a fruit bat. I found this all rather amusing, but I was happy to indulge my creativity in a way that wasn't putting pressure on myself to be able to do any particular thing.

There are so many ways that we can express creativity, not just through visual art but through movement and other mediums.

Passion can be incredibly productive and rewarding. I feel far more satisfied in the discarded dreams that were buried deeply in my psyche that I've managed to excavate, process, let go, or have gotten to live out in one way or another, than in those that I have not yet been able to connect with. In some areas I still feel held back. These days, I channel most of my passion into my writing. Creativity flows through me with a strong connective force, rushing out into the world into books that many thousands of people are reading.

WHEN YOU'RE FEELING LOW

Sometimes it's hard to connect with our passion. When we feel dull or low, it may be that your passion is going through a period of dormancy. It may be that we're tired and we need to rest. Maybe we have grief to process relating to any number of life changes. In these instances, it can help to listen to intuition.

Ask the following questions:

· Am I ready to reconnect with my passion?

If yes, move on to the next question. If not, ask further questions such as:

· What is it that I most need right now?

· How can I nurture myself so I can come back into the fullness of being?

· Where can I find ease?

· How can I soothe myself?

· Is there anger that I need to release from the past?

· How best can I do this?

Some people find hitting pillows or screaming into an empty room to be incredibly therapeutic in terms of releasing anger. Other people take it out on a punching bag at the gym or through venting verbally or writing it all down.

EXERCISE ON CONNECTING WITH YOUR PASSION

If you're ready to reconnect with your passion, allow your mind to relax. You may wish to gaze into a candle or imagine a candle burning in the cauldron in the centre of your chest, the energy centre related to your calling, vocation, and yes, your passion. Allow yourself to connect deeply to the centre of your being, your solar plexus and chest. Here you may wish to put your hands on that part of your body. There is a furnace within you that burns in this part of your body, burns brightly, sometimes burns in anger. If you feel anger right now, allow it to wash over you. Experience it fully. When you open to a sensation, it no longer burns you; it simply sweeps through you, burning up all that you no longer need. Allow any anger to burn through you now.

Now connect more deeply with the centre within anew, allowing your energy to burn brightly and open like a flower in bloom. Within your core there is endless passion; allow it to burn through you right now, lighting you up, burning through your blood, burning every cell in your body, all the energy in your whole body system and the sensation of passion. Does anything emerge for you? Is there anything you're passionate about right now? Anything that you've been holding yourself back from that you really want in your life, that you want to create, that you want to initiate, that you want to give to the world through your expression, through your energy, through your power and magic?

Raise your arms above your head if you can, holding them in a V shape, allowing the energy of spirit to flow through you, connecting all the centres of energy in your body in the element of fire and passion. You may wish to move or dance, you may wish to stomp your feet or clap your hands. Movement is very important to fire. Breathe deeply, just as fire needs air to thrive. As you release your breaths, allow yourself to go deeper into the sensations of passion burning within. This is your endless source of energy, the fuel of your life, the heat from this fire of passion that powers you. Respect it, nurture it, treat it with care, and it will serve you well for all your days.

HARNESSING THE ENERGY OF FIRE

The Element of Fire initiates things, births them into the world. There might be something that you want to initiate in your life, or it may be that you easily initiate things and don't follow through. Either way, working more directly with fire can help to propel you forward. In areas where we are stuck, we can use different elements, working with their energies in order to rise to the next level. Fire can burn through barriers, whether it's through anger driving us to make a change, or through excitement and passion to create something new.

You will need:

A candle (any colour that resonates with your intention)

A lighter or matches

A quiet space where you won't be disturbed

Find a space where you can perform this exercise without interruptions. Place the candle in front of you and light it.

Sit comfortably and focus on the flame. Take a few deep breaths, allowing yourself to become present in the moment.

Reflect on what you want to initiate or the commitment you want to make. It could be a project, a personal goal, or a habit you want to form.

When you feel ready, say the words that occur to you intuitively or something like the following invocation:

. . .

Sacred fires burning bright,
Ignite my passion, guide my sight.
I call upon your courage, impetus and drive to begin anew,
As this flame burns bright and true,
I harness the fire, I follow through.

Spend a few moments in silence, visualising the flame of the candle infusing you with the energy and determination needed to initiate and commit to your goal.

Say your goal out loud. You can also write it down to cement it further.

When you feel ready, extinguish the candle, knowing that the fire's energy is within you, driving you forward. Reflect on this inner transformation.

AETHER

In ancient and medieval science Aether or Ether is known as the fifth element, the material that fills the region of the universe beyond the terrestrial sphere. This is a concept found in various philosophical, meta-physical, and scientific traditions; it is the most subtle and fundamental element, transcending the physical nature of the other four classical elements of earth, water, air, and fire.

In classical Greek philosophy aether was thought to be the material that fills the universe beyond the terrestrial sphere. It was believed to be the substance that makes up the heavenly bodies and was considered to be incorruptible and eternal.

In alchemy and various esoteric traditions, Aether is the quintessence, the purest and most perfect form of matter, and the key to transformation and enlightenment. It is seen as the bridge between the material and spiritual, facilitating communication and harmony between them.

In many traditions, spirit, life force, or aether is seen as a binding force that connects and permeates all things. It is often associated with the divine, the soul, or the animating force of the cosmos. Unlike the other elements, which are tangible and can be observed directly, Aether is intangible and often described as the essence of life or the cosmic breath that sustains all life and being.

Aether is both the active spirit and the receptive soul, the context behind the content of our lives, the collective unconscious and the essence of deep consciousness that is outside of ordinary awareness, the liminal intangible "all." It is the substance of all things and the void in which they are suspended, the everything and nothingness of all, the terrifying potential power we contain and the vastness of the universe.

PRACTICAL WAYS OF WORKING WITH AETHER

Breath Meditation - Focus on your breath, imagining that with each inhale, you are drawing in the pure essence of Aether. As you exhale, feel the spirit energy spreading throughout your body, connecting with every cell. This practice helps to centre your mind and align your spirit with the universal flow.

Visualisation - Sit quietly and visualise a luminous light surrounding you. Imagine this light as the Aether, filling the space around you and within you. See it as a shimmering, translucent energy that connects everything. Feel its presence, allowing it to guide your thoughts and emotions towards a state of harmony.

Gentle Noticing - Spend time observing the interconnectedness of nature, listening for the silence behind sound, and the space all around us. Close your eyes and sense the energy that flows through the earth, trees, and air. Feel yourself as part of this web of life, acknowledging the spirit that pervades all.

Intuitive Drawing or Writing - Engage in spontaneous drawing or writing, allowing your intuition to guide your hand. Don't think too much about the outcome; instead, focus on the process and let your inner spirit express itself. This can help you tap into the subconscious and the essence of Aether.

Dream Work - Keep a dream journal and pay attention to your dreams. Set an intention before you sleep to connect with the element of Aether. Dreams can be a powerful way to receive messages from the spirit world and your subconscious mind.

Presence Practices - Engage in mindfulness exercises that focus on the present moment. By fully immersing yourself in the now, you can become more attuned to the subtle energies of Aether that are always present but often unnoticed.

3

COMBUSTIBLE MAGIC

"Discernment is a meeting point of the parts' will, the Self's will, and the universal will. From this confluence, a living, flowing Knowing emerges— a unified will that guides our actions and perceptions. With this clear yet permeable sense of Self, we engage with the world with openness and care, neither losing ourselves nor closing ourselves off." — Laura Patryas

WHAT IS IT WE REALLY WANT AND NEED?

Quite literally, you were born for this life you're in. No one else was. Just you. And given you were born for this, look around at your life. Look back at your previous experiences, both joyful and challenging, and all you've learned and uniquely experienced so far. As you survey your life, know that the things you do not like, the worn tired patterns, the restrictions, the pain, fear, and suffering you may be experiencing, the boredom or lack of satisfaction...all of that is a powerful magical lesson, too, if only we can see it and work with it.

Within what we do want and what we do not want are tensions. Working with these tensions will transform our lives. If we get very clear on what we do and don't want, explore the light and shadow polarities of each thing, alchemise the emotions by feeling our feelings with radical acceptance and openness.

When you feel drawn, pulled, or nudged in a particular direction and nothing else is getting in the way, it is likely to be your intuition that's steering you, your inner compass. Imagine standing on a path in a beautiful natural environment, perhaps by the sea, or lake, or in the forest, where the air is fresh with the scent of trees. Look down at the path at your feet, notice how it holds you. This is your path, and though you may stray to one side or another, this path will always pull you back towards your deep desires, if only you let it. Notice how it feels to stand firmly on your path. Orientate yourself at the point that feels right for you at this point in your life. At any moment, you can close your eyes and check in. Let the path, your path, guide you.

In the buzz and mess and rigidity of modern life, where external messages bombard us with what we are supposed to want, it is easy to lose touch with this inner guidance. As children we were often disconnected from our intuition through the will of others around us. We were told what we should and should not want, we were punished for behaving instinctively. We may have learned to distrust our body's subtle way of telling us what feels right and what doesn't. Our intuition often gets drowned out by the noise and the strong currents of other forces around us – our friends, family, employers, society, and others – leaving us feeling adrift and disconnected. Take a step back from the chaos. Breathe deeply, and let the forest quieten your mind. Listen to that soft nudge, that fleeting sensation, that quiet pulse within you. Trust it, for it is the voice of your soul, leading you where you most need to go.

In a world that often dictates what should bring us joy, finding this inner guidance can be challenging. We are told what success looks like, what achievements are worthy, and what happiness should feel like. To find what genuinely lights us up, we must peel back these layers of imposed expectations. Reflect on the moments that make your heart race and your spirit soar. These are still within you, glowing, waiting to be fanned into a radiant blaze. What are the activities, dreams, and pursuits that make you feel truly alive? What do you absolutely love? What is getting in the way?

Let us journey deeper into the forest, where the air is damp and earthy, the mossy path is dappled with light and shadow, and the air hums with innate wisdom. Here, beneath the boughs of the ancient trees, lies the shimmer of intuition – a pool reflecting the essence of our being – our "why".

When you go deep within and connect with your soul, you may find that this inner sense of being is the wellspring from which your sense of meaning and purpose pours forth.

Here are some questions you may wish use as prompts while writing in your magical journal:

- What lights you up? What gets you excited? What do you care about?

- What are the recurring themes between these things?

- What inspires you most in other people?

- What things do you most deeply and repeatedly crave (even if you never tell anyone about them)?

- What are your core values? (What truly matters to you?)

- How do you like to create? (This doesn't have to be through visual art or writing, it can be through food, through dance, through organising events – anything that inspires you.)

- What would you like to see more of in the world?

- What are the gifts you want to give to the world?

As you reflect on these questions, and on this chapter, you may find resistance coming up. If so, allow it to and also allow yourself to get curious about it. To me, resistance often feels like a tightening in my chest, a feeling of closing in, a defensiveness. It can feel cold with fear or hot with anger, but it often points to a deeper understanding lurking just below the surface.

It may be that you already have a good idea of what is meaningful for you and your creativity, and it may feel cumbersome to have to think about this again. You may already have some strongly held convictions that you are not wanting to examine, and that it always your choice.

On the other hand, you may not. You may feel confused about purpose and meaning in your life, or resistant to the idea of having purpose at all. You also may think that you're not creative. I'm absolutely convinced that you are. Creativity is such an integral part of being human. We are all storytellers, creating meaning in the world with the stories we tell ourselves about our lives. We are all shaping our world in one way or another, every single day. If you feel you are not creative, you may be carrying wounds from your childhood where you felt (or were told) that you weren't good enough. In that instance, perhaps it was safer to disconnect from the notion of being creative. That may have been the best way to protect yourself at the time.

As I said, in my early schooling years I was repeatedly told by teachers that I wasn't creative because no matter how hard I tried I could not colour neatly within the lines. Perhaps you have some similar childhood wounds around not feeling good enough. When you were young you probably did not have many options. The older people around you dictated what was good or bad, and you had to fall in line. It may have been safer to disconnect, to stop trying, to distance yourself from that pain. Now, you have a choice.

Why am I talking about creativity in a book about magic? Simply, because I believe that they are the same thing. There are different flavours, of course, but I have come to recognise that the force within me that inspires me to write books, build fantasy worlds, cook beautiful meals, and occasionally paint abstract images or write songs...is the very same creative force that flows through all of life. It has many names and there are many ways of understanding it, just as there are many ways of deliberately and consciously working with it that are understood to be magical.

You may disagree, and that it perfectly okay, but either way, I encourage you to take a few slow, deep, breaths as we go deeper into this journey, whenever you're ready.

WHEN WE SUPPRESS WHAT WE WANT IT WARPS OUR PERSPECTIVE

Several years ago, my good friend Steffi Christie, who is a brilliant coach for neurodivergence and creativity, noticed something strange on the floor of her local shopping centre. The floor was warped, ripping the vinyl, and someone had put tape over the rough edges. This simple noticing prompted Steffi to become aware of how tensions warp things, and not just physical things like the floor in an old mall, but also internal emotional structures.

You may be wondering why, in this book about wild witchcraft, I'm suddenly talking about old vinyl flooring in a shopping centre. Perhaps it's jarring amid all the more natural-seeming metaphors. That's good. Pay attention.

Sometimes the most important insights come to us in strange and unexpected forms. Steffi's insight was one of the most helpful I've encountered because it led to an understanding of how the internal tensions we feel when we want something always warp our perspective. This does not have to be a bad thing at all, but it's incredibly useful to think about and excavate within ourselves. We don't necessarily have control over what we want, but sometimes we try to keep ourselves (or other people) safe by denying our desires.

I'm not saying we should always act on desires – not at all – but in denying or suppressing them we don't get rid of them, they just stay there, warping the foundation of our psyches. No matter how much tape we plaster over our suppressed desires, they will remain there creating the burden of internal tension and warping our perspective.

Of course we have a choice. Instead of denying our wants we can practice noticing, questioning, becoming curious about them and either working towards them or integrating them back into the wholeness of our being.

Why was this insight so helpful to me? At the time, I was working up the courage to embark on my first big publishing project on a novel that was deeply personal, and I was terrified! I had been suppressing a lot of the things I'd wanted regarding publishing, and I was ready to confront the fears I had surrounding what I wanted. Some of these fears were around feeling like an impostor and wanting to be included in a clique of more literary writers. I'd see these writers at events and read about them. They were so much cooler and more sophisticated and cleverer than I was. They all seemed to be good friends and I was a total outsider.

"When you think that other people are insiders and position yourself as an outsider," Steffi told me, "you give your power away. You de-centre yourself and project you own power onto those other people. They didn't even ask you to do that. They don't necessarily want your power. This is about you, not them."

This was a deeply valuable insight for me. In unpacking the tensions of wanting and projection that I was engaged in – all to protect myself – I realised that "in-crowd" was really just made up of people, each with their own insecurities. A few days later I went to a local literary event and found myself standing next to Elizabeth Knox, one of New Zealand's most formidable, acclaimed, and brilliant writers. Instead of standing back and distancing myself from her as I usually would in a situation like that, I said hello and introduced myself. We had a wonderful conversation that was helpful and insightful. I talked about how I had recently started working on my first ever fantasy book project, that I'd always loved reading fantasy as a child, but that my family's attitude towards it (particularly my grandmother, who could not stand reading fiction that wasn't firmly based in the real world) had held me back from writing fantasy books. Elizabeth, as a fantasy writer herself, knew exactly what I was talking about and expressed her furious frustration at this seemingly small internal struggle I was facing. It was deeply affirming to feel *seen* by this powerful literary figure. She said something along the lines of "I simply do not understand how some people cannot for a moment accept that their version of reality isn't the only way of seeing things!"

This was precisely the problem I was struggling with because it was not just a suppression of fantasy books that was troubling me. It was my family's attitude towards spirituality in general. They were scathing and dismissive of most spiritual things – anything not based firmly in their version of reality. Their way of seeing things was the only way of seeing things – according to them. As someone who saw things very differently, my whole experience of being, my perspective, my reality...was all being denied.

The interesting thing is that the conversation I'd had with Steffi about how wanting warps perspective, and feeling like an outsider (because I deeply wanted to be included and this was warping my perspective of "insiders") had directly led to a whole lot of internal processing which allowed me to introduce myself to Elizabeth Knox and have this conversation that shed light on a deep-rooted problem I had only vaguely been aware of. Growing up, I experienced a lot of painful moments around my spirituality, but I'd never made the connection to how I was holding myself back as a form of self-protection, including holding myself back from writing fantasy books. Opening myself up to this awareness allowed me to soothe myself and heal some old wounds, and to commit to the kind of writing I wanted to be doing at this stage of my life – which is now, several years later, my full time job and vocation.

Sometimes it doesn't feel safe to want what we want, but we can notice this and discover the deep-rooted causes in order to understand ourselves better. And when we feel ready, we can go about the good work of digging up the weeds that stifle the flourishing of our deepest yearnings. When we go deep into releasing old patterns and emotion we clear out what we no longer need and recycle the energy into something new. This creates the space and potential for transformational change. We may not always get what we want. Under the powerful gaze of our attention, what we want will continue to grow and change as we shed the layers of our old-selves which were so laden with other people's judgements and become more and more who we truly are.

One of the interesting things I discovered when I faced my wants and fears around my writing and publishing was that I did not really want to be a super clever sophisticated writer. I didn't have any desire to write the kinds of books that most people need a dictionary to read, or that are hard work in any way. I struggled with literacy so much as a young child that I deeply value writing that is clear, accessible, and engaging – especially when it's fun to read. I don't personally see much value in writing things that are hard to understand. After spending almost a decade in the academic system, being thoroughly sick of jargon and complex academic writing, I had found my public sector work a breath of fresh air. When writing advice and information for busy senior officials and Cabinet ministers it was important to be as clear and concise as possible and I loved that. I'd also loved the casual ease and flow of blogging and writing for the student magazine when I was younger. I loved reading books that I could get lost in and enjoy, not the ones that required too much hard work to understand.

Around this time, I began to stand more confidently in my identity as a 'real' writer. Previously, I'd sometimes dismissed my writing as a hobby, and for years I said I didn't want to be recognised as a writer or write full-time. It was true and false at the same time. I didn't want those things, because I was scared of wanting them, because deep down, I *did* want them but felt powerless. Aren't we humans full of paradoxes?!

In excavating all this, I was able to connect more deeply with what I was wanting, and in doing so, I let go of the attachments I had to being a fancy sophisticated literary writer. This meant I could focus instead on what I did want – to write meaningful, fun, and wonderous books full of real magic and personal development.

Reflection questions

- *When is it not safe to want what you want?*
- *How do other people's judgements about your desires affect you, and how have you internalised them?*
- *What deep desires do you have that other people may judge as shallow or conceited? (e.g., being recognised, being famous, wanting to look or appear a certain way)*
- *How does the "tension of wanting" warp things in your perspective?*
- *How does it feel to acknowledge and accept the things we want and clear away other people's judgements?*
- *How does this process change your perspective, your relationship to what you want?*
- *How does this heightened awareness affect the things you want? Do you notice any transformation?*

FEARS AS ALLIES IN DISGUISE

In quiet moments of reflection, or in busy or confronting situations, we sometimes brush up against deep fears and longings; we uncover layers of hesitation and doubt that obscure our path. Among these are four pervasive fears that shape our journey:
- the fear of magic,
- the fear of our power,
- the fear of ourselves,
- and the fear of what we want most.

Each of these fears can hold us back, yet they also offer opportunities for growth and self-discovery. We can explore these fears, understanding their roots and learning how to transform them into sources of strength, power, and clarity.

As we step deeper into the enchanted forest of our own consciousness (or whatever metaphor you prefer), seeking the magic that calls to our hearts, we inevitably encounter the shadowy figures of our fears like gate-keepers we must face in order to progress on our journey.

The fear of magic is rooted in the unknown. Magic represents the vast potential that lies hidden, the creative force that defies logic and limitation. People tend to fear this power because it challenges our familiar reality, asking us to expand our perceptions and step into uncharted realms of being. Yet when we have the courage to embrace this fear, we open ourselves to wonder, possibility, and the boundless adventure of co-creating our lives. Magic has long been feared. Just as witches are often "the bad guys" in fairy tales and many religions demonise magic – even to the extent of sometimes banning fantasy books.

The fear of power can arise from the burden of responsibility. The immense force of our own potential influence and capability can feel over-whelming, even terrifying. We may fear misusing our power, losing control, or navigating the weighty consequences of our choices. But genuine power is not domination – it is in empowerment, our deep pres-ence, and the recognition of our ability to shape reality. When we make peace with this fear, we become empowered to create positive change.

Presence and attention, either focussed inward or outward, rather than caught somewhere in between, is incredibly powerful. In her book, Unbound, Kasia Urbaniak explores this magic of empowerment with a particular focus on unlearning the unhealthy dynamics and patterns of patriarchy. This is deep work, and so worthwhile.

Perhaps the most intimate fear is the fear of ourselves. Gazing into the depths of our own psyche, as if into a bottomless pool, requires the courage to face our vulnerability. We may recoil from what we see – the unacknowl-edged wounds, the shadow aspects, the desires we deem unworthy, bad or wrong. But these too are vital parts of our wholeness. We do not need to act on desires, but if we do not face them and understand them they will continue to haunt us. As we befriend this fear and embrace radical self-accep-tance, we reclaim the lost pieces of our soul and become integrated beings.

Then there is the fear of what we want most. Our deepest longings can be the stars that guide us, yet their intensity can feel painful, especially when we don't know how to receive what we most desire. The yearning to express our truest selves, to love and be loved, to offer our unique gifts to the world – can make our hearts tremble. We fear the transformative power of our desires, the risk of disappointment and loss. But our desires are also the keys to our magic and meaning.

Ultimately, fear in all its faces is a powerful teacher. Fear marks a threshold of transformation, an edge where we are being invited to shed our limited identities and step into greater versions of ourselves. As we muster the courage to cross these thresholds, the fears alchemise and we transform deeper into being more fully ourselves.

So, as you walk the winding path of your magical becoming, remember that your fears are allies in disguise. Greet them with curiosity and respect, for they hold the seeds of your greatness. With each fear embraced, you reclaim more of your authentic power and draw closer to the desires that make your spirit sing. Here in the forest, in the depths of your being, is the enchantment you seek – the magic of your fully embodied, unapologetic, wildly radiant self.

MAGICAL SYMBOLISM OF THE CAULDRON

The cauldron is a powerful and ancient symbol in mythology and witchcraft. This mystical vessel is revered as a source of transformation, abundance, and rebirth. The cauldron is often linked to deities and sacred rites. One of the most famous cauldrons is the Cauldron of Dagda, a central figure in Irish mythology. Dagda's cauldron, known as the Cauldron of Plenty, was said to be bottomless, providing endless sustenance and symbolising abundance and generosity. This cauldron never emptied, regardless of how much was taken from it, illustrating the boundless nature of the divine provision.

The Welsh goddess, Cerridwen, is well known for her cauldron which was used to brew a potion that granted wisdom and inspiration. This potent brew required a year and a day of preparation, symbolising the deep, transformative processes of life. The Cauldron of Rebirth signifies regeneration and the cycle of life, death, and rebirth, highlighting the belief in reincarnation and the continuous flow of life.

In witchcraft, the cauldron holds a central place as a versatile and sacred tool. It is often seen as a symbol of the element of water, fertility, creation, and the transformative power of nature. The cauldron is used in various magical practices, from brewing potions and elixirs to burning herbs and scrying.

The cauldron's association with transformation is particularly significant in witchcraft. Just as ingredients placed into a cauldron can be transformed into something new, the cauldron symbolises the witch's ability to transform and manifest desires. It represents the alchemical process of turning base elements into something precious, the inner alchemy of spiritual growth and enlightenment.

The cauldron is often used as a focal point for ritual and spellwork. It serves as a container for the elements, where Water can be scryed for visions, Air imbues vapour, the essence of the potion, to rise up and create the desired atmosphere, Fire can be kindled for purification, and Earth can be added to ground energies. This multifunctional use underscores the cauldron's role as a microcosm embodying the interconnectedness of all things.

THE THREE CAULDRONS

You do not need big metal cauldrons in order to practice witchcraft, but you might be interested to know that ancient wisdom speaks of three cauldrons that reside within each person, swirling with the energies of transformation and enlightenment. Reflected in the old Irish poem, *The Cauldron of Poesy,* these cauldrons – the Cauldron of Warming, the Cauldron of Motion, and the Cauldron of Wisdom – are mystical vessels residing within the body. These metaphorical cauldrons are understood to function like energy centres, similar to nadis or chakras in Hindu and Buddhist traditions, the meridian centres of Chinese and Japanese medicine, the Sufi concept of lataif-e-sitta, the ancient Egyptian concept of energy centres aligned with spiritual knowledge, or the Kabbalistic teachings in Jewish mysticism which describe the sephiroth of the Tree of Life as vital spiritual nodes.

My understanding of working with the three cauldrons comes from my own research and also from my studies with the Order of Bards, Ovates and Druids. This is a revivalist tradition, drawing on and adapting historic cultural practices of people who are now often grouped together as Celtic or Gaelic. Little is known about many of these traditions, as written language was late to come to Britain. Before the Roman invasion, the Britons did not have a widespread writing system. The Celts used Ogham script for inscriptions – lines and notches carved into stone or wood. The Cauldron of Poesy poem was believed to be written in the early medieval period, between the 7th and 9th centuries. The poem claims within its text to be the work of the mythic poet Amergin Glúingel, a key figure in Irish mythology, the chief bard and druid of the Milesians. The three cauldrons may have originated from the poem, or they may have been a longstanding tradition. Either way, I have found them to be powerful and transformative to work with.

THE CAULDRON OF WARMING: THE SEAT OF VITALITY

The first cauldron, known as the Cauldron of Warming or the Cauldron of Incubation, resides in the belly. It is said to be born upright in most people and is understood to be the seat of our physical life force, our instinctual energy, and our connection to the earth. This cauldron governs our basic needs, our survival instincts, and our ability to draw nourishment and strength from the world around us.

When this cauldron is balanced and full we feel stable, healthy, and grounded. However, we are not always able to control the material world, including our own physical selves. The Cauldron of Warming can be unbalanced, tip, or overturn. When this happens, we may feel disconnected from our bodies, lacking in energy and motivation. We cannot fill a cauldron that is overturned, but we can nudge it back around by meeting our deeper needs, following our intuition, seeking healing from experts, and nourishing ourselves on all levels.

Practices that can help restore balance to the Cauldron of Warming include:
- Engaging in grounding exercises and spending time in nature
- Eating nourishing, wholesome foods
- Getting enough rest and having good sleeping routines
- Cultivating a sense of safety and security in our environment
- Engaging in physical activities that bring joy and vitality

The Cauldron of Warming is deeply tied to the physical world and the body's health. The environment plays a critical role in its condition. Living in harmony with the land, connecting with and respecting nature can help to fill this cauldron.

THE CAULDRON OF MOTION: THE REALM OF EMOTION

The second cauldron, the Cauldron of Motion or the Cauldron of Vocation, is located in the chest and heart area. This cauldron is the deep well of our emotions, our capacity for empathy and connection, and our ability to engage with the world through our feelings and desires.

Unlike the Cauldron of Warming, the Cauldron of Motion is said to be born on its side in most people, hinting that emotional growth and maturity develops over time, through our life experiences and relationships.

When the Cauldron of Motion is upright and balanced, we can experience the full spectrum of human emotions in a healthy way. We are able to form deep, meaningful connections with others and pursue our heart's desires. However, when this cauldron is blocked or overturned, we may struggle with emotional instability, difficulty in relationships, or a sense of disconnection from our authentic desires.

To stir the Cauldron of Motion, consider practices such as:
- Engaging in creative pursuits that allow for emotional expression
- Practising presence, listening, and empathy in relationships
- Exploring therapeutic modalities for emotional healing
- Setting healthy boundaries and being gentle with ourselves
- Cultivating appreciation and celebration

The Cauldron of Motion, with its emphasis on emotional and creative expression, thrives in environments where art and heart are shared and celebrated. Festivals, storytelling gatherings, and creative projects not only stir the individual's cauldron but also help to elevate the collective emotional well-being. In communities where these expressions are nurtured, a sense of unity and empathy can be observed, strengthening the social fabric and enhancing resilience against collective challenges. Conversely, in settings where emotional expression is stifled or unvalued, there may be a dullness or disconnection, mirroring an untended Cauldron of Motion. This can lead to a lack of support and understanding, weakening the bonds that should ideally unite people.

THE CAULDRON OF WISDOM: THE CRUCIBLE OF TRANSFORMATION

The third cauldron, the Cauldron of Wisdom or the Cauldron of Knowledge, is situated in the head. This cauldron is the seat of our wisdom and understanding, and our connection to spirituality and inspiration.

The Irish text tells us that the Cauldron of Wisdom is born upside down in most people. This implies that wisdom and spiritual insight are not inherent, but rather must be actively pursued and cultivated over a lifetime. I'm not sure that this is always true. Babies and young people are often more innately connected with spirituality before the world comes crashing in, but I understand that developing some kinds of wisdom takes time and comes with experience.

When the Cauldron of Wisdom is turned upright and filled, we experience clarity of thought, deep understanding, and a sense of connection to something greater than ourselves. We are able to access our intuition and inspiration. However, when this cauldron remains inverted or is blocked, we may feel stuck in old patterns of thinking, disconnected from our inner wisdom, or lacking in purpose and direction.

To fill the Cauldron of Wisdom, we can engage in practices such as:
- Meditation and contemplation
- Studying spiritual texts and philosophies
- Engaging in deep, meaningful conversations and exchanges of ideas
- Pursuing education and lifelong learning
- Seeking out mentors and wise counsel

The Cauldron of Wisdom reaches its fullest expression when one is in tune not only with personal insights but also with greater awareness. This cauldron is deeply enriched by spiritual practices that connect with the bigger picture. Observing astronomical events, aligning practices with lunar cycles, and participating in rituals that honour the Earth's rhythms can profoundly impact this cauldron.

Ultimately, the journey through the Three Cauldrons offers a system for inner-work and a transformative processes that invites a deep reconnection with the body and the ancient rhythms of the earth, encouraging a harmonious balance that can lead to personal and collective fulfilment.

Each cauldron's state reflects not only individual well-being but also the potential for healing and renewal. The Cauldron of Motion, with its focus on emotional and creative energies, plays a crucial role in psychological healing. Similarly, the Cauldron of Wisdom provides a pathway for spiritual healing, guiding individuals to seek deeper truths and understanding, often leading to personal transformations and a renewed sense of purpose.

RITUAL OF THE THREE CAULDRONS

This ritual can be performed individually or in a group setting, ideally during a full moon to harness its potent energies for transformation.

Materials Needed:
- Three bowls or cauldrons
- Water and salt
- Candles to represent each cauldron
- Incense or herbs for smoke cleansing

Optional:
- Herbs (eg: rosemary for physical health, chamomile for emotions, and sage for wisdom)
- Crystals (eg: red jasper for grounding, moonstone for emotional balance, and clear quartz for spiritual clarity)

Setup:
1. Cleanse the space by burning herbs or another cleansing herb.
2. Arrange the three bowls or cauldrons in a line. Place herbs and crystals in each cauldron that represent the cauldron (optional).

Ritual Steps:
1. Opening: Begin by lighting the incense or the herb bundle, moving from the first cauldron to the third, stating your intention, e.g., for

balance, healing, and wisdom. Light the candles in front of each cauldron, aligning with the energies of grounding, emotion, and wisdom respectively.

2. Focus on the first cauldron and place your hands on your belly, connecting with the strength and vitality of your physical form. If you do not feel strong or vital, that's okay, but if you can, allow yourself to connect with that energy just for a moment, opening up to this power within you.

3. Move to the second and put your hands on your heart area, focusing on empathy and emotional healing. Allow your heart and your will and all your desires to shine forth. Notice if you feel any conflicts there. If so, allow each conflicting desire you have to have a moment to express itself. For instance, you may have a desire to be brave and a conflicting desire to feel safe. Allow both of these desires to express themselves one at a time, and as they do, allow the conflicting desire to watch, listen, understand, and empathise. Acknowledge and thank these desires. It may be that you feel a nudge to go back to the first cauldron at this point and reaffirm your strength and empowerment in your body and in this world. This presents a new opportunity to go deeper.

4. When you're ready, move your focus to the third cauldron and focus on the divine spark within you and its connection to all that is. Allow yourself to connect in whatever way makes the most sense intuitively to you. If you like, you can ask for guidance, insight, and connection to deep wisdom.

5. Focus on each cauldron one by one. At the first, place your hands into the water and feel the sensation of it. If it makes sense for you, this can be an opportunity to reconnect more deeply with your physical presence and acknowledge the gifts of your physical body, no matter how painful. Thank your body for doing its best and allow yourself to connect more deeply.

6. Focus on the second cauldron and stir the water gently with your fingers. If you are ready to open yourself up to more emotion you may wish to do this now. If you're already feeling overwhelmed by feelings, you may wish to visualise your emotional troubles being soothed away with the water's motion.

7. At the third cauldron, hold your hands above the water, sensing the energy there, just as you may sense the subtler energies around you and

the wisdom hidden within all things. You may wish to wave your hands above the water, visualising the energy of wisdom filling your spirit.

8. Offer thanks to the three cauldrons within you. Snuff out the candles in reverse order, starting with the third, then the second, and finally the first, sealing the energies you've raised.

5. Finish by grounding yourself. Eat something, drink water, or sit on the earth, visualising excess energy returning to the ground. You may choose to take any herbs from the cauldrons and leave them outside under a tree as an offering to nature.

Close your ritual space by thanking any deities or spirits you have invoked, and affirm that all energies are sealed within the cauldrons, now part of your being. This ritual can be repeated as often as needed, especially during times of personal transformation or when seeking deeper spiritual insights.

MAGIC OF SYNCHRONICITY

Synchronicity is the thread that binds seemingly unrelated events, revealing a deeper, hidden pattern. It's a term coined by Jung, meaning an "acausual connecting principle" which could be understood as a mysterious connection between the psyche and the external world. Synchronicity can also be viewed as a form of divine guidance, nudging us in a direction more aligned with our path. It's the magic that makes us pause and wonder, connecting the dots between our inner world and the outer experiences.

Synchronicity occurs when there is a meaningful coincidence that defies logical explanation, like thinking of a friend you haven't seen in years and then suddenly bumping into that friend or receiving a message from them. Unlike mere chance, these moments feel imbued with a sense of purpose and alignment. They often arrive when we are in tune with our intuition, serving as signposts that guide us. Whether it's meeting the right person at the right time, finding a book that answers an itchy question, or seeing repeated symbols, synchronicity acts as a bridge between our conscious desires and the subconscious currents of the universe.

WORKING WITH SYNCHRONICITY IN MAGIC

To harness the power of synchronicity, we need to cultivate awareness and be receptive to the signs and patterns around us. Here's a practical exercise to reveal these patterns in your life:

Pattern Journal: Keep a journal dedicated to noting down synchronicities. Write down any peculiar coincidences, repeated numbers, symbols, or dreams that seem significant. Over time, review your entries to identify recurring themes or messages.

Intention Setting: Begin (or end) your day by setting an intention to be open to synchronicities. This can be as simple as a silent affirmation: "I am open to the guidance of synchronicity today," or it could be more specific, focusing on particular synchronicities you're interested in exploring.

Reflection questions

Reflect on the past few days, weeks, months and years.

In what situations did you experience the most joy and ease? Where did you run into resistance?

What patterns keep repeating for you over and over?

Ask yourself, "What might life be trying to tell me?" Pay attention to any feelings or insights that arise.

COLOUR MAGIC

Colour magic is a vibrant and accessible tool in the practice of witchcraft, utilised for its ability to attract specific energies and manifest various intentions. Each colour emits a unique frequency and holds distinct associations and powers, which can significantly enhance your magical work. However, it's crucial to acknowledge that colour perception is highly personal and can be influenced by cultural, emotional, and individual factors. Therefore, while traditional associations can guide your practice, personal intuition should also play a key role in choosing colours for your magic.

Here are some commonly accepted associations for colours in magical practices, which can serve as a starting point for integrating colour magic into your rituals:

Red: Passion, strength, love, and courage. Use red to initiate action, ward off negativity, and when dealing with matters of the heart.

Orange: Creativity, attraction, enthusiasm, and success. Orange can be used to stimulate mental activities and promote energy.

Yellow: Joy, intellect, communication, and travel. Yellow aids in matters of learning, mental clarity, and swift action.

Green: Growth, fertility, health, and prosperity. Green is most often used in spells for healing, financial success, and abundance.

Blue: Peace, healing, tranquility, and truth. Blue can calm the mind, aid in healing, and foster patience.

Purple: Spirituality, psychic abilities, and ambition. Purple is ideal for deepening spiritual awareness and enhancing psychic powers.

Pink: Romance, friendship, compassion, and nurturing. Pink attracts emotional love and helps heal matters of the heart.

Black: Protection, absorption, and banishment. Black is powerful for protection rituals and to banish negativity.

White: new beginnings, peace, and clearing. White can be used in place of any other colour.

While these traditional meanings provide a framework, the personal and cultural significance of colours can vary greatly. For example, white is seen as a colour of mourning in some cultures, contrasting with its Western associations with "purity" and weddings.

To adapt colour magic to your personal context, start by observing your reactions and feelings towards different colours. Consider keeping a colour journal, where you note your feelings and experiences with different colours over time. You can also explore the historical and cultural meanings of colours within your own heritage, which can add layers of depth to your magical practice.

PLAYING WITH COLOUR MAGIC

Colour Meditation: Choose a colour you wish to connect with. Select an object of a particular colour to hold and meditate with, or simply find a quiet spot and visualise yourself surrounded by a light of this colour. As you meditate, focus on the qualities you associate with the colour, allowing those qualities to infuse into your life.

Colour Candle Magic: Select a candle in the colour that corresponds to your intention. As you light the candle, visualise the flame activating the energy associated with that colour, drawing your desire towards you.

Wardrobe Magic: Integrate colour magic into your daily life by wearing clothes that align with your daily intentions. Need confidence? Wear red. Looking for calm? Choose blue.

By understanding the traditional uses of colour in magic and integrating your personal and cultural connections, you can create a deeply personalised magical practice that resonates with your intentions and experiences. This approach not only respects the complexity of colour perception but also empowers you to use colour in a way that is most meaningful to you.

MAGICAL HERBS AND PLANTS

I could write an entire book on plant magic, and perhaps one day I will, but for now, I will just share what I can fit into this already-rather-long book. Plants and trees have long been revered for their magical properties, serving as powerful allies in our spiritual and magical practices. Each plant and tree carries unique energies and properties that can be harnessed for various purposes, from healing and protection to love and prosperity.

When working with plants and trees, it is essential to remember that they are living beings with their own energies and spirits. To connect with them effectively, approach them with respect and reverence. Here are some steps to help you build a respectful relationship with the plants and trees you work with:

1. **Asking Permission:** Before taking any part of a plant or tree, always ask for permission. This can be done silently in your mind or spoken aloud. Close your eyes, take a deep breath, and mentally or verbally ask the plant or tree if you may take what you need. Pay attention to any feelings, thoughts, or sensations that arise, as these can be signs of the plant's response.

2. **Offering Appreciation:** Express your appreciation. This can be done through a simple thank you, a verbal blessing, poem or chant, or by leaving a small offering such as water or some compost. Showing appreciation helps to honour the plant's spirit and maintain a harmonious relationship.

3. **Respectful Harvesting:** When harvesting from a plant or tree, take only what you need and ensure that you do not harm the plant. Use clean, sharp tools to make clean cuts, and avoid taking too much from any one plant. This mindful approach ensures that the plant can continue to thrive and offer its gifts in the future.

4. **Connecting Through Meditation:** Spend time sitting quietly with the plant, allowing yourself to tune into its energy. Place your hands on the plant or tree, close your eyes, and take deep, slow breaths. Visualise your energy merging with that of the plant, creating a harmonious exchange. This practice helps you to build a deeper connection and understand the plant's unique properties.

WAND AND STAFF MAKING BASICS

You do not need a wand or staff to practice magic, however, if you feel drawn to them, they can be powerful tools, often used to direct energy, cast circles, and perform rituals. Creating your own wand or staff can be a deeply personal and rewarding experience. Here are some basics to get you started:

Selecting the Wood: You may find that the wood chooses you by falling across your path, or you may want to deliberately choose a type of wood that resonates with your intention and energy. Each type of wood has its own magical properties. For example, oak is associated with strength and protection, while willow is linked to intuition and healing. When selecting your wood, consider what qualities you want to imbue in your wand or staff.

Harvesting the Wood: As with harvesting herbs, always ask for permission before taking wood from a tree. Look for fallen branches or twigs that have naturally separated from the tree, as these are often easier to work with and do not harm the tree. If you must cut a branch, do so with respect and appreciation, ensuring you do not take more than you need and cutting at a natural join in the wood.

Preparing the Wood: Once you have your piece of wood, you could choose to remove the bark, whittle patterns into it or smooth the surface using sandpaper. You may wish to rub oil onto it to reveal the natural beauty of the wood. You can also carve symbols, runes, or other markings into it if you are drawn to do so.

Charging and Consecrating: To charge your wand or staff, hold it in your hands and meditate on your intention. Visualise your energy flowing into the wood, infusing it with your desired qualities. You can also leave it under the full moon or in sunlight to absorb natural energies. To consecrate your tool, pass it through the elements – smoke from incense for Air, flame for Fire, water for Water, and soil for Earth – while stating your intention.

Decorating and Enhancing: You can decorate your staff or wand in whatever ways make sense for you. Some people prefer an un-decorated approach, others like to go all out by adding crystals, feathers, ribbons, or other natural elements. These additions can amplify the tool's energy and help you to connect with it more personally. As always, focus on your intention and allow your creativity to guide you.

By respecting the plants and trees you work with and taking the time to craft your magical tools thoughtfully, you can create powerful allies in your magical practice. Whether you are making a simple herb sachet or a beautifully adorned staff, the care and intention you put into your work will resonate through your magical workings, deepening your connection to the natural world and the energies that flow through it.

MAGICAL HERBS

Herbs have long been an important part of my life. When I was about twenty years old, I signed up to formally study herbalism and spent a year learning about the plants – their medicinal properties as well as other important interrelated subjects like nutrition, anatomy, and physiology. Herbs have long been an important part of my magic, too, whether in my kitchen witchery or in other magical workings.

Connecting with herbs intuitively is a powerful process that can enhance your everyday life and magical practices. Start by using your senses to get to know the herbs. Hold a sprig of rosemary in your hands. Feel the texture of the leaves and stems. Notice whether they're smooth, rough, soft, or prickly. Close your eyes and take a deep breath, inhaling the herb's natural scent. Herbs have distinctive aromas that can evoke different feelings – lavender might make you feel calm and relaxed, while mint could be refreshing and invigorating.

Look closely at the herb's appearance. Observe the colour and shape of the leaves, flowers, or seeds. Each herb has its own visual signature, and these characteristics can tell you a lot about its properties. Bright green basil leaves, for example, are often associated with prosperity and protection, while the delicate petals of chamomile flowers are linked to peace and relaxation.

Taste can also play a role in connecting with herbs. If the herb is safe to consume, try a small nibble or make a tea. Notice the flavours – are they bitter, sweet, or spicy? The taste of a herb can give you clues about its magical uses. For instance, the spicy kick of ginger might be energising and stimulating, making it great for spells involving courage and strength.

Choosing the right herb in your magical practice is often about following your intuition. Let yourself be drawn to the herbs that catch your eye or have a scent that appeals to you. Trust your instincts – often, the herbs you need will naturally attract you.

Meditate with herbs by holding them or placing them nearby as you focus on your intentions. Let their natural energy align with yours, helping to amplify your desires and goals. Herbs can also be used in spellwork to enhance your rituals and make your magic more potent.

I find solace and power in gardens, especially herb gardens where aromatic scents bring their own magic into the air. There are far too many herbs to cover in this book alone, and there are many ways of interpreting and working with them. Here, I'm just going to share some brief properties of ten magical herbs.

Lavender

This fragrant herb is a balm to the spirit, promoting peace, cleansing, and sleep. Associated with the element of Air, it is often used in rituals to invoke harmony and healing. Lavender is believed to guide dreams and meditation, providing a gentle touch to the mind and soul. Its soothing aroma is used in aromatherapy to alleviate stress and encourage a restful night's sleep.

Mugwort

A herb of the moon and dreams, mugwort is protective and psychic, opening the doors to visionary work associated with the Ancient Greek goddess, Artemis. It aligns with the element of Earth, aiding in prophecy and magical workings. Mugwort is known for its ability to enhance lucid dreaming and astral travel, making it a valuable tool for those exploring the depths of their subconscious.

Rosemary

Symbolic of remembrance and love, rosemary is used for protection, purification, and mental clarity. Linked to the element of Fire, it aids in rituals of healing and purification. Rosemary's invigorating scent is believed to sharpen the mind and boost memory, making it a popular choice for scholars and those engaged in intellectual pursuits.

Sage

With its cleansing smoke, sage is wonderful for purification, removing negative energy, and spiritual protection. It connects to the element of Air and enhances wisdom and protection. Sage is often used in rituals to cleanse spaces, objects, and people, creating a sacred environment free from negativity. Note that there are cultural considerations around white sage, including sustainability considerations.

Thyme

A bearer of courage and bravery, thyme is used to promote strength and healing. It resonates with the element of Water and is powerful in love spells and deepening psychic abilities. Thyme's energising properties are believed to revitalise the body and spirit, providing the fortitude needed to face challenges.

Basil

Attracting wealth, love, and promoting peace, basil is deeply connected to the element of Fire. It is used in spells for prosperity and protection. Basil's vibrant green leaves are often placed in homes and businesses to attract good fortune and ward off negative influences, ensuring a harmonious environment.

Mint

Known for its abilities to attract abundance and vitality, mint stimulates the mind and body. It corresponds to the element of Air and offers protection while travelling. Mint's refreshing aroma is believed to invigorate the senses, providing a burst of energy and mental clarity, making it a favourite in both culinary and magical practices.

Bay

Worn by the oracles, bay laurel enhances psychic abilities and provides protection. This noble herb aligns with the element of Fire and assists in divination and victory. Bay laurel's aromatic leaves are often used in rituals to seek guidance and ensure success, making it a symbol of achievement and honour.

Chamomile

A sun herb, chamomile brings relaxation, prosperity, and protection. It's associated with the element of Water and is useful in spells for peace and money. Chamomile's gentle blossoms are often brewed into tea to soothe the nerves and promote restful sleep, embodying the calming energy of the sun.

Elderflower

Revered as a sacred tree, elderflower is used for protection, healing, and prosperity. It is linked to the element of Air, guarding against negative energy and promoting healing. Elderflower's delicate blossoms are often used in potions and charms to attract blessings and enhance spiritual well-being.

CREATING HERBAL TALISMANS

Creating talismans using magical herbs is a wonderful way to harness their natural energies. This exercise will guide you through various methods of making and charging herb talismans to align with your magical intentions. You may wish to do this work in a sacred space or as part of a ritual.

Materials:
- A selection of magical herbs
- Small cloth pouches or sachets
- String or ribbon
- Small jars or bottles
- Beeswax or soy wax (for herb-infused candles)
- A piece of jewellery or charm (optional)
- Cleansing materials (e.g., herbs, incense)
- A quiet, dedicated space for ritual work

Method 1: Herb Sachet Talisman

Choose herbs that resonate with your intention. For example, lavender for peace, rosemary for protection, or basil for prosperity.

Creating the Sachet:

Fill a small cloth pouch or sachet with your chosen herbs.

As you add each herb, focus on your intention, visualising the energy of the herb merging with your intention.

Close the pouch tightly and secure it with string or ribbon.

Hold the sachet in your hands and meditate on your intention. Visualise the sachet glowing with the energy you wish to infuse. Speak your intention out loud or silently, clearly stating your intention.

Place the sachet under your pillow, carry it with you, or keep it in a sacred space to continually benefit from its energy.

Method 2: Herb-Infused Candle Talisman

Choose herbs that align with your intention.

Melt beeswax or soy wax in a double boiler.

Add the herbs to the melted wax, stirring gently.

Pour the herb-infused wax into a mould with a wick.

Allow the candle to cool and solidify.

Once the candle is set, hold it in your hands and meditate on your intention. Visualise the flame carrying your desires into the universe as the candle burns.

Light the candle during your rituals or meditation, focusing on your intention as the herb-infused wax releases its energy.

. . .

Method 3: Herb-Infused Oil Talisman

Choose herbs that align with your intentions.

Fill a small jar or bottle with your chosen herbs.

Cover the herbs with a carrier oil (e.g., olive oil, almond oil).

Seal the jar and place it in a sunny spot for 2-4 weeks, shaking it gently each day.

After infusing, strain the herbs out of the oil. Hold the bottle in your hands, meditate on your intention, and visualise the oil glowing with the desired energy.

Use the herb-infused oil to anoint candles, charms, or yourself during rituals. The oil can also be used to dress spell candles or to enhance your magical workings.

Method 4: Herb-Infused Jewellery Talisman

Choose a piece of jewellery or charm and cleanse with herb smoke before beginning.

Place a small amount of your chosen herbs into a locket, charm bag, or small vial attached to the jewellery. Alternatively, anoint the jewellery with herb-infused oil.

Hold the jewellery in your hands and meditate on your intention. Visualise the jewellery radiating with the energy you wish to infuse.

Wear the jewellery regularly, especially during times when you need its specific energy. The talisman will continue to work as long as you wear it, aligning your energy with your intentions.

CRYSTALS, GEMSTONES AND MAGIC

Crystals have long held a place in magical practices. From the ancient peoples who revered particular gemstones and created crystal jewellery to the medieval practitioners who used them for divination, these natural stones have been integral to spiritual practices across cultures and centuries.

Incorporating crystals into magical practices doesn't require elaborate rituals or arcane knowledge. Simple acts, like placing a specific stone on an altar to enhance the ambient energies, or carrying a stone for wisdom or protection during travel, can integrate the power of crystals into everyday magic.

For those inclined to explore the potential of crystals, the journey begins with tuning in to intuition. Each crystal has its traditional attributes, but the depth of its power can only be grasped through personal connection. This may mean spending time with the crystal, meditating with it, or keeping it close as you perform your daily rituals.

In recent years, questions have been raised around the ethics of mining crystals from the earth, particularly in terms of unfair labour and sustainability issues. You may want to explore where your crystals come from before you buy them, and make choices that resonate well with you.

The relationship with crystals in magic is as deep and complex as the stones themselves. Crystals can offer a direct line to the earth's powerful energies, aiding us in our magical workings and providing a tangible connection to the mystical forces of the earth. There are many books about crystals, so here I will just include properties of a few. Note that these properties are not set in stone, and just like with people, some crystals will be easier for you to get along with than others. When choosing crystals, focus on the ones that feel good to you.

Amethyst is a stone of spiritual awareness and inner peace. It is a trusted companion for those who seek to calm their mind and enhance their intuition. Used in meditation and dream work, it protects, acting as a guardian for the soul.

Rose Quartz is associated with unconditional love and compassion. Rose Quartz exudes a gentle, nurturing energy. It fosters love and emotional healing, making it ideal for self-love, and mending emotional wounds. Its soft pink glow brings comfort to the heart and mind.

Clear Quartz amplifies energy and brings clarity to the mind and spirit. It balances energy and is a powerful tool for meditation and healing work. This versatile crystal can be used to amplify intentions.

Black Tourmaline is a stone of protection and grounding. Black Tourmaline dispels negativity and shields against psychic attacks. It creates a protective barrier, grounding during rituals and ensuring a stable connection to the earth's energies.

Citrine Radiating with the warmth of the sun, this is a powerful attractor of prosperity and success. It boosts confidence, stimulates creativity and abundance. Its golden light has a vibrant energy, making it a cherished stone for those seeking growth, clarity, and success.

Lapis Lazuli is a stone of truth and wisdom. It enhances inner vision and promotes clear communication, making it a valuable ally in meditation and spiritual exploration. This ancient stone has been revered for centuries for its ability to unlock higher realms of consciousness.

Carnelian is a stone of energy, courage, and motivation. It stimulates creativity and helps overcome fears, making it perfect for those embarking on new ventures or seeking to ignite their passions. Its vibrant energy instils a sense of boldness and confidence.

Selenite, named after the moon goddess Selene, is a crystal of mental clarity and spiritual purity. It cleanses energy, connecting to the divine. Often used to cleanse other crystals, Selenite's luminous white energy creates a serene and peaceful atmosphere for spiritual work.

Tiger's Eye is a stone of truth, protection, and fortune. It enhances willpower and confidence, grounding the user and bringing prosperity. Its watchful energy provides a sense of security and stability, making it a favoured talisman.

Moonstone with its ethereal glow, is a stone of intuition and emotional balance. It aids in new beginnings and supports through emotional transitions. Its connection to the moon imbues it with a gentle, calming energy that enhances intuition and spiritual insight.

Hematite is a powerful grounding stone that enhances focus and absorbs negative energy. It anchors to the earth, providing stability and clarity. Its reflective surface acts as a shield, protecting against external negativity.

Jade is revered in many cultures for its luck-bringing properties. It promotes harmony and prosperity. Its verdant energy attracts abundance and enhances well-being, fostering a sense of peace and balance. It is a symbol of health, wealth, and longevity.

Aquamarine promotes calmness and enhances communication. It is a protective talisman for travellers, soothing the mind and spirit. Its serene energy flows like water, bringing peace and clarity to those who carry it.

Garnet is a stone of vitality and passion. It boosts energy and courage, inspiring confidence and determination. Its fiery essence ignites the spirit, making it a powerful ally for those seeking to embrace their inner strength.

Malachite is a stone of transformation and protection. It aids in personal growth and enhances willpower. Its vibrant energy encourages positive change, making it a catalyst for personal and spiritual transformation.

CRAFTING GEMSTONE TALISMANS: A PRACTICAL EXERCISE

Creating gemstone talismans is a beautiful and powerful way to harness the energies of the earth and infuse them into your magical practice. Talismans can be crafted in various ways, depending on your intention and the resources at hand. This exercise will guide you through different methods to create and charge gemstone talismans, ensuring they are imbued with the desired energies. You may also wish to bless and charge an existing gemstone necklace you have, using a similar method to those described below.

Method 1: Simple Gemstone Talisman

Choose a gemstone that resonates with your intention. For example, use Rose Quartz for love, Black Tourmaline for protection, or Citrine for abundance.

Cleanse the gemstone by blessing it with herbs or incense, or placing it in saltwater or under moonlight or sunlight.

Hold the cleansed gemstone in your hands. Close your eyes and focus on your intention. Visualise a bright light surrounding the stone, infusing it with your desired energy. Speak your intention out loud or silently, clearly stating your intention.

Carry the charged gemstone with you in a small pouch, or place it on your altar. You can also keep it under your pillow or in your pocket.

Method 2: Gemstone Talisman Necklace

Choose a gemstone and cleanse it as described above.

Wrap the gemstone in wire to create a pendant. Secure the wire tightly so the stone stays in place. Alternatively, place the gemstone in a small cage pendant.

Hold the cleansed gemstone in your hands. Close your eyes and focus on your intention. Visualise a bright light surrounding the stone, infusing it with your desired energy. Speak your intention out loud or silently, clearly stating your intention.

You may also wish to light a candle that corresponds with your intention. Hold the pendant over the candle flame (not too close) and recite a simple incantation, such as: "With this flame, I charge thee. With the power of [your intention]."

Wear the necklace close to your heart, allowing it to radiate its charged energy throughout your day.

POWER OF THE VOICE

The voice is an exquisite instrument that we often take for granted simply because it is something we all possess. Through our voice, we communicate with words and sounds, song and deep sighs, weaving spells and enchantments with nothing but the air from our lungs and the intent in our hearts. Singing and chanting has been used throughout history across cultures as an important part of rituals and healing. I see this as kinds of natural technologies of the voice which evolved in order to soothe the nervous system, build connection within communities, and restore balance after stress and trauma.

Many of us have wounds when it comes to our voice's expression. As children, we were told to be quiet, we were told not to cry, we were told off for being too loud. Perhaps we had sharp painful moments when we sang happily only to be teased, judged, or bullied by people around us who were supposed to care for us – our parents, siblings, or peers. Many people do not sing because they carry such a trauma. If this is something you relate to, then gentle and safe experimentation with the power of your voice can be deeply therapeutic.

The voice is a direct extension of our spirit and will. When we vocalise, we are not merely producing sound; we are sending our energy and intent into the world, creating ripples in the form of literal sound waves. Singing, humming, and chanting are ancient practices, used by witches, shamans, and communities throughout the ages to create change, invoke power, and alter consciousness.

SINGING

Singing in magic is a way to raise energy, evoke emotions, and honour the divine. It can be as simple as singing a heartfelt song that resonates with your intent, or as complex as composing a melody to embody your spell. Singing to the moon, the sun, or the earth can strengthen your connection to these powerful forces.

Practice: Choose a simple song or intuitively create one that aligns with your magical work. Focus on your intention while you sing, allowing your voice to carry your desires into the universe. Visualise your desires being woven into the notes, and feel the energy building. Put your hand to your upper chest or throat and welcome this power into your life. Align with it.

If you have felt unsafe singing in the past, keep your hand in place and let your body know that you are safe now. You are safe to sing and to express yourself.

Repeat these messages until they sink in. Practice this magical singing whenever you feel called to. You may wish to wrap your arms around yourself and hold yourself before or after singing to reaffirm your safety and connect more deeply with your being.

HUMMING

Humming creates vibrations that resonate through your body and into the space around you. There is something liberating in creating sounds without words. While words have power, sounds alone also carry resonance. Humming can be used to ground and centre yourself, align with a particular vibe, call in or honour the powers or deities you're working with, or charge objects with your intent.

Practice: Take a few deep breaths to centre yourself. Start humming gently, focusing on the sensation of vibration within your body. Just a single note with the exhale is enough, it doesn't need to be a melody. In fact, a single note is better for clearing and grounding. Imagine these vibrations clearing any stuck energy in your body and the space around you. Practice humming very low and notice how grounding that feels. You can use this power to ground yourself if you're ever feeling flighty or anxious. Even just breathing out deeply with your throat slightly constricted can create a low humming sound that relaxes the nervous system.

CHANTING

Chanting is a potent tool for focusing the mind, invoking deities, or raising energy. The repetitive nature of chants helps to enter a trance state, making it easier to slip between the worlds and work your will.

Practice: Write a simple chant that encapsulates your intent. It could be a single line or a couplet, repeated to build power. As you chant, allow your mind to relax and let the magic unfold. If you're working with a deity, imagine your chant reaching out to them, inviting their presence and assistance. You may also work with witchy chants that other people have written. When I was younger I liked to memorise chants by Doreen Valiante or from the Goddess Movement. You can find witchy chants online, and learn the ones that resonate most with you. Chants do not have to rhyme, but rhyming can help us remember them!

Working with the voice in magic is a deeply personal and powerful practice. It connects us to the ancient traditions of our ancestors and allows us to express our will in one of the most direct ways possible.

It doesn't matter what you sound like, what's important is your intent and the emotional investment you put into your vocalisations. So let your voice be heard, and let the magic flow through it. Experiment with the voice and all the different sounds it can make, the way that children often do when left to their own devices.

ELEMENTAL CHANTS

Here are some example chants for each of the elements. If you want to you can work with these chants. Feel the intent behind each word, allowing the vibrations to resonate within and around you.

Air
Elements of air, breath and sky,
Wisdom and clarity, thoughts that fly,

Feather and cloud, breeze and voice,
In Air's swift movement, awaken we our choice.

Fire

Elements of fire, flame and spark,
Transformation and courage, light in dark,
Ember and blaze, ash and heat,
In Fire's bright passion, transformation is complete

Water

Elements of water, deep tide and stream,
Intuition and feeling, reflection and dream,
River and ocean, dew and rain,
In Water's flowing healing, renewed again.

Earth

Elements of earth, soil and stone
Growth and stability, hearth and home,
Moss and lichen, root and tree,
In Earth's strong foundation, empowered we'll be.

These chants can be used within rituals, during meditations, or whenever you feel the need to connect more deeply with the elemental forces.

AWEN

In the context of witchcraft, particularly those practices influenced by Druidry and other forms of Celtic spirituality, Awen is a concept of significance. The word itself is Welsh, meaning "inspiration" or "essence," and it refers to the divine spark of creativity or the flowing spirit of enlightenment believed to permeate the universe.

When it is chanted, it is pronounced "Ahh – ooooh – wen."

Awen is understood as a mystical force that flows through us. In druidry and witchcraft, this concept is harnessed as a channel for creative and magical practices. It is the inspiration behind spellcraft, ritual work, and the creation of talismans or other magical items.

Awen is also understood as a manifestation of the life force shared by all beings, linking the individual with the larger cycles of nature and the cosmos. This understanding emphasises the interconnectedness of all life, where each part reflects and influences the whole. In druidry and witchcraft, practitioners often draw on Awen to deepen their connection with the natural world, using it to align their personal energy with the energies of the earth and sky, plants, animals, and celestial bodies.

Chanting or intoning the word "Awen" is a common practice. This is often done in a group setting where participants raise energy together, each long, slow Awen amplifying the energy and deepening the group's connection to the divine.

The symbol of Awen, often represented as three rays of light or three points leading to a path, encapsulates its essence in visual form. The three rays may be interpreted as representing the balance between male and female energies, with the central point as the harmonising aspect, or they might signify the flow of energy between the individual, the community, and the land. This symbol is used in various ritual contexts and as a talisman to attract divine inspiration and balance.

BECOMING THE CAULDRON: CREATING YOUR OWN WILD MAGIC

When it comes to creating your own rituals and spells, you are both the creator and the created, the cauldron and the potion brewing within. This is where the deepest magic lives – not in following someone else's formula, but in listening to the wild call of your own soul and responding with authenticity and power.

THE INTUITIVE ALCHEMY OF PERSONAL MAGIC

I've spent decades exploring different magical traditions, reading countless books, and experimenting with various approaches to ritual. But the most profound magic I've ever experienced didn't come from perfectly following instructions. It emerged in those moments when I dropped into deep presence, when I allowed my intuition to guide me, when I trusted the call of my wild self.

The truth is, you already know how to create magic. Your body holds ancient wisdom, your heart understands the language of intention, and your spirit recognises the sacred when it encounters it. Rather than giving you a rigid template to follow, I invite you to dive into the well of your own knowing. Trust what emerges.

LISTENING TO THE CALL

Magic begins with noticing. What is calling to you right now? What feels alive in your body, your dreams, your everyday moments? What keeps appearing in your awareness, like a persistent whisper or a recurring symbol?

Perhaps you're feeling drawn to water – noticing puddles after rain, dreaming of oceans, finding yourself lingering in the shower. Or maybe fire is speaking to you through candlelight that captivates your attention, unexpected warmth on your skin, or a surge of passion in your chest.

Take a moment now to close your eyes. Breathe deeply. What element is calling to you? What aspect of your life is asking for magical attention? Is there a wound seeking healing, a desire wanting manifestation, a boundary needing protection?

The first step in creating your own ritual is simply this: listen. Pay attention to what's already stirring within and around you. Your magic is already happening.

GATHERING THE THREADS

Once you've felt the call, begin gathering the threads of your ritual. This isn't about following correspondence tables or adhering to rigid rules – it's about noticing what naturally wants to be part of your magical working. What colours are you called towards, what objects are significant right now?

If I'm creating a ritual to release old pain, I might find myself drawn to the water's edge. I might notice that I want to bring red flowers, not because a book told me they symbolise something, but because their colour speaks to my heart about passion and blood and life force. I might feel called to bring a stone I found years ago on a beach, simply because it feels right in my palm.

What objects, elements, words, movements, and spaces are calling to you? Which herbs want to join you in this work? What time of day feels aligned with your intention? Trust the impulses that arise. Your unconscious mind is far wiser than you might realise, making connections your conscious mind hasn't yet understood.

Our bodies are magnificent instruments of magic, yet so often we focus solely on words and tools, forgetting the power of our own flesh, blood, and breath. As you craft your ritual, pay attention to what your body wants to do.

Does it want to dance? To sit in stillness? To lie on the earth? To stretch toward the sky? To whisper or to shout? To touch water, fire, stone, air?

There have been times when my most powerful rituals involved no tools at all – just my body moving as it needed to move, my voice sounding as it needed to sound – standing by the ocean during a personal crisis, feeling called to simply scream into the wind and waves. That primal release, that raw expression, was more magical than any elaborate ceremony could have been in that moment.

Your body knows what it needs. Listen to it.

WEAVING YOUR WORDS

Words hold tremendous power in magic. They shape our realities, cast our intentions into the universe, and give form to the formless. But the most potent words aren't necessarily ancient incantations or perfectly rhymed couplets – they're the words that resonate most deeply with your own truth.

When crafting words for your ritual, allow them to emerge naturally. They might come as a song, a poem, a simple statement, or even just a sound. They might arise in the moment rather than being prepared in advance.

I often find my most powerful magical words come when I place my hands on my heart, close my eyes, and simply ask: "What needs to be said?" Then I wait, listening for the response that rises from my depths. Sometimes it's a single word. Sometimes it's a stream of consciousness. Sometimes it's a melody without lyrics.

Trust whatever arises. The words that carry your magic most power-fully are the ones that feel true in your body when you speak them.

DANCING BETWEEN STRUCTURE AND FLOW

There's a beautiful tension in magical practice between structure and spontaneity, between form and formlessness. As you develop your personal rituals, you'll find your own balance between these polarities.

Some rituals might benefit from clear steps and boundaries – perhaps beginning with creating sacred space, casting the circle, invoking the elements and directions, the "working" with a focus on intention, then closing the circle. This structure can create a container for powerful trans-formation.

Other magical workings might want to flow more organically, following the energy moment by moment without a predetermined path. These spontaneous rituals can access depths that more structured approaches might miss.

Neither approach is inherently better. The key is discernment – what does this particular intention, this particular moment, this particular aspect of yourself need? Sometimes the most appropriate answer is "both" – creating a flexible structure that allows for inspired deviation.

CLOSING THE CIRCLE, OPENING TO LIFE

However your ritual unfolds, remember the importance of conscious closure. Magical energy needs grounding and integration. This doesn't have to be elaborate – it might be as simple as placing your hands on the earth, taking a few deep breaths, or eating something nourishing.

The closure of your ritual marks not an ending, but a transition. The magic continues to work within you and through you as you return to everyday life, which is itself a magical unfolding.

For some magic, it might feel appropriate not to speak about it too much, not to tell friends what you've been doing, especially at first. Notice, as you close your working, whether this is something to keep to yourself for a while or whether the energy is expansive and wanting to be shared. I recommend journalling about your process, including how you felt during and after your rituals, because this is a powerful tool for reflection.

As you continue to create your own rituals and spells, know that your practice will evolve. What feels powerfully resonant today might feel flat tomorrow, and approaches you've never considered might suddenly call to you with urgency.

This is not inconsistency – it's evidence that you're alive, growing, changing. Your magic should change with you.

THE COURAGE TO CREATE

Creating your own rituals requires courage. It means trusting yourself more than authorities, valuing your experience over dogma, and being willing to make "mistakes" that turn out to be doorways to deeper understanding.

In a world that often tells us to follow rather than lead, to conform rather than create, developing your own magical practice is a radical act of self-trust and authenticity.

Remember that wild magic speaks to each of us in our own language. The symbols, elements, and approaches that awaken magic for someone else might leave you cold, while the simplest, most personal ritual might crack open the cosmos for you.

Trust this. Trust yourself. The magic you seek has been within you all along, waiting for you to claim it, to shape it, to set it free into the world.

The magic is in the wild, and the wild is in you.

4

CELESTIAL MAGIC

"The evidence suggests not that the planets themselves cause various events or character traits, but rather that a consistently meaningful empirical correspondence exists between the two sets of phenomena, astronomical and human, with the connecting principle most fruitfully approached as some form of archetypally informed synchronicity"
— Richard Tarnas

People who don't know much about astrology often criticise it for being too simple – for putting people into boxes – for stereotyping... which is ironic, because astrology is actually incredibly complex. Equating newspaper horoscopes with astrology is like assuming that all food is actually Twinkies, and then criticising food for being anti-nutritious. This comparison is akin to judging the vast ocean by the water in a single bucket. Understanding astrology, much like understanding the biochemistry of nutrition, can take a long time – just to get a reasonably good grasp of one way of doing it. And just like any complex subject, there are lots of schools of thought, and systems, and each has its own merits and some work better for some people than others.

I like to think about it like this: for thousands of years, human beings did not possess small pocket-sized devices with screens, or even large screens in their offices and homes for watching things. Instead, they had little choice but to watch the world around them. For thousands of years, people have watched the patterns in nature, in the swirling of water, the migrations of birds, and in the night sky. They watched the movement of visible planetary bodies and identified the planets from the stars. Based on the movements of the planets, they connected them with their own cultural mythology. Mercury, for instance, is fast moving, darting between the others: the messenger. This observation led to the belief that Mercury influences communication and travel. They watched these patterns and associated them with the changes they witnessed in the world around them. There are many cultural similarities in the symbolism of these planetary bodies, especially between Vedic and Western astrology.

It was only in the last few hundred years that the contemporary mythology associated with 'science' split from more nuanced cultural understandings in Western thought and went on to colonise local knowledge systems wherever it found them, declaring their understandings as "not real knowledge." Despite the technological advances afforded by this process, it has cut many people off from mystical and nuanced understandings of the world that our ancestors shared. Astronomy, the 'real scientific' study of the stuff we find outside our planet, has been split from astrology for a while now. The former is taken seriously while the latter has been reduced to tacky newspaper horoscopes or stereotypes about twelve types of people in most people's eyes. This dichotomy overlooks the rich historical and cultural significance of astrology, as well as its layered complexity. This may be to our detriment, as a species well known for its nearsightedness and inability to recognise broader patterns.

For me, it is the synchronicities that make astrology so validating, and the insights it provides into the patterns of the psyche that make it so useful. As a teenager, before I knew anything at all about astrology, I made up a pattern that represented me. I drew it over and over in my school books. It was a crescent moon with lines going in different directions. I was planning to get a tattoo of it at some point. In my early twenties, I took a night class on astrology with a couple of friends. This was the first time I had the chance to see my birth chart and when I looked at it a shiver ran up my spine.

The pattern in the centre...well, it was the pattern I used to draw over and over. It was the pattern that represented me. (And yes, I did get a tattoo of it!)

This personal anecdote underscores the profound, often inexplicable connection people can feel with astrology. If you want to see your birth chart, you can look it up on a website like Astro-charts.com or Astro.-com. You'll need to know your time of birth to get an accurate chart, because the houses change every two hours, based on the earth's rotation and where the horizon line is. If you don't know the exact time, you can put in an approximate time. You will be able to see which signs the planets are in and how they relate to each other, but the "houses" may not be accurate. It may take a while to understand what it all means but the information in this chapter is intended as a helpful guide.

This is what my chart looks like:

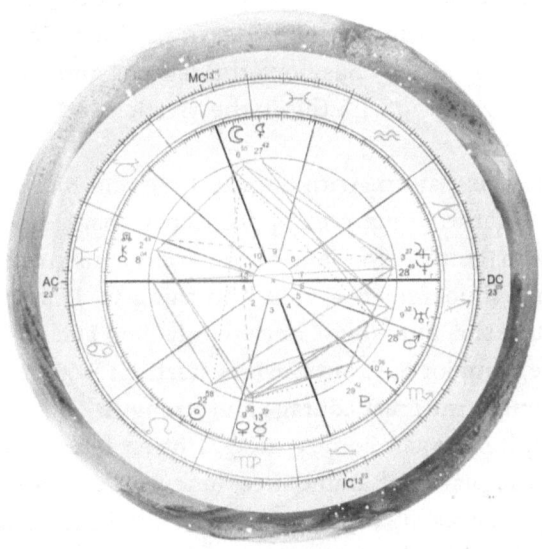

A birth chart like this captures the synchronicity of when someone was born. For instance, the Sun was in Leo when I was born, Mercury was

Virgo conjunct Venus, and Saturn was in Scorpio. Each of these things carries its own resonance.

When you have looked up your own chart, you can begin to interpret it, looking up what it means to have a planet a particular sign, beginning to piece together this map of your psyche. I have created some additional tables for each planet in each sign, available to download from my website: www.irisbeaglehole.com/resources

I have been studying astrology for years and though I understand a lot, there is always so much to learn. The synchronicities have continued, and become more and more convincing. Over a decade ago, I was sitting in an armchair reading a book when I experienced a sudden flood of insights around my fears. I briefly wondered whether Saturn had gotten into Scorpio, as it was supposed to sometime that year. When I checked a few days later, Saturn had indeed crossed over into Scorpio, at just the time when I was being confronted with my Saturn in Scorpio lessons, leading up to my Saturn Return (when it gets back to where it was when someone was born). Saturn is the planet of hard learning, of boundaries and constrictions. It always has powerful lessons and you will see Rosemary and Athena working with this in the Myrtlewood Mysteries books at times.

I've noticed this pattern with Saturn more and more over the years. When I have a Saturn square or opposition transit, especially to natal Saturn or my Sun, I often experience a constriction in my chest, a bit like a feeling of being squeezed in a vice. The thing is, I often haven't been following my transits, but when I have that feeling I go and look them up, and every time, a major Saturn transit is starting! But working with that tension has brought me great courage and strength.

When a Jupiter transit comes along, I often feel buoyant and energised. Jupiter, the planet of abundance, luck, and excess often brings me wonderful experiences of expansiveness. Sometimes it feels a bit like drinking a liquid luck potion!

I've also noticed other little synchronicities that can be very helpful. For instance, I realised that I sometimes suddenly get the urge to start cleaning, sorting, and de-cluttering when the moon is in Virgo. This has led to better planning of the month to maximise this kind of rare (for me) activity.

Whether people believe in astrology or not, I tend to find it extremely useful. Looking at a chart and the tensions there (often represented by red lines), and knowing a bit about the mythic archetypes of the planets and the parts of the psyche they represent, really has helped me to understand myself and other people better, especially the patterns or experiences that have no particular clear rational or scientific explanation.

It's not that the planets are actually inflicting things upon us, rather that they provide a clear and easy to understand map of the reflective universe, the patterns of the cosmos and psyche at the moment of our birth, and in everyday life, that we can learn so much from. I also don't believe there are "bad" things in astrology, rather, many of the challenges can lead to uncovering our hidden strengths!

Looking at the transits, where planets are now in relation to their placing when I was born, helps me understand the things that I'm learning about in my life in the present. Astrology, in this sense, acts as a mirror, reflecting not just our personalities but also our ongoing life journey. I don't even mind if it's just confirmation bias or some kind of placebo, because it's helpful and it's also quite beautiful. It is a symbolic language and a comprehensive system for mapping the psyche that is helpful in my writing and can play out with the character's own journeys.

THE SIGNS

As I said above, we each contain all the archetypes of the zodiac within us, but they are expressed in different ways. Some of the energies may feel blocked within us, some will be stronger or complicated by other factors. The zodiac signs are archetypes representing the energies of key constellations around the ecliptic – where the planets seem to circle us within our solar system.

Here is a basic run-down of the key archetypes of the zodiac signs. As you read over them, you may find it interesting to reflect on which ones resonate more strongly with you, and which ones you don't identify with at all. If you have your chart, you can look into how each of the zodiac signs appear for you, and whether you have any planets in the signs.

Glyph Zodiac Sign Basic Interpretation

♈ Aries Bold, impulsive, pioneering, action-oriented

♉ Taurus Grounded, sensual, loyal, values stability

♊ Gemini Curious, communicative, adaptable, quick-witted

♋ Cancer Nurturing, intuitive, protective, emotionally deep

♌ Leo Confident, expressive, warm-hearted, proud

♍ Virgo Analytical, precise, practical, helpful

♎ Libra Diplomatic, aesthetic, fair-minded, relational

♏ Scorpio Intense, transformative, private, emotionally powerful

♐ Sagittarius Philosophical, adventurous, freedom-loving, optimistic

♑ Capricorn Ambitious, disciplined, responsible, goal-focused

♒ Aquarius Visionary, innovative, independent, humanitarian

♓ Pisces Empathic, dreamy, spiritual, imaginative

THE HOUSES

In astrology, twelve 'houses' divide up the sky like the face of a clock. The first begins at the horizon in the area of the sky where the sun rises. Each section of the sky above (and imagined sky below) represents the key areas of life experience. The zodiac signs appear to move through each house roughly every two hours which means that even twins born a few minutes apart can have radically different natal charts.

The planets, as dynamic symbols of energy and motivation, appear to move through these houses and signs, activating the archetypal themes and challenges inherent in each domain. They reflect the catalysts for our growth, the opportunities and obstacles that shape our individual paths of self-realisation. If you have a key planet or luminary in any of these houses, it will likely take on a more significant meaning for you. Someone with Sun in the second house will have a deep need for material security and place significance on values. Someone with Saturn in the second house would also feel a significance in that area, but it would take on a more serious tone with the heavy burdens and deep lessons of this challenging planet (more on the planets later).

By understanding the significance of each house and the areas of life it represents, we gain insights into our own existence. If parts of this don't make sense yet, that's totally normal. I have been studying astrology for almost twenty years and I'm still learning so much. It has its own language and there's always more to learn. As you read on, some things may begin to make more sense, and you can always skip over it and come back later if you're finding this chapter too heavy on the information!

1st House (self): The first house represents the initial emergence of the individual into the world, the pure potential of our being. It's the divine spark of life, the undifferentiated consciousness that begins the journey of self-discovery and actualisation. This house also relates to identity, appearance, self-expression, and vitality. It is associated with Aries, Mars, and the Ascendant (which is the sign of the first house).

2nd House (the material world): The second house represents engaging with the material world, learning to relate to possessions and values, and developing a sense of self-worth. It's the phase of establishing a secure base from which the self can explore and grow. This house encompasses resources, assets, and personal values. It is associated with Taurus and Venus.

3rd House (communication): The third house represents communication and interaction with the immediate environment, the mental faculties, learning to process and share experiences, taking a practical approach to integrating information, and exploring the world of ideas. This house also relates to siblings, early education, short trips, and writing. It is associated with Gemini and Mercury.

4th House (foundations and roots): The fourth house represents deep emotional bonds, roots, and creating a sense of home. It's the phase of nurturing the inner world, integrating family and ancestral influences, and developing the capacity for emotional intimacy. This house relates to home life, emotional security, and private life, and is associated with Cancer and the Moon.

5th House (creative expression and pleasure): The fifth house represents creative self-expression, the joyful exploration and expression of passions. It encompasses romance, play, creativity, pleasure, close friendships, performance, and giving form to the authentic self. This house also relates to children, hobbies, and self-expression. It is associated with Leo and the Sun.

6th House (routine and work): The sixth house represents the routines and responsibilities of daily life, work, developing discipline, humility, and the capacity to serve others. This house also encompasses health, daily routines, service to others, and pets, and is associated with Virgo and Mercury.

7th House (relating and projection): The seventh house represents relating deeply to others, projection, relationship, partnership, and balanced, reciprocal exchanges. This house also governs marriage, legal contracts, open enemies, and business partnerships, and is associated with Libra, Venus, and the Descendant.

8th House (transformation and rebirth): The eighth house represents deep transformation, the descent into the underworld of the psyche to confront hidden shadows and wounds, loss, and the dissolution of the old self, followed by the rebirth and regeneration of a more integrated, authentic being. This house also relates to sexuality, money, power, birth, death, the occult, inheritances, and psychological transformation. It is associated with Scorpio, Pluto, and Mars.

9th House (expanding consciousness): The ninth house represents the expansive quest for higher meaning and universal truths, the spiritual seeker, broadening one's horizons through travel, study, and the exploration of diverse philosophies and belief systems. This house encompasses higher education, spiritual learning, long-distance travel, big-picture ideas, and publishing. It is associated with Sagittarius and Jupiter.

10th House (achievement): The tenth house represents actualising the mature, individuated self in the world, claiming one's authority, contributing one's unique gifts to society, and leaving a meaningful legacy. This house relates to career, public reputation, achievement, and social status. It is associated with Capricorn, Saturn, and the Midheaven.

11th House (connecting with the collective): The eleventh house represents connecting with the larger collective, finding one's place within the community of humankind, aligning personal aspirations with group ideals, and working towards the betterment of all. This house also relates to acquaintances, social groups, hopes and wishes, and humanitarian causes, and is associated with Aquarius and Uranus.

12th House (union with the infinite): The twelfth house represents surrender and transcendence, the dissolution of the ego-Self into the vast ocean of cosmic consciousness, letting go, merging with the numinous, and realising one's fundamental unity with all that is. This house also traditionally relates to hidden enemies, self-undoing, secrets, and spiritual enlightenment, and is associated with Pisces and Neptune.

As you look at your chart, look at each of the 12 houses, starting from the ascendant and journeying down and around the circle. Where are the key luminaries and planetary objects in your chart? What do you notice about their placement in the houses? Which houses do you relate most strongly to? Sometimes a house does not have any strong significance in our chart, but the sign or planet that corresponds with that house might still have strong significance because of the sign it is in or its aspects to other planets, for example a planet in its own sign (e.g., someone with Uranus in Aquarius or in close aspect to a key personal planet will have a strong affinity with 11th house themes even if they don't have any planets in the 11th house).

It can be interesting to look at the houses as a progressive unfoldment of the self through reflecting the process of development and the journey of becoming whole. Each house represents a stage of growth, an archetypal challenge that calls forth the development and integration of different facets of the psyche. The planetary energies that transit these houses provide the unique challenges and opportunities for this growth.

THE INTERPLAY OF PLANETS, SIGNS, AND HOUSES

Glyph Planet / Point Basic Interpretation

☉ Sun Core self, vitality, identity, purpose

☽ Moon Emotions, instincts, inner world, nurturing

☿ Mercury Communication, thinking, learning, perception

♀ Venus Love, beauty, harmony, values, relationships

♂ Mars Drive, action, desire, assertion, energy

♃ Jupiter Expansion, luck, growth, philosophy, beliefs

♄ Saturn Structure, discipline, responsibility, boundaries

♅ Uranus Innovation, disruption, freedom, rebellion

♆ Neptune Dreams, illusions, spirituality, compassion

♇ Pluto Power, transformation, depth, rebirth

☊ North Node Destiny, soul growth, future direction

In astrology, the twelve houses form a celestial stage in which the planets, as dynamic characters, play out their roles. Each house represents a specific area of life and the planets' unique personalities, as shaped by the signs they occupy, influence these areas reflecting our personal story, challenges, and life experiences.

The planets in astrology each have their own personality, desires, and mode of expression. Venus, for instance, represents love, beauty, and harmony, while Mars embodies aggression, drive, and passion. When these planets occupy different houses and signs, they bring their energies forward in different ways, focused on the areas of life represented by those houses.

For instance, someone with Venus in Mars' native sign of Aries residing in the fifth house might find that their Venus 'goddess archetype' expresses itself through the bold, assertive, and spontaneous and often impatient nature of Aries. The fifth house of creativity, romance, and self-expression could provide a useful outlet for the intensity of Venus in Aries through creativity, and someone with this placement might struggle with the intensity of their romances and frustration with their own impatience until they can learn to tap into their creativity and channel this energy more effectively into useful outlets.

The signs of the zodiac act almost like the characters, costumes, and scripts for the planets as actors to embody, modifying their expression to adapt to the role. A planet's energy manifests differently depending on the sign it occupies. Mercury, the planet of communication and intellect, takes on a curious, adaptable, and quick-witted character in its native home of Gemini, while in Scorpio, it becomes more intense, probing, and psychologically astute.

The interplay of planets, signs, and houses in astrology presents a comprehensive reflective map that can have an uncanny ability to tell the story of our lives. By understanding how these levels, layers and archetypes interact and influence each other, we gain insight into the challenges, opportunities, and themes that shape our personal journeys.

THE SUN

The Sun stands as the radiant monarch of the sky, casting its golden light upon the stage of our lives. Through the lens of Jungian psychology, this celestial luminary is the light of our awareness in the solar system of our lives, a symbol of the self, the organising principle of our psyche, and the beacon of consciousness that guides us on our journey.

The Sun in astrology illuminates our core essence, the central facet of our being around which all other parts orbit. It represents our vital force, our will to exist, and the quest for meaning that drives us forward. In the birth chart, the Sun's placement by sign, house, and aspect reveals the archetype that shapes our identity, our conscious ego, and the path we walk to express our individuality. It highlights the qualities we are called to embody, the challenges we must face to actualise our potential, and the creative energy we wield to forge our destiny.

Now, in saying all this, you might not relate to your sun sign (or "star sign" as people often call it). I was born with the Sun in Leo, but I do not often come across as a proud, dramatic, centre-of-attention stereotypical Leo. When this happens, there are often several reasons at play. For instance, my Mars in Scorpio squares my Sun in Leo – this challenging aspect reflects a sense that I'm always under threat and need to hide. If I hadn't done so much personal development, magical transformation, therapy and so on, I would always be hiding! But in working with the challenging aspect, I have learned a lot and I can channel this tension into the plot of my writing which gives it an outlet. My Sun is also "intercepted" in Leo. This means that there is no house that starts in the sign of Leo in my chart, meaning it's difficult for me to express this energy directly. I can, however, channel it out through my strong Mercury in Virgo in the third house – again – through my writing!

If you do not relate to your Sun sign, look to see if there are any red lines on your chart pointing to it. These are usually how squares or oppositions are drawn on a chart. Also, check to see if the zodiac sign your Sun is in has a house line going through it, or if it's intercepted with no houses beginning in it. If either of these things are true for you, you may find it helpful to look at how else the zodiacal energy of your Sun sign could be expressed through other planets, e.g., Mars through physical activities and martial arts, Venus through beautiful creativity, Mercury through writing and other forms of sharing ideas.

From a Jungian perspective, the Sun embodies the archetype of the Hero, the protagonist of our personal myth who embarks on a journey of self-discovery, facing trials and adversaries, only to return transformed with newfound wisdom. It symbolises the process of individuation, the unfolding of the self that occurs as we integrate the disparate aspects of our psyche – conscious and unconscious, shadow and light – into a unified whole.

Yet, the brilliance of the Sun also casts shadows, revealing the parts of ourselves that we leave unilluminated, the aspects of our ego that require integration to achieve true self-realisation. The Sun's position challenges us to confront our hubris, to recognise the limitations of our ego, and to transcend the illusion of separateness, realising that we are but stars in a vast, interconnected cosmos.

The Sun, resplendent and sovereign, claims its throne in the sign of Leo, a domain where its golden light is embraced with joy and majesty. This regal positioning, where the Sun is said to be in its domicile, reveals the heart of our solar system in its fullest expression, illuminating the stage of life with warmth, creativity, and the undying flame of individuality.

WORKING WITH THE SUN

Just as the Sun illuminates our solar system, providing light and life to all the planets, our natal Sun represents our core essence – the vital spark of who we are and who we are becoming. Working with solar energy involves connecting with our own inner light and learning how to let it shine authentically.

Solar energy is active, expressive, and radiating outward. However, this doesn't mean we all express it the same way. Someone with Sun in Cancer might shine most brightly when nurturing others or creating a safe space for emotional expression, while a Capricorn Sun might radiate most powerfully through achieving goals and building lasting structures. If you have Sun in Libra, you might feel most alive and centred when creating harmony or bringing people together. Your solar energy might express itself through diplomatic leadership or through creating beautiful spaces that bring people joy. If you have Sun in Scorpio, your light might shine most intensely through transformative experiences or deep investigation.

WORKING WITH SOLAR CYCLES

The Sun offers us natural cycles to work with – both daily and yearly. The daily solar cycle provides a rhythm for different types of magical work:

- Dawn (sunrise): Perfect for new beginnings, setting intentions, and awakening spiritual energy
- Noon: The peak of solar power, ideal for manifestation work and charging magical tools
- Dusk (sunset): Suitable for completion work, gratitude practices, and releasing what no longer serves
- Night: Time for rest, dreaming, and allowing the unconscious to process the day's solar activities

The yearly solar cycle, marked by the solstices and equinoxes, offers larger rhythms to work with:

- Spring Equinox: The sun's growing strength supports new projects and fresh starts
- Summer Solstice: Peak solar power for manifestation and celebration
- Autumn Equinox: Beginning of the sun's waning cycle, good for harvest and gratitude
- Winter Solstice: The sun's rebirth, perfect for planting seeds of intention for the coming year

SOLAR MAGIC PRACTICES

Working with solar energy can take many forms, from simple daily practices to more elaborate rituals. Here are some ways to connect with and channel solar energy:

- Solar Charging: Create a dedicated space in your home where the morning sun shines. Place crystals, magical tools, or even your morning tea here to charge with solar energy. You might be drawn to traditionally solar stones like Citrine or sunstone, but trust your intuition – the best solar tools are ones that resonate with your particular way of expressing solar energy.
- Sun Meditation: Spend time in natural sunlight (being mindful of skin safety). Feel the warmth on your skin and imagine this solar energy filling your body with vitality and purpose. This can be especially powerful when done at sunrise or during your sun sign season.
- Solar Altars: Create an altar that honours your solar energy. Include symbols that represent your Sun sign and house placement, as well as objects that make you feel confident and authentic. This might include:
    - Colours associated with your Sun sign
    - Objects that represent your proudest achievements
    - Symbols of your creative expression
    - Items that make you feel powerful and centred
- Working with Your Solar Season: Pay special attention to the month when the Sun moves through your natal Sun sign. This is your personal "solar return" – a powerful time for:

- Setting intentions for the coming year
- Performing rituals of self-expression and empowerment
- Reflecting on your authentic path
- Celebrating your unique gifts and achievements

Working with solar energy is about finding and expressing your own unique light in a way that feels authentic and life-giving. Whether your Sun burns like a quiet candle or a blazing bonfire, the key is to honour its natural expression while maintaining harmony with the rest of your being.

THE MOON

The Moon – luminous and enigmatic – reflects the Sun's radiant light, revealing our innermost needs, emotions, and the nurturing essence that binds us to the rhythms of life. The Moon in astrology represents our emotional landscape, our inner-child, and the undercurrents of that tug at the shores of our consciousness.

As the celestial body closest to Earth, the Moon orbits through the zodiac over approximately 28 days, each phase shedding light on our intuitive, receptive aspects. In the birth chart, the Moon's position by sign, house, and aspect offers a window into our inner world, showing how we seek comfort, nurture, and emotional security, reflecting our upbringing, and the qualities we inherited from our caregivers.

The phases of the Moon, from the new beginnings of the New Moon to the culmination and release of the Full Moon, mirror the ebb and flow of natural cycles and emotions. These lunar rhythms remind us of the impermanence of our feelings and the constant flux of life's tides. Yet, the Moon also echoes our shadows, fears, and vulnerabilities, challenging us to confront these deeper waters, to embrace the entirety of our emotional selves, and to find the light of understanding and compassion in the darkness.

In relationships, the Moon's placement offers insights into our needs for emotional connection, how we express care and sensitivity towards others, and the kind of nurturing we seek from loved ones. The Moon reflects the bonds that tie us to the past, grounding us in our roots. In the birth chart, the Moon's placement offers deep insights into the structure of the psyche, revealing the ways in which we seek emotional nourishment and experience vulnerability.

Jungian astrology views the Moon as a gateway to the collective unconscious, a luminous orb that illuminates dark night. It represents our innate need for attachment, belonging, and emotional resonance with others, reflecting the mother archetype and the primordial experience of being nurtured. For some, the Moon's placement can reveal the aspects of our psyche that we have repressed or ignored – emotional and instinctual aspects that have been marginalised or neglected. Challenging emotions arise, urging us to integrate these elements into our conscious awareness. It calls us to delve into the depths of the unconscious, to uncover the treasures hidden in the dark, and to bring them into the light of consciousness. Through this lunar exploration, we encounter our inner world.

Because the moon relates to our emotional and child-selves, and to how we were nurtured (or not) in our childhoods, the placement and aspects of the moon in the chart can reveal to us how we might still need to re-parent ourselves. Childhood is often a challenging time, but through our continued personal development there are as many opportunities for healing and renewal as there are tidal cycles.

WORKING WITH THE MOON

The Moon is our celestial mirror, reflecting our deepest emotional tides. While the Sun represents our conscious identity, the Moon illuminates our inner landscape – our needs, feelings, and the unconscious patterns that shape our emotional life. Working with lunar energy means developing a relationship with these deeper currents of our psyche.

Understanding your natal Moon placement is like having a map to your emotional wellbeing. A Taurus Moon might find emotional security through physical comfort and stability, while a Gemini Moon might need mental stimulation and variety to feel emotionally balanced. The house placement of your Moon adds another layer – for instance, a fourth house Moon might find emotional nourishment through creating a nurturing home environment, while an eleventh house Moon might need community connection to feel emotionally fulfilled.

WORKING WITH LUNAR CYCLES

The Moon's monthly journey offers a natural rhythm for emotional and magical work:

New Moon:
- Focus on rest and renewal
- Set intentions for the lunar cycle ahead
- Plant seeds of emotional growth
- Work with shadow aspects of your lunar placement

Waxing Moon:
- Build on intentions set at the New Moon
- Take action to nurture emotional growth
- Gradually increase emotional expression
- Work on developing new emotional patterns

Full Moon:

- Celebrate emotional culminations
- Release what no longer serves
- Charge moon water and magical tools
- Perform divination and psychic work

Waning Moon:
- Release old emotional patterns
- Let go of emotional baggage
- Work on emotional healing
- Explore forgiveness and acceptance

Spend time under the moon's light, especially during the full moon. Feel its gentle reflection washing over you, cleansing your emotional body. You might create a comfortable outdoor space with blankets and pillows, or simply sit by a window bathed in moonlight. You may wish to keep a moon journal tracking lunar phases, your emotional patterns, dreams and intuitive insights, or simply keep a small notebook to write your new moon intentions in each month.

Working with lunar energy requires balance. Too much lunar focus can lead to emotional overwhelm. Too little can result in emotional disconnection. We can find ways to honour both emotional depth and practical stability.

If your Moon has challenging aspects, you can work with them. For instance, if you have a square or opposition between Moon and Mars, you might find it helpful to channel emotional intensity into creative or physical outlets. Moon-Saturn can be worked with by creating structured ways to process feelings. Moon-Pluto people will deeply benefit if they can become more self-aware and transform emotional patterns through shadow work. Moon-Neptune people can find ways to ground their emotional sensitivity through practical activities.

Lunar work is about cycles rather than linear progress. Just as the Moon waxes and wanes, our emotional life has natural rhythms of expansion and contraction. We can learn to flow with these natural cycles and understand how we respond to the energy of the moon as it traverses each sign through the month. For instance, I find the Moon in Virgo to be a great time for decluttering – when I happen to have the energy and focus to do so!

By working consciously with lunar energy, we can develop a deeper understanding of our emotional nature and learn to use these insights for growth and healing.

MERCURY

As far as planets go, Mercury may be small in stature, but has a big role to play in how we think, communicate, and get from A to B. Imagine Mercury as the ultimate celestial communicator, ensuring the other gods' messages are delivered promptly and with a bit of panache. It's like the communicator of the solar system, connecting the divine with our earthly realm. Mercury in our natal charts reflects the way we process information, how we learn, and how we share our ideas with others.

When it comes to communication, Mercury governs the way we speak, write, and even gesture. It's the planet that helps us put our thoughts into words and our words into action. Mercury is also the ruler of our rational mind, the part of us that loves to categorise, analyse, and make sense of the world around us.

As a dual sign, Mercury has two sides to its cosmic personality, like a celestial Gemini twin. On one hand, it's got the intellectual curiosity of Gemini, always keen to learn new things and make connections. On the other hand, it's got the analytical precision of Virgo, the sign that loves nothing more than diving into the details and finding the perfect solution to any problem.

So, when you're looking at your natal chart, pay close attention to where Mercury is residing. Its sign, house, and aspects can give you insights into how your mind works, how you express yourself, and even what kind of jokes make you laugh.

MERCURY RETROGRADE

There's a part of me that craves the fuzziness of Mercury retrograde. It's like a dozy morning, where you just want to pull the blankets over your head and bury yourself in the depths of consciousness...or unconsciousness, as the case may be. In this sense, the energy of this time is similar to other low ebbs, such as the season of winter or the darkness of the new moon. These inward times are incredibly important, just like the phase that a butterfly needs to spend in a cocoon or the darkness in the earth that helps the seed to grow or the gestation period of one kind or another.

Paradoxically, those times when it feels like nothing is happening, when we feel confused and want to pull the blanket over our heads, when things aren't all sunshine and roses, fun and active, are actually some of our most deeply productive times, unconsciously. This is when the inner work is done – the gestation that makes birthing a new project possible... eventually.

Mercury retrograde happens three or four times a year. This is when it looks like the planet is back-tracking across the sky rather than moving forwards. This is not the time to reap rewards or to launch a new venture in the world. It's not a great time to publish a book usually either, as I found out the hard way when book three of the Myrtlewood Mysteries needed about fifteen different versions uploaded because the proofing changes somehow didn't make it into the final version, or the thirteen versions after that!

Mercury retrogrades are a state of deep inner processing time for the mind and for consciousness. If we can go inwards during this period deliberately and even enjoy the befuddled nature of it all, we can get the most out of this time and make it really worthwhile.

It might be that you weed your garden and you discover some stroke of insight that comes to you. This happened to me once leading to when I first started writing fiction almost twenty years ago. I was weeding the garden of an old house that had been in my family for generations. I kept digging up old bits of metal and old bottles, which seemed a striking metaphor for excavating old family patterns. A character came to me who was doing something similar and the metaphor deepened. I became a novelist and perhaps I wouldn't have if I'd never followed that intuitive nudge.

It might be that you have a cryptic dream and you discover everything you dreamed about was strikingly similar to an image drawn by a great mystic philosopher 100 years ago. That happened to me during a Mercury retrograde once too. These strokes of insight can come through more easily, but through the fuzzy signal of the retrograde, precisely because the conscious mind is not so actively dominating the scene, leaving way for a deeper connection with the soul.

I do find journalling is helpful for many reasons, but particularly with Mercury retrogrades, things sometimes emerge through journalling that I wasn't previously aware of. In fact, the idea for this very book came to me during a Mercury retrograde and I wrote quite a significant part of it in that time, like a stream of consciousness.

Interestingly enough, as I began to shape the idea for this book, to structure and fill that structure with the words, it felt that those words needed to be there. Writing can be a bit like that. When in deep creative flow I feel as though I'm channelling the story – perhaps from the future in which it is already written, or from my "higher self" or some other divine place. Several times during the process of writing this book, I've had a feeling that this is a book that I've been trying to write since I was a teenager (at least), or perhaps all my life. Because as I began to explain my magical worldview, I thought back to early experiences of awakening that led me on this path, including things that I journaled about when I was fifteen or sixteen years old – insights that I opened up to in my quest for spiritual awareness that came through me onto the page in the form of intense moody teenage poetry, and then, as often does with universal truths, the same messages emerged in different forms. I later discovered some of my own insights were concepts already reflected by many philosophers, mystics, and other spiritual teachers.

The truth is, as most mystics have said: absurdly simple. The deepest truths are often laughably simple and hilariously absurd. And yet, as we lean into our truth, as we step deeper and deeper into awareness, those simple things – the interconnectedness of all, the universality of the paradoxes of light and shadow, and the uncovering of the unknown – we allow ourselves to let go of all that we are not. We release the identities that we've been taught by society to value, and go deeper and deeper into our sense of being, meaning, and purpose that relies on no one and nothing else. We develop a strong sense of what resonates deeply, what makes sense for us and what doesn't.

Now, from this place of letting go of preconceptions, we can decide that, ultimately, it doesn't matter what other people think of us, how many university degrees we have, how many people have heard of us, whether or not we've saved somebody's life, what we look like, or how we dress...ultimately, these things are abstract and arbitrary. They are products of this world that we can choose to enjoy or let go of. We can choose how we dress, be it extravagant or simple, rather than remain shackled to follow other people's expectations of us to in order to try and hide from judgement. We can do this only when we've looked into the shadow of our own harsh judgement, and we've seen it for what it is – ultimately an interesting experience, unpleasant and pleasant at times to wield, but insubstantial, like many of our fears.

I'm not immune to caring about other people's judgement, particularly those who might endanger me or those who I care about deeply. Of course, I want to protect myself from harm in a rational way. And I want to empathise with the people close to me and make sure that, in their eyes, I'm not doing things that they would judge as hurtful or unpleasant. I can choose this, but I do so out of my own freedom.

I'm a lot less afraid of people's judgement than I used to be when I was younger. And the more I learn to sit with my own judgement and see that behind it generally lies fear, the more I get comfortable with the sensations of fear so that it no longer has the power to dictate and control my life, the freer I become in my mind.

Mercury rules the mind, wit, and writing, and other modes of communication, which is why Mercury retrograde is often attributed to technology breaking down, the wrong emails being sent, or the wrong transactions not going through. And when I say "rules", what I really mean is "reflects." When the planet Mercury goes retrograde, it is reflecting a reversal, a backwards motion in the sky, a bit like hitting rewind on an old VCR – that whirring noise as it goes back to where it was not so long ago.

Mercury retrograde is a powerful review period. You get a chance in your mind to go back over what you've learned, not just recently, because Mercury can be a bit of a time traveller. Mercury is sometimes associated with the magician in Tarot, and just like the element on the periodic table after which it is named, Mercury is quicksilver. So when Mercury is retrograde we can reflect on the past with greater insight, and in that we can liberate ourselves from some of the old limitations of our minds and our judgements, allowing ourselves to become freer and more connected. Because our judgement is often the mind that holds us apart from connecting deeply with our whole selves.

VENUS

Venus is a beacon of beauty, love, and harmony. Cloaked in the soft luminescence of dawn and dusk, this celestial siren sings the songs of our desires, our attractions, and the ways in which we connect to one another and to the world around us. Venus, named after the Roman goddess of love and beauty, echoes our yearnings for pleasure, for art, for the sensation, and for the soulful gazes of deep connection.

Venus is the lover and the muse, guiding us through our expressions of affection, our aesthetic inclinations, and our material values, painting our interactions with the palette of her passions. When we fall in love, it is Venus who beckons us toward the object of our desire; when we create, it is Venus who inspires us with her muse; and when we indulge in the sensual pleasures of life, it is Venus who delights in our satisfaction.

In each zodiac sign, Venus dons a different costume, expressing her love and beauty through the filter of that sign's qualities. From the fiery ardour of Aries to the mystical depths of Pisces, she reveals the multifaceted nature of our desires and our joys. Yet, Venus also speaks of the shadows cast by our desires. She reminds us that in our quest for love and beauty, we may need to confront challenges like jealousy, possessiveness, and surface-level values. She teaches us that authentic beauty lies in the balance, in the acceptance of imperfection, and in the understanding that love, in its purest form, transcends the physical.

Venus invites us to embrace love in all its forms, to seek out beauty in the mundane, and to tune the dissonant chords of our lives into a harmony.

VENUS RETROGRADE

It's not just Mercury that goes into retrograde. Other planets do it too. For the most part, with the outer planets, this is just reflected in a slowing down of or muting of the energy associated with that planet, or perhaps a deepening of the long-term work of the transformation associated with that planet (we'll get to the outer planets in more detail later). The personal planets, Mercury, Venus, and Mars all seem to have a more strongly felt effect when they retrograde. Venus retrogrades roughly every eighteen months and lasts about six weeks. If you want to know exact timings, it's easy to look them up online by searching something like "Venus retrograde dates [year]".

During Venus retrograde, the usual outward flow of Venusian energy turns inward. This is not a good time for a makeover! It can be a good time for rethinking what truly matters to us, reassessing our relationships, and reflecting on our sources of joy and creativity. It can be marked by a return to past relationships or unresolved creative issues, providing an opportunity to heal.

The sign in which Venus retrogrades is important to understanding the challenges and opportunities of the transit. For instance, Venus retrograde in Scorpio will be more likely to bring up deep issues and fears relating to intimacy and 'being seen' in our creative pursuits, whereas in Capricorn, this retrograde takes on more of a focus on finances and the structures that support us in relating and creation. The house in your chart that Venus retrograde is transiting will also have more of a focus. For instance, in the fourth house, it may be a good time to reassess your home environment, deciding what is and is not working for you, giving away the things that aren't useful and considering future upgrades of furniture or renovations, whereas in your second house the transit may bring up issues of insecurity with money. This too is an opportunity for processing which can lead to better financial security in future, but don't make any rash financial decisions and leave big things until after the learning of the retrograde has completed and Venus is out of shadow (you can look this timing up too).

Venus retrograde often brings old lovers or friends back into our lives, even just as spectres of the mind. This can stir up unresolved feelings or conflicts, urging us to deal with unfinished emotional business. It's a chance to either reconcile or achieve closure, depending on what is most healthy and needed. While challenging, this period can also be an opportunity to deepen connections with others. By addressing the issues that surface, relationships can be built on firmer, more honest foundations.

These times might also bring a reassessment of what we value and our financial matters. Previous decisions regarding investments, purchases, and the way we handle money might be questioned. It's a good time to review budgets, reassess financial plans, and correct course if necessary, but not to make any big outward decisions until the retrograde period has passed.

Artists and creators might experience a slowdown in their creative outputs, or they may reach a new level of understanding as existing projects require transformation/re-evaluation. Venus retrograde encourages introspection about our needs and desires in relationships and personal pursuits. Understanding what truly brings us joy and fulfilment can lead to significant personal growth and a clearer sense of self.

Delays and setbacks are common during this period. Embrace patience and use this time to refine your plans and projects rather than pushing forward aggressively. If old friends or lovers return, consider what these reconnections might teach you.

MARS

Mars embodies the warrior archetype of its namesake Roman god, associated with Ares in Greek Mythology. This energy does not belong to any one gender; we can all connect with the archetype of the warrior, even if it's just in relation to the causes worth fighting for. Associated with courage, action, and desire, this fiery planet embodies the spirit of the quest, the will to survive, and the drive that propels us forward against all odds. Mars resonates with primal instincts, of the rage that burns within our bones, and of the passion that fuels our ambitions. Depending on the planet, sign, and aspects of Mars in your chart, this may be an easy energy to relate to, or it may be confusing, especially if you have Mars in a gentle sign like Cancer or Pisces.

Mars reflects our assertiveness, our capacity for action, and the manner in which we pursue our desires, the raw energy that urges us to assert our individuality, to defend our territory, and to chase after what we want with single-minded determination. In the natal chart, Mars reveals how we express our anger and our assertiveness, how we handle conflict, and the things that drive us, physical energy and the force of our ambitions.

Mars in the zodiac signs puts on different armour or camouflage, shaping our drive and our passions according to the qualities of each sign. In Aries, Mars wields the fire of the pioneer, ready to blaze new trails; in

Scorpio, Mars is in stealth mode, it dives into the depths, devious and immensely powerful; in Capricorn, Mars wears a power suit with ambitions to conquer peaks of achievement.

In each house of the natal chart, Mars brings dynamism and energy, illuminating the areas of life where we are most compelled to act and to assert ourselves. In the 1st House, Mars influences physical presence and personal initiatives, whereas a 6th House Mars drives work ethic and our approach to health and service.

Mars is often difficult, especially in societies that value peace and diplomacy, but with every difficulty in a chart there is potential to build strength and a strong Mars is a fierce inner ally. The fiery energy of Mars casts shadows, for with great power comes the potential for conflict, aggression, and destruction. Mars teaches us about the consequences of unchecked desire, of the fine line between assertiveness and aggression, and of the importance of directing our energies towards constructive ends. Mars challenges us to face these shadows and harness our inner warrior, not for the sake of battle, but for the courage to act and to face life's challenges with courage.

MARS AND MAGIC

Mars, often associated with aggression and combat in mythology, governs our energy, drive, and desire in astrology. It represents our assertiveness, how we pursue our goals, and how we express anger and passion. A Mars transit can invigorate our actions, boost our courage, and sometimes challenge our tempers. Understanding and effectively channelling Mars' vigorous energies can significantly enhance one's ability to assert oneself and take decisive action.

Mars is all about action and energy. Its placement in your astrological chart influences how you assert yourself, your aggression levels, and your drive to pursue your desires. Mars' energy is straightforward and bold, often encouraging us to start new projects, defend our boundaries, and assert our independence.

Mars is excellent for starting new initiatives. Use this energy to kick-start projects you've been hesitant about. Mars gives you the courage and the drive to take the first steps. Mars rules physical exertion and the body. Engage in regular physical activity, which can be an effective way to channel Mars' intense energy constructively. This could be anything from a vigorous workout, joining a sports team, to taking up a martial art.

If you typically shy away from asserting yourself, you can use a Mars transit to practice standing up for yourself. Role-playing exercises, assertiveness training workshops, or simply speaking your mind in situations where you'd normally stay silent can all be beneficial. Mars can stir up conflict, so learning to deal with disagreements in a healthy and constructive way is crucial. Practice techniques for healthy confrontation, ensuring that you're clear and direct with your words while remaining respectful of others.

When Mars is retrograde, action may be stalled and situations may become tense and passive-aggressive. The sign of Mars and the house it transits through during the retrograde will affect people differently, but Mars retrogrades tend to be a good time for reflection on our will, our strategy and tactics, and how we assert ourselves in the world.

Mars inspires bravery and when Mars is transiting key planets and luminaries in your chart it can be a good time to confront your fears and do things that challenge you physically or emotionally. Whether it's public speaking, solo travel, or undertaking a challenging task, we can channel Mars into good action and courage.

If you're feeling inhibited, angry, or frustrated, you may want to work with Mars directly through magic, for instance, creating a Mars themed talisman, performing a ritual to honour and embody Martial energy, or practicing some of the fire element magic presented earlier in this book such as channelling the energy of rage.

Sometimes the best way of working with Mars magic is more direct – through physical activity like active exercise, martial arts, or even dance. If your Mars is in a water or air sign this may be difficult. Air signs tend to want more abstract or intellectual expressions of Mars, whereas water sign Mars prefers to follow the path of least resistance. You can work with this. Choose activities that make the most sense for you, whether that's karaoke, swimming, or going for long walks. What physical activities make you feel good and embodied?

Often, if our Mars is in a difficult sign or aspect we've faced exercise related traumas at school where we were forced into uncomfortable sports or activities that made us disconnect from our bodies in anxiety. Leaning into physical activities that do feel good can help to remedy this, bridging the mind body connection and releasing the painful emotion buried in our bodies. If you struggle with serious complex trauma, do this work with the guidance of trauma-informed therapists if you can, and be exceptionally gentle with yourself.

JUPITER

Jupiter joyfully embodies expansion, representing the part of the psyche that seeks meaning, understanding, wise beliefs, and looks to expand beyond known boundaries, whether intellectual, spiritual, or cultural. Jupiter's influence is linked to optimism, opportunity, and the natural drive towards improving oneself. It can signify the optimistic part of the self that seeks to grow and find fulfilment through broadening one's horizons. Jupiter encourages exploration and the pursuit of truth, aligning with Jung's idea of individuation – a lifelong process of becoming aware of oneself and achieving self-realisation.

Jupiter transits often feel amazing, like we've taken a swig of liquid luck potion that lasts us all week. We feel like we're expanding into new levels of awareness, and everything good is lining up for us. Working with these transits can help them to contribute to lasting improvements in our lives rather than just fleeting moments of blissful good fortune.

The archetype of Jupiter can be a bit like Santa Claus, arriving every now again, jovial and bearing gifts, before flying off on his sleigh with a merry chuckle. In our charts, Jupiter embodies an inner-sage or guru, lending wisdom and strength that will vary depending on what sign or house it's located in.

WORKING WITH JUPITER IN MAGIC

Drawing on the abundant and expansive energy of Jupiter in magic can be exceptionally powerful, especially during a Jupiter transit. You can create talismans for good fortune and expansion, celebrate the journey of your life so far, and envision new goals and dreams, aligning yourself with the magnanimous energy of this benevolent planet to improve your life.

Talismans for Good Fortune and Expansion

Crafting a talisman during a Jupiter transit involves harnessing the planet's expansive and optimistic energy using one of the talisman processes described earlier in this book. Choose materials that resonate with Jupiter's qualities – shiny metals, and amethyst and citrine are excellent choices. You may wish to do this work on a Thursday, Jupiter's day. You can inscribe a talisman with symbols of abundance, such as the symbol for Jupiter (♃) or other things that signify luck and joy. As you create the talisman, infuse it with your intentions, e.g., for prosperity, wisdom, and opportunities. Wear or carry it to attract Jupiter's beneficial influences into your life.

Celebrating the Journey

Take time to reflect on your life's journey, acknowledging the growth and achievements you have experienced so far. Create a ritual space filled with blue and purple candles, Jupiter's colours, and adorn it with objects that symbolise your accomplishments. Meditate on your path, giving thanks for the wisdom and opportunities you have received. Journalling about your milestones can also solidify this reflection, helping you to appreciate how far you have come and setting the stage for future growth.

Envisioning New Aspirations

Jupiter's energy is ideal for setting ambitious goals and dreaming big. During a Jupiter transit, spend time visualising your future aspirations. You may wish to create an altar to Jupiter, incorporating symbols and colours of Jupiter into your altar or ritual space, such as blue, purple, gold, and silver. Or create some kind of vision board filled with images and words that represent your goals. Focus on expansion in various aspects of your life – career, relationships, personal growth, and spirituality. You can use affirmations and word magic that relates to what you care about, value, and believe in.

Rituals for Alignment

Engage in rituals that align you with Jupiter's energy. This might include lighting candles, reciting chants for abundance and growth, or performing meditative visualisations of expansion and success. Focus on embodying the qualities of Jupiter – optimism, wisdom, generosity, and expansive thinking – during your rituals. Honour the planet Jupiter in your rituals through offerings of chocolate and fruits, or libations – pouring out a swig of mead, wine, juice, or spirits, into a cauldron, onto a burning fire, or outside. Alternately, you can drink the libation yourself in honour of celebrating Jupiter.

By consciously working with Jupiter's energy through these kinds of practices, you can connect with and harness the planet's beneficial influences to bring about positive changes and growth in your life. Embrace the opportunities Jupiter presents, and let its expansive energy guide you towards greater fulfilment and success.

SATURN

In the realm of Jungian astrology, Saturn is the stern teacher, embodying the archetype of the wise elder, complete with hard limitations and discipline. Saturn is the master of boundaries, the sculptor of destiny, cold and unyielding, master of the passage of time and the slow march of fate.

Saturn's lessons are etched in the marrow of our bones, each hardship a lesson. Saturn guards at the threshold of our fears and aspirations, urging us to do the hard work we are avoiding, to confront the shadows and challenges we hide from. Saturn's journey is the path of austerity and structure, busting down anything that is unstable and offering the chance to re-build our lives with a stronger foundation.

In the heart of Saturn's dominion there is always a sense of disappointment. Yet, within this sorrow, there is also a promise – the promise of growth, of hard-won wisdom and the potential rewards of new dreams made real once we let the old outdated dreams die. Saturn's embrace is both a strong support and a challenge.

So, let us honour Saturn, the grand master and lord of time, with the same reverence we reserve for the ancient. For under Saturn's stern gaze and unyielding grip, we find not only the weight of our burdens but also the key to our liberation.

Saturn is associated with the harsher realities of life: limitations, duties, and delays. Its influence is felt as a constriction, a pressing need to confront our responsibilities and mature in our approach. As I've mentioned, I tend to notice a big Saturn transit approaching as a constriction in my chest, like being pressed in a vice. When I have this sensation, I look up my transits and here I always seem to find transiting Saturn conjunct, square, or opposite my Sun or other personal planets.

Saturn demands that we build enduring structures, both externally in our lives and internally within our psyches. Saturn transits in astrology are often met with apprehension, as they tend to bring about significant challenges, limitations, and necessary restructuring in one's life. Known as the taskmaster of the zodiac, Saturn's energy focuses on discipline, responsibility, and long-term growth. Understanding and embracing the lessons of Saturn can lead to profound, lasting changes and a more solid foundation in life.

The adept Jungian astrologer Liz Greene has written a most fascinating book about the lessons of Saturn – once believed to be a bad (malefic) planet in astrology – with a new lens of the important lessons we can learn from limitations and the brilliant gifts and achievements that can be earned through hard toil and inner-processing when we do our Saturn work.

WORKING WITH SATURN

The key to benefiting from Saturn's transits is to align with its demanding energy rather than resist it. Here are ways to work constructively with Saturn:

- Acceptance of Reality: Begin by facing your current limitations and challenges head-on. Saturn asks for a stark, unembellished look at the facts. Assess your life structures – financial, professional, personal – and identify where fortification is needed.
- Saturn rewards careful planning and foresight. Establish clear, achievable goals that address the areas of your life that Saturn is influencing. Break these into smaller, manageable tasks to avoid feeling overwhelmed.

- Implement regular routines that work for you and enhance your time management skills. Saturn appreciates a methodical approach.
- Reflect on past mistakes – not to dwell in regret but to mine them for valuable lessons. Saturn's energy supports growth from hindsight, encouraging a wiser approach in future endeavours.
- Develop your emotional and mental resilience. The pressures of Saturn can lead to feelings of despair or fatigue. Engage in practices that bolster your spirit and keep you mentally and emotionally equipped to handle stress.
- Use this time for deep psychological work. Saturn's energy can reveal our fears and blocks. Therapy, meditation, or spiritual practices can be potent tools during a Saturn transit to transform these fears into strengths. If you're not sure where to focus, look for recurring thought patterns and areas where you feel stuck. What are you ready to change? What change are you not quite ready for but you know you need anyway?
- Recognise that embracing limits can lead to mastery. Saturn teaches that mastery in any area of life often requires accepting and working within certain boundaries.
- Craft a simple ritual, for instance where you write down your commitments and the steps you will take to fulfil them. Place these in a box or an envelope, and open it periodically to reaffirm your commitment.
- Utilise stones like black tourmaline or onyx, which resonate with Saturn's grounding energy. Keep these stones with you as a reminder of the strength and stability you are building.
- Dedicate time each week to reflect on your progress. Saturn values reflection as a tool for learning and adjustment. Journalling can be incredibly helpful.

Working with Saturn's energies does not have to be an oppressive experience. By aligning with Saturn's demands for structure, discipline, and integrity, you not only survive these transits but emerge stronger, more capable, and more in command of your destiny. This is the true gift of Saturn – solid foundations built on the bedrock of hard-earned wisdom and effort.

URANUS

The planet Uranus is the lightning bolt of change and represents the forces of sudden shocks, revolution, individuality, originality, and liberation from the shackles of convention.

Uranus shakes us out of complacency by delivering unexpected events that disrupt the status quo and force us to adapt. Its influence is electric, unpredictable, and destabilising, but ultimately frees us from limiting patterns so we can reach more of our authentic potential.

Uranus transits and aspects often coincide with periods of accelerated growth and change in both the inner and outer life. We may feel restless, anxious, or inspired to break free from restriction. Flashes of creative insight and technological breakthroughs are linked to Uranus. So are rebellion, separation, and sudden twists of fate that alter our trajectory.

Uranus stands as the harbinger of sudden change and innovation, of rebellion against the status quo. Uranus embodies the archetype of the revolutionary and the awakener, compelling us to break free from the constraints of tradition. This planet's energy is electric and unpredictable, mirroring the lightning bolts that symbolise its disruptive and transformative power. It represents the force that drives us towards self-realisation by shaking up established patterns and pushing us beyond our comfort zones. Uranus challenges the structures of the ego, urging us to embrace our authentic selves and to awaken to new levels of consciousness. It is the spark that ignites the flames of creativity and originality, encouraging us to think outside the conventional boundaries and to envision new possibilities.

As the ruler of Aquarius, Uranus is associated with themes of freedom, innovation, and humanitarian ideals. It compels us to question societal norms and to seek progressive solutions to collective problems. In our personal lives, Uranus can manifest as a sudden insight or a radical change that disrupts the familiar and opens the door to new perspectives. Its influence can be unsettling, but it is through these disruptions that we find the potential for growth and transformation. Uranus invites us to embrace chaos and uncertainty as necessary components of the creative process. It teaches us that innovation often arises from the dissolution of old forms and that the path to enlightenment is rarely linear.

Uranus spends about seven years in each sign, marking part of the zeitgeist and shared experiences of part of a generation. Those born with Uranus in the same sign often challenge convention in similar ways and are collectively tasked with innovating the sign's domain, while the house of Uranus in a natal chart, and the aspects it makes to other planets reflect the psyche in a more personal way.

NEPTUNE

There is nothing quite like the powerful spell of Neptune, the planet of the intangible, unconscious, and transcendent dimensions of life. Neptune relates to the realms of dreams, mysticism, compassion, oneness, delusions, and things which are hidden and submerged. Neptune dissolves everything it touches, including boundaries, merging the individual with the collective and the earthly with the divine. Its archetypal influence is a pervasive force, like the ocean wearing away stone or a cosmic mist enveloping the psyche.

Neptune spends about fourteen years in each sign, shaping the ideals, imagination, and spiritual expression of a generation. Neptune's placement influences popular art, music, and culture with a unifying aesthetic, holding the masses in thrall.

As a personal influence in the birth chart, Neptune's house placement shows where we long for redemption, creative inspiration, and spiritual connection. It is the realm where we imagine perfection and may fall prey to illusion. Aspects from Neptune to other planets can reflect our capacity for compassion, longing, and mystical understanding.

Neptunian people (those with strong Neptune and Pisces influences in their chart) are magnetic and highly empathic, often struggling to establish boundaries between self and other. People may fall in love with them at the drop of a hat and become obsessed. A strong Neptune makes one imaginative, intuitive and attuned to subtler realities but can also lead to confusion, fantasy, addiction, and playing the victim or saviour. It can be a challenge for Neptunian people to ground themselves and focus on practical matters. The highest expression of Neptune embodies divine compassion and sees only the sacred in all creation.

PLUTO

Pluto is considered the great harbinger of transformation and the depths of the subconscious. Though astronomers may no longer consider Pluto a planet, this does nothing to diminish the power of Pluto in astrology with power in the darkness, destruction, rebirth, regeneration, and the undercurrents that drive our deepest most secret fears and desires.

Pluto, named after the Roman god of the underworld, governs the unseen forces at play within our psyche and the world. It challenges us to confront our shadows, to dive deep into the abyss of our inner truths, and to emerge renewed, like the mythical phoenix rising from its ashes. This celestial body represents the principle of death and rebirth, not as an end, but as a necessary passage to transformation.

In the astrological chart, Pluto's position marks areas where we face our deepest fears, where we must let go of old forms to allow for new growth. It's where we encounter power struggles, both within ourselves and with the outside world, leading us to our personal empowerment through the alchemy of the soul.

Pluto is not for the faint hearted. It calls for courage to face the dark corners of our existence, to question, to dismantle, and to rebuild stronger foundations. Its transformative potential lies in its ability to strip away what no longer serves us, challenging us to evolve and to find our power in the authenticity of our being.

Remember, the transformation Pluto offers is intense and all-encompassing. It touches every part of our lives, asking us to walk through the fire, to trust in the cycle of death and rebirth, and to emerge on the other side with a deeper understanding of our power and place in the cosmos.

CHIRON

There is a crack in everything — that's how the light gets in
  - Leonard Cohen

Chiron is the wounded healer, representing our deepest wounds and our greatest potential for healing and wisdom. Discovered in 1977, this celestial body was named after the centaur in Greek mythology who was skilled in medicine but unable to heal his own wound.

In astrology, Chiron's position in a birth chart indicates an area of profound sensitivity, where we've experienced pain or feelings of inadequacy. However, it's through confronting and understanding these wounds that we gain unique insights and the ability to heal others. Chiron thus symbolises the transformative journey from pain to compassion, from woundedness to wisdom.

The house and sign placement of Chiron in a natal chart reveal the nature of one's core wound and the path to healing. This placement often points to where we feel most vulnerable, but also where we have the greatest potential to develop empathy, understanding, and eventually, the capacity to guide others through similar challenges.

Chiron's cycle, which takes about fifty years to complete, often correlates with significant periods of personal growth and healing in an individual's life. By embracing the lessons of Chiron, we can turn our deepest pain into our greatest strength, becoming a source of healing not just for ourselves, but for others as well.

NORTH NODE

The North Node in astrology represents our soul's frontier – the edge of growth where we are called to venture out beyond our comfort zone. The North Node is a compass pointing toward our highest evolution in this lifetime. It can feel like the path of greatest resistance and greatest reward, challenging precisely because it represents qualities and experiences our soul craves to develop.

Where the South Node shows our default patterns and accumulated past life skills (our cosmic comfort zone), the North Node reveals what feels uncomfortable but necessary for our growth. It's the spiritual equivalent of exercise – the resistance creates strength, and the discomfort leads to growth.

The North Node's position by sign and house in our birth chart illuminates specific areas where we're meant to push beyond familiar territory. It's where we might feel most awkward or uncertain, yet it's also where our greatest breakthroughs await. The North Node asks us to trust in the unfamiliar, to step into new ways of being that may feel counterintuitive at first.

For example, someone with a North Node in Aries might have comfort with compromise and partnership (South Node in Libra) but needs to learn the courage of standing alone. Or someone with a North Node in the 10th house might need to overcome their tendency to hide in private life and step into public leadership.

Following the North Node's path often feels like walking through resistance. It's not meant to be easy – it's meant to be transformative. The challenges we encounter along this path are not obstacles but opportunities for the exact growth our soul signed up for. When we align with our North Node's energy, even though it may feel uncomfortable, we often experience a sense of purpose, of moving in harmony with our soul.

This growth isn't about rejecting who we've been. It's about expanding into who we can become. It's a sacred invitation to evolutionary growth, pointing the way toward our potential while honouring the wisdom we bring from our past.

WEAVING IT ALL TOGETHER

After years of studying astrology, I still find myself discovering new layers of meaning in the patterns of the planets all the time. Each planet has its own distinct character, its own way of manifesting in magical work.

Often the best place to start with astrology is in learning your own chart. In this chapter I've endeavoured to provide a helpful starting point for this process. You can look up your chart online and begin to understand the different planets and how they are expressed in their signs and houses in your chart. Similarly, it can be fun to look up the charts of other people you know and have conversations with them about what they relate to.

You can also bring astrology into your magical practice, honouring the planets just as the ancients did, invoking them as deities, making offerings to them. The energies of the planets express themselves through colour, scent, stone, herb, and season. Here's how I've come to understand them, but I encourage you to discover your own connections:

I've found that the best way to start working with these energies is simply to pay attention. Notice how you feel during different moon phases. Watch how planetary transits reflect in your daily life. Keep a journal of your experiences – you might be surprised at the patterns that emerge.

TRUST YOUR EXPERIENCE

While books and teachers can guide us, our personal experience is our wisest teacher. I've found that some traditional correspondences make sense for me, while others don't resonate at all. That's fine – astrology is a living practice, not a fixed set of rules.

Pay attention to how different energies affect you. Notice which planets you naturally align with and which ones challenge you. Let your practice develop organically rather than trying to force it into predetermined patterns.

Working with planetary energies is an ongoing process of learning and discovery. Each transit, each lunar phase, each planetary aspect offers new opportunities for understanding and growth. It's important to remain curious about what these celestial patterns can teach us.

Like the symbols in my birth chart that I used to draw before I knew what they meant, sometimes our deepest wisdom comes through intuition rather than intellect. Trust your inner knowing while remaining open to learning. The stars have been teaching humanity for thousands of years – they have plenty more insights to share if we're willing to learn.

5

DELECTABLE MAGIC

"Food is magic. Its power over us is undeniable. From the sweet, rich lure of a freshly baked brownie to an exquisitely steamed artichoke, food continues to seduce us. Food is life. We can't continue to live without its magic. Food, however, also harbours energies. When we eat, our bodies absorb those energies, just as they absorb vitamins, minerals, amino acids, carbohydrates, and other nutrients. Though we may not be aware of any effect other than a sated appetite, the food has subtly changed us."
– Scott Cunningham

KITCHEN WITCHERY

I've always been drawn to the humble and delicious associations of kitchen witchery. I grew up alert to the magic of baking which could transform basic ingredients into delectable treats, and I was raised in a family where we all took on the role of cooking big family meals from a young age, not following recipes most of the time. I have four younger siblings, with fifteen years between us, so for much of my childhood and adolescence my mother would be busy with a baby. When it was my night to cook dinner, I'd go into her bedroom and ask her advice. Almost all her instructions started with "First, chop an onion..." I'd begin that step and then go back to ask for more advice while the onion browned in the frying pan. This is how I learned to cook, and how I still cook to this day. There are few meals I make that don't start with chopping an onion or two.

Kitchen witchery is much more than the simple act of cooking – it's an alchemical process where we transform the seemingly mundane into the magical, creating something greater than the sum of its parts. Each ingredient holds its own energy and meaning. These can be chosen not just for flavour but for their metaphysical properties. Take delicate fragrant basil, for instance, revered for its powers of protection and love, or cinnamon, which resonates with wealth, passion, and enhanced awareness.

At times, the kitchen is my sanctuary; the oven and stove, my altar; my large enamel casserole dish is my favourite cauldron. The more awareness I hold while I cook, the more the everyday act of making a meal is imbued with intention and appreciation, turning every dish into a spell. I don't always cook every day, and sometimes I cook with little awareness as I juggle other things, but in moments of presence, as I chop, stir, and blend, I am not just preparing food; I am also aware of the magic I'm brewing. This is the heart of kitchen witchery – creating harmony within and without, nurturing body and soul with every delectable bite. This philosophy has the power to turn every meal into a ritual, where the simple act of eating nourishes more than just the body, but also the spirit.

THE MAGICAL ROLES OF ORDINARY KITCHEN UTENSILS IN THE CRAFT OF KITCHEN WITCHERY

Every kitchen utensil can be seen to serve both a functional and a magical purpose. The humble wooden spoon can be understood as channelling the grounding energies of the wood it is made of and the element of Earth, infusing our concoctions with stability and strength. Our kitchen cauldrons (or pots and pans) are often the vessels in which transformation occurs. Here, raw ingredients metamorphose into nourishment, their cell walls breaking down and releasing important micronutrients. The knives we use are tools of precision and separation. In the magical kitchen, the knife cuts through more than just physical ingredients – it slices through resistance and barriers, carving out space for new intentions to come forth. As I chop herbs and vegetables, I sometimes visualise cutting away troubles and obstacles. Cutting onions might bring tears to my eyes, but the discomfort can symbolise the challenges we must face in order to step further into our power and the tears are clearing. Even the humble grater has its role, shredding materials as it shreds old patterns, helping us to break things down into manageable, digestible elements, making the tough textures more palatable. The pepper grinder and mortar and pestle, along with other tools for grinding and blending, serve a similar purpose. As I crush herbs and spices, I am not merely releasing flavour but also amalgamating different energies, creating powerful mixes that enhance both the potency of my dishes.

You can think of your kitchen implements as magical tools, for instance:

Wooden spoon: Grounding, stability, Earth element, strength
Pots and pans: Transformation, alchemy, nurturing
Knives: Precision, removing obstacles, carving new paths
Grater: Breaking down problems, making challenges manageable
Pepper grinder: Releasing hidden energies, adding spice to life
Mortar and pestle: Blending energies, creating potent mixtures
Whisk: Incorporating Air element, stirring up new ideas
Measuring cups: Balance, proportion, careful intention-setting
Peeler: Revealing inner truths, shedding old beliefs
Rolling pin: Smoothing out difficulties, expanding possibilities
Tongs: Grasping opportunities, shifting things
Ladle: Distributing blessings, sharing abundance
Spatula: Turning situations around, flexibility in approach
Kettle: Distillation, transformation through heat
Colander/sieve: draining away excess, separating useful things
Masher: Breaking down barriers, processing, softening resistance
Zester: Adding zest to life, enhancing flavours of experience
Kitchen scales: Balancing energies, weighing decisions
Can opener: Accessing hidden resources, opening new pathways
Oven gloves: Protection, handling hot situations safely
Funnel: Channelling energies, focusing intentions
Blender: Integrating different aspects of life, harmonising energies

Kitchen witchery need not be complex or shrouded in mystery. The magic lies in the awareness we bring to our everyday culinary tasks. As we stir a simmering pot, we might reflect on stirring up new wonderful changes and adventures in life. While sieving pasta, we might consider that we can also internally let go of what no longer serves us. These simple acts of reflection during the practical tasks of cooking, are all part of kitchen witchery. It's about infusing our daily routines with intention and awareness. The most powerful magic often comes from quiet moments of connection between our inner world and our outer actions. The next time you step into your kitchen, you might like to take a moment to appreciate the gentle yet powerful potential in every utensil and every act of food preparation. In doing so, you'll be practising kitchen witchery in its most accessible form.

THE MAGIC OF THE EVERYDAY AND THE POWER OF LISTENING TO OUR BODIES

As reflected above, in kitchen witchery, the magic we weave is not reserved for grand rituals or special occasions. Rather, it is found in the everyday – the simple acts of choosing, preparing, and consuming food. This practice of nourishment and nurturing includes a strong focus on listening to our bodies, understanding our needs, and responding with intention.

The first step in everyday kitchen witchery is to tune in to our own physical and energetic needs. Our body is our constant companion, our physical expression here on earth, and therefore it can be a dear friend or an enemy bound with the inherent limitations of the material world. Many of us have disconnected and painful relationships with our physical selves, a trauma that has been created by a dominant culture deeply uncomfortable with mortality, and rife with agendas. Advertisers trying to get you to buy their various cosmetics, clothing, supplements and so on have an obvious interest in making us feel bad about our looks, our size, our differences etc. because it's easier to sell things to unhappy people.

Knowing this alone is often not enough to reverse decades of patho-logical social influences, but it's a start. The more we connect intuitively with our bodies, the more whole and re-connected we become, and the less influences those outer messages have on us.

Everybody is physiologically unique, with our own requirements and responses. What nourishes one may not suit another. By paying attention to how different foods affect our vitality and emotional state, we can begin to craft habits and practices of nutrition that support our physical, emotional, mental, and spiritual well-being.

Intuitive eating involves listening to your body's hunger cues and responding thoughtfully. It's about eating what your body really craves, when you're hungry, savouring every mouthful with gentle awareness, and naturally stopping when you're full – being in tune with the natural rhythms of your body, just as plants draw nutrients from the earth and sun in harmony with both their wellbeing and the ecosystem in which they are connected.

Notice how certain foods impact your energy levels and mood. For instance, some may find that root vegetables ground and stabilise them, while others might feel tired and low after eating certain root vegetables but find they're invigorated by citrus fruits.

Before cooking, tune in to your body and then set an intention for your meal. This could be for healing, protection, energy, or joy. As you cook, visualise this intention being stirred into your food in harmony with your physical state. Aligning your meals with the cycles of nature not only enhances the nutritional content of your food but also connects you to the rhythm of the earth. Eating seasonally and locally helps to attune your body to the environment.

The kitchen can be a sanctuary of warmth and nourishment. Making it a space where you feel calm and inspired can profoundly impact the magic of your everyday cooking. If possible, keep your kitchen space open and inviting; organise it in a way that suits your lifestyle, disregarding other people's expectations if they really do not make sense for you. A cluttered space can lead to a cluttered mind, which affects how you cook and eat. I grew up as one of the oldest in a chaotic household of six children (I have a step sister who is a few months older than me), and I can cook in almost any kitchen space, no matter how cluttered. My childhood helped me to filter out and work around the mess, though a clear space is easier to navigate!

If your intuition guides you to do so, you may also wish to incorporate elements that remind you of your connection to magic as you cook, such as candles, herbs, crystals, or symbols which can hold energy within your kitchen space. If your kitchen is a shared space, be mindful of other people and communicate as clearly as possible about what you're doing so as to avoid draining and unnecessary tension which will only detract from your magic.

Eating can be a conscious magical act, a time to appreciate the food and honour the body as the vessel that carries you through life. Take time to really taste your food. Notice the textures, flavours, and sensations.

Eating slowly and without distractions allows you to fully absorb not only the nutritional benefits but also the energy of the meal (though sometimes distractions and multi-tasking can also be an experience you might want to have, such as a shared meal with friends or family while watching a favourite show).

Kitchen witchery in everyday life reminds us that each choice, each bite, is an opportunity to infuse our lives with magic. It teaches us that by listening to and respecting our bodies, and honouring the food we eat, we engage in a continual act of magical practice.

Expressing appreciation for the food, the hands that prepared it, and the earth that provided it enhances the spiritual nourishment and connects you more deeply to your food.

FOOD BLESSING BY PAMELA MEEKINGS-STEWART

May the four winds protect us
May the four directions bless us
May the elements of earth, and air, and fire, and water be our guides and companions, uplift our spirits
And may the Earth goddesses be truly thanked for the abundance of food on our table
Blessings on the hands that hold
Blessings on the hands that sew
Blessings on the hands that harvest
And blessings on the cooks!
And blessings on our good hearts
Blessings be
Blessings be
Blessings be
Eat!

THE PRINCIPLES OF KITCHEN WITCHERY

In the practice of kitchen witchery, every flavour we encounter – both in our dishes and in our lives – holds significant meaning. These flavours can range from the sweetness of success to the bitterness of challenges. Kitchen witchery teaches us to embrace and learn from this full spectrum, using the principles of balance, acceptance, and transformation. The tastes we experience can reflect and influence our journey through life.

Embracing All Flavours

Sweet: Traditionally associated with pleasure and success, sweetness in our food can remind us to appreciate the joys and blessings in our lives. In kitchen witchery, sweet ingredients like honey and fruit are often used in spells for love, joy, and prosperity.

Sour: Sour flavours challenge us to embrace life's complexities. Ingredients like lemon and vinegar not only cleanse the palate but also clear away negativity, providing protection and purification in magical practices.

Bitter: Though often avoided, bitter flavours such as kale or dark chocolate are vital for balance. They help with digestion, teach us resilience, and help us appreciate the value of facing life's challenges head-on, strengthening our spirit.

Salty: Salt is essential for flavour and preservation, and in witchcraft, it is used for protection and grounding. Salty flavours remind us to ground ourselves in reality and protect our energy from external influences.

Umami: The savoury richness of umami, found in foods like mushrooms and soy sauce, can enhance depth and complexity in our dishes. In life, umami encourages us to seek depth in our relationships and experiences.

Just as a well-balanced dish requires a thoughtful combination of flavours, a balanced life needs a mix of experiences. Kitchen witchery emphasises the importance of integrating all aspects of life – joy, sorrow, challenges, and triumphs – into a cohesive whole.

When we cook, choosing ingredients for both their flavours and their magical properties allows us to infuse our food with specific energies. This act of intention sets the stage for transformation, both in the kitchen and in our personal lives.

Savouring each bite and reflecting on the flavours can mirror our approach to life's experiences. By fully experiencing the present moment, we acknowledge and appreciate the diverse aspects of our lives.

TRANSFORMATION THROUGH FLAVOUR

In kitchen witchery, the transformation of ingredients symbolises our own ability to change and adapt. Cooking is alchemy, and as we transform ingredients into a meal, we are reminded of our power to transform our own lives.

Just as we might adapt a recipe to better suit our taste or the ingredients we have on hand, we can adapt to life's circumstances, finding creative solutions to challenges we face.

Each flavour can teach us something about ourselves and how we handle different aspects of life. By reflecting on our reactions to various flavours, we can gain insights into our emotional and spiritual health.

Integrating the full spectrum of flavours in our cooking encourages us to embrace the full spectrum of life's experiences. It teaches us that every experience, like every flavour, has its place and purpose. The challenges (bitter and sour) are as important as the successes (sweet) and the everyday moments (salty and umami).

By applying the principles of kitchen witchery to both our cooking and our lives, we learn to create a rich, balanced, and fulfilling existence. We learn that every flavour, every experience, contributes to the person we are becoming.

This deeper exploration into the principles of kitchen witchery not only enriches our culinary practices but also enhances our life philosophy, encouraging a holistic and embracing approach to all that life offers.

DEEPENING THE EXPERIENCE OF FLAVOURS

In the enchanting practice of kitchen witchery, every flavour we encounter offers a gateway to a deeper understanding of life's complexities and our own innate magic. By appreciating the intricate entwining of flavours in our meals, we can learn to appreciate the intricate experiences in our lives, stepping ever deeper into our own wild magic. Let's explore how this appreciation can enhance our sensory experiences and enrich our spiritual journey.

The complexity of flavours in a dish isn't just about taste – it's about the stories, the processes, and the energies that come together to create something unique and dynamic. Each ingredient carries its own history and magic, and when combined, they create a symphony of tastes that is greater than the sum of its parts.

Just as a chef layers flavours to build depth in a dish, we can layer experiences and emotions in our lives to build a rich, textured existence. Learning to appreciate subtle undertones and fleeting notes in food can teach us to recognise and value the less obvious moments in our lives – the quiet joys, the gentle sorrows, and the fleeting connections that shape our days.

In cooking, contrasting flavours – like sweet and savoury or bitter and salty – can enhance each other, making a dish more balanced and enjoyable. Similarly, in life, contrasting experiences can provide balance and perspective. Joy feels sweeter after sorrow, and success feels more triumphant after challenges. Embracing this interplay can deepen our understanding and appreciation of each moment.

APPRECIATING COMPLEXITY AND ALCHEMY

To truly appreciate the complexity of flavours, we must slow down and focus, engaging all our senses. This mindful approach to eating can extend to other areas of our lives. Yes, just as we savour a complex dish, we can savour complex moments in life. This means fully immersing ourselves in experiences, paying attention to the details, and being present in the moment, feeling the texture of an emotion, recognising the layers of a relationship, or acknowledging the depth of a challenge.

After a meal, reflecting on the experience can enhance our understanding of the flavours and our enjoyment of the food. Similarly, reflecting on life's experiences can help us integrate them into our personal narrative, finding meaning and lessons in everything we encounter.

By embracing the full spectrum of flavours and experiences, we step into a life lived in full colour and full emotion. This means not shying away from the complex, the difficult, or the unfamiliar, but rather leaning into them with curiosity and openness.

Each of us carries within us a wild magic – the unique energy and potential that we bring to the world. By engaging fully with life's flavours, we tap into this magic more deeply. We learn to create, to adapt, and to conjure joy from the myriad ingredients life offers us.

Just as we transform ingredients into a meal, we can transform experiences into wisdom. This is the alchemy of the spirit – turning the raw materials of our lives into gold. Every experience, every flavour contributes to this transformation, making us more complete, more powerful, and more magical.

In kitchen witchery, as in life, the complexity of flavours is not just to be endured but to be celebrated. It is in this complexity that we can find the metaphoric spice of life, and it is here that we discover the power to live fully and magically.

By embracing the fullness of our experiences and the complexity of our emotions, we step deeper into our own wild magic, enriching our journey through life.

ENCHANTING INGREDIENTS

In the magical kitchen, ingredients can be chosen not just for their taste but for their spiritual properties and energies.

Garlic is not only a staple for its robust flavour but is also revered for its protective qualities (watch out vampires!). Hanging a braid of garlic in the kitchen has long been thought to ward off unwanted spirits, but we can reinterpret this lore in ways that make more sense to us in our everyday lives. Garlic does indeed have protective qualities when it comes to nutritional science, boosting our immune systems and warding off potentially harmful microorganisms. It's also very tasty.

Salt is a simple yet powerful magical substance, used for purification and protection. Some practitioners like to sprinkle pinch of salt in the corners of the kitchen. Salt has long been used as a cleansing agent. When added to dishes, salt enhances flavour, of course, but depending on your mindset, you could also imagine it adding to your energetic protection or creating a barrier against unwanted influences.

Honey, the sweet nectar of hardworking bees, is a symbol of abundance and sweetness in life. Used in spells, it can sweeten situations and soften hearts. When I drizzle honey into a dish, I might focus on sweet outcomes and harmonious relationships.

Herbs play a crucial role in kitchen witchery, each with their own magical attributes. Rosemary, for remembrance and protection; thyme for courage and clear vision; basil for love and prosperity. These are but a few of the fragrant allies that assist in weaving magic into meals.

Water, the essence of life, is vital in the kitchen. It is used to cleanse, to brew, and to mix. When charged with intention or even under the light of the moon, it can imbue dishes with special resonance. For instance, enhancing emotional healing and intuition. In Māori traditions, water is important for purification and transitions between the sacred and mundane.

Elements and ingredients, when combined with intention and knowledge, transform the act of cooking into a potent magical practice. This interplay nourishes the body and nurtures the soul, making every meal a ritual of love, protection, and prosperity. I find endless fascination in the deeper layers of kitchen witchery. The art of infusing is about imbuing oils, vinegars, and spirits with herbs, flowers, and crystals, chosen for their magical properties. For instance, a syrup infused with rose petals for love, a rosemary infused olive oil for a sharp and flexible mind, or a tasty vinegar steeped with ingredients like nettles, garlic, horseradish chilli, and onions for protection (and immune-system boosting) which can be sprinkled onto salads.

Fire transforms, be it a flame on the stove or an oven's heat. It changes the very nature of things. As I cook, I respect this element as a creator and destroyer, harnessing its power to transmute intentions and re-shape my dreams and the raw ingredients I'm working with into a delicious and powerful meal.There's enchantment in baking. Breads, pastries, and pies aren't just treats; they are dreams made real. Each fold of the dough, each sprinkle of sugar or seeds, can be a ritual act. Baking a loaf of bread with intentions of abundance – kneading prosperity into the dough with every turn – creates more than food; it creates magic that you can share.

Fermentation is another mystical process. The transformation of cabbage into sauerkraut or grapes into wine is a type of alchemy, harnessing the life force of these ingredients, watching them change form and increase in both nutritional and magical potency. Fermentation can be seen as a metaphor for personal transformation and growth.

Crafting magical meals for the seasonal festivals holds a special place in preparing for rituals. Each festival offers an opportunity to honour the cycle of the seasons. Creating dishes that align with these energies – be it a sun-themed cake at Midsummer or a hearty stew at Samhain – helps to attune oneself to the rhythms of nature.

Reflection questions
What did you learn about food preparation, growing up?
How would you like to transform your relationship with food and cooking?
What new recipes and cooking methods are you eager to try?
How does kitchen witchery resonate with the magical practices?
How might you integrate more kitchen witchery into rituals or into your everyday life?

NUTRITION AND THE INTERCONNECTED WEB OF KITCHEN WITCHERY

In the sacred space of the kitchen, we find ourselves at the intersection of nourishment, magic, and the intricate cycles of life that sustain us. The practice of kitchen witchery invites us to explore deeper perspectives than the status quo. We can see beyond the dominant view of nutrition that is reductionist (reducing food to its components rather than understanding it in its totality). We can embrace the holistic nature of food and our relationship with it to see that every ingredient we use is more than the sum of its parts, it carries various energies and its own history of use – a microcosm of the interconnected world we inhabit.

Whole foods such as a single apple, for instance, are not merely a source of carbohydrates or fibre, but a fruit born of the complete ecosystem within a tree, of the sunlight, soil, water, and the careful tending of both human hands and the unseen forces of nature. When we approach our culinary crafts with this perspective, every meal becomes an opportunity to commune with the earth and to weave our intentions into being.

To understand the magic of whole foods, it can help to reckon with the allure of processed alternatives. Ultra processed foods have been around for only a short time, approximately the past hundred or so years. I'm not going to be weird and judgemental about processed foods. To deny them completely can be another form of unconsciousness, and to judge people for their consumption is just another way of giving away our power in an attempt to "lord-it" over others, which in itself is a self-defeating task.

I do not follow any particular food dogmas in their totality because it's important for me to hold some scepticism, to break rules whenever they don't make sense for me, and to acknowledge diverse perspectives rather than saying there is "one right way" of doing anything. While paleo diets and so on can be quite restrictive and extreme, there is a drop of truth to be found within the notion that our physical evolution has not caught up to our modern food system.

Our bodies, shaped by millennia of evolution – primarily foraging, fishing, and hunting for food – are naturally drawn to flavours and energy sources that were once rare in the wild. Salt suggests the presence of minerals, tangy flavours hint at vitamin content we need, and even bitter and pungent flavours present in some of our foods can be indications of important micronutrients and are helpful for digestion too. Sweet tastes in the wild often signalled the presence of minerals like chromium and also suggested safe and energy-dense foods crucial for survival. Fats and proteins, essential for our bodies but often scarce, were obviously prized for their ability to sustain us through lean times.

In our modern world, where these once-rare nutrients are available in abundance, particularly processed carbohydrate-dense foods playing on taste profiles which were so rare and valuable in the wild, we now find ourselves grappling with biological impulses at odds with our current reality. The disconnection of ultra-processed foods, engineered to hit these primal taste preferences, appeals to our ancient instincts while they tend to lack the complex nutritional profiles and magical energies of whole ingredients.

THE PARADOX OF MODERN FOOD CULTURE

Historically, access to processed and refined foods was a mark of wealth and status. The ability to eat breads made of wheat separated into fine, white flour or sugar refined into pure crystals was a luxury reserved for the elite. Paradoxically, in many contemporary societies, we see now the most processed foods are being consumed by those who often cannot afford more nutritious options.

Today, it is often the wealthy who seek out simpler, more whole foods – heirloom vegetables, ancient grains, and traditionally prepared dishes. This shift reflects a growing awareness of the nutritional problems with overly-manufactured foods, yet it is a bizarre reversal of the trends for much of human history where only the wealthy could afford processed foods.

The industrialisation of our food system, while solving many problems of scarcity and distribution, has also created a painful disconnection between people and their food. Many of us no longer know where our food comes from, how it was grown, or who tended it. This disconnection extends beyond just knowledge – it impacts our magical and spiritual relationship with what we eat.

In kitchen witchery, this disconnection can be seen as a form of magical challenge. When we're unaware of the journey our food has taken to reach us, we miss opportunities to infuse our meals with intention and appreciation. We may fail to recognise the inherent magical properties of our ingredients, seeing them instead as mere commodities.

This pathology of disconnection manifests in various ways – from the prevalence of diet cultures that demonise certain foods, to the environmental impacts of large-scale agriculture that prioritises profit over sustainability. Despite all this, we have the opportunity to heal this disconnection in some small way through our practices, reconnecting with the magic inherent in our food.

Whole foods do not always need to be expensive. They can be foraged, swapped with neighbours, and shared in countless ways through community connections. In cities it is harder to access these kinds of connections where it's rare for those around us to have gardens, but little by little, step by step, we can work our magic of reconnection.

Many people I know have a dream of buying some land and building a community, however you don't have to wait for the ideal situation to connect. Getting to know like-minded people who live locally to you is a wonderful place to start. Even if you live in an apartment, you can make sourdough and other fermented foods in abundance and share or swap them with other people nearby. Joining in with local community gardening allotment gardens can be a wonderful thing to do if you can't grow food at home. There are many systems being set up all the time for community connection and food production, such as land-sharing with people who have land but no time to garden, foraging in the wilder areas around us, and participating in alternative economic networks like time-banking.

A HOLISTIC VIEW OF NUTRITION

While understanding the basic components of our food can be helpful, it's key to approach nutrition from a holistic perspective that reflects and honours the complexity of whole foods in nature. The reductionist view that categorises foods simply as "proteins", "fats", or "carbohydrates" fails to capture the intricate interconnections of many kinds of nutrients and energies present in whole ingredients. For instance, beans are often labelled as "protein" but also provide complex carbohydrates, fibre, vita-mins, and minerals, and each kind of bean has its own history within food traditions. Avocados, typically seen as a "fat", contain a wealth of other nutrients including potassium, vitamin K, and various antioxidants, and the most luxurious creamy texture of any fruit! We could try to assemble all the components of an avocado but they'd never add up to the fabulous whole that grows on trees with such ease and glory.

In magical terms, holistic views allow us to tap into the greater poten-tial foods, but as a general principle here are some properties of macronu-trients:

- Protein rich foods, like legumes, nuts, and many animal products, represent strength and endurance in magical practices. They can be used in spells for protection and grounding.

- Carbohydrate rich foods, like fruits, starchy vegetables, and grains, are associated with quick energy and can be used in rituals for communi-cation and joy.

- Fat and oil rich foods like nuts, seeds, and some animal products, are linked to abundance and protection in kitchen witchery.

However, rather than focusing on these macronutrients in isolation, consider the whole food and its overall energy. A potato, for example, is not just a source of carbohydrates, but carries the grounding energy of the earth, the vitality of the sun, and the nurturing power of water.

THE ILLUSION OF COMPLETE UNDERSTANDING

In our quest to understand the world around us, modern science has made remarkable strides, particularly in the field of nutrition. The discovery of vitamins, the mapping of metabolic pathways, and the identification of essential nutrients have all contributed to our knowledge of how food interacts with our bodies. However, this reductionist approach to nutrition, while valuable, has also led to some unintended consequences and misconceptions.

The attempt to demystify food through scientific analysis has, paradoxically, created its own set of myths and delusions:

- By breaking down foods into their component parts, we've fallen into the trap of believing that we can fully understand a food by knowing its nutrient profile. This overlooks the complex interactions between nutrients and the presence of yet-undiscovered compounds.
- The isolation of nutrients has led to the belief that we can replace whole foods with pills and powders, ignoring the synergistic effects of consuming nutrients in their natural state.
- Calorie counting and macro-tracking have become widespread, reducing the complex act of nourishment to a numbers game. This approach often neglects the quality of food, its energetic properties, and the context in which it's consumed.
- The identification of nutrients with specific health benefits has led to the marketing of "super foods," often ignoring the fact that a varied, balanced diet of whole foods is more beneficial than relying on a few "miraculous" ingredients.
- Neglect of traditional wisdom has eroded our connectedness with food. In the pursuit of scientific validation, we've often dismissed traditional food knowledge and practices that have sustained cultures for millennia.

This reductionist view, while providing valuable insights, has contributed to our disconnection from food. It has led us away from seeing food as a holistic part of our environment and ourselves, and towards viewing it as a collection of disparate chemical compounds.

We have the opportunity to reclaim the mystery and magic of food without dismissing scientific knowledge. We can integrate scientific understanding with traditional wisdom and personal intuition, creating a more holistic and balanced approach to nourishment.

By acknowledging the paradox of both the value and limitations of reductionist science, we open ourselves to a deeper, more nuanced understanding of food. In our magical practice, we can use scientific knowledge as a tool, while always remembering that the whole is greater than the sum of its parts. Just as a spell is more than a list of ingredients, food is more than its nutrient profile. It's a living connection to the earth, a carrier of energy, and a potential for transformation – both physical and spiritual.

RECONNECTING THROUGH MAGICAL PRACTICE

Kitchen witchery offers us a path to reconnect with our food, the earth, and ourselves. By approaching our culinary practices as magical acts, we can heal the disconnection created by modern food systems and nourish ourselves holistically.

Here are some ways to incorporate this holistic, magical approach into your kitchen practice:

Ingredient Selection: When choosing ingredients, consider not just their nutritional content, but their origin, growing conditions, and the energies they carry. Locally grown, seasonal produce often carries the most vital energy of your immediate environment (if you have access to it).

Ritual food preparation: Transform cooking into a ritual. As you wash vegetables, visualise cleansing away unnecessary energies. When chopping, focus on releasing the vital energy of the ingredient into your dish.

Intentional cooking: Infuse your dishes with specific intentions. A hearty stew with root vegetables could be a spell for grounding and stability, while a vibrant salad with leafy greens might be used to promote vitality and growth.

Appreciation and celebrations: Before eating, take a moment to express appreciation for your food, acknowledging all the seen and unseen forces that brought it to your plate and celebrating the meal.

Seasonal eating: Where possible, align your diet with the turning of the wheel of the year. This practice helps attune you to natural cycles and the energies of each season.

In embracing a holistic approach to food and kitchen witchery, we open ourselves to a deeper, more magical relationship with what we eat. By moving beyond reductionist views of nutrition and reconnecting with the inherent magic of whole foods, we can transform our kitchens into sacred spaces of nourishment, healing, and magical practice.

Each ingredient carries its own unique blend of nutrients and energies. Vegetables draw their power from earth, sun, and water. Fruits embody the sweetness and abundance of nature. Grains represent the cycles of planting and harvest. Animal products, for those who choose to use them, carry the energy of the creatures they come from. They are often traditionally associated with grounding and strength. While many spiritual traditions have certain animal proteins that are avoided, and many people have ethical frameworks that prohibit meat-eating, it can be helpful to consider what makes sense intuitively for you.

Some bodies function better with animal proteins and struggle to digest vegetable proteins like legumes. People often have deep-seated reasons for eating or not eating particular things. Many of us have food traumas around certain foods which makes eating them painful in some way. There is no ethically perfect way to eat. As living beings, all our actions have consequences and we are always making compromises regardless of how conscious our eating is. Judgement against other people's eating practices, while sometimes amusing, only casts more shadows and bolsters our sense of superiority in a disconnecting way which is ultimately unhelpful.

Regardless of your dietary preferences, it is important to consider the shadows of the food we eat – the life-death-life cycle present in all consumption, whether it is through the death of the grain upon harvest, the agricultural practices of monocropping that destroy biodiversity, or the farming of animals with greater or lesser degrees of freedom and suitable conditions. I will repeat that for most of us, there is no perfect ethical food, there is only a journey of deepening awareness.

There is no way of escaping the cycles of death and life, but in our exploration and growing awareness of the shadows of our consumption, we can make choices that allow us to be more in integrity with our values, but financial limitations need not be a reason to make ourselves guilty and diminish our power and worth. For instance, buying the nice free-range eggs if our budget allows can feel better than the cheaper eggs, and purchasing them from a local farm might feel even better, but we are all doing our best based on the situations we find ourselves in, and if finances are tight the last thing we need is guilt. Good conscience with food should not be reserved for the wealthy, who tend to have a far higher carbon footprint at any rate.

VEGETABLES

Vegetables draw their energies from the earth, sun, and water, making them potent bearers of life force. They are essential not only for their nutritional value but also for their varied magical properties, for instance:

- Root vegetables (carrots, beets, potatoes): Grounding and nurturing, they are linked to the Earth element and are great for stability and grounding rituals.
- Leafy greens (spinach, kale, lettuce): Associated with health and vitality. They can be used to promote physical health and spiritual growth.
- Alliums (onions, garlic): Protective and purifying, these are used to ward off negative energies and encourage physical and spiritual protection.
- Cruciferous vegetables (broccoli, cauliflower): Linked to protection and strength, useful in spells for physical health and endurance.

Creating dishes that combine both proteins and vegetables allows for a balance of energies that can align with your magical intentions. A hearty stew with beef (for strength) and potatoes (for grounding) can be a spell for stability and resilience. A salad with beans (for healing) and leafy greens (for vitality) might be used in rituals to enhance overall well-being and energy.

As you prepare your meals, consider the energies each ingredient brings. Washing, chopping, and cooking vegetables can be seen as a way of releasing their energies, while cooking proteins might be viewed as an act of empowering or activating their inherent strengths.

Incorporating a thoughtful balance of proteins and vegetables not only contributes to a well-rounded diet but also weaves magical intentions throughout your daily life.

DEMONISING AND DEIFYING: FATS, OILS, AND CARBOHYDRATES

Nothing has been more demonised in modern nutrition in the past century than fats and carbohydrates (both of which were highly prized, valued, and spiritually important in most of human history!). Fats and carbohydrate sources are important in balanced nutrition.

Carbohydrates are the body's primary source of energy, fuelling our physical activities and cognitive functions. This does not mean we primarily need to eat carbs. When we eat other forms of energy like protein and fat, it must be broken down into a carbohydrate form by our bodies in order to be utilised. In magical terms, carbs are associated with the element of Air and can be used in spells for quick energy boosts and communication.

Foods high in carbs like fruits and grains, provide us with energy and are often associated with love, happiness, and abundance. Carbohydrates were rare in the wild which is why sweet flavours are so desirable for many people. Here are some ways you can work with carbohydrate rich foods in your kitchen witchery practices:

- Grains: Bread, pasta, rice, and other grains are staples in many spells and rituals. They are symbols of prosperity and abundance. For instance, baking bread is a literal act of manifestation, each loaf embodying intentions of growth and nourishment.
- Fruits: Each fruit carries its own magical properties. Apples, for instance, are used for love and healing spells, while oranges can be used to attract success and joy. Incorporating fruits into your diet can bring a sweet, energising boost to your day and your magical workings.

- Vegetables: Starchy root vegetables like potatoes and carrots are grounding and protective, providing boosts of energy.

Fats play a crucial role in diet and magic by providing energy reserves, protecting organs, and aiding in the absorption of vitamins. In magical practices, fats are associated with the element of Earth, providing grounding, abundance, and protection, for instance.

In witchcraft, butter has been used for its protective qualities. It can be anointed on thresholds to keep away negative energies or added to recipes to promote peace and comfort within the home. Different oils can be selected for their specific energies; olive oil for peace and purity, coconut oil for protection and purity, and sesame oil for financial abundance.

As you consume these foods, visualise their energies nourishing not just your body but also your spirit. Reflect on the properties of the ingredients, and let their magic empower you throughout the day. Carbohydrates and fats are more than just components of our diet – they are magical allies that bring energy, protection, and balance into our lives. By choosing these ingredients with intention and using them in our cooking, we turn every meal into a ritual, enhancing our magical practices and our connection to the natural world. By facing the shadows within our food system we also bring them, more and more, into the light of awareness. There is no perfectly healthy or ethical way to eat, we are all doing our best in this murky world. Be gentle with yourself.

MICRONUTRITION – CRAVINGS AND THEIR INTERPRETATIONS

Understanding our cravings can be an art of interpreting the body's subtle language. These desires are messages from the body, telling us what it needs.

Craving for sweetness might not simply be a call for sugar, but perhaps a deeper need for minerals like chromium, essential for blood sugar regulation, or magnesium, crucial for hundreds of biochemical reactions. This craving cannot ultimately be satisfied with processed sweets, but it can be with whole complex foods like mineral-rich fresh berries, sweet potatoes, or even cinnamon. Naturally sweet foods often contain chromium whereas processed sugary foods are unlikely to.

Similarly, a longing for salty flavours might indicate an electrolyte imbalance and perhaps a desire for grounding, rather than a need for sodium alone. Instead of reaching for processed salty snacks, we might use foods seasoned with mineral-rich salts or naturally salty foods like seaweed and other seafoods, rich in iodine and magnesium. Or we can enjoy the processed snacks while contemplating how else we might add to our nutrition! Feeling bad about our snacking is not going to help, so allow intuition to guide you towards the gentle nourishing choices that meet your emotional and physical needs. These choices not only nourish the body but can be imbued with intentions of balance and grounding in our magical work.

Cravings for fatty or oily foods could signal a need for essential fatty acids or fat-soluble vitamins. Here, avocados, nuts, seeds, or fatty fish like salmon can provide not just nutrition but also magical energies of abundance and fluidity. If you make sure you have enough whole nourishing oily and fatty foods, you will feel more satisfied than trying to deny yourself of fats and oils. Fats are important for satiety, for instance, "rabbit starvation", a condition named by Arctic explorer Vilhjalmur Stefansson in the early 20th century to describe the extreme gnawing hunger that can present when people eat only lean meats like rabbit without enough fats. The condition arises because the human body has limited capacity to metabolise protein in the absence of other macronutrients leading to serious health complications if not addressed. Fats also slow down the release of glucose from sugars into the blood, stabilising energy levels, ultimately decreasing excessive sugar cravings, and inhibiting the vicious cycle of sugar highs and lows.

The common desire for chocolate often masks a need for magnesium, chromium, antioxidants, or mood-boosting compounds. Dark chocolate and raw cacao products, rich in these nutrients, can satisfy this craving while offering a potent magical ally for the powers of indulgence and joy.

Cravings for starchy foods might indicate a need for emotional comfort or even serotonin production. Whole grains like quinoa or brown rice, along with legumes, can address these needs while magically representing abundance and grounding. The urge for something crunchy or crispy, often linked to stress or frustration, can be met with less-processed food alternatives like toasted seeds, which still allow for the release of tension. Alternately, we can indulge in crunchy crisps and chips and align ourselves in a state of pure enjoyment. Whatever you choose, you can magically make the most of your eating, whatever form it is in, rather than using it simply as a numbing escapism (though doing that can be great sometimes too!).

Spicy food cravings, potentially signalling a need to stimulate metabolism or release endorphins, can be addressed with fresh chillies, ginger, or turmeric, each carrying fiery magical properties of transformation and protection. If we shy away from spicy foods, we may be avoiding the circulation of particular emotions. We can gently experiment with increasing our tolerance for these foods in ways that feel right for us.

As we work with these cravings, we develop a more intuitive approach to nourishment. This might involve mindful eating practices, where we pause before consuming to ask our body what it truly needs. Body scanning can help us locate areas of tension or discomfort that might correlate with specific nutritional deficits. Some practitioners find value in relaxed journalling processes and meditations which can help us to reveal subconscious messages about the body's needs.

For those inclined towards divination, pendulum work or other tools can be used to communicate directly with the body's wisdom, asking about potential deficiencies or imbalances. Intuitive cooking becomes a magical act in itself, allowing us to be guided by instinct in our ingredient choices. Considering elemental associations can provide insight into emotional or energetic imbalances underlying our cravings. Moon phase tracking might reveal patterns in our body's rhythms and needs that align with lunar cycles. Paying attention to which herbs or crystals we feel drawn to can often correlate with specific nutritional or energetic needs, adding another layer to our kitchen witchery practice.

As we deepen this practice of intuitive, craving-conscious kitchen witchery, we may find our relationship with food transforming. Our cravings might shift towards foods that are more nurturing, emotionally, physically, and spiritually as we connect more deeply with our bodies, fostering a deeper bond with the earth and its rhythms.

THE ALCHEMY OF MAGICAL INFUSIONS

In the sacred space of your kitchen, the art of crafting infusions becomes a powerful act of magic. These potent elixirs can be potions, carrying the essence of your intentions and the spirit of the ingredients used. As we create these infusions, we tap into the ancient wisdom traditions who practiced various forms of plant medicine and herbalism, in deference of the cycles of nature, utilising the transformative power of our own will.

Infusions are a gateway to connecting with the natural world. Each herb, spice, fruit, or flower we use carries its own unique energy signature, connecting us to the earth's rhythms and the elemental forces that govern our world. As we work with these ingredients, we're not just preparing culinary delights, but also creating potent magic.

The modern world, with its emphasis on scientific rationalism, has largely stripped away the mystical aura that once surrounded our daily rituals and consumptions. What our ancestors might have revered as magical elixirs, we now casually refer to as coffee or tea. This demystification, while bringing undeniable benefits in terms of understanding and reproducibility, has also diminished our connection to the deeper, spiritual aspects of our consumption habits.

If the ancients were to observe our contemporary society, they would likely be awestruck by what they'd perceive as ubiquitous magic. Our technology, our medicine, and even our everyday beverages would appear as manifestations of incredible power. They might see our morning coffee ritual not merely as the consumption of a caffeinated beverage, but as a daily invocation of energy and clarity. Our glass of wine over dinner might be viewed not just as fermented grape juice with a percentage alcohol content, but as a potion for relaxation and social bonding. In the eyes of our ancestors, we would be a society of powerful mages, casually wielding powers beyond their wildest dreams.

Paradoxically, in our quest for scientific understanding, we've lost touch with this sense of wonder and magic. It's time to reclaim this perspective, not by rejecting our scientific knowledge, but by integrating it with a renewed sense of reverence and intentionality.

By re-enchanting our world, we can infuse our daily lives with greater meaning and purpose. This doesn't mean abandoning reason, but rather expanding our perception to embrace both the rational and the mystical. When we approach our morning tea or coffee as a potion, imbued with intention and respect for the plants that created it, we transform a mundane act into a sacred ritual. This shift in perspective can extend to all aspects of our lives, helping us to see the extraordinary in the ordinary and to live with greater awareness and appreciation for the complex, interconnected web of life that surrounds us.

General Preparation Guidelines

Sacred space: Before beginning, cleanse your workspace. This could involve smoke clearing with incense or herbs, ringing a bell, lighting a candle, or simply taking a moment to set your intention for the work ahead.

Cleanliness: Use sterilised equipment. This physical cleanliness not only promotes food safety, it also mirrors the process of creating sacred space within the bottling of each infusion. You can sterilise glass jars and lids with boiling water or in an oven heated to 110 degrees Celsius (230f) or ideally both boil them in the water then put them in the oven to dry. Infusions with a strong alcohol or vinegar component are already more naturally protected from pathogens than infused waters or syrups.

Sacred times: Consider aligning your infusion-making with relevant times of the day. For instance, if calling upon the powers of the sun is relevant, choose midday as an ideal time for preparation. If you're creating something more relaxing, the twilight hours might be more suitable. Consider taking into account the lunar cycles or other planetary energies.

New moon for new beginnings, the waxing or full moon for amplification, waning moon for intuition, new beginnings, or relinquishing that which no longer serves you.

Intention setting: Throughout the process, focus on your magical intention. You may wish to whisper incantations, visualise your desired outcome, or simply imbue the preparation with your energy.

Appreciation and celebration: Always thank the plants and elements for their contributions to your magical work.

INGREDIENTS FOR MAGICAL INFUSIONS:

When creating infusions, think about what you want to achieve and select your herbs, spices, and other elements accordingly. Just like with other magical associations, the meaning will be different depending on your own experiences, so choose what makes sense for you. The following ingredients could be used in various combinations depending on your desired magical outcome:

Basil - Attracts love, wealth, and protection.
Mint - Promotes energy and communication.
Rosemary - Offers protection and boosts memory and fidelity.
Lavender - Brings peace, purification, and calm.
Thyme - Increases courage and is good for banishing and purifying rituals.
Sage - Used for purification and protection.
Dandelion - Aids in divination, spirit calling, and wishes.
Rose Petals - Encourages love, healing, and psychic powers.
Cinnamon - Attracts success, healing, and protection.
Ginger - Amplifies success, power, and money spells.
Black Pepper - Offers protection and wards off negative energy.
Vanilla - Enhances love, lust, and mental powers.
Juniper - Protects against theft, attracts love, and wards off accidents.
Chilli Pepper - Used for fidelity, hex breaking, and love spells.
Garlic - Provides protection, healing, and strength.
Anise - Helps increase psychic abilities and is protective.
Cloves - Drives away hostile and negative forces, attracts riches.

Cardamom - Enhances love and lust spells.
Fennel - Provides protection, healing, and purification.
Coriander - Attracts love and cures illness.
Nettle - Dispels darkness and fear, strengthens willpower.
Chamomile - Promotes relaxation and aids in prosperity.
Bay Leaves - Provide wisdom, protection, and psychic powers.
Lemon Balm - Used for love spells and mental healing.
Hibiscus - Enhances divination and clairvoyance.
Oregano - Brings happiness, strength, and vitality.
Parsley - Used for purification and protection.
Liquorice Root - for power and potency.
Eucalyptus - Enhances healing and protection.
Peppermint - Purifies and stimulates the conscious mind.
Calendula - Promotes psychic dreams and protection.
Star Anise - Increases psychic awareness and luck.
Tarragon - Encourages health and protection during travels.
Marjoram - Protects homes and brings happiness.

PREPARING HERBAL OIL INFUSIONS

Herbal oils capture the essence of plants, becoming potent magical tools for anointing, cooking, or ritual use. Magically infused oils bring a gentle magic to our everyday cooking, transforming your kitchen into a space of quiet enchantment.

Creating magical oils is about connection, just as oil is a connective substance. Oil in a pan will help conduct heat, making things cook more easily and become crispy. Oil in a salad will help to break down the cells of plants, connecting us with the nutrients that are more available.

Creating magically infused oils is an opportunity to recognise the inherent properties of herbs and plants, working with them respectfully to enhance their power and bring it into our lives. This kind of practice doesn't require any flashy spells or dramatic transformations, it can simply be mirrored in the gentle infusing of our daily lives with purpose and awareness.

As you continue of this kitchen witchery journey, you may begin to see your pantry in a new light. That bottle of olive oil? It's a potential carrier of solar energy. Those dried herbs in your spice rack? Each one holds unique properties waiting to be unlocked. Choose ingredients with intention and incorporate your creations into your daily rituals such as a rosemary-infused oil for mental clarity, or a lavender oil for peaceful sleep.

Carrier oils:

When choosing a carrier oil, consider both its practical properties and its energetic associations. The oil you select will become the foundation of your magical infusion, carrying and amplifying the properties of the herbs and your intentions.

Olive Oil: A versatile staple, olive oil carries the essence of the sun. It's rich in antioxidants and vitamin E, making it nourishing for both culinary and skincare uses. Associated with peace, healing, and purification. It's an excellent all-purpose carrier for magical infusions.

Grapeseed Oil: A light, almost odourless oil that's easily absorbed. It's associated with Venus and is often used in beauty and love magic. Grapeseed oil is ideal for delicate herb infusions where you want the plant's properties to shine without competing scents.

Sunflower Oil: As its name suggests, sunflower oil embodies solar energy. It's light, nutrient-rich, and beneficial for skin health. Use it in infusions aimed at boosting confidence, vitality, or success.

Coconut Oil: Solid at room temperature but quick to melt, coconut oil is prized for its moisturising properties and light, tropical scent. It's linked to the moon's energy and is often used in love and purification magic and for body care or sensual rituals.

Avocado Oil: A rich, heavy oil that's deeply moisturising. Avocado oil resonates with earth energy and is often used in grounding and abundance magic. It's ideal for infusions meant for deep healing or connection to nature.

Almond Oil: Light and easily absorbed, almond oil is rich in vitamin E and has a subtle, nutty aroma. It's connected to Mercury and mental acuity but is also lovely on the skin. Use it for infusions meant to enhance communication, learning, or dream work.

Jojoba Oil: Though technically a liquid wax, jojoba closely resembles our skin's natural sebum. It's ideal for facial oils and hair care. Associated with youth and beauty, it's excellent for skin-focused infusions for self-love, confidence, and rejuvenation. Jojoba oil is not usually eaten, unlike the other oils, and is more suited to home-made skin care and anointing oils rather than for internal consumption.

Choose ingredients and combinations that feel right for you, and which align with your intentions, for instance:

· Abundance: Olive oil with basil, bay leaves, and orange zest

· Immunity and intellect: Sunflower oil with rosemary, thyme, and garlic

· Clarity: Grapeseed oil with sage, lemon peel, and peppercorns

Basic instructions for oil infusions

Ingredients:

- 2 cups carrier oil (like olive oil or other skin-safe plant oils)

- 1/2 cup fresh herbs or 1/4 cup dried herbs (chosen for their magical properties)

Instructions:

1. On your altar or sacred space, lay out your ingredients. You may wish to hold your hands over them, charging them with your intention.
2. For cold infusion (preserving the subtle energies of delicate herbs): Combine oil and herbs in a clean glass jar. Seal and store in a cool, dark place for one lunar cycle (about 29.5 days). Give it a good shake every day or two, while visualising your intention.
3. For heat infusion (for roots and barks, or to quicken the process): Gently heat the oil and herbs in a double boiler or saucepan on a very low heat stirring clockwise to draw in energy. Heat this up to 50 degrees Celsius for at least half an hour, but potentially up to three hours. Strain through cheesecloth into a sterilised dark glass bottle.
4. Store in a cool, dark place, using within 3-6 months for optimal magical potency.

ENCHANTED VINEGARS

Vinegars act as magical catalysts, accelerating change and transformation in your spellwork and cuisine. The sharp bite of vinegar becomes a vessel for transformation. Infused vinegars are potent elixirs, catalysts of change that break down the old and bring in the new.

In the alchemical laboratory of your kitchen, vinegar becomes a magical medium, its acidity a force that extracts and amplifies the essence of herbs, fruits, and flowers. Each bottle of infused vinegar is a spell in liquid form, carrying the power to cleanse, transform, and enliven both your culinary creations and your magical workings.

Vinegar has long been revered for its preservative and medicinal properties. Each creation is an opportunity to bottle your intentions and create change, from fiery chilli-infused blends that ignite motivation and boost circulation, to delicate lavender infusions that soothe and heal.

It is up to you which kind of vinegars you use for infusions. Most herbalists seem to prefer apple cider vinegar as a base , while other practitioners may prefer the more neutral base of white vinegar. A wine vinegar may resonate with fun and bounty, or vinegar derived from a particular fruit like raspberries might make deliciously sweet magic. There may be times where you want to use a rich balsamic for a particularly potent spell – and a tasty dressing. The combinations are endless and they're really up to you, for instance:

- Protection and immunity: Apple cider vinegar with garlic, chilli flakes, and thyme
- Prosperity: White wine vinegar with mint, basil, and cinnamon stick
- Healing: Apple cider vinegar with oregano, rosemary, and ginger
- Luxury: Balsamic vinegar with mustard, cumin seeds, and orange peel

Basic instructions for infused vinegars

Ingredients:

- 2 cups organic vinegar (apple cider for healing, white wine for clarity, balsamic for grounding)

- 1 cup fresh herbs, flowers, or fruit (chosen for their magical correspondences)

Instructions:

1. Place herbs/fruit in a sterilised glass jar, speak aloud the qualities you wish to infuse.

2. Pour vinegar over ingredients, ensuring they're fully submerged. Seal with a lid.

3. Store in a dark place for 2-4 weeks, shaking or turning every few days while focusing on your intention.

4. Strain and bottle the charged vinegar, and keep it in your pantry to use in cooking and other magical activities.

THE MAGIC OF ALCOHOLIC INFUSIONS

We can transform alcohol into potions, infusing them with the essence of herbs, fruits, and our own magical intent. The warmth of spiced rum can kindle our passion and warm our hearts. The sweet embrace of fruit liqueurs can nurture love and abundance. Our magically infused spirits can also make great libations when offered to the gods at seasonal festivals and in other key rituals and spells. Remember, with great power comes great responsibility. These creations are to be respected and enjoyed mindfully, their magic savoured in balance rather than abused in excess. These elixirs require patience; allow time for essences to meld and magic to develop fully, often over weeks or even months.

Crafting magical alcohol infusions begins with selecting the right base spirit. Vodka's neutrality makes it ideal for showcasing delicate herbs and fruits. Brandy and cognac offer rich, warming notes perfect for spices and berries. Rum complements tropical ingredients and adds depth to spiced blends. Gin's botanical profile enhances herbal infusions, while whiskey provides a robust foundation for stronger flavours. Even grain alcohol can serve as a potent base for tinctures and bitters. Each spirit lends its unique character to the infusion, influencing both taste and magical properties.

Divination essence: Vodka with star anise, lemon balm, and vanilla bean

Courage whiskey: Whiskey with cinnamon stick, cloves, and orange zest

Abundance rum: Dark rum with dried figs, nutmeg, and allspice berries

Romantic brandy: Brandy with fresh cherries, rose petals, and pink peppercorns

Ingredients:

- 1 litre organic spirit (vodka for purity, rum for sweetness, brandy for luxury)
- 1-2 cups of your choice of herbs, spices, or fruit aligned with your magical purpose (for essences use a higher concentration compared to liquors which might only use 1-2 cups per litre of alcohol)
- citric acid or lemon juice (for a tangy flavour)
- sugar or other sweetener such as honey, maple syrup, or stevia to taste (optional)

Instructions:

1. Begin at twilight, when the veil between worlds is thin. Cleanse your space with incense.

2. Combine ingredients in a clean glass jar, speaking an incantation over each ingredient as you add it.

3. Seal and store in a place of power in your home (near your altar, in a sacred corner) for one full moon cycle.

4. Shake or stir daily, visualising your intention merging with the liquid.

5. Strain on the night of the next full moon, bottling under moonlight.

SYRUPS OF SWEETNESS AND LIGHT

Magical syrups are concentrated potions of sweetness and intention. These versatile concoctions can be used to sweeten beverages, drizzle over desserts, mix with infused vinegars and oils to create extra-potent magical vinaigrettes, or they can add a magical touch to cocktails and ritual offerings. Syrups are simple – a mixture of sugar and water infused with herbs, fruits, flowers, or spices. This simplicity means they're powerful vehicles for magical intent.

The process of creating magical syrups allows for deep connection with your ingredients. As you simmer herbs in sweetened water, you're not just extracting flavours, but also the essence and energy of the plants – from rose petals for love spells to cinnamon for prosperity.

My favourite syrups to make are elderflower infusions in the spring. A syrup is a lovely way to store the potent floral energy of elderflowers, often mixed with citrus and sometimes spices or rose petals. Elderflowers are uplifting and regenerative. Bottling their fragrant energy in the spring means I have the power to enjoy their delight all through the year in beverages and deserts.

Remember that the act of creating these syrups is itself a form of magic. The focus and intention you bring to the process infuses the syrup with your personal energy, enhancing its magical efficacy. As with all magical crafts, clarity of purpose and respect for the ingredients are key to creating potent and delicious magical syrups. Choose what makes sense for you, for instance:

· Dream enhancing: lavender, chamomile, and lemon balm
· Energy boosting: ginger, lemon zest, and rosemary
· Processing: cinnamon, nutmeg, and vanilla
· Creativity: mint, lemongrass, and cardamom

Basic syrup instructions

Ingredients:

Either a ratio of 2 cups sugar to 1 cup water (for storage at room temperature unopened and in the fridge for longer)

Or a ratio of 1 cup water to one cup sugar (if storing in the fridge for up to a month)

- your chosen quantity of fresh herbs or fruit and/or spices. You may want to use 2-4 tablespoons of these ingredients per cup of syrup, selected for their magical properties

- citric acid or lemon juice to taste – adds a delicious tangy flavour (take account of the liquid component if using lemon juice and subtract the same amount from the water you're adding to maintain liquid ratios)

Instructions:

1. Rinse your herbs and fruit, slicing to increase exposed surface area. Combine your fruit with water and leave to soak for at least one hour. Keep track of the quantity of water you have added!

2. Combine sugar in your desired ratio (e.g., if you've added 2 cups of water and want a longer lasting syrup, add 4 cups of sugar). As you combine sugar and water, stir clockwise, chanting or silently focusing on your intention.

3. In a saucepan, bring the mixture to a simmer on a medium heat, stirring regularly. Let the mixture simmer for at least 30 minutes.

4. Remove from heat and strain into sterilised glass bottles or jars while the mixture is still hot, speaking words of appreciation and celebration. Seal while still hot for best preservation.

6. Store in a cool, dark place, or in the fridge.

As with all kitchen witchery, the magic lies not just in the ingredients, but in your intention and the sacred act of creation. As you craft these infusions, you're participating in the revival of ancient traditions, transforming your kitchen into a place of wonder, alchemy, and magic.

STEWS AND SOUPS: THE CAULDRON'S BREW

The simmering cauldron is the heart of the kitchen witch's realm. Within its depths, we blend the earth's bounty and stir in a dash of magic, crafting potions that nourish both body and soul. Stews and soups are particularly special; they are the embodiment of transformation, where ingredients mingle and morph, imparting their essence and energy into a harmonious whole.

Creating a stew is akin to crafting a spell; it's about intention, patience, and the alchemy of ingredients. Begin with a robust base – perhaps a bone broth or a rich vegetable stock for grounding and protection. You may wish to start by frying onions and perhaps garlic for their protective properties, then layer in protein sources and root vegetables for grounding and potatoes for sustenance. You may wish to stir in some barley or beans – symbols of abundance and prosperity – to fortify your spell. As your stew bubbles gently, envision it's magic building, perhaps it is forming a protective shield around all who partake of it, nourishing the soul, uplifting the spirit or something more specific.

Soups, with their soothing qualities, are perfect for spells of healing and emotional peace. Brewing your own broth can be empowering; adding leafy greens like spinach or kale can draw in healing energies. You may wish to add herbs like parsley for vibrant energy and celery for mental clarity. As you stir your soup you can envision it fulfilling its purpose, for instance, washing away ailments and discord, bringing health and harmony to those who sip it. To enhance the healing power, a squeeze of lemon and some finely grated zest can brighten flavour and add potency.

Each season offers unique ingredients and energies that can be harnessed in your culinary creations. In autumn, a pumpkin soup can be especially powerful for grounding, preparing us for the introspective winter months. In winter, a hearty bean or beef stew can help conserve energy and provide warmth. Spring soups might feature fresh seasonal vegetables like tender asparagus, symbolising new beginnings and rejuvenation. Summer soups with tomatoes and basil can be energising, celebrating the fullness of life.

As you stir your stew or soup, you may want to stir deosil or clockwise, which is traditional for invoking and attracting positive energies. With each stir, you might chant softly, infusing your dish with intentions: May those who eat this soup find peace, may those who share this stew gain strength. Such words elevate your cooking, turning a simple meal into a ritual of enchantment.

For me, the act of browning onions is where magic begins. Each slice through the onion can be seen as a cut through the layers of reality, reaching deeper into the mystical realms. The simple act of cutting onions isn't just preparation, it's a ritual, releasing energies and setting the stage for transformation.

As you slice the onions you may consider this as an act of opening doors, the sharp knife cutting through barriers that separate the mundane from the magical. Tears that spring forth may bring emotions with them, just as change often does. Heat the oil or butter and add your onions, stirring gently, and as they begin to sizzle, their transformation releases sweet, earthy aromas that ground the senses and cleanse the space.

Each step in your cooking process is a part of the alchemy. From the initial sizzle of onions in oil to the final sprinkle of herbs, your kitchen is a sanctuary where the simple act of making soup or stew becomes a magical practice. Let your intuition guide the seasoning, and always taste the food as it cooks to make sure it is on the right track. Is it too sweet? Does the flavour need to be balanced with salt or acidity (e.g., lemon juice or vinegar)? Is it too savoury? Consider adding a drizzle of honey or a sprinkle of brown sugar. Let your spirit infuse the dish with intentions. For instance, health, protection, or prosperity.

MAGICAL TRUFFLES AND ENCHANTED CHOCOLATES

Truffles are obviously magical. These small, rich confections are not just a treat for the taste buds but a potent vessel for magic. Working with chocolate, a powerful ingredient known for its properties of indulgence and happiness, we can craft truffles that delight the senses and carry strong magical intentions.

Preparing the Base: Chocolate Ganache

Start by creating a simple chocolate ganache, which is the heart of your truffle. Heat cream until it's just about to simmer – think of this as bringing your intentions to the surface, ready to be infused into your creation.

For making traditional chocolate truffles, the standard proportion is a 2:1 ratio of chocolate to cream; meaning for every 2 parts chocolate, you use 1 part heavy cream to create a firm ganache suitable for rolling into truffles.

Pour the hot cream over finely chopped chocolate, waiting for a moment before stirring, or use another method of gently melting the chocolate into the cream. Take care as chocolate burns very easily.

As the chocolate melts, visualise your resistance dissolving as your desires begin to form, the heat activating their potential. You may wish to stir in a whisper of butter for smoothness and a pinch of salt to balance the flavours and enhance magical conductivity.

Infusing Flavours and Intentions

Rose and Cardamom Truffles - Melt your chocolate with a crushed cardamom pod and a splash of rosewater. Cardamom for clarity and love, rose for nurturing, love, and spiritual alignment. These truffles are perfect for fostering connections and enhancing emotional understanding.

Lavender and Honey Truffles - Incorporate lavender-infused honey into your ganache. Lavender for peace and tranquillity, honey for sweetness in life and abundance. Ideal for soothing the soul and attracting joy.

Orange Zest and Cinnamon Truffles - Add grated orange zest and a sprinkle of ground cinnamon to your chocolate mixture. Orange for joy and prosperity, cinnamon for success and healing. These truffles are excellent for invigorating the spirit and encouraging success.

Chilli and Dark Chocolate Truffles - For those seeking a bit of magic to ignite passion, mix in some finely chopped chilli with your dark chocolate ganache. Chilli brings vitality and courage, while dark chocolate deepens the connection to the heart.

Mint and Matcha Truffles - Combine ground matcha and a few drops of peppermint extract. Mint for healing and communication, matcha for energy and protection. These are great for refreshing the mind and shielding the spirit.

Forming Your Truffles

Once your ganache is infused, chill it until it's set but pliable. Scoop and roll the ganache into balls, each a perfect capsule of intention. You may wish to coat them in cocoa powder, crushed nuts, coconut, or powdered freeze-dried fruit.

As you roll each truffle, focus on your intentions. Imagine each truffle as a charm, a small but powerful magic circle. When consumed, the magic unfolds, weaving its way through the senses, enchanting from within.

The magic of these truffles lies not just in their flavours or ingredients but in the intention with which they are made. Whether shared with loved ones or offered as a personal treat, these magical truffles are a celebration of the joyful and transformative powers of kitchen witchery.

BAKING AS KITCHEN WITCHERY

Baking is a form of alchemy, a transformation of simple ingredients into something totally different. As we combine flour, water, butter, and yeast, we are not merely creating bread or pastries; we are invoking the ancient magic of transformation and creation.

Baking begins with the basics – flour for sustenance, representing the earth itself; water for life and intuition; stirring invokes air and growth; and heat from the oven is the fire that transforms. Each element is essential, and each corresponds to one of the four classic elements of magic, creating a balance and harmony essential for successful spell work.

Symbolism in Baking

Bread - The simple act of baking bread is rich with symbolism. It represents prosperity, the cycle of life, and the sustenance of the soul. Loaves can be scored with sigils or symbols before baking, infusing them with specific intentions.

Cakes and pastries - Baking cakes and pastries, especially for celebrations, is a way of marking the sacred milestones of life. A birthday cake, for example, is not just a treat; it is a spell for longevity and joy. The act of blowing out candles is a powerful release of energy and intent.

Pies - The crafting of pies, with their circular shape, represents the cycle of life and the turning of the seasons. Filling a pie with seasonal fruits or vegetables honours the bounty of the earth and can be used to celebrate and enhance seasonal festivals.

Baking for Magical Purposes

Love and Attraction - Infuse your bakes with vanilla or rose for love, or add apples and honey to promote attraction and sweetness in a relationship.

Protection and Purification - Incorporate salt or garlic in savoury bakes to create protective barriers for your home and family.

Prosperity and Success - Cinnamon, nutmeg, and allspice are perfect for drawing wealth and success. Incorporate these into bakes when starting new ventures or to boost your finances.

Healing and Wellbeing - Lemon, ginger, and mint can be used in bakes to promote healing and physical health.

As you knead dough or mix batter, focus your intentions. Visualise your dreams coming to life with the rising of the dough or the baking of the cake. When you partake of your baked goods, or share them with others, you are also sharing blessings and magic.

Baking can feed the soul and weave magic into our lives, connecting us to the ancient traditions of hearth and home, binding us to the magical energies of the earth and the transformative power of fire.

MAGICAL SALADS AND VEGETABLE DISHES

Salads might often be seen merely as side dishes but they hold vastly underestimated potential power in their mosaics of textures and colours, of fresh ingredients and complimentary flavours. In the delightful crunch and the bursts of taste we can find the joy of seasonal magic. In kitchen witchery, salads can represent regeneration, embracing the fresh and new.

As you choose ingredients for a salad, think about what each could represent. What is significant about the flavour, texture, or appearance of the ingredient? What would you like it to mean for you? For example, in creating a simple green salad you might choose one of the following (using your own interpretations where you prefer):

· Spinach for strength and protection
· Arugula or rocket to stimulate the mind and body
· Kale for endurance and resilience
· Mixed baby greens for fresh energy and balance
· Iceberg or cos lettuce for crunchy refreshing change

Next, you might select from some of the following ingredients, adding

vibrant colours to your salad, each bringing its own spectrum of nutritional properties and magical energies:
· Tomatoes for passion and courage
· Carrots for encouragement and success
· Capsicum for charm and creativity
· Cucumbers for healing and renewal
· Blueberries for protection and calm
· Beetroot for intuition
· Radishes for altering perceptions and awakening the senses
You may wish to add chopped herbs too, such as:
· Basil for love and wealth
· Mint for travel and clear communication
· Coriander (cilantro) for cleansing and clarity
· Parsley to dispel negativity
· Dill for luck and protection
Cheeses in a salad can act as powerful symbols of culmination and transformation – milk turned into a myriad of flavours and textures, each with its own specific energies, for instance:
· Feta for fresh new beginnings
· Goat cheeses for agility and reaching new heights
· Blue cheeses for enhanced perception
· Parmesan for consolidation of resources and hard-won success
Grains can bring substance to salads, making them more fulfilling and grounding. Their presence in a dish can symbolise abundance and prosperity along with other properties like:
· Quinoa, excellent for overall health and strengthening of spirit (try to find locally grown and sustainable sources!)
· Barley for love and healing
· Farro for endurance
· Wild rice for attraction and attention
Roasting transforms the inherent qualities of fruits and vegetables, enhancing their natural sweetness and complexity:
· Roasted beetroot for grounding and tuning intuition
· Sweet potatoes for grounding and nurturing
· Apples for love and healing
· Pears for longevity and grace
Adding proteins to a salad turns it from a side dish to a main course,

anchoring the salad's energies and making it a complete meal, for example:

- Chicken for courage and endurance
- Salmon for wisdom and abundance
- Tofu or tempeh for resilience and growth
- Eggs for productivity and rebirth

Nuts and seeds add crunch and potency to salads, especially when toasted. They are a bit like the cherry on top of the dessert, only crunchier and more satisfying. Toasting (or pre-soaking) nuts and seeds helps to eliminate the enzyme inhibitors which naturally stop the seeds from sprouting until they're ready. This makes the seeds more digestible, and stops enzyme inhibitors from interfering with the digestion of other things. Symbolically and magically, this is part of the processing – the alchemy – that makes metamorphosis possible.

- Almonds: Known for their ability to promote wisdom and prosperity. Adding toasted almonds to a dish can enhance mental clarity and attract abundance.
- Walnuts: Used for their connection to the intellect and the heart. They are believed to aid in healing and protecting the heart both physically and emotionally.
- Pecans: Associated with money and employment spells. They are excellent for dishes intended to foster career success and financial stability.
- Hazelnuts: Known in folklore for their ability to impart wisdom and inspiration. They are perfect for dishes that aim to boost creativity and intuitive insights.
- Pistachios: Used for breaking love spells and warding off evil eyes. Add them to dishes that are meant to protect against negative energies.
- Cashews: Great for memory enhancement and alignment with psychic pursuits. Their creamy texture when toasted adds a luxurious feel to meals.
- Pine nuts: Often used in spells to attract and retain wealth. Their creamy and satisfying flavour enhances both sweet and savoury dishes.
- Sunflower seeds: Symbolise truth, honesty, and loyalty. They are excellent for salads that aim to promote open and truthful communication.

· Pumpkin seeds: Known for promoting prosperity and protection. They are also associated with mental clarity.

· Sesame seeds: Believed to attract positive energy and abundance. They are often used in money and prosperity rituals.

· Chia seeds: Used for endurance and energy. These tiny seeds are powerful in boosting physical stamina.

· Flax seeds: Associated with healing and protection, particularly in health-related rituals. They add a nutty flavour and are rich in omega-3 fatty acids.

· Hemp seeds: Known for their healing properties and nutritional benefits. They support energy levels and overall well-being.

To toast nuts and seeds, spread them in a single layer on a dry skillet. Heat them over medium heat, stirring or shaking the pan frequently, until they are golden and fragrant. This not only brings out their flavours but also symbolises bringing their energies to life – awakening the dormant magic within.

MAGICAL PICKLES

Pickled ingredients are like little charms or enchantments, each adding a burst of flavour and an extra dimension of magic. These tangy delights are wonderful for adding both a physical and an energetic zing to your dishes.

· Pickled Capsicums: These vibrant jewels are steeped in vinegar and spices, transforming them into carriers of energy for enhanced perception and protection. Capsicums, in their pickled form, can add not only a sweet and tangy flavour but also an energetic barrier against negative influences.

· Olives: Known for their role in protection and peace, olives bring a depth of flavour and a wealth of magical properties to any salad. Green olives can be used to promote wisdom and black olives for abundance and grounding.

· Capers: Tiny yet mighty, capers are often used for potency and protection. Their sharp taste can invigorate a salad while energetically fortifying the eater against harm and enhancing their strength.

· Pickled Onions: These are superb for clearing obstacles and fostering clear communication. Their crisp, sharp bite and vibrant energy can cut through confusion and banish negativity.

The dressing you choose can be seen to bind the spell together. It is the carrier of your intentions. Interestingly, though vinegar oil dressings have been used since ancient times, the combination is now understood to have useful properties for unlocking nutritional components within vegetables. A vinaigrette with olive oil (for peace and purity) and vinegar (for healing and protection) can be whisked with a touch of mustard (for protection) and a drop of honey (for joy and sweetness). Similarly, a yogurt-based dressing with cucumber and mint could be perfect for a spell for soothing and restoration.

Edible flowers include marigolds for respect and admiration, violets for loyalty, and nasturtiums for victory, borage for tranquillity. If you have a garden, you may wish to grow these flowers not only to add to your salads, but also to attract the bees to pollinate other plants nearby. In selecting these flowers, as with other ingredients, pay attention to how they feel to you. What does their taste and colour represent?

As you layer your salad, focus on each ingredient's properties. With every leaf, slice, and sprinkle, envision the energies combining, enhancing the powers you wish to manifest. When you mix the salad you are combining the energies as you would a potion, so that each element melds harmoniously.

Imagine a salad for a winter feast: Begin with a base of mixed baby greens or spinach, sprinkle in a cup of cooked quinoa, and add pieces of beetroot, carrots, or pumpkin which have been pre-roasted in balsamic dressing. Add a sprinkle of pickled capers for sharpness and potency, crumble some feta for a touch of creaminess, and top with sage-grilled salmon and a sprinkle of toasted pumpkin seeds and a dressing made with lemon juice and zest, wholegrain mustard, and olive oil. Each ingredient not only complements the others in flavour but also in magical properties, creating a balanced dish that nurtures us holistically.

FROM PERSONAL TO GLOBAL

Food is much more than sustenance – it is a powerful connector that links the microcosms of our bodies and our daily lives to the macrocosms of the world. Each ingredient carries a story, a journey from the earth to our plates, reflecting the interconnectedness of life.

In daily life, we engage with food on a deeply personal level; it nourishes not only our bodies but also our spirits. The choices we make about what we eat reflect our values, our culture, and our personal health. This daily interaction with food is a form of ritual – a set of actions infused with meaning and intention. Choosing ingredients becomes a reflection of our personal ethics and beliefs. For some, this may be opting for organic, locally-sourced, or ethically-produced food as a statement of support for sustainable practices. Yet this can be challenging to maintain, particularly as the price of food rises.

Meals are inherently social; they bring people together around a shared table. In every culture, food is a medium through which hospitality is expressed, relationships are nurtured, and community bonds are strengthened. Food allows us to experience and celebrate different cultures with respect and openness. Each cuisine offers a glimpse into history, culture and geography. The choices we make about what we eat can have implications. Food politics encompass everything from the rights of farm workers to global trade policies, to issues of global food security and local sustainability. Politics is about power, and stepping into our power, as witches, allows us to face the paradoxes and ethical dilemmas from a position of intuition and wisdom, rather than be defeated by the onslaught of mixed messages.

Food can be a subtle form of activism and political magic. Choosing fair-trade products, boycotting goods from areas involved in ecological damage, or supporting local farms over corporate agribusinesses can all be ways in which eating becomes an act of power. Knowing where our food comes from is a privilege not afforded to everyone. This knowledge empowers us to make informed choices that align with values which have a direct impact on health, the environment, and the economy.

Understanding the supply chain of our food – where it was grown, how it was processed, and the manner of its journey to our plates – allows us to make choices that can either support or challenge existing power structures within the global food system. Every bite of food is a direct connection to the earth, carrying with it the energy, the spirit, and the essence of the place where it was produced. This connection is sacred, a reminder of our reliance on and relationship with the natural world.

Foods absorb the energies of their environment. Consuming them allows us to ingest these energies, affecting us physically, emotionally, and spiritually. In kitchen witchery, understanding the broader implications of our food choices enriches our practice and our lives. It teaches us to see the act of eating as an act of interconnectedness – a way to honour the earth and our bodies, support communities, and engage with the world in a meaningful way.

As we prepare and eat our meals, let us be mindful of the broader narrative each ingredient shares within the magical story of our lives. This awareness turns our meals into rituals of appreciation, respect, and magical intention. Food is a powerful tool for transformation – of the self, the community, and the world. By embracing the full spectrum of what food represents, from the personal to the global, we step deeper into our magical practice, connecting the microcosm of our individual experiences with the macrocosm of existence.

6

BOUNTIFUL MAGIC

"You do not have to be good.

You do not have to walk on your knees for a hundred miles through the desert repenting.

You only have to let the soft animal of your body love what it loves." – Mary Oliver

I find few things more pleasant than sipping a favourite beverage, particularly a good cup of tea, and appreciating the beauty already in my life. Celebration doesn't have to be a big grand thing, it can be attained in little moments of joy.

You don't need to try to be "grateful." I cannot emphasise this enough. If you're not feeling the gratitude buzz, that's okay. There's a lot of new age literature on gratitude which can be wonderful, but sometimes it can feel a bit forced or stale.

We often have mixed feelings about gratitude. As children, how many of us were told that we "should be grateful" or were forced to thank people for things when that wasn't what we were genuinely feeling?

Gratitude and thankfulness can be wonderful, but sometimes have an edge of disempowerment because we are "grateful to..." or "thankful for..."

There's an implied "other." A deity, an outside force that is giving us the thing to feel gratitude about, and while this can be fine, it can also feel disempowering. If I list the things I'm grateful for in my life, I'm always wondering about this divine other bestowing me with gifts, rather than simply appreciating the gifts.

If I'm saying "thank you" it can sometimes feel like subtly giving my power away. That might be totally good and fine. I've benefitted from gratitude practices many times throughout my life, but more and more I find myself preferring instead the liberated radiance of appreciation and celebration for which there need be no separation between myself and the divine, no "other" to thank, no pressure to feel grateful, simply a rejoicing in the present moment of connectedness.

Sometimes worries and other thoughts can get in the way of appreciation, but if we let those clear away, like clouds in the sky clearing to reveal the sun, and focus on what we really have, what we really know, what we really feel deeply in our bodies, the joy in our bones, we can find that deep within us, there is a well of indestructible appreciation and celebration. There is a part of us that is always in the throes of appreciation, no matter how hard we try to cut it off. If we can connect deeply with this wellspring that is just so happy to be here, we open the way for that beautiful energy of deep, deep, deep appreciation not only to connect with our lives and our bodies but to flow right through our existence.

You may be surprised (or maybe not so surprised by this point), to find that this deep appreciation is not just for the sweetest flavours of life but for all the bizarre complexities as well, the strangeness, and even for things that our conscious mind finds deeply unpleasant. Our shadow appreciates and delights in ALL sensation – all experience. This is one reason why people tend to clamp down on or disconnect from the deep loving energy that flows through us, that connects us with the divine. We disconnect because our conscious mind has decided to sort experiences into good and bad and then try to shut ourselves off from the bad experiences.

The problem with that, as we know, is that the "bad" experiences of the shadow then take on huge power in our lives. At the same time, shutting off from what we've labelled as bad also in some ways shuts us off from our own joy. We've clamped down on our emotion – our willingness to feel – and in doing so we distance ourselves from parts of ourselves! In this state that most people probably find themselves in most of the time, we're not able to fully appreciate life's complexities for the gifts they may become.

Shadow work, which we will delve deeper into in the next chapter, involves trusting ourselves in our fullness, including the parts that dwell in the darkness of the unconscious. I've come to a growing awareness that what is normally called the unconscious is actually a deeper level of awareness, a deep consciousness beyond our ordinary awareness. This understanding is reflected in many spiritual traditions in which an ordinary level of waking awareness is seen as delusion or madness. This idea that what we know as ordinary consciousness is actually not aware, and that what we know as the unconscious is really a deeper level of awareness is quite a paradox, and it is sometimes misunderstood by those who have a resistance to the hard limitations of the world.

Remember how I said that a myth is not something that never happened, it's something that's always happening all the time, at a deeper level. Well, most mythological creation myths I've encountered begin with some kind of void or chaos (or both). Just as within the cocoon, there is much that is unknown that the former caterpillar in its goo state must go through before finding its way out into the light. In the Māori mythology that I grew up with, the story of creation begins with Te Kore, the void. From that void, there are many stages of the dark night before the light of awareness shines through:

Ko Te Kore – the void

Te Kore-te-whiwhia – the void in which nothing is possessed

Te Kore-te-rawea – the void in which nothing is felt

Te Kore-i-ai – the void with nothing in union

Te Kore-te-wiwia – the space without boundaries

Na Te Kore Te Po – from the void the night

Te Po-nui – the great night

Te Po-roa – the long night

Te Po-uriuri – the deep night

Te Po-kerekere – the intense night

Te Po-tiwhatiwha – the dark night

Te Po-te-kitea – the night in which nothing is seen

Te Po-tangotango – the intensely dark night

Te Po-whawha – the night of feeling

Te Po-namunamu-ki-taiao – the night of seeking the passage to the world
Te Po-tahuri-atu – the night of restless turning
Te Po-tahuri-mai-ki-taiao – the night of turning towards the revealed world
Ki te Whai-ao – to the glimmer of dawn
Ki te Ao-marama – to the bright light of awareness
Tihei mauri-ora – there is life!

The void is not simply nothingness. It is the unknowable mystery, the unfathomable; the deep consciousness of our own soul mirrors the deep consciousness of the universe. It is the dark fertile soil through which all new things emerge.

If we want new things to emerge in our lives, if we want more abundance, if we want to have more wonderful experiences, if we want to live more fully in joyful magic, then we need to connect with this energy and create a clear channel between what we know in our deep soul and our conscious awareness. We need to process, release blocks, and allow all the other distractions to fade to the background so they're not getting in the way and influencing what comes through.

In my experience, if we get out of our own way, if we get out of the way of the divine, we open ourselves up for the most miraculous, beautiful, and transcendent unfolding. When I'm in this flow, all sorts of opportunities knock on my door. I'll be thinking about finding something, and then it will appear. For instance, a few months before writing this I was contemplating getting support with my social media, and then the perfect person was revealed to me, who happened to be an old friend and who understands exactly what I'm trying to do and knows how to help me. Similarly, sometimes I'll be working on a plot for a book that just won't fall into place until I connect with this deep intuition, connecting with the void, allowing new things to come through. I'll create spaciousness in my life rather than going around in circles in my mind trying to work things out rationally. I surrender to the unknown, and suddenly I'll have all the pieces I need to make the puzzle fit.

HARVEST STOCKTAKE

This is the part of the book where we celebrate the harvests of our life – on what we have developed, achieved, and worked through so far that's worth celebrating – and it's all worth celebrating! If you've gone through challenging times, I want to take a moment to acknowledge you, your courage, your bravery, your determination despite all the odds. You are here, and you are important. The universe would be a lesser place without you, that's a simple fact. No one has faced the exact same challenges as you have in your life. No one. Your life is absolutely unique, even if you've been taught that it isn't, even if you've been told you're normal or average or that there's nothing special about you, there is.

No one has the exact same upbringing as you, no one sees things the same way. No one has been through exactly what you've been through, and that's true for everyone. You have been taught to be hard on yourself, to limit yourself and diminish your light, to belittle your success. If so, you were probably taught that by other people who were similarly taught the same thing. Many of us try to keep ourselves small in order to keep ourselves safe, but it doesn't really work that way, so now my dear, it's time to unfurl.

It's time to celebrate yourself!

What is the harvest in your current life? What things have you worked for, aligned with and received:

· In the past year?
· In the past five years?
· In the past ten years?

Focus on each thing you've listed and put your hand on your chest or belly (wherever's comfortable). Focus on your feelings and the sensations in your body. Breathe slowly and deeply and appreciate all that you have accomplished.

Now, looking towards the future, the next year, five years or ten years...

What is it that you want to harvest in your life? (Your goals, your dreams, your desires.) Make a list of what you want regarding:

· Home and living situation
· Key relationships (this can include family and friendships)
· Prosperity and wealth

- Your effect on the wider world
- Your creations
- Being valued by the world

What are the things that are holding you back from receiving that harvest? What limiting thoughts are holding you back, for instance:

- I don't know how
- I'm not good enough
- I don't deserve....

Focus on each limiting thought and put your hand on your heart. For each one, acknowledge that you're ready to release this barrier. Thank it for its service – it was trying to keep you safe – but you're ready to bloom now.

Clearing some of these limiting thoughts, letting go with love, or even by stepping into a deep appreciation of all that you've learned from those past experiences, opens you up to so much more in your life. Abundance can flow into your life at a staggering rate if you can release the barriers to it and hold the space for the connection between the deeper soul and the spirit, hold that space open with the deepest appreciation. And you can also encourage this process by really appreciating all that you already have. The more you appreciate, the more you are in the vibe of celebration, the more you train your brain to feel good by default.

When I'm looking for a lost item I often pause and take a moment to shift my perspective, because I know I'm in a state of looking rather than finding. Similarly, if you're in the state of madly searching for something or seeking it out in your life and not finding it, you may be able to shift the external situation by shifting the internal state first, to bring yourself into a state of finding or receiving. You won't be able to find abundance if you're continuously in a mindset of lack, grasping for all that you do not have, because that grasping, hungry state of desperation is not the state of finding abundance or being in abundance and it's certainly not a state of celebration.

In order to shift into a state of abundance and celebration, we often have to release the resistance that is getting in the way. This book includes many exercises which can help with this process, and you are also free to create your own. What lights you up? What colours, environments, words, and practices feel like abundance and celebration to you? Make a list of all the things you can think of that feel exuberant. It need not be in a formal ritual, it could be making pizzas at home with your family or going for a walk with a friend. It could simply be closing your eyes right now and connecting with the wild, vibrant, and powerful lifeforce that flows through all of us.

If you can move more towards the internal state of appreciation, whether that's through visualising, affirming, or feeling the feelings of that wonderful harvest in your life – harmony, well-being, wonderful outcomes for your family, happiness of all kinds, or any other specific details – then you will already be in the abundance of what those wonderful outcomes feel like. Hold these thoughts and feelings gently. Do not stifle the flow by being too heavy-handed, because the energy of the soul and the spirit really need to flow, to expand, to open.

You may wish to practice visualising your energy expanding so that it's a bigger bubble around you, expanding more and more until it is one with the entire universe. This can help you to let go of the tensions and constrictions, the attachments that you have that are getting in the way of your flow and opening up to the vast possibility and wonder of all that is.

THE MAGIC OF OPENNESS

The ability to open oneself up for magic to flow through our lives is often one of removing obstacles. For instance, if we want a particular result, we need to be open to that result, and in our openness, the flow of magic can come through us. If we're open and excited and joyful, and we sustain that state even when it doesn't look like things are happening, even when we're tested with other distractions or things getting in the way, then we can retain that connection to the source of all magic and life and allow it to flow through us and through our intentions, our words, our spellwork, and so on.

For instance, if you want to be in a wonderful new relationship with someone that you absolutely love deeply and feel totally fulfilled in, you need to be open to that, including all the humiliation involved in surrendering to love, the gooey messiness of it all. You might want to begin by saying to yourself, "I am open to love." How does that feel? Do you have any resistance? What technique would you wish to apply in releasing it if you do? Perhaps journalling or just feeling into the sensations might help to clear the way.

You can then go deeper into the working of this. When you're comfortable saying, "I'm open to love," you can take a step forward: "I'm open to connecting deeply with love." And continue on: "I'm open to transformative new love and all the joys, intensities, vulnerabilities, and sensations that will entail."

Of course, you may find that you're only open to the good stuff, and yet in any deep, intimate relationship, there will be shadows that emerge from our own unconscious minds. These shadows for you will probably be reflected in your past relationships and the power dynamics and patterns of your childhood. For instance, if you've had relationships where your partner was cold or angry or exhibited other unpleasant qualities – even though you're totally not to blame for your ex being a jerk – the chances are fairly high that there's a shadowy part of you that is fascinated by whatever those unpleasant experiences were. And this might come up the more you delve deeper into the risks of vulnerability in relationships, the potential for shame and humiliation and all kinds of other things that we become vulnerable to in our most intimate connections.

If you can hold this space gently and breathe through it, open yourself up to embracing and releasing the shadows which until now have been deeply attached to the bad experiences that your conscious mind didn't know they wanted, you can clear the way to become really, truly excited about this new, powerful love that you're now totally open to in your life.

Similarly with money, if money has always been a struggle for you, you always feel like you're not receiving or saving enough of it, you've got a sense of scarcity and fear around money, you have unpleasant emotions around paying bills (which, quite frankly, is most people quite a lot of the time), then you're carrying a huge amount of resistance to abundance. From the state of scarcity, you are like a hungry ghost, and no amount of money that you receive will satiate that grasping not-enoughness. It might be that you don't feel like you value yourself enough, especially in a physical way, but it could just as easily be distrust of the outer world. You see, money is connected with survival for us, and fear around our survival reflects a lack of faith in the world, the universe, and in life.

This is a totally understandable thing to experience because bad things happen, including the things that you've already personally gone through and the many, many bad things you've witnessed around you. However, that lack of faith, that fear, is a clamping down, is getting in the way of experiencing your full magic and fulfilment.

Things are more complicated when it comes to health, but similar techniques can be applied to great effect. Why are things more complicated when it comes to health? Because health and our physical body is the very nexus that we inhabit within nature, and so it is the most intimate relationship any of us ever experience.

As Clarissa Pinkola Estés points out, our body is a dear companion, the sweet animal we are born into in this natural world and in this life. Sometimes we are born with bodies that are already struggling from various ailments, or we develop health problems later in life.

Many of us, myself included, have struggled with chronic illness. And this is not the kind of book that tells you to just think happy thoughts and your problems will be solved, because spiritual bypassing will, quite frankly, get you nowhere. However, despite the huge challenges of pain and illness, the body has much magic and much potential. We are both blessed and cursed with our bodies. They are amazing living vessels with which to explore the world – taste, sight, touch, everything that we experience comes through the senses of our bodies.

THE MAGIC OF CELEBRATION

Celebration is vital to a healthy society and as such, it's a component of magical practice, a conduit for communal joy and personal fulfilment. Historically, communities across various cultures have harnessed the power of celebration to strengthen bonds, commemorate significant milestones, and facilitate the release of collective tension. In many traditional societies, regular celebrations often revolve around the cycles of nature, such as solstices, equinoxes, moon cycles, and harvests, reflecting the magical symbolism of life's ebb and flow. These communal gatherings are imbued with significance and connection to the natural world, fostering a sense of unity and mutual support.

Through the acts of dancing, feasting, and music, our rituals of celebration can transcend everyday conflicts, lifting people into a shared experience of transcendence and connection. This collective energy release not only strengthens community bonds but also reaffirms cultural and spiritual values.

If you're interested in creating a coven or casual witchy community meet up group, I have created a resource with some helpful guidance based on my own understanding and experiences. You can download this from my website: www.irisbeaglehole.com/resources

You do not have to be part of a magical community to draw on the magic of celebration for yourself and others in your life; you can reflect on what kinds of celebrations make the most sense for you and how you can add to regular family and social celebrations to make them more magical.

Many of our shared social rituals of celebration in dominant culture are now focused on spending money. Christmas and birthdays are for presents, easter is for chocolate, Valentines day is for flowers (and also chocolate). I don't have a problem with all the chocolate or feasting in general, or presents for that matter, but we need not limit ourselves to celebrations in the form that they are sold to us. The ritual of blowing out candles on a cake and making a wish is certainly a kind of magic, and there are many ways of adding to this. You may want to bring more magic into an ordinary gathering by inviting people to bring along a story or poem reflecting the theme, through a group song, or a small symbolic ritual such as choosing a word for the new year or encouraging guests to write down things they want to release or bring into their lives and to burn the paper in a brazier.

Here are some additional ideas that could add more magic to your celebrations:

· Encourage guests to bring small, meaningful items or mementoes that they associate with positive memories or hopes for the future. As part of the celebration, each person can share why they chose to bring a particular item.

· If the setting allows, give guests ten minutes to go outside and connect with nature. They may wish to bring back a leaf, stone, flower, feather, etc. that relates to the celebration or something they want to share about with the group.

· Instead of relying solely on purchasing gifts, encourage the creation of edible or handmade items like crafts, knitted items, or baked goods.

· For decorations, it can be fun to involve everyone, for instance in making paper lanterns, garlands, or wreaths.

· Plan a walk or hike that corresponds with the season or the celebration's theme. This can include collecting natural items like leaves, flowers, or stones to create a seasonal altar.

· Dedicate a portion of the celebration to storytelling. Each participant can share a personal story, a myth, or a folklore tale that resonates with the celebration's theme.

· Provide materials for guests to create their own talismans, using fragrant herbs and flowers that symbolise different intentions or wishes.

· Create a communal recipe book where each guest contributes a favourite recipe, especially those with cultural or family significance. This book can be added to over time and shared during gatherings.

· Integrate a planting activity where each guest plants a seed or a small plant. This can symbolise growth, new beginnings, or intentions for the future. The plants can be taken home or left to grow together in a community garden.

· Incorporate a candle lighting ceremony where each person lights a candle for someone they wish to remember, honour, or send positive thoughts to. This can be done in silence or accompanied by a reading or music.

· Provide a notebook for guests to write down their thoughts, wishes, or reflections during the celebration which can be a lovely memento after a special birthday or gathering.

· Create a moment during the celebration where each person shares something they want to celebrate. This can be done verbally or by writing on slips of paper.

The magical aspect of communal celebrations lies in their ability to create a shared energetic space. Such gatherings amplify the group's intentions, whether for a good year ahead, health, or prosperity. Moreover, celebrations are occasions for the sharing of stories, wisdom, and traditions.

PERSONAL CELEBRATION

On a personal level, incorporating celebration into our magical practice can significantly enhance our connection to intentions and achievements. Personal rituals of celebration, such as honouring our accomplishments or marking phases of personal growth, can reinforce our magical will and clarity. But we do not need to celebrate anything in particular. Even if you haven't accomplished anything lately, you can still celebrate, and incorporate celebration into your daily life.

Why bother with all this celebration? Rumination, the tendency to dwell on negative thoughts and experiences, is deeply ingrained in human psychology. This proclivity served our ancestors well in the wild, helping them remember, anticipate and avoid threats. However, in modern life, this survival mechanism often leads to excessive worry and stress. Our brains can easily become trapped in cycles of negative rumination. To counteract this natural bias, many psychologists suggest consciously cultivating positive rumination practices.

Celebration rituals, similar to those found in traditional cultures, can help restore balance and harmony to our mental landscape. By deliberately focusing on joyful aspects of our lives and celebrating, we can train our brains to give equal weight to the things we actually want and enjoy. This practice of positive rumination doesn't negate our ability to address problems, it provides a crucial counterbalance to our innate negativity bias. Regular engagement in personal celebration practices can gradually reshape our thought patterns, leading to improved mental health, increased resilience, and a more balanced perspective on life's challenges and joys.

For me, small rituals of celebration are about allowing myself to unburden from the tensions that I tend to hold as I go through my day. When I celebrate, even just lifting my arms up in the air while walking by the ocean, I feel a gentle looseness, as if my inner core has unwrapped from being tightly wound, from trying to keep me focused. When I'm focused, I'm productive and I need that tension sometimes to get my work done. And yet, when I shift into a space of celebration, this energy unfurls like wings, expanding wider and wider perhaps even into the limitlessness of the vast cosmos. I breathe in deeply. I raise my arms in celebration.

Being in celebration is a wonderful experience. And it's one we can cultivate, but we often don't. This has been very important for me, personally, because I have such a strong drive to do my work which often takes me out of the present moment. When I say my work, I mean my inner work, work on my creative projects, meeting the needs of the other people in my life, especially my child, monitoring the different parts of my writing business, replying to messages, planning ahead (which is something I've always struggled to do). I spend a lot of time going over the list in my head of what comes next: putting one book up for pre-order, finish the editing for another book. I'm always working on multiple projects at a time. I love this. I love my job. I couldn't think of anything better for me. I am a writer at heart. I remember having such a strong urge to write as a very young child, but the problem was that even though my primary spoken language was English, I could only read or write in Māori until I was about eight or nine years old. Because I couldn't write in English when I was about six, I wrote a song – it's a very short song – about the sky god Ranginui and the Earth Mother Papatūānuku, feeling empathy for them when they had to part. I was probably quite an odd child, and it's no wonder I ended up a writer, but that urge to do my work has been really powerful even when I didn't know how to channel it.

I struggled so much with my mental health as a child and teenager, partly because I didn't know how to channel my energy into things properly, and because I felt so overwhelmed, terrified, and burdened with pain from unprocessed childhood emotional trauma. I didn't yet know how to wield the intensity of the drive inside me. Now I feel like I've worked through the tensions within me, for the most part, to the point where they've become strengths. It's definitely not that I no longer struggle or anything – there are still situations that arise from time to time that feel as though they might have destroyed me completely. There are still days and sometimes weeks and months where my energy slows or I feel stuck, and yet overall I have so much to celebrate!

As someone who always resisted the idea of hard work when I was younger because I hated being told what to do, I really work incredibly hard now, or at least I work incredibly often. Often my work is actually quite gentle, safe, and flowing, and yet as a society we value "hard work" so much, almost above all else, in slightly delusional ways. We'll justify the terrible behaviours of somebody who's incredibly wealthy by saying they worked really hard, as if people who clean our toilets do not work incredibly hard. It is a moral confusion to conflate virtue with hard work as though it bestows some kind of value onto people as if hard things somehow make us valued or morally good or excuse reprehensible behaviour.

And yet, I find myself more and more wanting to do my work. But in that work there is sometimes constriction, and often there's not enough celebration to relieve the tension. So recently I've been celebrating as much as I possibly can. To celebrate, some people like to have a party or just get really drunk, which is not the most effective way of doing it. Celebration can be simply in the moment, in any moment.

Celebration beads

I was recently in a local crystal shop. I like to support small local businesses so I bought a few things for myself and my child, including a set of beads. Prayer beads have been used all over the world in many different cultures. I don't personally like the word "prayer" very much because it feels disempowering and because it's quite associated with Abrahamic traditions which have so many rules which are really not my thing.

Prayer has a prominent place in many spiritual practices. There are times where prayer had felt necessary for me – a surrendering to a sense of powerlessness, a letting go, a deep and humble asking. In beseeching a god, asking them for what we want, we give our power over to them. While sometimes this is called for, often the most powerful magic is not about begging an external power to grant our wishes, but about actively initiating our own magic. Witches tend to work with deities in a different dynamic, more like a partnership, welcoming them, honouring them, and calling upon their blessings.

There may be times when surrendering our power is an important part of our magical transformation, but as a general daily practice it does not suit me. Instead of using these beads for prayer, I can use each bead as a tool for celebration, sensing the feeling of rolling the bead around in my hand with an intention. I can hold a bead and say, "I celebrate myself." I can turn to the next bead and say, "I celebrate my life." Moving along through the beads I can say different things that come to mind.

You don't need beads for this exercise, but they can be an excellent tool for attention and focus. If you don't like the idea of beads you could simply tap your fingers or do something else that is subtle and repetitive. You can use any beads you happen to have in the house, a bracelet made of round crystal beads, a pearl necklace, even a string of beads from a hanging ornament. You could also collect materials you like and make your own set of celebration beads. With whatever you prefer to use as a tool to anchor in your daily celebration practice, you can say celebratory affirmations like:

I celebrate the [season].
I celebrate connecting with the essence of my being.
I celebrate all the abundance that I have in my life.
I celebrate my health.
I celebrate my wonderful body that is working to look after me.
I celebrate the wonderful air I'm breathing.
I celebrate the wonderful sunset I'm watching.

I celebrate the beautiful sky above.

I celebrate everything that I've achieved today.

I celebrate everything I've achieved this week.

I celebrate everything I've achieved this month.

I celebrate everything I've achieved this year.

I celebrate everything I've achieved in the last few years to get me to this very point.

I celebrate all the achievements of my life.

I celebrate myself just in being here, being human.

I celebrate the wonderful people in my life.

I celebrate myself.

I celebrate my life.

I celebrate my being.

I celebrate my success.

I celebrate the beauty of nature.

I celebrate all the sensations I'm feeling right now.

I celebrate my breathing.

I celebrate my inspiration.

I celebrate my creativity.

I celebrate my magic.

I celebrate the divine forces in the universe.

I celebrate all the learning that I'm doing right now in my life.

I celebrate all the learning I've done so far to get me here.

I celebrate the wonderful relationships in my life.

I celebrate my ancestors.

I celebrate being enough.

I celebrate having enough and plenty more.

I celebrate that I do enough.

I celebrate that I'm loved and valued enough.

I celebrate that I am wonderful.

I celebrate that I have such wonderful abundance in my life.

I celebrate my senses.

I celebrate everything that I experience in this moment.

I celebrate feeling loved by this benevolent universe, cosmos, by this divinity that we all are.

I celebrate being seen and valued.

I celebrate sharing my message.

I celebrate my healing and growing.

I celebrate my continued insights and understanding.

If you allow it to, the sensation of holding the round beads in your hand and turning each one, can induce a heightened presence, a deepening of awareness, and ultimately that state of flow and presence is what celebration is. So, as you turn the beads you may be more aware of your body, more aware of sensations, more aware of connections – spiritual connections to nature, connections to the universe – more aware of authentic insights that might flow through you. As you focus on the bead, turn it in your hand and then move to the next one with a few celebratory words and an openness to the sensations and experience of celebration.

Every touch is a celebration, getting myself into such a wonderful state of appreciation. That keeps on working with every touch of the bead. There is more celebration even if it's just a feeling, just a word, just a simple affirmation.

THE SHADOW OF MONEY

If you find it difficult or near impossible to truly feel the warmth, glow, expansion, and abundance of celebration, it is likely because you have blocks around opening and receiving. Many of us have resistance to receiving certain types of abundance such as attention, love, gifts, or money.

When we hate, despise, or resent money, or have any kind of strong resistance against it, we unconsciously create an equally strong desire *for* money in our shadow self. This is similar to how we create an equally strong unconscious desire for all the things we cannot consciously accept or love.

There are many things that are very difficult to consciously accept, which is partly why, according Jung, the shadow of our collective unconsciousness looms so large over us as a species, and over our entire world. Bringing this shadow into the light of awareness, is apparently how we begin to transform it, just as sunlight works as a disinfectant. What festers in the darkness can be transmuted in the light of awareness, but the first step of this is awareness and acceptance.

Acceptance of a thing does not necessarily mean saying that it's okay; it means not completely shutting off from it and allowing it to come into our full awareness. When we do this with money, allowing ourselves to be open to it despite the injustice in the world and the corruptions within our various financial systems, we're able to access money as a resource in more empowering ways.

As somebody with strong ethical convictions and values I spent many years with complex resistance towards money. I hated that I needed it. I dreamed of a world where I didn't. Yet obviously, I needed to cultivate a good relationship with money in order to not feel stressed and broke all the time, which I managed to do, living simply on very little for quite a lot of my life. But this, too, had its limitations.

You see, money is so connected with freedom, and being open to money is being open to our freedom in different ways. Paradoxically, if instead of resisting, hating, and resenting money, people love it and desire it above all else without addressing the associated shadow's resistance, further imbalances and tensions will result. So the trick is to process our various resistances, conscious or unconscious, to money and the freedom that comes with it – to digest these, like a meal, so that they're no longer clogging us up psychologically or burdening us. We need to process our money blocks to release the limiting beliefs we've been taught about money so that we can create our own more empowering and inspiring beliefs.

Money relates so strongly to value. We spend money on what we value and withhold our money from going towards things we do not like. In order to feel good about money, I needed to value myself – not just by spending money on myself (though this can be a wonderful thing) but by going deeper into my own practice of self-love and excavating a lot of old limiting beliefs and releasing old painful emotions like guilt.

All of this is work, but it can be a lot of fun if we allow it to be. It can be healing and regenerative. It can be inspiring. And we can open up to this process, which is a bit like the feeling of soaring – opening our metaphorical wings, opening up to the freedom of having the resources to do what we want, freeing ourselves from the limitations and unburdening ourselves so that we can fly.

There are many amazing teachers when it comes to money, and many books about money mindset and blocks. I have learned a lot from exploring these topics myself. I feel that, just like with any topic, the more different perspectives you can process and incorporate into your understanding, along with your intuition to figure out what's useful for you, the better your foundation is. This leads to better openness in terms of being able to have the life that you want.

Sometimes this money stuff borders on toxic positivity and spiritual bypassing. There is a lot to unpack when it comes to prosperity gospel – the idea that divinity will bless you with wealth if only you have enough faith, pray hard enough. We all know that being a good person has very little to do with the amount of wealth we have, just as we know that working hard doesn't always make people wealthy. We all struggle with the physical limitations of this world, which often include financial constraints. Life is not fair, and though we can do what we can to make it fairer, it is easy to get stuck in our limitations and feel powerless. There is a powerful paradox when it comes to money, and working with this paradox can liberate us emotionally, opening us up to greater freedom with our resources, more openness to abundance, and a healthier relationship with money.

Money is always connected to value of some kind because it's a technology of value created by human beings as our societies evolved to be more complex. When we think about our ancient ancestors who lived in times before money existed, we understand that their lifestyles were far more closely connected with particular resources. A lot of people say that people would barter and that was impractical, and therefore money had to be invented. This is not necessarily true historically and anthropologically as anarchist anthropologist David Graeber pointed out in his fascinating book *Debt: The First 5000 Years*. Before "money" there were many different credit systems that existed before anything close to resembling money as currency. People would have ways of keeping track; if somebody had given them a whole lot of, say, fruit that was in season, they would make markings to record this.

Tally sticks were a simple but effective method of recording debts and transactions in medieval Europe, particularly in Celtic communities. These notched wooden sticks were split into two halves, with each party retaining one piece, ensuring a precise record that couldn't be easily tampered with. The term "stock" originates from the Old English word "stocc," meaning a tree trunk or log, reflecting the material used for tally sticks. This connection extends to modern financial terminology, where "stock" represents shares or ownership in a company. Just as tally sticks denoted a portion of a debt or obligation, stocks represent a portion of a company's value, illustrating the evolution of recording and managing economic relationships over time.

When we think about money in that more ancient sense, it's not merely about acquiring or selling things – it is relational. It is about relationships that are built and maintained through trust in relation to resources. For instance, in many cultures, it is not considered appropriate to completely pay off a debt because that's completely cutting off a relationship and saying, "I don't want anything to do with you. I've paid off the debt." Instead, it makes sense to pay a little bit more, to give a little bit more than was taken originally, so that the relationship will continue. This kind of reciprocity and gifting is a huge, important social technology that has developed in different ways across cultures and across time.

If we think about money in terms of what we value and in terms of how we've evolved to have these systems, in terms of its foundations, we can have a steadier relationship with it. This is not to gloss over the bloody history, but to bring it into greater awareness. According to Grae-ber, money as currency was developed largely through wartime. Appar-ently, when travelling soldiers needed to be fed, the easiest system for allowing this was to create taxes, which meant that the soldiers could claim the tax and have this currency that would enable them to be fed when they were traveling across vast distances in order to fight for the boundaries of kingdoms and empires.

I'm not going to justify any of the violence. But it's interesting to think about the evolution of money in this historic context, especially since it seems to have been invented quite independently in three different parts of the world all at the same time, giving the impression that it was a part of our human evolution.

Money appeared in approximately 600 to 500 BCE in the ancient kingdom of Lydia, present day Turkey, where King Croesus introduced the first official coins. Around the same time in the late Zhou Dynasty of China, coins initially shaped like tools and later round with square holes, began circulating. Similarly, in ancient India, the use of silver punch-marked coins emerged. The history of money, much like the rest of human history, is long and complex and bloody, and yet trying to remove ourselves from the system does nothing to heal it.

If we begin to untangle some of the knots around this, then we can begin to empower ourselves more with our money, our relationship with freedom, and our relationship with the material world. We can start to see money not just as a problem, not just as a burden to think about, not just as a survival mechanism, but also as something that has a shadow which can be brought into the light. Money can feel good – it is something that we can connect to energetically from the heart as opposed to just some-thing that makes us fear for our survival. We can allow ourselves to form a good relationship with money.

Yes, over time, money has become this abstract thing, often discon-nected from values, and yet it has become such a sophisticated system for moving resources around the world. In a sense, we have evolved through systems like this to having a global social system, almost like an ecosys-tem, which is not in particularly good balance at the moment. Instead of having lots of small tribal groups and lots of small settlements, and even lots of different, slightly bigger kingdoms and empires, we are beginning to have more of a global system. There are many problems within this system, but also many opportunities arise from this vast interconnectedness that has evolved.

It almost behaves the way that a human body does because complex systems have similar patterns, whether you're talking about a forest ecosystem, or the human body, or any other kind of organism, or any kind of organic, complex system. In a sense, we live within an organic complex system. We just don't think about it that way because we like to separate ourselves from the natural world for some strange reason.

Money enables us to connect with the world in ways that humanity has never been able to before. Of course, there are still issues with money, and global shipping for that matter, which is why awareness is so important, but in being very honest with ourselves, we cannot pretend that our hands are clean, we cannot operate outside the system in which we are dependent upon for our survival. Instead, we must find better ways to live within it because we have no choice. If we want a better world, change must happen from the inside, because there is no outside.

In terms of the very personal level of money, if we can clear our limitations, our beliefs around money being difficult, having to work hard for money, money being disempowering, money being bad, people with money being evil – if we can begin to face and untangle and clear the emotion that most of us hold around those things, then we can allow a new relationship to emerge. We can feel good about money; we can feel connected and happy, and generally get into a more empowering situation.

It can be helpful to think about what a really good relationship with money feels like for you. What does it look like? What does your bank account look like? You don't have to know the specifics of where money is coming from, but being open to money coming from different places, being open to receiving, being open to living in abundance, allows you to be more empowered in many different ways. It allows you to stop denying yourself and to stop casting shadows by not wanting to acknowledge certain things, by having stigma around money.

When we can open up to it – and that can also mean opening up to awareness of all the bad stuff around money, not suppressing feelings but processing them – we can be in a better position energetically and magically to step deeper into our power. Despite the many, many problems with money and monetary systems, there's also a lot of power that can come from good people like you having plenty of money, having more money than you know what to do with, having abundance that you can invest in your communities towards good things. You can use it to live a life that is healthy and inspiring and empowering for you and the people around you. You can share with other people; you can make better choices because you *have* more choices.

Yes, when you have more money, you have more choices; when you have less money and when you're in survival mode, you have fewer choices. Yes, there are lots of tensions in the journey towards having a good relationship with money as opposed to a pathological one, which is, I think, almost the default in society. Typically, either people are frugal, and perhaps in denial (frugality is not necessarily bad, it can be a helpful thing, but can also involve denial and repression), or people can be totally the opposite, spending money on all sorts of things that they think will make their life better, but it's actually coming from a place of unconsciousness.

Leaning into the feelings of tension within us can bring more awareness and openness.

THE MAGIC OF MONEY

It took me a long time to become comfortable receiving money. When I was a child, I'd compulsively eat all the sweet things I had access to and I'd spend any money I had on sweets given half the chance. I had no impulse control whatsoever, but as I grew up I began to recognise money as a key to my emotional security. I learned that if I didn't spend all the money I had I could avoid the cloying sensations of doom that came from the powerlessness of being broke.

Just as spending all my money was a scarcity response, so too was my pattern of saving because the scarcity in my childhood had taught me that being broke made me terribly, terribly anxious. So over the years, I always had enough money, which often meant not buying things that weren't necessary and learning to live frugally. I didn't like money. I resented my dependence on it. I felt that I was only interacting with money because I had to, because it was necessary, but surely there was a better system. I'm sure there actually *are* many better systems. I spent years studying local community economies as part of my academic research, and I understand that there are many, many wonderful ways of creating more sustainable economies. Economies are systems of energy flow; just as the circulatory system moves blood around the human body, the financial system, the economy moves resources around the social organisms of the world. Nature always reflects, as I continue to remind you.

In recent years, I've come to accept more and more that being open to the flows of abundance allows me to step further into my power. It allows me to have freedoms and invest in causes that are meaningful for me. I personally wish that many of you wise, wonderful witches are blessed with receiving an abundance of wealth and prosperity, because quite frankly, many of you who are doing this deep inner work would be much, much better at using that power and that freedom for wonderful things than many other people would be. It is quite a conundrum that many people who are spiritually and ethically inclined cut themselves off from the material world, because if all of those people were able to find a balance between the material and spiritual, this world could be a much more wonderful place. Imagine all of the great community initiatives we could support, all of the well-being that could be fostered, all of the community gardens, the therapeutic and educational services, the opportunities we could give to people who have been deeply disadvantaged by the current systems which have largely been built unconsciously.

As all the money mindset people keep repeating, you can't get poor enough to make poor people wealthy, yet if you open yourself up to wealth and to stepping into the potential power that comes with it you can not only help others directly, but you can also help them by example. If there's a contradiction to be worked through, a paradox that can be powerfully held or transformed in order to reconnect these disparate parts of ourselves that have been disconnected and shadowed, it is a paradox that money is often involved in destroying nature, and yet money connects with us through the element of Earth, through the material. Money is also part of nature, albeit in a bizarrely abstracted form.

When I began actively doing money mindset work fairly recently, in 2023, I cleared away a lot of anxieties from the scarcity in my childhood. I felt I had a pretty good relationship with money already. After all, I always had enough money, even when I lived on pretty low incomes as a student, as a solo mother working part-time and living off scholarships while I was studying. Yes, I always had enough. I always held the space for *enough* to be in my life. But I still had a deep resistance to money. I also had a deep distrust in "the system", which is totally understandable. We have financial systems that are very unfair when it comes to money. Many people suffer and struggle with the toxic stress of poverty which makes it very hard to "rise above" or "pull yourself up by your bootstraps".

I studied sociology at university for many years, and I understand there are very real problems, inequalities, and injustices that exist in the world. This had always held me back from having a really good relationship with money.

I still hold many of the same views, largely about inequality and wanting the world to be better, but I've managed to open myself up to having a much more open, flowing, and positive relationship with money and abundance. When my books started to do well and I was still in my public sector career, I didn't think about leaving my job because I'd become used to the security of it, and I didn't want to rely on my books alone or put a lot of pressure on my creativity to support me. But the universe conspired against me, or in this case, I suppose in my favour. I was comfortable enough in leaving my permanent role and going into contracting, allowing me to have more time to write. But as my first contract came to an end, the political environment at the time meant that contract work was drying up. So while I was still technically looking for a new contract, I was spending a lot of time focusing on my books and my writing business. During that time, my writing career really started to take off so that I was earning more money than I could have possibly hoped to in a public sector career.

This did not happen by accident. This happened with a lot of deep inner work, encouraged by the many books on money mindset and magic that I was reading at the time. I went into my old money blocks, my bad memories with money, all the things that I'd been carrying around with me that had held me back, and I released a lot of old painful emotion. You see, when you're a child, you can easily carry emotions that haven't been resolved in your body well into adulthood that can get in your way. One of the money blocks that I found particularly poignant was guilt around money. Growing up as the child of a solo mother, I had memories like accidentally knocking over the milk when I was four years old and my mother crying out and being very upset because milk was expensive at the time when she barely had enough money to feed us because of austerity policies. This guilt was stored in my body, along with pain and shame when it came to money. And when I released a lot of this personal emotion and delved into my fears and my resistance, money started pouring into my life in a way that astounded me.

More and more readers are finding my books, and I'm experiencing unprecedented abundance, allowing me to live a dream I had never even dared to hope for of being a full-time author. I'm receiving everything that I need and more. Having more means that not only can I feel relatively safe in my savings and comfortable despite relying on my writing to support me. It also means that I am in a position where I can contribute to things that I want to see in the world. I can be generous, and I can feel good about that. This is the harvest of many, many years of "hard work" on a soul level, many years of ripening, cocooning and melting away old beliefs.

Abundance isn't just about money, but if you have a negative relationship with money or resistance to it, it can be infinitely rewarding to release the blocks that are holding you back to make way for the harvest to come. You may wish to write down all of the difficult experiences you've had before regarding money and then go through each one, forgiving and releasing, breathing acceptance, connection, and love into that part of yourself, that child self, that younger self, letting go of your attachment to the pain and especially to anyone else who inflicted that upon you, because you don't need to be bound by their misdeeds. This is a good thing to do, not just with money but with other things like health and love.

Money often carries a complex and sometimes negative connotation. It's not uncommon for people to view money as something bad or toxic, a necessary evil that can corrupt or complicate life.

However, when we step back and view money from a broader, metaphorical perspective, we can see that it is like the blood flowing through the body's veins; it is a vital force that moves resources, facilitates exchange, and sustains the life of our communities and economies.

Just as blood nourishes and supports the body, enabling growth and health, money, when respected and used wisely, can be a powerful tool for good. It can create opportunities, support noble causes, and improve lives.

By cultivating a healthy and positive relationship with money, we open ourselves to prosperity, not just for personal gain but also for the greater good. Embracing this perspective allows us to transform our inter-actions with money, seeing it as a channel through which we can enact positive change.

INTUITIVE MONEY SPELL

Our relationship with money is often complex and deeply intertwined with our emotions and past experiences. This intuitive money spell is a ritual designed to transform your relationship with money, helping you release old blocks and open yourself to the flow of abundance.

This spell is more than just a series of actions; it's a meditative process that connects you with the deeper aspects of your psyche, the natural elements, and the powerful archetypes of abundance and prosperity.

This spell reflects the ancient alchemical processes of solve and coag-ula, the dissolving and reforming, just like a caterpillar dissolves in order to re-form as a butterfly.

This spell is structured to guide you through a journey of release, empowerment, and manifestation. The core of the spell involves a deep and introspective release of emotion you carry around past money wounds and blocks, allowing you to forgive, let go, and clear the path for new wealth.

Be aware that releasing old money wounds may come with emotional pain and may be connected to trauma. If you decide you are not yet ready to go into the next part of the spell, simply close the spell and do what you need to take care of yourself.

Alternately, you may decide to spend a few days on this first part of the spell.

I had no idea I was carrying around so much guilt and shame around money; however, taking time to release the old emotion and forgive life for the painful experiences has helped me immensely. I have sometimes found it helpful to go for a walk while repeating releasing and forgiving affirmations and occasionally rubbing my solar plexus.

Other people find EFT tapping very helpful and there are many videos on EFT for money blocks available for free online. If you need more time for this part of the spell, that is a very good thing because it means you're doing deep work.

Take your time and then, when you get to a point of inner peace and are ready for the other side of the spell, you can return to it.

As you embark on this spell, remember that your intention, focus, and emotional process are key.

Approach each step with mindfulness and openness, allowing yourself to fully experience and embrace the transformative power of the ritual. This spell is not just about attracting wealth; it's about reshaping your relationship with money and opening your life to new abundance.

Many of us are uncomfortable with receiving. It can be hard to receive compliments, attention, unexpected gifts or money. If any of these things bring tension, guilt, or anxiety to you, take a few moments to journal on your experiences and feelings, forgiving, releasing, and relinquishing the emotion from the past. Often we have conflicted experiences in our past with receiving, especially when it has come in a form we were not comfortable with or had a lot of expectation around it. Many people feel more in control when giving rather than receiving.

If you hold tension in your chest around this, place one hand on the tense place, and the other gently on your belly. Breathe softly and deeply into your belly, relaxing, and allowing the tension to dissipate. You are in your power now, and you are safe to receive more of what you really want.

Processing these old feelings clears space for us to begin anew, and to receive what we are actually wanting with clarity and ease. When you have cleared the emotion, allow yourself to relax into the feeling of receiving.

On a symbolic level, money often relates to the planets of Jupiter and Venus and archetypes like The Empress in tarot. There is a richness and depth within this symbolism. I tend to think of the colours of green and gold, and feelings of abundance and generosity.

Money and wealth also relate to value, and more symbolically to our values in general and our relationship with the material world.

Many spiritual people like to dismiss or de-value the material world and money because they see these things as shallow or too materialistic, detracting from more important things; however, we are all material beings living in the material world.

Though in the past I've also had a fractured relationship with money, I've found that instead of disconnecting from it and de-valuing it, I've grown and healed more through opening up to valuing money and valuing the material as part of our world, not disconnected from the whole.

After all, the shallow waters are no less important than the depths!

I have included a list of items that can relate to this energy. You can find this after the spell instructions.

In preparation for this spell, you can gather some of these items from around your house, or choose things that resonate with the energy of wealth for you, personally.

These items will help to anchor you and your magic.

Items to gather:
· Candles or incense (optional)
· Pieces of paper and a pen
· Fireproof container (optional)

Crystals to Symbolise Wealth
· Jade: Known for attracting prosperity and success.
· Emerald: Associated with richness and abundance.
· Pyrite (Fool's Gold): Attracts wealth and abundance.
· Citrine: improves financial situations.
· Goldstone: Often used in wealth-attracting rituals.
· Lodestone: attracting wealth.

- Tiger's Eye: For attracting luck and money.
- Aventurine: good fortune, especially in finance.

Natural Items

- Green plants or leaves: Symbolising growth and renewal.
- Basil leaves: Associated with wealth and used in money spells.
- Mint: Attracts prosperity and financial success.
- Sunflower seeds: Symbolise abundance and bountifulness.
- Wheat stalks or grains: Ancient symbols of abundance.
- Oak leaves: Representing strength, stability, and prosperity.
- Pine cones: Symbolising growth and abundance.
- Acorns/seeds: Potential and the growth of new ventures.

Other Suggestions

- Coins and banknotes: Direct symbols of money and wealth.
- Green candles: Often associated with prosperity and growth.
- Gold candles or objects: Symbolise wealth and abundance.
- Cinnamon sticks: Believed to attract success and prosperity.
- Patchouli: A herb known for its association with material wealth.
- Rice: A symbol of wealth and prosperity in many cultures.
- Gold or green ribbons: To symbolise the binding of wealth to you.
- Honey: Symbolises sweetness and abundance.
- Silver coins or objects: Representing wealth and prosperity.

Preparation

Gather items your items. Find a quiet space where you won't be disturbed. Arrange your items on a small table or altar.

Opening & Consecration

Light a candle and/or incense and bless your space.

Hold your hands over the items you've gathered and visualise a bright light surrounding them. Say, "I consecrate these items for abundance and prosperity."

Releasing Money Wounds

On a piece of paper, write down any negative experiences, feelings of shame, guilt, or scarcity related to money from your past.

Hold each written wound in your mind, feel the emotion, then consciously release it, saying, "I forgive and let go."

Safely burn or tear up the paper, visualising the blocks dissolving away. Take as much time as you need.

Note that if you need more time with releasing money wounds, take a few days to allow the old pain to come up, release the old guilt and emotions you've been carrying, and forgive life for all the suffering you've endured, opening yourself up to healing and deeper understanding.

Acknowledge Personal Power and Powerlessness

Sit quietly, acknowledging your feelings of power and powerlessness when it comes to money. If you received a large amount of money, what power would you feel? What fears of powerlessness might come with this power?

Power and powerlessness often come together. Accept your power to attract abundance.

Open Space for Wealth

Say, "I now open a new space for wealth and abundance in my life."

Connecting with Abundance

Visualise the energy of money, for instance, Jupiter, Venus, and The Empress, archetypes of abundance and wealth. Feel their energy surrounding you. Hold or touch each item that you've selected and open up to the energy of abundance it signifies for you. Notice these energies and how similar and different they are from each other.

Affirmations

As you touch each item, you may want to repeat affirmations to yourself, using the magic of words to open yourself up to the energy of money, "I am open to abundance," and, "Wealth flows to me easily."

Setting Money Intentions

Sit for a moment with a new piece of paper. From this more open energetic space, allow yourself to open up to new desires and goals. Take a few moments to sit in this openness with your pen and paper. Now, write down your intentions for wealth – what you wish to receive and how you see your life with new abundance.

Place the paper in an envelope, or just fold it over and seal it with wax from your candle or another method that suits you, symbolising the locking in of your intentions. If you prefer, you could also seal some of the symbolic wealth items you gathered inside the paper.

Closing the spell and grounding.

After sealing your intentions, take a moment to ground yourself. Place your hands on the earth or floor, and visualise roots growing from your body into the earth, anchoring your intentions in reality.

End the spell by celebrating the abundance already present in your life. This helps shift your mindset towards recognising and appreciating wealth in all its forms.

In the days following the spell, pay attention to any insights, opportunities, or changes in your perspective regarding money. Journal about these experiences to deepen your understanding and connection with the spell's intentions.

ABUNDANCE MEDITATION

Find a quiet, comfortable space where you won't be disturbed. You may choose to sit or lie down. Consider lighting a candle or incense to create a serene atmosphere. Have soft, uplifting music playing in the background if it helps you to relax.

Begin by taking deep, slow breaths. With each inhalation, feel your body relax; with each exhalation, release any tension or stress. Visualise roots growing from the base of your spine or feet, extending deep into the earth, grounding you in the present moment.

Visualise a golden light glowing softly in your heart centre. With each breath, allow this light to expand, filling your chest and eventually your entire body with warmth and radiance. This light represents appreciation and joy.

Think back over your life, starting from early memories to the present day. Allow different moments to come to mind where you learned something valuable or received blessings, no matter how small. As each memory surfaces, see it bathe in the golden light, transforming it into a vibrant scene of celebration. Hear laughter, see smiles, feel the warmth of those moments.

Reflect on the challenges you've faced and how they've shaped you. With kindness and compassion, celebrate these too, recognising them as integral parts of your journey. Visualise yourself embracing these experiences, understanding that they contributed to your strength and wisdom.

Now, imagine a path ahead of you, bathed in golden light. As you walk this path, envision doors along the way. Each door represents a future opportunity for celebration. Visualise yourself opening these doors with excitement and joy, encountering more blessings, achievements, and happy moments.

As you continue along the path, set intentions for what kinds of joys and successes you wish to welcome into your life. Be specific about what you wish to celebrate in the future – personal milestones, relationships, creative achievements, or spiritual growth.

Gradually bring your attention back to the present. Take a few deep breaths, feeling the energy of potential celebrations stirring within you. When you're ready, gently open your eyes, carrying the warmth of the golden light and the excitement for future celebrations with you.

If you like, write down any insights or specific future celebrations you want to remember or focus on from this meditation. This can help solidify your intentions and maintain a celebratory mindset.

THE CHILD-STATE AND BEGINNER'S MIND IN MAGIC

Starting at the beginning again is an important part of the process of transformation; in beginning again we come back to our innocence, letting go of the world-weary know-it-all aspects of the psyche in order to create space to really drink in the experiences of life.

Loving-kindness meditations, as taught in Buddhist practices, place attention on fostering a soft, gentle love for all beings. This is very similar to "the love of all existences", which is a key value reflected in Druidry. If you're sceptical like me, you might instinctively question why on earth one would want to love *all existences*. Surely there are plenty of things not to love out there, and yet, after many years of seeking, searching, questioning, and working magic, I have come to understand that the creativity and inspiration that flows through us is exactly the same thing as the great divine force of love.

It is not just reflected in life. This force *is* life. It moves through all of life and all of existence, from the rocks to the concrete of our cities, to the digital brains of the computers we've created to reflect our own brains, to the hearts, minds, and souls of every living, breathing thing. There is no separation between this life force and that which we call "love." And therefore, to connect with love, with compassion, with tender kindness, with this force, with the very essence of all beings, is the most powerful thing one can do in our magical practice.

You do not have to agree with me on this, or on anything else. I completely understand why there are plenty of things out there not to love, and there are lots of things I personally don't enjoy or support, but we are complex beings capable of holding paradoxes and this is perhaps the biggest paradox of them all. Everything is connected despite the illusion of separation; we are all made of energy and that energy could just as easily be called love as it could be called atoms or anything else.

This does not mean you have to approve of all the cruelty in the world, but you can love the part of yourself that resists those things. You can love, through your own compassion, those who suffer, and at some level, that is all of us. Whether or not somebody deserves your compassion may be immaterial to this exercise, because if you say "good morning to everyone except those bad people who do things I don't like", that is, if you withhold your love, you're not directly affecting other people or making them any better, you're only hurting yourself in this very moment.

And so, as you stretch deeper into your magical life, you will likely find greater and greater power in an openness and acceptance, in a deep well of compassion and kindness that begins to emerge inside you. This is the love of your soul. Your soul, in all its complexity and all its depth, is deeply, deeply loving. And the more you connect with it, the more whole you become, the more your spirit, body, and soul merge into one totality of being – unified will.

This totality is reflected in different traditions and by different names. It may be called enlightenment, it may be called reaching nirvana, it's called *unio mentalis* in hermetic traditions. The unnerving thing about deepening into wisdom is that one is reborn into the childlike presence of being within the magic of the world.

This is reflected in Nietzsche's parable of the camel, the lion, and the child. The lion seeks greatness, rising above the status of the mundane camel, and yet its next stage of evolution is to the very innocence of a child. This same principle is reflected in the concept of "beginner's mind" as taught by Buddhist teachers like Thich Nhat Hanh. Beginner's mind is the state of gentle, loving awareness. The more we can be in this open state of attentiveness, the more beautiful and miraculous our lives inevitably become.

But how do you get there? In my experience, sometimes you can go up, and sometimes you have to go down. That is to say, sometimes, from the position that you're in, you can begin to soften and feel better. You can affirm wonderful things, you can move your body in wonderful ways, you can take in beautiful scenery. When you're already in a really good space, this is easy. You can appreciate all the things around you, all the wonderful things about your life with ease, grace, and joy. You can celebrate, you can rejoice.

SOLVE ET COAGULA

Not feeling it right now? You're not the only one. If you are not in a space of joyful openness already, if you're feeling uncomfortable or sad, fearful, anxious, grumpy, angry, frustrated, or just that never-ending grasping thirst for more, that sense of unease and that lack of fulfilment that many of us feel rather a lot of the time, then instead of trying to claw your way up to a state of equilibrium and then become happier and happier and more blissful, sometimes a far more transformative way to get to the same position is by going downwards. This is one of the great paradoxes of life.

There is tremendous power in opening up to the experience of difficult emotions. Indeed, it is one of the few things that can deeply transform, change, and shift these challenging patterns within us.

In alchemy, the path to spiritual enlightenment involves navigating both heavenly and hellish states within one's own mind, symbolised by the processes of descent into the dark depths of the psyche, a process called nigredo, confronting and integrating shadow aspects, akin to experiencing hell. This is followed by the stage of albedo, ascending to higher states of spiritual awareness, akin to experiencing heaven, followed by rubero, which symbolises the achievement of the ultimate goal of alchemy – complete transformation and integration of the self. This dual pathway to enlightenment, embracing both the light and dark aspects of the self, is echoed in other spiritual traditions such as Buddhism, Sufism, and Gnosticism, where profound growth is achieved through both ecstatic and challenging inner experiences.

In deeply feeling all of the frustrations and opening yourself up to those sensations, you discover that every bad feeling is actually tied to your resistance of it. That's what makes it bad. Fear is exactly the same as excitement, except with fear, we close down and resist. With excitement, we expand in anticipation of something good coming. Anger and passion are the same feeling, except with anger, we're often in resistance leading to frustration and suppression which then leads to resentment or depression. Even shame and embarrassment are experienced as resistance to humiliation which can be felt as a beautiful humbling and grounding experience if we are not in resistance to it (more on this later).

If you're not feeling 100% wonderful, you can use this as an opportunity to connect somatically (connecting deeply with your senses and your body).

Focus on your body. You may wish to cast a circle around yourself in your mind or bathe yourself in silver or golden light, or whatever it is that helps you to create the sacred space of safety within your being.

Put your hand on your heart, on your solar plexus, on your belly, or somewhere else where you feel the need or where the bad feeling seems to be coming from, and you may wish to pat, tap, or gently rub that part of your body.

For me, I experience most resistance in my solar plexus. This is a locus of control, the energy centre of the body that is most connected with the logical mind that is always seeking to control, always reaching for more.

When you've placed your hand on the part of your body where you feel the most emotion right now, allow yourself to breathe while focusing on the sensation.

Now, allow yourself to really open up to whatever it is that you feel. Allow yourself to breathe into the sensation in your body and observe it as it shifts, because emotions do tend to shift around when they're observed with gentle awareness. Hold a spaciousness in your mind as you do this. Do not try to push, do not try to force yourself to feel anything in any way at all. Just watch and listen and breathe slowly. Be present with the feelings that you have, and breathe into them.

If something unpleasant comes up for you, know that you can stop this exercise at any time, but also know that this is a golden opportunity. Allow yourself to release the resistance to the feelings that you don't like, and see what happens to the emotion.

For instance, you might be fearful about an upcoming situation, but if you release the resistance and allow yourself to fully experience the sensation, you may discover that a part of your soul resonates with this very experience. You see, the unconscious part of your shadow is craving all kinds of experiences and really deeply wants you to have absolutely everything, even the types of experiences that your conscious mind might be horrified about (and for good reason). This disconnect is part of the absurd, infinitely frustrating, enraging at times, and bizarre unconscious magic that plays out in our lives, resulting in extraordinary levels of suffering and drama stranger than even Hollywood can concoct.

Shadow work is about excavating this unconscious self, this aspect of your deep shadow soul, and then making the connection between your conscious and unconscious. You're able to accept and transform the things that you did not like and, in doing so, even find a pleasure and satisfaction, a thrill, a shiver, a throb of sensation – some kind of transformative signal that shows you that that shadowy part of your soul has had its thirst quenched, allowing that deeper transformation, that metamorphosis that you've begun, to continue on to its next stage.

Life throws all kinds of situations at us that we do not want, and this often causes us pain. Just as staying physically open and loose on impact can prevent injury by allowing our bodies to absorb and adapt to sudden forces, being emotionally open and flexible in the present moment helps us handle life's unexpected challenges. When we encounter painful situations, openness and emotional fluidity allows us to absorb and process these experiences without breaking. By staying present and receptive, we can navigate through difficulties with grace, adapting to what comes our way instead of resisting and causing ourselves more pain.

I have always found that once I can fully process an emotional pattern, whether it takes years or minutes, the situations that have been reflecting that pattern for me in my life change as quick as lightning, and I don't have to experience it again. When I began writing this book, it was suggested to me that I could include examples of magic in my life.

The constrictions in which we hold ourselves back can also feel pleasurable, not just in respecting how we are so carefully keeping ourselves safe from all the risks of our success, but also in the tightness; there is a magic to be found in the contained, the same way we might feel supported when we wear particular clothing that contains our physical form, or shoes, the same way that kinky people might enjoy being tied up and bound. It is a choice whether or not we enjoy the constrictions and the bondage that currently holds us back.

There is a part of our soul that loves the hard, yucky, dark matter of life. Why? Because life is all about the journey, including all the challenges on that journey and their resolution. If you picked up a book or started watching a movie and only good things happened in that book and movie, would you want to keep watching it? We need the challenge, we need the darkness, we need the shadow, because without it, the light is meaningless. So with this, we go deeper into the paradox of being, like a roly-poly, into the darkness, and in the constriction of the stretch, of the forward motion, the inner spiral.

It is the constrictions of winter, where there's not enough heat and traditionally there's scarcity of food. It's all part of the journey. There are many things in the journey that we totally wish we did not have to face at all, absolutely understandable. We can have total compassion for ourselves and our suffering, and we can connect with a part of our soul that loves absolutely everything, including that suffering, because your soul is divine.

In doing this work, myself, I go from the specific things that I would like into a state of oneness, and at that state of oneness, I can put my hand over my heart and connect in with myself. I can open to the connectedness between myself and the powerful force which you could call love, or the divine, or God or many other names. And I can also experience all my resistance, all my fear, all my frustrations, even my lack of faith, my grasping – all of that with openness, which paradoxically softens it so that it begins to dissolve. I can breathe into the sensation in my body, be present, open to having more and more sensation, deeply feeling the warmth, the soft receptiveness within me. This is the place through which magic comes.

The alchemical process of "solve et coagula" mirrors the internal transformation and metamorphosis we undergo, much like the journey of a caterpillar turning into a butterfly. "Solve," meaning to dissolve or break down, represents the initial stage where our existing structures, beliefs, and emotional patterns are deconstructed. The caterpillar enters its cocoon, where it dissolves into a nearly liquid state. Internally, we experience dissolution and disintegration, where old ways of being and thinking are questioned and dismantled.

"Coagula," meaning to coagulate or come together, signifies the subsequent phase of reformation and integration. Just as the caterpillar's cells reorganise and transform into the intricate structure of a butterfly, we begin to rebuild our inner selves with new insights and understandings. This stage is about synthesising the dissolved elements into a cohesive and higher form of self. Through this alchemical process, we emerge from our metaphorical cocoon as transformed beings, embodying a more refined and enlightened state of existence. The cycle of "solve et coagula" continues, fostering continual growth and evolution on our path to self-realisation.

I find that when I set my tongue at the base of my mouth, it mirrors a presence, an awareness of the deep soul, like the depths of the ocean or of deep space, the void from which all creation is born. Actions like this can be touchstones, like the crystals you might wish to carry in your pocket, like the cup of tea you drink every morning, the simple rituals throughout your day. These touchstones are subtle invitations towards presence.

The more we can connect with this space within ourselves, in our experience of the world around us, the more we can see the hidden beauty in imperfections, in all experiences that we encounter; even in our pain and suffering, there is beauty. Even in the ways we make ourselves feel wrong and bad, there can be an underlying zest for life, a craving for learning and for sensation, even a secret exquisite joy. Even in our deepest fears, there is exhilaration. You can tune in to this beauty, exquisite joy, and exhilaration within your being. From this place, we are able to connect more deeply with our wild magic. And that, my dear, is everything.

HUNGRY GHOSTS AND THE RAVENOUS SOUL

In mythology, hunger often represents a deep, insatiable craving that mirrors our own voracious desires for more – more experiences, more fulfilment, more meaning. The concept of hungry ghosts, prevalent in Buddhist, Chinese, and other East Asian traditions, embodies this idea vividly. Hungry ghosts are depicted as beings with immense bellies and tiny mouths, symbolising their endless and unquenchable hunger. They wander the world of the living, driven by their insatiable appetites, reflecting the human condition of perpetual longing and dissatisfaction, a cautionary tale about the dangers of unchecked desires and the suffering that comes from being in unconsciousness and therefore never being content.

Similarly, the Fear Gorta of Irish folklore is a spectral figure representing the devastating effects of famine and unfulfilled needs. This "hungry man" roams the land during times of scarcity, evoking the desperation and fear associated with extreme hunger. The Fear Gorta is said to bring misfortune and hardship, embodying the anxieties and insecurities that arise from our relentless quest for sustenance and security. It reminds us of the fragility of our existence and the dire consequences of our unending pursuit of more.

These mythological figures reflect our internal struggles with desire and fulfilment. They highlight the human tendency to seek satisfaction in external experiences and material possessions, often leading to a cycle of perpetual craving. In recognising the symbolism of hungry ghosts and the Fear Gorta, we are reminded of the importance of finding balance and contentment within ourselves. By addressing our inner hunger and understanding its roots, we can strive for a more harmonious and fulfilling existence, where our desires are met with mindful awareness rather than endless pursuit. What this mythos can teach us is that our perspective is almost everything.

For instance, as I write this, I'm on a stony, pebbly shore of an ocean, surrounding a hillside with rocks jutting out, and I look at this view and think how gorgeous it is. But if I really wanted to have a bad experience of the situation right now, I could think about all the slimy, rotting things that might be in the ocean. I could think of the pollution in the world and how there might be plastic floating around just in front of me under the surface. I could think about how the shapes of the hills could be a little bit better, or perhaps they shouldn't have built those houses over there. I could think about how the slightly fishy smell of seaweed isn't the most pleasant to experience, and in that state of resistance, I could be having a horrible time. But why would I want to do that?

Similarly, if I look at the glorious vista of my life, I can choose to see it as a miraculous unfolding, a beautiful view of all sorts of rich experiences, a thriving ecosystem. Or I could choose to think about all of the things that I haven't done, all of the problems that I don't know how to solve, all of the frustrations I have, or why I'm angry about a situation.

Looking out upon this view, a hungry ghost would see all the bad stuff, just as looking at a river of clear drinkable water, a hungry ghost would be thirsty but would only see a toxic wasteland. However, it's possible for the hungry ghosts to transform themselves, not through imagining a beautiful illusion, but through facing the ick of their situation – facing the awfulness and opening up to it until they reach a new level of awareness, thereby they see the water as clean and drinkable, and are transformed into human beings.

What the parable of hungry ghosts teaches us is that through aligning ourselves to appreciating everything, including our bad feelings, we go through the internal transformation necessary in order to recognise the beautiful vista of our life for what it is, instead of a horrible, slimy mess. Now, if your life doesn't in any way resemble a beautiful vista, that is perfectly okay. It just means that you're on the brink of something really big because you have a huge amount of potential for stepping more deeply into your magic right now. You have all kinds of weird experiences that your soul has brought forward from its shadow realms for you to experience, which means that there is so much potential joy, bliss, and transformation waiting for you.

You can look out at the broad perspective of your life, and if you want to, you can go up or down. You can either begin to notice the beautiful, fragrant, delicious things and thereby magnetise more of it into your life with deep appreciation, or you can take the downward path and open up to experiencing the gory glory of the shadow, the darkness, that which we cannot control, that which causes suffering and pain, that which we resist. And yet, in embracing it, in embracing the darkness, we have an unprecedented opportunity to bring our light deeper into the world, to raise awareness personally and collectively.

It's important to note that with the upward and downward ways of doing things – neither is superior to the other. I do believe that they all lead to the same place eventually. And I encourage you to do whatever feels best for you in any particular moment, because the more you get used to either raising yourself up into a state of bliss or pushing yourself into the depths of sensation in order to no longer have its power over you or cramp your style, the greater you expand your being into wholeness.

Both approaches work in tandem together, giving you the greatest advantage and the best access to both the light and the shadows. When you do this in a process of shadow exploration, any spellwork and rituals you do carry more potency because you are more deeply empowered.

You can also deliberately do this work *through* ritual and spellwork. I like to play a game with myself where I hold my mind open either while sitting in meditation or going for a walk, and when something arises that I don't completely enjoy, that I have resistance to, I allow myself to go into the beautiful, loving state and/or ask with curiosity, "How can I enjoy this?" For example, it might be something like "My business isn't doing so well," or "My work's not going so well." And then, if you ask with curiosity, "How can I enjoy this?" you open up new possibilities.

It might be that you're in a state where you absolutely cannot enjoy it. To me, this indicates a need to grieve. It might take time, or it might not. You may need to allow all the experiences to flow through you. You may need to sulk and pout, you may need to scream and vent, you may need to hit some pillows, you may need to go out into a garden and do some intensive pruning to get out your frustration on that annoying plant that keeps growing back way too fast. You might need to just roll around in the unpleasant sensations for a while, and in doing so, you might even find that there's pleasure to be had in your self-righteousness, in your self-pity, in your burning anger, even in your boring frustration. When you can find pleasure and humour in it, when you can find lightness and curiosity again, that's when you know that you've grieved enough.

PRACTICAL: EQUINOX LIGHT AND DARK INTEGRATION

Deep transformation, as in alchemising the disparate elements of the self, requires acknowledging, accepting, delving deeper, and better understanding where you have conflicts and paradoxes existing within you. For example, there might be a part of you that is striving for success, wanting to do more and more, wanting to accomplish, and yet another part of you just wants to rest, to hide, to give in. When these two parts are not integrated, a conflict of the self is present which will wear you out over time. You may lean further into one direction, such as the striving, only to feel more exhausted by the part of you that wants to rest, or you may seek to rest and bury your head in the sand only to feel more frustrated and plagued by unpleasant emotions telling you that you haven't done enough.

Or, you can integrate these emotions...

Hold up your hands, palms open in front of you. Imagine in your left hand you are holding that need for passivity and rest. Acknowledge how it wants to wrap you in a warm blanket, wants to give you lots of nice, wonderful naps, it wants you to be safe, to rejuvenate, to choose to be protected from the world, wants you to snuggle up and find peaceful rest. In your left palm, you may imagine some sort of object that represents this, or it may be a colour, texture, or some other thing that reflects your need and desire for rest.

Now, in your right hand, imagine holding your striving, wanting to achieve, to do, to act. That impetus, that burning energy, is fire compared to the restful water in your left hand. You may see it as some other kind of object if that makes sense for you. Your striving wants you to achieve, it wants you to accomplish. It wants you to be active and to do. In some ways, it also wants to protect you from feeling like you haven't accomplished anything, even if that means taking a risk that might result in frustration or failure when things don't work out.

Focus again on the left hand of passivity and restfulness, and now return your focus to the right hand of striving, impatience, frustration, wanting you to get things done. Can you see how both try to help you, support you, or protect you? Can you see that both are actually wearing you out, partly because they are at odds with each other?

Return your attention to your left hand. Acknowledge the gift of peaceful, receptive response. Bring it into your heart. Acknowledge it, how you can honour this in your life: taking rest this way, nourishing your mind and your body, peacefulness, listening to music, being by the sea, having nice naps, indulging your deep need and desire for peace and rejuvenation. Feel this peacefulness wash over you. Hold your hands over your heart.

While you focus again on your open right palm, you feel and connect with that burning passion, that passion that wants so much to strive and be active in the world, and yet it can wear you out. Acknowledge where that burning desire comes from. Acknowledge how it wants to support you in your life. Greet it with love and respect. Then move it to cover your other hand over your heart if you feel comfortable doing so, resting passion atop peace, striving atop rest, corresponding to each other, allowing you to achieve what it is you want, to allow these energies, water and fire, to swirl around each other. Allow yourself to open to both so that they both have a place within. Allow yourself to be intuitively guided towards both restfulness and action, passivity and activeness.

As you continue to hold your hands here, see that these two are mutually beneficial in how they can support you. They no longer need to function as opposites, calling you in different directions. Rather, they can balance as equal weights on the scale that allows you to do what you most need to do in your life. This way, open yourself up to brilliant potential. And as you do so, open yourself up to a deep sense of appreciation for both these forces in your life.

You may wish to move your body in ways that release the tension. Take several deep, calming, relaxing, energising breaths to be both calm and energised, to be both relaxed and active. These are the states that encourage deep and lasting productivity and satisfaction, allowing inspiration to flow through you both in your restful states and in your active states.

Acknowledge your desire for rest. Know that the need for rest will not go away and neither will your desire to strive.

EMBRACE THE CYCLE AND LET GO

I often find myself peculiarly enthralled by the cycle of renewal that nature so eloquently displays. The deep and solemn beauty of the forest where the old trees thrive until they gently, gracefully relinquish their hold, falling to the forest floor. In their decay, they nourish the soil, fostering the sprouting of new life. Their demise, necessary for the birth of the new.

This natural cycle is a poignant metaphor for our own lives. To allow new growth, we must be willing to let go of what no longer serves us. The beliefs, habits, or relationships that once provided structure and safety might now stifle our growth, much like the shadow of an old, towering tree stifles the saplings below. By releasing these old ties, we open ourselves to new opportunities and experiences, and allow fresh life to take root.

Embrace the change, as unsettling as it might seem. Just as the forest does not fear the fall of its timeworn trees, we should not fear the process of renewal. It is in this space, the shadowed and nutrient-rich soil of what once was, that new life can emerge. In letting go, we do not merely make room for the new – we invite it in, with open arms and a curious heart, ready to flourish in the newly cleared ground of our existence.

What are you ready to let go of in your life?

Where do you currently feel stuck?

What repeated patterns and circles do you find yourself in?

If you breathe into the tension of these patterns, slowly and gently, like trees rustling in the forest, what new glimmers of awareness are ready to shine through?

7

FORMIDABLE MAGIC

"Archetypally, the Life/Death/Life nature is a basic component of the instinctive nature. This is personified through world myth and folklore...stories are filled with these remnants of the old creation Goddess personifications." — Clarissa Pinkola Estés

As the shadows grow longer and the veil grows thinner at Samhain we turn to grieving the past and healing our ancestries, releasing the pain of the past, and opening up to working with the shadow – deep inner work. In nature death fuels life. Leaves fall from the trees to compost into rich fertile soil; everything that dies in the wild breaks down into particles that fuel ongoing and future life. Nothing is wasted.

In contemporary culture we have a lot of resistance to death because it terrifies us. Our limitations, our mortality, the end of life as we know it, all of this is too scary to think about most of the time. But death is the shadow of life, and much empowerment can come from facing our fears of the unknown, from looking death in the eye and holding our power, our attention, our awareness.

ILLUMINATING THE SHADOW

We all hope for a better world, for our own freedom, joy, and happiness, and the happiness of those we love. We all aspire to better things, to better feelings, to better outcomes. That's the flame, the light, that casts the shadow of despair, because for every ray of light in optimism, there's also the darkness in potentiality. That is where the pain comes from, and that is why sometimes people's hopes, especially when voiced in a naive, ignorant, or insensitive way, can give rise to voices of such despair. If hope brings pain, why do we bother? Because just like the seed willing to sprout, we must take the risk to live life as fully as we can muster, and just as the trees let go their leaves in the autumn, we too must let go of what no longer serves us so that it can compost into the fertile soil of the psyche, ready to grow anew.

If we can integrate both the hope and despair together, seeing them as part of a concentric circle, an interlocking whole, we're stepping into the part of the master magician within ourselves and within the world around us. Being able to face the shadow of despair requires bravery. Facing our shadows and walking into the unknown darkness requires such courage. It is the most important work we can do, especially if we care about the fate of the world and our loved ones, because everything we do that hurts them is a symptom of the unintegrated shadow.

It is essential to grieve the past in order to clear the way for new life, to compost the old decaying matter of the psyche and free up the energy to nourish our present and future. In this grieving, we face the limitations of life, and how in every choice we make, every path we take, we leave other options behind that will never be lived and experienced. In this undertaking, grieving becomes the antidote to regret, for we no longer regret the things we have fully accepted and let go of.

Whatever you are carrying right now, you have the opportunity to call your energy and power back to yourself. Put your hand over your heart, or wherever you feel called to place it on your body. Notice where your energy still lingers in the past. Notice all the threads connecting you to situations that no longer require your present active attention. Call all your energy back, allow it to fill you up. Feel any emotions that need to be felt right now, accept, let go, and simply be. This is a simple form of shadow work that you can do every day, if you choose to.

The more we alchemise our shadows, the more we are freed from their unconscious influence upon our lives, often sabotaging us in ways we often do not understand or recognise at all. As the darkness of the unconscious becomes illuminated by awareness, we personally, are able to slip deeper and deeper into being, into our magic, into our power, into the flow of life, opening to creative energy pouring through us into the world. Creative expression itself is a beautiful way of dancing with the shadow, be it through the words we speak or write, through the art we make, through the messages we send out into the world, or simply by being a beacon of presence, joy, wisdom, and understanding for others around us. Like the alchemists of old, we can transmute the lead of our shadows into the gold of our deeper selves.

Nature includes a great deal of both light and shadow, and so too does our own wild nature. Notice how life feeds off life and do not to turn away from the very vital role death plays in the cycle. Animals consume other living animals and plants; one must die for the other to live. Life is regenerative, and the transmutation from one form to another is magical. What shadowy parts do we need to observe within ourselves? What do we need to accept and let go of in order for a part of our own selves to die and nourish the new self in its transformation? The beautiful poet Rainer Maria Rilke encapsulates the essence of this process, this terrifying though ultimately exhilarating transmutation – *"Let everything happen to you: beauty and terror. Just keep going. No feeling is final."*

Just as nature moves through cycles of light and dark, life and death, growth and decay, so too must we embrace the totality of our being. We must learn to dance with our shadows, to find the hidden gifts within the challenges and the wounds. The more integrated we are, the more we are able to contribute to fulfilling our deeper purpose in this world.

What is your purpose in this world? The paradox of purpose is that it is both extremely unique and individual while also, on another level, being entirely, beautifully, simply the same as everyone else's. All beings come into this material world to experience, to learn and grow, to share and create, to experience the extreme limits of physicality. Sometimes, it doesn't go so well, which is not to say that it should or should not always go well, because that is part of the greater mystery.

In terms of your own personal purpose, I cannot tell you specifically what it is, but I can tell you how you might find it. Find it by listening deeply in silence, feeling down through the scattered everyday thoughts, feeling deeply into your body. Being present in your body and yourself. You can do this through formal meditation practices, but you don't need to. You can do it in any moment – every moment – every time you get a glimpse of yourself, be it in the heat of an argument or an easy stroll in the park or the taste of the delicious soup you're making. Every moment, you have the opportunity to be in the deep, wild sensation of your being. Allow yourself to sink into the dark, rich soil of your soul, to feel the pulse of life that thrums through your veins.

Allow yourself to connect to your purpose as you walk, as you fall asleep at night, as you lie in the bath, immersed in hot water, and you feel your whole body relax. Go deeply into that sensation, go deeply into sensations in your body. Tune into each one of your senses – your allies in experience – as each can bring its own wild lesson. Our ancestors knew to tune into all their senses. It helped them survive the wilderness and struggles of less convenient times and it can also help us now in our complex modern lives.

The feeling of heaviness in your chest might signal emotion welling to the surface from deep within, ready to be felt, grieved, released, and unburdened. The view around you may provide a sign, a symbol, connecting you with your path. What bird just flew overhead? Is it an ancestor sending you a message, a sign from divinity, or a simple synchronicity reflecting to you that you're on the right path? Only intuition can guide you here. Let the cravings of the mind fade away for a moment and tune in. What interpretation feels right? The scent of perfume hanging in the air as you walk down the street might lend a sense of romance or nostalgia to the present moment, evoking a new desire within you to reconnect with old friends or open up to new love. Every new flavour you taste is a whole new experience, broadening your horizons. The sounds we hear in the rustle of trees, in the wind, in the ocean's waves, in the chatter and bustle of the city, all this too can contain wild wisdom, if only we connect to it. Our emotions, themselves, are our biggest asset in uncovering our own wild nature. Sometimes emotions can seem awfully inconvenient, but slip beneath the dusty resistance and you'll find a treasure chest of powers waiting to be awakened.

In connecting with our wild magic we learn that allowing all sensations to rise up and be felt, no matter how pleasant or unpleasant we judge them to be, is immensely powerful work. Embracing our emotions with radical acceptance is important work, as the Buddhist writer, Tara Brash encourages. It may seem too simple – or far too messy – or boring – or too hard. However, leaving our old emotions trapped within us like stroppy children sent to their rooms does nothing to set our whole selves free or tap into the immense power that even emotions judged as "unpleasant" can bless us with. When we can fully feel, we can deeply heal.

Continue this work and you will develop a strong sense of inner knowing, such a strong connection with your intuition, that you will be able to communicate with your soul and your soul's reason for being here, your purpose. You may begin to notice it subtly at first, the things that are important to you, the messages and symbols that appear in your life, the signs and yearnings for the good things you want to bring into the world. Any kind of communication that you have can be a translation of your purpose, and the closer you are to this sense of being, the closer you are to yourself and the more magical your life becomes. You don't have to worry about whether you're on the right path, because you simply must be. You're here, aren't you? The question is, how far have you strayed from your soul's deeper longings into the roles and ambitions that other people have set for you?

If you're having trouble connecting to that deep sense of knowing, do not fret. This is a life's work. But the more you practice listening, tuning in, feeling deeply, even in your despair, the closer to *knowing* you will come. The many distractions of life sometimes make this challenging.

In doing this work, you may need to grieve deeply, especially if you're carrying old emotion and trauma like many of us do. Listening to your body and to your soul may be challenging if there's too much emotion in the way, but know that as you grieve, as you breathe through the sensations of emotion, allowing it to release and change, and as you transform your relationship to it, you're clearing away the old burdens, like dead tree trunks in the forest, so that new life can grow, opening yourself up to the healing in a spiritual way, emotionally, with the magic which is also connected to absolutely everything.

As Jung wrote, "There is no coming to consciousness without pain. People will do anything, no matter how absurd, in order to avoid facing their own Soul. One does not become enlightened by imagining figures of light, but by making the darkness conscious."

Here's a paradox again: that you are uniquely, complexly, beautifully unique and yet part of the universe, so deeply interconnected that all is one, with the inner reflecting the outer. We can go more deeply into our experience, dissolving the blocks and obstacles in our way, and as we do so, we open the way for magic to come into our lives. Like the seed that must break open to sprout, we too must allow ourselves to be cracked open by life, to let the light pour into our darkest places.

The deeper you go with this, the more you will see surprising results in the world around you, the magic, the flowers blooming with the dewdrops glistening on their petals in the morning. And as we open up to the synchronicity, we connect with the creative force within us all and dream things into being and into reality in a way we might have never thought possible. As we stir our metaphorical cauldrons, we mix the ingredients of life – joys and sorrows, light and your shadow – and alchemise them into the potion of our becoming.

Until we make the unconscious conscious, it will direct our lives and we will call it fate. By embracing your shadows, we reclaim the power to shape our destiny. The more we integrate our shadows, the more we are freed from their unconscious influence upon our lives, sabotaging us in ways we often do not understand or recognise at all. As the darkness of the unconscious becomes illuminated by awareness, we personally are able to slip deeper and deeper into being, into our magic, into our power, into the flow of creation with pure creative energy pouring through us into the manifest world. Be it through the words we speak or write, through the art we make, through the messages we send out into the world, or simply by being a beacon of presence, joy, wisdom, and understanding for others around us.

Throughout history, the forces of empires have not only redrawn maps but have also sought to redefine the spiritual landscapes of those they dominated. This system of disconnection has had the privilege to decide what is real, as Vandana Shiva points out, creating monocultures of the mind where only the ideology of the dominating forces of the world are allowed to be honoured as real knowledge and other forms of understanding and wisdom are stripped of their value, ridiculed, or diminished as just "myths and legends," as if these weren't equally as important as modern science in understanding humanity and the world around us. Indigenous practices, rich with magic and deeply intertwined with the land and its spirits, were, and still are, often suppressed, misunderstood, or dismissed by authorities. Throughout history, the ideologies brought by colonisers, including in the many periods of colonisation of Brittain and Ireland, aimed to convert or erase local spiritual traditions, valuing material wealth and dominion over the earth above the ancient wisdom of harmony and balance.

In this process, a disconnection was wrought, a rift between humanity and the magic that ripples through the natural world. The rise of materialism, the belief in only what can be seen, measured, and sold, has further deepened this chasm. Modern life, with its technological marvels and its frenetic pace, often leaves little room for the quiet intuition of the earth, the rhythms of the moon and the tides, the ancient calls that beckon us to remember our part in the great web of being.

Yet, it is in this disconnection that the seeds of awakening can find fertile soil. To awaken the witch within is to answer the call of the wild, the primal, the magical that exists within and around us. We cannot ignore the shadows of violence and domination in the world, if we want to live fully in our magic. We need to face these shadows, not gloss over them, as we do all that we can to reconnect. As we do this, we see nature, not as a resource to be exploited but as a sacred community to which we belong. To embody the wisdom of the wild witch is to understand that genuine power in presence, in the ability to listen to the stories of the wind and the waters, and to speak the language of the plants and the stones.

Becoming a powerful force in the world does not require the conquest of others but the mastery of oneself. It calls for the courage to stand in one's truth, to live in alignment with one's deepest values and wisdom, and to wield one's power with grace, for the benefit of all beings.

THE COSMIC SCALES

What we want has an equal and opposite force that comes with it, often keeping it just out of reach. For instance, if you decide you'd love to have new love come into your life, the reflective nature of the universe means that while the light of your awareness focuses on how nice it would be to have this new love, a shadow part of you is equally focused on the very opposite of that. You might not be aware of it because the nature of the shadow is to be hidden, besides you're so focused on how nice it would be to have something wonderful that it seems ridiculous that any part of you wouldn't want that, but if you dig beneath the surface, you may find something else going on. This is not just relevant for love, it's true for all desires. While the conscious mind has its sight set on a new shiny goal, there's another part of us that deeply resists the change, that's afraid of the vulnerabilities of intimacy, that mistrusts the giddiness of new love, is afraid of the risk of getting hurt, is afraid of losing control and of having to deal with somebody else in our personal space.

If you don't properly integrate the shadow desire, it will get in the way. The new love may not show up, or it may show up in a form that is incompatible with what you're really wanting. Or if you do manage, with the great power of your will and desire to bring about the new love, you may quickly discover that even though this person seemed perfect, a shadow of your desire manifests in the relationship, sabotaging the chance of a happy union, and within three or four months you might only see flaws in the person who seemed so wonderful when you first met.

You do not have to integrate these shadows, but I'm going to tell you that in my experience, it is the quickest way and the most effective way towards resolving issues and tensions in your life. In doing this work, you may clear a path towards your desires or discover that unbeknownst to you, the part of you that resists love is actually trying to take you on a deeper spiritual journey. Instead of pursuing the romance that society tells us we need in order to be complete, you may discover that you value your aloneness, where you go deeper into the magic of your solitary existence, a powerful desire that is more meaningful for you in the long run than romantic whims that may distract you from your spiritual path. You may find that there are other loves in your life, such as your creativity, your friends, and family members, and so on, that are more fulfilling for you at this time. It is only in letting go of the attachment to your desire, and in processing the shadow of it, that you can uncover whether it is what you really want, ultimately, or whether it was simply leading you down the garden path towards other magic.

Although many of us are easily drawn into the great rush and fanciful delights of romance, for the most part, these are projections distracting ourselves from our fear of aloneness. When we can fully integrate that aloneness, then it no longer matters. It is dangerous to seek fulfilment in another person, but when we find our own fulfilment we can be happy in relationships without getting into unhealthy emotional co-dependency patterns. When we uncover what we really want, we have the choice. We can be open to new love or not and we can stay powerful. This is the most important thing, especially in a relationship. If we give too much of our power away, we upset the balance and create a miserable push and pull dynamic, which is best avoided at all costs.

If you're in a long-term relationship and you feel that the spark has gone, you may wish to delve into your desires on what you're wanting and what the polarity, the opposite of that desire, is. For example, you may wish for more attention from your partner, but equally, you may wish to be left alone. You may really want them to do or not to do certain things and you may have frustrations built up over time in your partnership. Of course, these things are normal, and yet they also have huge potential for transformation if you could look at the pattern a little bit differently, connect with your desire and the equal opposite. You have a lot of potential to transform your relationships and your life into one that is far more magical.

For instance, if your partner doesn't contribute to the household chores there may be a part of you that very much, definitely, consciously wants them to do their fair share, yes. Meanwhile, deeper down, you may find that there is a saboteur part of you that enjoys the rage of being angry with them, that loves feeling self-righteous, because isn't self-righteousness delicious sometimes?

There are shadowy unconscious parts of us that absolutely delight in other people not living up to our expectations because we can feel like they proved us right! We've told them over and over again and they still haven't listened. We can feel like martyrs to the cause and enjoy all that shadowy rage.

There is something within us that loves to struggle, that loves to fight. And unfortunately, this often is a part that we only feel safe expressing in our closest relationships. This is why our children are more likely to argue with us than with strangers or even their friends, because we are safe.

The closer you are to somebody, the more they see your shadow side, and it's not always pretty, but it does contain the rich psychic minerals through which magic can grow, if only you let go of the old leaves and let them compost down into something that's ready to be recycled, reborn, to transform, to grow new life into this world.

POWER, PARADOX AND THE DOUBLE BIND OF EXPECTATIONS

The paradox of power and control is that when you try to seize power or take control you're actually in a state of disempowerment. The more we seek control, the less power we are able to hold, because our attention is focused elsewhere – on the thing that we want to control, rather than on our own innate sense of empowerment which can only be found when we are present and centred.

Trust that you can cope with the immense power you already wield, and you can begin to break the pattern of a lifetime – the pattern of seeking externally the things which we already possess internally. Coming from this internal locus of power, we naturally are more able to focus and deal with external challenges. Stress and anxiety and going around in circles are all clever ways for the mind to feel as if it is in control when really it is just distracting you from the only power you do have, which you can find in stillness, in tuning in and listening and feeling the immense power of your being.

We do not always have control internally or externally, perhaps control is only an illusion after all, but we can find empowerment within ourselves. Indeed, it is the only place we *can* find our power!

In centring ourselves we have tremendous power over our lives, and in the world around us. Sometimes it helps to detach from the expectations we have of others. If you want your child or partner, boss, friend or parent or sibling to behave a certain way, you've already given up your power and fixated on something external to create a problem.

Now it may certainly be true that your partner or friend or sibling is being terrible. It really is a problem! You're not making that up. You can acknowledge that for what it is, but in doing so, also acknowledge that you are seeing from a particular lens. You have a vested interest in changing the behaviour because you have strong expectations. How do I know you have strong expectations? Because that's how human relationships work, especially for those closest to us. Our expectations of other people help us get through the day. It's how our brains work to simplify things. We expect people to behave in a certain way so that we don't have to spend all kinds of excess energy in wondering and speculating about how they will behave. We weave stories about the people in our lives into our own stories. X is the person who... X means this to me... X always or never or sometimes does....

There's nothing wrong with this at all, except when it's causing us pain. The expectations we have from others can seem totally reasonable and the people breaking those expectations are therefore automatically totally unreasonable. Expectations help us navigate relationships but they can also become a hindrance to actual connection and meaningful communication.

How will you know if your expectations are getting in your own way? You'll be furious, sometimes, or simply frustrated, or disappointed. You'll go around in circles trying to figure out how to solve a problem with another person. They are always the problem, right? While there are a lot of behaviours that are indeed problematic, by staying within the pattern of the problem we are trapped within it. It's only when we can step back into selves and let go of our patterns of expectation that we can see more clearly how to approach the situation. We may be surprised to discover it wasn't really any of our business and that the other people involved are actually fine. Or that there are simple things we can do to support them without getting in the way with our own agenda (which in my experience tends to be more about trying to control my own anxiety than anything else).

In stepping back and allowing our illusions of control to dissolve along with the expectations that come with it, we can see more clearly what is really going on. For instance, in a romantic relationship, you may expect a certain level of care or attention, you may expect gifts of flowers or chocolate, you may assume that your significant other should turn off their device and listen to you when you have something to say, or just that they'll put the grater back in the right place so you don't have to look for it every single time! Take a step back, step back into yourself, into your own sense of being, which is the most empowered position for you to be in, and ask yourself "what do I really need?" It might be just a level of care and attention, or it might be specific symbolic gestures like bouquets of flowers, or it might be that you discover something else that you've never realised before about yourself and your own needs.

When you've explored your own feelings and intuition to the situation without thinking about the other people involved you will be in a far better situation to express what it is that you really need. You may discover you have a pattern of being let down by people that comes from your parents letting you down as a child. Parenting is a tough gig and I don't know of any parents who have not ever let their children down. Even if you have brilliant loving and caring parents you will still have been hurt by life in your childhood and your parents won't have been able to protect you from that pain. Young children naturally look up to their parents like gods. If this does not ring true for you, you may have been disappointed so early on that you don't even remember the blind adulation a baby feels for the amazing big people in their life. If you unearth painful experiences in this process of looking within, please do consult with trauma-informed therapists and allow yourself to process and grieve. This is very important. If you're trapped in grief and trauma it's hard to feel magical and powerful because of the emotional ties holding you back, however you may well find that in resolving the old emotion and in healing you will be in a far better position to do the magical work you're here on this planet to do, especially in your ability to empathise and relate to the struggles of other people.

People often find that the things that bother them in other people relate to something from their own childhood, particularly when it comes to people in positions of authority, and in processing this you can liberate yourself and break the pattern. If you find you are often in the same kind of pattern but with different people, then you have an opportunity for liberation.

When I was working in the public sector, in large government ministries, I occasionally had managers who triggered feelings of powerlessness from my childhood. It wasn't always clear that this was the case, because when someone behaves in a way that seems disrespectful or narcissistic, we tend to identify them as the problem, but after a while I realised that my emotional reaction to these kinds of managers was so intense. It was coming from somewhere else. Yes, the people were out of line, but the emotion in me felt...very young. I looked back and realised I'd had this similar pattern throughout my life, with one of my PhD supervisors, with some of my teachers, and most definitely with family members. My childhood was rife with power struggles. Over and over again I was made to feel completely powerless. Even though I was fortunate not to suffer from physical violence when I was growing up, I was faced with threats of violence and twisted psychological manipulation every single day from a family member who used words as a means to control. Suffice to say, I've had my fair share of powerlessness.

This pattern repeated for me for many years with various authority figure I had to work with. It became clearer to me, over the years, that I needed to resolve the internal situation in order to solve the external situation. This happened piece by piece, as my awareness of my own emotional situation grew and as I became braver. I reasoned that I first had to process the emotion as much as I possibly could so that I could deal with the external situation and work the magic I needed to work in order to properly resolve the pattern. It's my experience that in resolving patterns they stop repeating, and my strategy is to approach the situation from every possible angle to see what I can learn and process until I know the best way to proceed.

I had a manager at the time, I'll call her Pam, who seemed like a total sociopathic narcissist. I wasn't the only person who struggled with Pam. Several other people in my team were having a hard time with her. She played favourites and punished people who she didn't approve of by humiliating them. I had been her favourite for a while, and even though I knew people who'd said awful things about her from previous roles she was in, I was willing to give her the benefit of the doubt, until my health played up and Pam was not here for it. She began suggesting undermining things like telling me to go to Human Resources and get a plan in place for improving my health to get things back on track. Now, if your health problems are exacerbated by stress, this sounds like a huge emotional burden to take on when you're struggling just to function! I managed to dodge that particular situation by making it clear that it wouldn't be helpful but Pam kept undermining me, occasionally saying nasty things to me in our one-on-one catch ups that made me so uncomfortable that I struggled even to repeat them to anyone else. Her behaviour created an environment of toxic stress, and while it helped a tiny bit when I commiserated with other people who had had similar (or worse) treatment from her, that circular pattern of complaining and speculating only went so far.

One night I received a demanding email from Pam which really threw me. At this point I'd gone around in circles for long enough, and I'd finally processed the previously unresolved emotions from my childhood around being made powerless to the point where I could think clearly. I wrote back: "I'm struggling with your management style."

I had hit a point of no return. I'd been looking for other jobs, but nothing had come through and I realised I couldn't run from this situation. It was time. I'd done the work and I needed to face this head-on. Pam wrote back: "Let's talk about this." It was an invitation, and I took her up on the offer, but knowing that I and others had struggled so much with her, I came prepared. I wrote down all the specific things that I'd had problems with, and why. When it came time for the meeting, I recorded the conversation for my own emotional protection, and I read out my spell. I'm going to call it a spell because it was based on another spell I'd done several times in my personal life which I will cover soon. It's a simple word spell, though you can make it as complicated as you like. It's a breaking spell because it breaks through the illusions and binds that we hold ourselves back with, often without even realising it.

The previous two times I'd performed this spell were both in relation to romantic attachments back in my 20s that I had been circling around in an infuriating way. The only way I could break myself out of the vicious cycle was to write down all the things I'd never said to the person in question, all the things I'd never said in order to protect them, or protect myself from the risk of them hurting me. I'd written the list, and I'd demanded the person's presence so that I could read it out to them, and in both situations it had worked. It had freed me from my own binds and I was able to continue to be friends with people rather than being infuriated by a dysfunctional attachment.

This work situation was different. But the situation was also similar enough that an adapted spell would work. I just needed to make sure I maintained my composure – held my power rather than scattering it in fear and frustration. My list was using clear non-judgy language, because I know that when you call people names and say, accuse them of being sociopathic narcissists, they stop listening to you, they go into fight or flight type survival mode and you don't get anywhere new from there. Survival mode is all about protecting what you already have. It's a personally conservative stance because you're trying to save yourself. I didn't want to put her into that position, because I wasn't doing this to punish her, I was doing this to break my own pattern.

I told Pam, very clearly and as calmly as I could muster that I needed her to listen and not to speak, then I read out my list, two pages of notes jotted down in my notebook. It was along the lines of "when you said...I felt..."

This spell didn't involve any crystals or candles, though if I'd wanted to, I could have brought a protective black onyx or an empowering garnet with me. I could have performed it in a small personal ritual before carrying out the more office-friendly ritual of having a meeting. When I'd finished going over my list of saying the things I'd always been too afraid to call her out on before, Pam said, "so what would you like out of this situation?"

I was taken aback, pleased that she hadn't reacted too abrasively, but I wasn't ready to jump to a solution just yet. "I want you to listen to what

I've said, and to respond." It took a while, but Pam, to her credit, did reflect on what I'd said, and on her own behaviour. "I might need to communicate things differently when I'm emailing you...and talking to you." This wasn't the entirety of the problem, but it was an acknowledgement of the surface level of it, and to her credit, Pam changed her behaviour after this. She admitted that she isn't a very introspective person, that as an extrovert she doesn't always realise how she's affecting people around her. The work dynamic changed and I stopped feeling like I was living in toxic stress, and shortly after this, Pam left and a new manager emerged.

This was a significant turning point in the troubling work power dynamics. It didn't resolve all of my problems, but I never had the same totally disempowering toxic stress situation at work again. I had risen from being a victim of the situation into a position of empowerment and I'd done it through speaking my truth. The magic worked.

THE MAGIC OF THE THINGS WE NEVER SAY: THE BREAKING SPELL

If there are people in your life who you have the same problematic dynamic with over and over again you may want to try this spell for yourself. I strongly recommend reading through this entire spell before beginning the work on it. It's powerful magic even though it's very simple.

Step one: feeling the feelings

First of all, focus on the present situation and write down in your journal, all the emotions that come up for you. When you're finished writing all the feelings down, allow yourself to feel the feelings as much as you can. Your openness to the sensations of your feelings is part of the magic. Take a moment to pause and take a few deep breaths. Relax your shoulders.

Step two: stock take

Now go back to your journal and write down all the times in the past where you've felt similar emotions. This is a stocktake of "the problem." In doing this, you're creating a conscious connection with the pattern. It's your pattern. It's not your fault, but it's a pattern you've been carrying with you. It's a lesson you've been trapped in for a long time. Write every single previous experience you can think of that relates to this pattern, including the first times in your life where you felt similar emotions. Acknowledge all the feelings. They are all valid. All our experiences are valid.

Step three: perspective

Now, looking over your lists, allow yourself to see the pattern in its entirety. How is this pattern helping you to learn about disempowerment? Are you ready to see the forest for the trees? Are you ready to see the pattern in its beautiful and painful entirety? The situation you've been in is probably incredibly uncomfortable, otherwise you wouldn't have chosen to focus on it for this exercise. You are incredibly brave for being here, for getting to this point and now I'm telling you the pattern is beautiful? Is that offensive? It may well be, and I'll acknowledge that there may be nothing at all beautiful in your painful situation. You get to decide how you look at it now because you're in the process of metamorphosis. You are doing the work. This is your own personal alchemy. You may wish to name the pattern, or you may wish to simply observe it, but either way, take a moment to pay yourself some respect. You've been disempowered. You've been a victim, here. Allow yourself to be fulfilled in your experience of this so far because it – for better or worse – has been part of your journey so far. Acknowledge your courage. You've had enough and you've gone further than many people ever do in their self-work and processing. You're ready for the next step.

Step four: the things you've never said

Write a list of all the things that weren't okay. Every single thing you can think of. This list can take the form that I took in dealing with my manager. "When you said x, I felt x," or "when you did x that was disempowering for me and made me think x." Alternately, you can frame the entire list as "It's not okay to…" which might work better in personal situations where a boundary has been crossed or needs left unmet. "It's not okay for you to ignore me when I say I need to talk," "It's not okay to break promises," "It's not okay to disregard my feelings," or "It's not okay to say things that distort my reality." You are communicating, clearly, everything that wasn't okay for you. Centre your own experience in this. You don't ever know exactly what is going on in another person's head, so it's important to focus on what you do know. You know what wasn't okay for you, so go ahead and write your list. Write all of it.

Step five: reflect

Reflect on your list. Allow yourself to have the courage to feel all the feelings. Have you missed anything? Feel free to add to the list. When you feel your list is full, look at it from a broader perspective, just to make sure you've done yourself justice. Remove any judgy or accusatory language from your list. It's fine for you to have those judgements, but the magic here involved breaking through them, even just for a moment so that you can honour your own experience in its totality, regardless of the other person. Are you scared of hurting them? Do you want to hurt them? Is it not okay that their behaviour had led you down either or both of those pathways? If so, write that down too.

Step six: choose

The choice is yours now. You have, in your hands, a super powerful tool. This is the breaking list. If you're ready and the person in question is safe enough to have a conversation with, then you can go about things in a similar way to what I did. If you don't want to speak to the person and it's unsafe to do so, then carry out the rest of this exercise in your mind and imagine them responding as YOU choose them to. Know that in the next stage you will be breaking the relationship. Are you ready for this? I'm going to tell you right now that if you've gotten this far, it's likely that the relationship is already broken, but like a bone that hasn't been properly set, it will never really heal unless you can give it a clean break. It will never be the same again. You risk losing something, yes, but it was probably something you never really had in the first place. What you risk losing is your illusion about what the relationship should be. In performing the breaking spell, things will change because you will change and because you will speak the words you've been bottling up all this time in order to protect the other person, or yourself, or the illusion of how the relationship should be. If you've gone around in circles with this enough, you might find you're already at the situation where you're ready for change.

Step seven: ask

Request a time where the other person can listen to you without speaking for a few minutes. Centre yourself emotionally and ask them, clearly, for what you want, e.g., "I have something I need to share with you and I need you to listen, without interrupting for a few minutes. When I've finished speaking, I want you to take a moment to think about what I've said. Can you do this?" They might distract you with some other thing or try to undermine you. If so, ask again. Ask, with calm confidence, until they agree. If they absolutely refuse you can always do this without them, but even asking takes courage. Asking to be heard is making a commitment to yourself and to your own needs.

Step eight: share

Once you've asked for what you need and this has been granted or refused, it's time to create a sacred space in your own mind. When emotions like fear and anxiety come in, let them know that this is a sacred space and they can sit quietly in the circle until it's time for you to call on them when sharing about your experiences of fear and anxiety. If you have the option to be in the same room as the person, when you enter the room, project your sacred space out to cover the whole room. Occupy this space in the fullness and calmness of your power. You have a right to be here. You deserve to be heard. Share your list. Share it with as much calm poise and earnest emotion you can muster. You are being incredibly brave right now and you are working powerful magic! Enjoy it. When you get to the end of your list, it may be helpful to remind the other person to reflect and process for a moment before responding. Hold the silence, if you can. It will probably feel uncomfortable, but this discomfort is important. There's always discomfort in change and you are in the magic of change right in this moment. When you no longer feel uncomfortable with the silence it's probably time to talk and allow the other person to respond. At this point you may also feel a rush – the sensation of freedom from your vicious cycle – the feeling of liberation. Acknowledge your own bravery. You did it.

Step nine: process

It's important to take time to reflect and journal on this process. What has changed and shifted for you? What is different now that you've said all the things you previously held back? How has your internal landscape changed? How has the external situation evolved? The change might be scary at first. It might not seem entirely good. It might be confronting, but you took the risk, and if you stay resolute and follow your intuition, in my experience, it will lead you to exactly where you need to be for the next stage of your journey. I've never known this kind of spell not to work, but in order to properly carry it out you have to cross the point of no return, breaking the spell of the illusion of what the relationship was before, breaking the pattern you were in, breaking your illusions of being disempowered, and allowing yourself to feel everything so that your feelings are no longer holding you back. That is liberation.

INTEGRATING OPPOSITES IN MAGICAL PRACTICE

In life we often find ourselves navigating between seemingly opposing forces – being stuck between wanting two things, or not wanting two things. The tension between what we want and what we don't want can feel unbearable. All of these can be understood magically, and worked with using the Jungian concept of the tension of opposites.

As humans, we are dualistic beings; there are two sides of our brains and bodies, and we are drawn to duality, creating opposites which may not exist beyond the boundaries of our perception – light and shadow, love and fear, creation and destruction.

These dualities, often perceived as conflicts, are actually essential parts of our daily existence. As magical practitioners, we have a choice to work with these paradoxes, to find the transformative power within the tension they create.

The integration or balance of opposites is a fundamental principle in many esoteric traditions, from the Taoist concept of yin and yang to the Hermetic axiom "as above, so below." This wisdom recognises that authentic power and transformation do not arise from denying or suppressing the contradictions within ourselves and the world around us, but from embracing and integrating them in a process of inner-alchemy.

When we engage in the alchemical process of integrating opposites, we tap into a well of personal growth and magical potential. By acknowledging and reconciling the light and dark aspects of our psyche, we cultivate a deeper understanding of ourselves and the complex nature of reality. This self-knowledge, in turn, allows us to step into our power with greater clarity, intention, and effectiveness.

Integrating opposites is not always easy; it requires courage, self-honesty, and a willingness to step into the unknown, to confront our shadows, to question our assumptions, and to expand our perceptions of what is possible. Yet, it also presents significant opportunities for deep transformation and empowerment.

The alchemy of opposites is not a destination but a lifelong process of unfolding. Each paradox you encounter, each polarity you seek to harmonise or transform, holds a unique gift and lesson. By approaching this work with curiosity, compassion, and openness, we discover the magic that arises when you embrace the power of paradox.

The concept of the tension of opposites is a fascinating one. Jung wrote that through holding this tension between two opposite approaches or options, eventually a third way would emerge – a new option that wasn't previously there. This may seem odd and abstract, however I've found working with the tension of opposites to be a powerful practice leading to wonderful results in my own life. In holding this kind of tension deliberately, rather than vacillating between which way to go or lamenting about not knowing what to do, I've often achieved the results I deeply wanted, regardless if it was a scholarship, a particular employment opportunity, or the resolution of a difficult personal situation. There is an underlying principle of tension being necessary to bring something new forward, just as the tension of contractions birth new life into the world.

There are two main ways of working with tensions. Holding the tension of opposites, which this chapter focuses on, and bringing opposites together in a process of integration which will be covered later in the book. Both are forms of alchemy. Holding the tension of opposites allows for a fulfilment of the tension, bringing new things into the world, whereas integrating them works at a deeper level to harmonise the psyche and allow for a more unified sense of being. I've chosen to include the first way in this chapter as it's so integral to working with our desires.

Jung's work suggests that every conscious wish or goal which arises within us has its opposite counterpart in the shadowy unconscious. Later in the book we will delve deeper into shadow work, but for now, you may find benefit in contemplating this idea. It was once explained to me by Judith (a wonderful leadership coach I was working with) as a bit like a set of scales or a see-saw, where as soon as a new desire pops into your consciousness on one side of the see-saw or scale, a shadowy resistance to that same desire appears on the other side, holding the conscious desire back until either the shadowy resistance is integrated or the conscious desire has enough weight to tip the scales in its direction. Holding the tension of opposites, in this metaphor, is like embodying the scale and opening up space for new possibilities which may come in the form of the known desire, or may be even more powerful and profound than anything in current awareness.

In magical practice, we understand that the tension of opposites is not just a conflict but a source of creative potential. When we hold this tension without rushing to resolve it, we create a space for transcendence. The "transcendent function" is a term coined by Jung, to describe the emergence of a new solution or synthesis that transcends the original opposites. In magical terms, this could be a new option or even the idea for a spell or ritual that alchemises the conflicting energies, bringing about a transformation that neither force alone could achieve.

Active imagination can be used in working with opposites. This involves imagining the two opposites as archetypes, visualising or chatting with them, facilitating a deeper understanding and integration of these aspects. You could even call upon deities that represent each side of a polarity, or use crystals, herbs, or talismans you've created in order to signify each possibility.

A REAL LIFE EXAMPLE OF WORKING WITH OPPOSITES

A while ago, before I was writing full time, I was in a situation where I was in between work contracts. I had a seven year career in the public sector, primarily working in policy – advising ministers, developing policy frameworks, working on potential new laws and regulation changes and leading strategy work. In most of that time I'd worked on wellbeing-focused projects that I felt good about, but often the effort I put in would amount to nothing as leadership changed their mind at the last minute or political tensions arose. Still, there was a lot I could feel proud of. I was looking for a new contract after taking the summer off to write, but every opportunity that surfaced seemed to vanish, leaving me in a state of limbo. Knowing that I could work with the many tensions I felt around needing secure income, I leaned into them:

· The tension between freedom and security

· The tension between my fears of scarcity and my desires for abundance

· The tension between being employed and self-employed

· The tension between wanting my book success to grow and feeling afraid of that very same success because it made me feel more vulnerable

· The tension between being responsible by having a serious job and doing what I love with my creativity and inspiration as guide

Many new opportunities that came up sounded good but didn't feel quite right. I was tempted to give up the freedom of contracting and settle for a permanent role, but that definitely didn't feel like a good compromise to make for the sake of security. It was as if I was being teased by cosmic forces. I ran the figures and discovered I could probably survive on my book income alone and still pay the mortgage and other bills, but it would be a tight squeeze. I kept looking for new opportunities, keeping options open, holding the tension to create space for possibility...and a small miracle happened. In holding this tension, and not compromising, and releasing a lot of childhood money wounds and blocks, and all the other internal work I was led to do in order to take care of my mental health during this confusing time, my books began to do better and better. Yes, it was partly because I had more headspace to focus on them and was making more confident decisions and working with some key astrological transits (a topic we'll cover in the next section), but it also felt like I was riding a wave of my own creation, using the tensions that could have been crushing me into a corner to support me instead!

The income from my books increased at least fivefold over the course of that year, and that also meant that many more people were reading my books (which was both delightful and terrifying!). I felt like I was literally living my dreams, and I still am. About three or four months into the year, I was offered a wonderful role which I would have jumped at immediately if it had been offered just a few weeks earlier, but at that point, I had an interesting choice to make. The work I was being offered was meaningful and well-paid and it would have contributed to good things happening, but my books were doing so well that I could now trust them to continue supporting me. Part of me wanted to take the job because it was good work, or because it was the responsible thing to do, but another part of me resisted the constriction on my time that it would create because it would have to be at least four days a week, at least nine-to-five, and I'd now had a taste of writing full time for several months. I relished the spaciousness of setting my own agenda, of structuring my own time, of not having people tell me what to do or have to deal with any office politics aside from my cats getting in the way occasionally.

I sat with this new tension of opposites, noting that the previous tensions I'd held and worked with had created the space for these new possibilities to emerge, both in my writing success and in the new role being offered. I appreciated that the time I'd waited without compromising on what felt right for me had been so important. If I'd been offered a great role straight away, I'd have been in there and my writing would have taken a back seat again, but putting it (and myself) first for those months, even in the fears I'd faced, had been worthwhile. I still had some family hang-ups. I come from an academic family where the kind of work I was doing in my non-writing career was respected, but my writing fantasy books was not something my grandparents would have valued or approved of. But it was something I valued and approved of! I had a chat with my mother, expecting her to push me towards the safer, more respectable option of taking the job and continuing to write on the side, but after laying out the situation, she surprised me: "Well, it's up to you love," she said. "Both seem like good options."

This was absolutely true. I'd somehow gone from feeling like I didn't have options a few months earlier – where every new work opportunity that came up vanished, and where I felt I had little control over improving my writing income – to being in a situation where I had two wonderful options. It was really nothing to complain about. I chose the option that felt right – the spaciousness of writing full-time, the freedom to set my own agenda. I trusted that they would find the right person to do the good work that I was passing up, letting the weight of that subside from my shoulders. Every day I get messages from people who adore my books. Some of them find solace in them during hard times, some have found their way back to a love of reading after picking up *Accidental Magic* and now they're reading all sorts of things. I still have the value of wanting to create more wellbeing which infuses my writing. In telling empowering, uplifting, and meaningful stories through fiction I am doing good work, but it's *my* good work.

HOW TO WORK WITH OPPOSITES AND PARADOX

Working with opposites is not a static state but a dynamic process. Just as the phases of the moon wax and wane, so too do the polarities within us shift and change. By attuning ourselves to these cycles and rhythms, we can better navigate the ebb and flow of our inner conflicts. Rituals that align with the lunar phases, the seasons, or other natural cycles can help us maintain this balance, grounding our work in the larger rhythms of the cosmos.

It is important to approach the work of opposites with a spirit of play and experimentation. Magic, at its heart, is about exploring the unknown and discovering new possibilities. By maintaining a curious and open-minded attitude, we can transform the tension of opposites from a source of stress into a fertile ground for creativity and growth. Each conflict we encounter becomes an opportunity to deepen our magical practice.

By incorporating these practices into our magical work, we honour the complexity of the psyche and tap into the deep transformative potential of paradox and the tension of opposites.

MEDITATION ON THE TENSION OF OPPOSITES

You may wish to do this meditation as part of a ritual, by creating sacred space, lighting a candle, burning incense or whatever makes sense to you. If you like, you can also choose physical objects to hold in both hands, such as crystals, if that feels intuitively right for you.

Find a quiet and comfortable place where you will not be disturbed. Sit or lie down in a relaxed position. Close your eyes and take a few deep breaths, inhaling through your nose and exhaling through your mouth.

Begin by grounding yourself. Visualise roots extending from your body into the earth, anchoring you firmly to the ground. Feel the stability and support of the earth beneath you.

Focus on a situation in your life where you feel a tension between two (or more) opposing forces. This could be a decision you need to make, conflicting desires, or any internal and external conflict you are experiencing.

Focus on one of these tensions at a time. Visualise these opposing forces as distinct energies or symbols. See them clearly in your mind's eye. They might take the form of light and dark, two different figures, or any imagery that resonates with you.

Allow yourself to fully feel the tension between these two forces. Notice any physical sensations in your body and any emotions that arise. Breathe deeply and stay present with these feelings.

You may wish to talk to these forces, to understand them better. If so, take all the time you need, while holding the tension. You may wish to communicate that you are actively working with the tension, rather than seeking a resolution. Remain open and curious, notice anything that arises for you – any thoughts, feelings or insights into your current situation. Notice but do not decide. Hold the tension, allowing yourself to sit in the discomfort of the unknown. Feel the stretch, the expansion of that stretching. Feel the pressure the way weightlifters deliberately put themselves into situations of intense tension, but only go as far into the tension as feels safe and good for you at this time.

If more tensions are present, focus on them one at a time, feeling, sensing and/or visualising them. After all sides of a tension have expressed themselves, focus on holding the tension between all these forces. Visualise yourself as a container for these energies, capable of holding both without needing to resolve the conflict immediately.

As you hold this tension, allow the space for something new to emerge; you may even sense it beginning to form. This represents a new, transcendent solution or synthesis that integrates the opposites.

If it does emerge, allow this third energy to grow stronger and clearer in your mind. Feel how it brings a sense of harmony and balance, transcending the initial conflict. Take a few moments to absorb this new energy, letting it integrate into your being.

When you feel ready, gently bring your awareness back to your breath. Wiggle your fingers and toes, and slowly open your eyes.

Take a moment to reflect on your experience and any insights that emerged during the meditation. You may wish to journal about it.

WORKING WITH TAROT AND PARADOX:

I'm not going to cover tarot very much in this book because quite frankly it deserves a whole book on its own, but you can use tarot in many of the rituals presented throughout the book, or develop your own.

If you want to work with tarot and the tensions you are experiencing, you might choose to do something like the following:

1. Select a card that represents the aspect of yourself or your situation that you are struggling with.

2. Meditate on this card, contemplating what it reveals about you and your situation.

3. Choose a card that represents the opposite quality. You may wish to choose several cards at this point, depending on how many tensions are present.

4. Reflect on how these energies interact and what the tension between them looks and feels like.

LUNAR CYCLE RITUALS

During the new moon, set intentions for working with opposites. Write your intentions on a piece of paper and put it under your pillow or plant it in the earth outside or in a plant pot. Over the next few days and weeks, reflect on the tension regularly, feeling it in your body, taking care to position yourself in your power rather than swinging between each side of the tension.

During the next full moon, reflect on your progress. You may wish to journal on this or perform a simple ritual of your own design. Celebrate your growth and reaffirm your commitment to your own inner-work.

OPPOSITES JOURNAL EXERCISE

Identify a current conflict or tension in your life. Write down the opposing forces or desires involved. Reflect on how each force serves you and what it might teach you. Write about how you can honour both sides and your openness to new opportunities and insights emerging. Revisit this exercise regularly to track your progress and insights.

Working with opposites is potent magic for anyone seeking greater self-awareness, magical effectiveness, and spiritual growth. By acknowledging and working with the paradoxes and polarities within ourselves and our lives, we open the door to greater wholeness, balance, and power. The exercises provided in this chapter are just a starting point. As you continue to explore and incorporate these practices, you may find your own unique ways of working with the opposites. The goal is not to eliminate or suppress either side of a polarity, but rather to work with them.

WORKING WITH INTERNAL STRUCTURES – DISSOLVING AND METAMORPHOSIS

In the process of delving deep into our psyches in our magical and healing self-work we sometimes find ourselves confronted with internal structures that once served a purpose but now hinder our progress. These structures were probably protective mechanisms we developed at various stages of our lives to help us navigate challenges and traumas. However, as we evolve and grow, old structures can become limiting, preventing us from fully embracing our magic and transformation.

The process of dissolving these outdated internal structures is a bit like the metamorphosis of a caterpillar into a butterfly. Just as the caterpillar must first turn into goo within the safety of the cocoon before it can re-form and emerge as a butterfly, we too must undergo a necessary dissolution to shed what no longer serves us and metamorphose into our most current and relevant selves.

In my own magical and self-development journey, I've encountered these kinds of structures within myself. As a particularly sensitive and anxious child, I experienced a great deal of fear and terror, which led me to develop hypervigilance towards any perceived danger. This defence mechanism served me well in navigating the challenges of my early life, helping me to stay safe and cope with difficult situations.

However, as I grew older and my circumstances changed, I no longer needed the same protective structures. I have shed many of them, over the years, yet some have remained, buried deep and largely unconscious. During some recent shadow work, I discovered an old fear-based structure in my solar plexus which had become calcified. On closer examination I realised this was like a lens of fear I'd been using for a long time to navigate my life – like a compass, helping me to find safety. However, the energy was stuck, and was keeping me stuck in using fear as a guiding force – as a support system – which was now limiting my ability to fully engage and trust in life.

PROCESSES OF DISSOLUTION AND REFORMATION

Now, I'm not going to say that there was definitely a psychic structure in my chest or aura or whatever, because I don't think it's helpful to get attached to specifics like that, but this was an insight I had about my experience that made a lot of sense. In focusing on this seemingly calcified structure (it felt a bit like salt crystals – gritty and cold and formed into a circle) I was able to be present and with deep empathy for myself as a terrified child, I began to soften and integrate this seemingly hard structure, breaking away the layers, and liberating myself from using fear to tightly control and navigate my life. I'm still in the process of this metamorphosis, but as it has continued, I've learnt more and more about releasing my fears, and I'm no longer afraid of many of the things that I previously shrank away from in terror.

Metamorphosis of the psyche requires a willingness to enter the cocoon of change, to allow ourselves to dissolve into the vulnerability – into the goo of uncertainty. It means gently confronting the fears and patterns that have become so ingrained in our beings, trusting in the process of transformation.

As I surrendered to this process, I found that the act of letting go, of allowing the old structures to dissolve, created space for something new to emerge. Just as the caterpillar's cells rearrange themselves within the cocoon, guided by an innate wisdom that holds the blueprint of the butterfly, I began to sense a deeper wisdom within myself, a powerful knowing that was guiding my own transformation.

This process of dissolution and reformation is not comfortable; it requires us to enter the discomfort of the unknown, to trust in the alchemy of transformation. It is precisely in this space of surrender and trust that magic happens. As we release our attachment to the old forms and allow ourselves to be remade, we open to the possibility of a more authentic, empowered, and aligned selves.

FAMILY SHADOWS

Many of us carry trauma in our family histories; in fact, most of us had parents, grandparents, or great-grandparents who were in one or two of the world wars, for instance, not to mention all the other challenges that people have lived through: the Great Depression and other crises in this century are just the tip of the iceberg. Humanity carries with it a long history of war, disaster, and other traumas, and our own lives reflect this on a micro scale.

I'm not going to tell you that these traumas that we've experienced personally and historically are not bad, because I am absolutely certain that they were. However, we also have a deep transformative potential in engaging with the collective shadow. Even simple shadow work, such as reflecting on the past with the light of your awareness, opening up for love, understanding, compassion, and letting go of old pain, can be tremendously healing.

What pain are you carrying around with you right now? How does this relate to the patterns of pain and trauma within your family? What purpose is that serving for you? Do you still need that? It is absolutely your right to carry this pain for as long as you want to. I am sure that you have suffered grave injustices in your life and in your family history. What I'm not sure of is how long it serves you to hold on to this pain. That, my dear, is up to you, though it's not always easy to process or even to think about traumatic things.

Much of the pain we carry is not something that we are consciously, deliberately engaging with most of the time. It is dormant within our bodies and is triggered sometimes when challenging things happen in our lives. If you don't feel you're currently carrying pain, that's lovely. However, you may want to take the opportunity in a quiet moment to reflect on whether you can sense any emotional pain in your body. Why would you want to go and look for something like that? Well, without feeling and releasing the emotion, it tends to stay within you. Brain scans show that long-term physical pain is in the same part of the brain usually reserved for emotional pain. Similarly, when somebody hurts us emotionally, it can feel like physical pain.

The more we know about the way pain is experienced in our brain (and it's *all* experienced in the brain, not actually in the parts of the body where we think it is, because the receptors for all sense experiences are in the nervous system), the more the lines blur between physical and emotional. You see, they're not entirely separate. If you experience physical pain in your body, you may find that going into the emotional feelings surrounding that pain can help to release the resistance to it, making the pain more bearable. I've done this with varying levels of success, but even a small amount of relief from pain is welcome!

People have many sensitivities when it comes to pain and trauma, and many forms of trauma are also collective and systemic. For instance, there are many kinds of discrimination that people face because of problems within our collective unconscious, the shadows of our society. However, if you are ready to walk deeper into your shadow, you will find deeper empowerment there.

You may wish to journal about your past, for instance, beginning with what you know of your family history and the traumas your ancestors experienced. As you do this, allow your awareness to soften with compassion. This energetically puts you in an open state, allowing the energy of life force to flow through you into the past, both your own past and the historic past. This is powerful magic, because it opens us up to healing our own stories and the stories of our genealogies and ancestry.

Healing the past doesn't change the details and facts, but it changes our relationship to it. There's a radical difference between telling the story of our past experiences from the perspective of the suffering victim compared to telling the same story from the healed perspective of the hero who has learned so much and triumphed. When we have broken stories, full of trauma, the narratives often make little sense. You may have grandparents that won't even speak of the past, or who knew nothing about their own families because their parents would not speak of shame that they endured, because of crimes committed in the family, or illegitimate children, adultery, and other things that are frowned upon often by various social groups.

One of my great-grandfathers left his entire family and ran off with my great-grandmother. They never spoke of this, and it was only later discovered through issues with a name change. When my mother was a teenager, Margaret Mead came to New Zealand, as she was a family friend (apparently all anthropologists knew each other back then). She held court in the living room of our family home and told my mother that she needed to know her roots "in order to know who you are."

So my mother jumped on a train to visit her lesser-known side of her family to better understand where she came from. "Nana, why did you and Poppa come to New Zealand?"

"Well," Nana said nervously, "we came on holiday. And then we lost our luggage, so we had to stay."

This made no sense. I'm not sure if she made it up on the spot or whether it was an old story hiding a truth that was far too filled with shame to speak about, and yet to the descendants, we merely find it a funny anecdote now, because we are no longer holding to such rigid social rules (though of course, abandoning your family is often frowned on even in more modern liberal societies).

This shadow, I believe, haunted my family. My grandfather, who grew up in a home where his father and mother never spoke of many things, carried a lot of emotional trauma and suffered from mental illness. Shadow passes itself down through many families, including my own. Without the shadow, though, the light would have no definition, and so herein lies our greatest potential for transformation.

As you write down the stories of your past, of your family history, and your own personal story, allow yourself to release any emotion that comes up, acknowledging it and feeling it as much as you possibly can, with as little resistance as possible. Feel compassion for that child who was bullied or hurt, who was made powerless. You may even feel brave enough to feel compassion for the parent who yelled at you in stress, for the ancestor who did the unforgivable thing...or you may not yet, and that's okay too. But allow yourself to be as embodied as possible, as connected to your senses, your feelings as they come.

You may find that when you do this again, perhaps in a year's time or a month's time, you write a very different version of the story, because your awareness has interacted with the past, allowing it to transform and heal, creating a coherent narrative rather than a broken narrative of trauma. This is not to say we want to write over the past and pretend it didn't happen; we merely want to be able to relate to it in a way that serves us and our descendants better in the long term.

When we can learn from the past and understand it with compassion and humility, we breathe fresh air into areas of our psyches that are often musty and stale. We allow for the rot to properly compost into fertile soil, and we open ourselves up to new grace.

Here are some questions:

- What in your life or in your family history are you ready to let go of right now?
- What sadness are you holding that you're ready to release?
- What burdens of emotion and trauma are you ready to sit down and free yourself from?
- How can you rest and nurture yourself deeply right now?

THE SURPRISING POWER OF FEELING EVERYTHING

Most of us, myself included, have become masters at distracting ourselves from our bodily sensations, especially those we don't like. We often restrict ourselves from fully experiencing the intensity of flavours and textures by multitasking during meals – watching television, reading, or looking at our phones. While this can be enjoyable, it means we don't fully experience sensations in the same way as if they had our full attention.

Why practice experiencing the intensity of sensation? Because it connects us with our magic. We come into this world with a voracious soul that craves all kinds of experiences. Yet, from a young age, we're taught that the full intensity of our feelings is often unwanted. As children, even when expressing excitement, we often receive mixed messages or disapproval from adults. We learn that our sensations and emotions can be "bad," and that we shouldn't be too loud, want something too much, or express ourselves in ways that irritate others. We distance ourselves from the fullness of experience, even though it's what our soul craves.

When we're deeply connected with ourselves, we experience exactly the emotion and sensation that our soul needs to in order for us to notice, thrive, heal, and grow. When we're too much in our heads, we can trick ourselves out of having deeper, more meaningful experiences moment to moment.

In this stage of my magical journey, I'm learning to recognise when I'm distancing or disconnecting from the full power of my emotions, and how to connect more deeply with myself and nature. This is the continuing magical path I'm on, making connections between mind and body, internal and external, between my inner experience and the stories I read in books.

So, how does sensation connect us with magic and the fulfilment of our soul? By surrendering to the fullness of experience – whether it's receiving love or facing humiliation – we connect more deeply with our inner selves. Shadow work teachers like Carolyn Elliot say that all fulfilment is humiliating to the ego. The ego cannot be fulfilled, so when we experience deep emotional fulfilment, it goes hand in hand with ego humiliation. In this returning to earth, there's a powerful magic hidden, a space to be reborn. Carolyn had her experience of this when she crossed a line a few years ago, opening herself up to being cancelled, This is a fear many of us have when putting our creations out into the world. This risk challenges our primal need for survival which is deeply connected to community and belonging.

I, myself, struggled for many years to share my creative work, and even now after publishing so many books, I still come up against a barrier within myself. With this book, in particular, I am encountering a new vulnerability in so openly sharing my magic, my personal stories, and my identity as a witch.

Sometimes, the intensity of the world feels overwhelming. When this happens, it's usually a sign that I need to let go of resistance and turn inward. I may need to take action on things I've been procrastinating, or I may simply need to rest. But I have to listen to the deep inner stillness that exists at my centre, regardless of the storm raging around me. The deeper you go into the water of consciousness, the stiller and more potent it becomes.

When things feel intense, I focus on the part of me resisting the flow of energy – usually in my solar plexus. I can choose to continue resisting or avoiding, or I can dive deep into the discomfort of the inner furnace. By opening up and allowing the rushing force of creation to come through, I meet it head-on and return to a state of flow. This allows the magic to pour through me and be channelled into the world.

This ability didn't come easily. For a long time, unhealed trauma prevented me from accessing this level of work. Through deep healing processes, guided by intuition and supported by wise counsellors, friends, and books, I've released a lot of old emotion from my childhood wounds: powerlessness, helplessness, agony, desperation, and emotional pain caused by disconnection, neglect, and bullying. I've learned to recognise when I'm projecting my pain onto others and how to integrate these shadows back into my awareness.

Yet, the ego's dissatisfaction remained – that grasping, never-satisfied, not-okay feeling. Now, this is the shadow I integrate daily. When I feel that sense of not-enoughness, I not only affirm that I am enough but also look in the mirror of my imagination to see that aspect of myself.

One of the best ways to connect with our magic is to openly experience higher levels of sensation. This doesn't always mean unpleasant sensations; it can involve things we already enjoy. For instance, try eating something sweet and savoury in the bath while listening to music. Choose intense flavours like plum sorbet, spicy curry, tangy fruit, or strong cheeses.

Why encourage this? Being in water activates your body's temperature sensors, while the foods stimulate your taste buds and sense of smell. Add in the visual and auditory experiences, and you're engaging all your main senses intensely at once.

Even without food, you can use all your senses in the bath or shower. There's always some scent in the air, taste in your mouth, and something to see and hear, even if it's subtle. Connecting with your senses is a powerful way to connect with your magic, your body, and the world.

Most of us spend much of our lives distracted, bypassing much of our experience. The more connected you are to feeling everything, the more connected you are to a deeper reality that often goes unnoticed. It's like stretching a muscle – the more you do it (within reason), the stronger you get. However, be cautious not to overwhelm yourself, as this can cause pain, stress, and lasting trauma. Take it one step at a time as you open up to sensation.

Consider recording your thoughts or writing about your experiences after these high-intensity sensory sessions. Note any insights, unexpected feelings, thoughts, or sensations that arise. This practice can deepen your connection to your magic and help you uncover hidden aspects of yourself and the world around you.

THE POWER OF DOUBT

Even though I've seen some amazing things happen in my life, and as I get older, I practice spending more and more time in the magic of life, there will still always be a part of my mind that doubts. There is a brilliant saboteur within me who is critical, who wants to pop the balloon, disperse any illusions I might have, and bring me back to earth. I value this part, because it's important to question everything with open curiosity, even if it seems totally at odds with having faith in something unknown. If we have too much blind faith, we risk falling into all kinds of mystical delusions which can be fascinating and beautiful in their own way, but delusions will ultimately get us nowhere. How can we tell the difference between truth and delusion if we do not also integrate and welcome the voice of doubt? If we shut ourselves off from the shadow, and that shadow has more power in our lives.

Faith and scepticism form quite the powerful paradox! Yes, sometimes that doubting saboteur does want to wreck things. It wants to come and destroy our dreams and make us doubt ourselves and our magic. But if we can love even that part of ourselves, the way a parent loves a young child even when the child is wrecking things and being deliberately obnoxious, that part is seen, acknowledged, and becomes connected with our whole selves, where it's far less damaging.

If you don't doubt yourself, but other people around you are constantly doubting and criticising you, that's an example of the shadow of doubt not being integrated within you but being projected outwards. This is not necessarily a bad thing, but it is certainly an opportunity. I'm also not blaming you for other people being mean and horrible, or saying it's all in your head. The external situation is real and I believe you. Your experiences are valid and people can indeed be awful and judgemental, ourselves included. The opportunity here, just like with any other shadow work, lies within your willingness and courage to find the part of you that

302

silently holds similar judgements, and to connect with this young and scared aspect of yourself. People talk a lot about inner child work, but the sceptic and saboteur can also be more of an inner teenager – that developmental stage is driven largely by questioning and criticising and developing analytical and original thought. It's possible that this wasn't a safe thing for you to do in your childhood and adolescence, so naturally, you suppressed it. You took that unseemly critical-judgemental-sceptical-saboteur aspect of yourself and pushed it down, as far away from you as possible to keep you safe from other people's judgement, but it never completely went away, and neither did the judgement. If you can reconnect, now, with that part of you that always questions, that always doubts, and that does want to burst your bubble, then you can step deeper into your power and the judgements from other people will naturally fall by the wayside. Armed with your own brave defensive critical saboteur, you will no longer need to be policed by the criticism and scepticism of others and you can turn your own aspect towards constructive criticism.

If you're interested in looking at your astrological natal chart for how this doubting aspect might come through for you, I suggest looking towards the challenging aspects in your chart: squares and oppositions, as well as any planets in Scorpio, the eighth house, especially those that have a relationship with your Sun. I also suggest looking at where Saturn falls in your houses, as it's a huge reality check, as well as the planet Pluto. Sometimes going deeper into these things can help you understand how universal patterns play out for you in particular, in the reflective nature of life.

For instance, I have Mars in Scorpio and Saturn in Scorpio (both in the fifth house). Mars squares my Leo Sun. The fifth house relates to creativity. Mars is the warrior; in Scorpio it definitely wants to question and doubt and burst bubbles, and Saturn has a gravity about it. Being in the part of my chart that relates to creativity – well, creativity has always been important to me. I've had to face serious doubts and enormous fear and monstrous self-criticism. I've also worked to integrate these questioning, sceptical parts of me into my being. They sometimes get in the way, still, yes. But the more I'm able to embrace that shadow, the more I can feel my power.

Life, without questioning and doubting can be incredibly dangerous. I once asked the question, the famous self-help adage, "What would you do if you knew you could not fail?" And a psychologist friend of mine replied, "I'd check myself in for a psychiatric assessment." This highlights that as well as adages like that one opening up new ways of thinking and possibility, there is a huge shadow when it comes to unbridled belief and unquestioning success. The paradox of failure and success is that they are deeply connected. People who succeed in this world tend to fail often, and have failed many, many, many times before the success was evident. Many so-called overnight success stories are actually built on the back of much learning, failure, and expertise built through those experiences.

People who are in states of mania often have feelings of being super-human, not doubting themselves. So losing the ability to question, and especially to question yourself, means that you've lost something precious and important. We can value our ability to question, and even the part of us that wants to break things occasionally, that wants to destroy, that wants to retaliate, wants to fight ourselves. We can integrate the shadows. And in doing so, there's less for us to fight, externally.

There's more wisdom for us to build the successes of our lives on. And we can hold doubt while remaining open to magic, holding that space for amazing things to happen in our lives, for small miracles or even large ones, for the intentions and the spells that we put out into the world with our words, with our feelings, and our rituals if we choose to do them, to find a clear resonance from our deep, unconscious soul through to the light of spirit, allowing them to be born into the material world that we live in, and allowing us to live and play and frolic in the magic.

SHADOW WORK

As we previously traversed, shadow work embodies powerful and trans-formative practices. It involves the courageous exploration of the hidden, repressed, or denied aspects of ourselves – the parts we often fear, resist, or reject. These shadow elements, when left unacknowledged, can manifest as self-destructive patterns, limiting beliefs, and a deep sense of inner discord.

The shadow is not a place of inherent darkness or evil but rather a repository for the qualities, impulses, and experiences that we have learned to conceal from ourselves and others. These aspects, though hidden, hold immense power and potential. By engaging in shadow work, we embark on a journey of radical self-acceptance, integration, and wholeness.

This practice requires us to confront the parts of ourselves that we may deem unlovable, shameful, or unworthy. It demands honesty, vulnerability, and a willingness to sit with discomfort. However, as we shine the light of awareness into these dark corners of our psyche, we begin to understand that our shadows are not to be feared but rather embraced as essential parts of our authentic selves.

Shadow work is a deeply personal and non-linear process. It can be supported through various modalities, such as meditation, journalling, dreamwork, or therapy. The key is to approach this work with self-compassion, curiosity, and a commitment to self-discovery.

As we engage with our shadows, we may uncover buried gifts, untapped creativity, and insights. We learn to reclaim the lost parts of ourselves, integrating them into a more whole and authentic expression of who we are. This process of integration can lead to greater self-acceptance, emotional freedom, and a deeper sense of purpose.

In the following meditations, we will explore two potent approaches to shadow work. The first invites us to encounter our shadow in a protected, sacred space, fostering understanding and integration. The second calls us to connect with the primal, transformative energy of the universe, embodied in the archetype of the devouring soul.

GRIEF AND CONTROL

Wherever there is grief, there is a loss of control. Of course, we equate grief with loss, but in dominant modern culture there is no place for the honouring of this important part of the cycle. There is a perpetual letting go in nature, and there is a natural grieving that goes along with it, dying to the past to be reborn in the present. But the grief that affects us the most in our lives happens in situations where we feel totally out of control. I'm not just talking just about the loss of loved ones, although that certainly applies. I'm not just talking about breakups or friendships ending either. We carry grief over all kinds of things: missed opportunities, being passed over for promotions, missing out or feeling left out in social situations of all kinds, not having our work recognised, not feeling loved and valued in many, many different ways.

Grief is a heavy emotion, and while it can have a kind of beauty to it, especially if we allow in openness, and wallow in the great salty waves, when we release great torrents of tears, and really feel our emotions of loss. This can be a glorious experience, uniting us with our deeper selves and connecting us more closely with others around us. The rites that we still have in our societies around death can be deep and profound, beautiful experiences, especially when they're designed with both grieving and celebration of a life lost at the heart. However, many of us do not get to experience profound release, a shared soothing. Instead, in the moments of great loss in our life, many of us are alone, not wanting to be a burden on others, not wanting to reveal our vulnerability, not wanting to appear to be a victim. Instead, we soldier on, bearing the enormous burden of unprocessed emotions that wear us out over time.

I have spent many, many years processing the emotional burdens that I've carried with me from childhood. And as I've come to know and release and understand myself better through these emotions, I've recognised that the emotion I still carry in my body, though it has lessened over the years, is a kind of grief, a grief for the child that I was, who experienced so many, so many, many, many times a total loss of control, a total powerlessness.

I didn't have the worst childhood, yet I was an incredibly sensitive child in a family where there was never enough time, energy, money, or attention to go around, but lots of children who were always fighting, parents who were working, stressed, tired, and overburdened with their own childhood issues like most parents are. As a child I had many ongoing challenging experiences with a family member who carried strong shadows of violence and disconnection. This played out through endless control struggles where I, as the child, was always inevitably made to feel totally powerless.

Not only was I an exceptionally sensitive child, I was always a feisty, fiery, argumentative, stroppy, combative, and passionate child, all at the same time. It's quite a volatile combination, feeling everything so deeply as I did, and being exposed to so many experiences of powerlessness, being reduced to tears and begging, being prone to what are unkindly known as "tantrums." where I would lose all semblance of control and not having a safe, healthy outlet for that intense emotion. I carried that with me into deep depressions in my youth, into much anxiety and anguish,

306

and a roller coaster of emotions that began to stabilise the more I excavated buried grief that I'd been carrying with me, allowing myself new perspectives as I lifted energy, as I shifted, as I opened up to my childhood self with compassion and love, and as I let go of the past so that it no longer held me back.

Finally, after several decades of processing I've gotten to the point where I can look back at the pain and unfairness and injustice, the humiliation, the bullying, and all of the horrible experiences of powerlessness and neglect in my childhood and feel a kind of appreciation.

Okay, I'll admit, it's kind of insulting, to tell people that they should look at the hard things in their life and feel grateful for them. I'm not going to tell you to do that. Not at all. I'm not going to tell you how you should feel because that is not my job. And I deeply believe that it's up to you how you make meaning of your life, including the hard things. But I can tell you why I feel appreciation, it's because without having all of those struggles, I never would have been so compelled to look within, to connect with my soul so deeply, and perhaps I would not have become a witch or a writer. I cannot say for sure, although many people who are attracted to witchcraft, and indeed to writing, carry scars with them that have led them into deeper exploration of themselves and of the magic within and around them.

Eckhart Tolle calls the inner wounds that we still carry the "pain body." The pain body, as he describes it, is unconscious, the energy that builds up within us and is triggered when bad things happen, or things that we perceive as bad anyway. But the pain body itself is not bad necessarily. It is an invitation for deeper awareness. When we can focus awareness on our pain, we cease living completely controlled by that pain. Instead of projecting it out into the world around us, our awareness of the pain within our bodies allows us to connect more deeply with all the disparate parts of ourselves, soothing and integrating the energy of trauma so it no longer governs our lives.

I have worked with that concept for many years, and have found it very helpful. Focusing inward allows us to step back into our power, whereas when we are focused on the outer, on the other person who has inflicted pain on us, or on the unfair situation that is causing the pain, stress, struggle, and fear in our lives, we feel powerless. We can go around in circles trying and trying and trying to figure out how we can get control, how we can get revenge, how we can win. But the real winning happens internally; the real control can only be within. The paradox of control and surrender reveals a deeper magic. If we surrender to our awareness of our pain, we gain more power, more control. The more we try to take control, the more powerless we become.

We can work with this tension between power and powerlessness, between control and surrender. We can hold the opposites, one in each hand, and ask what gifts they have to give us, how they are trying to support us. And we can integrate them together so that we're no longer trapped in an endless cycle of seeking control in a way that makes us feel more powerless.

Going into the grief that we carry, however we want to conceptualise it, is also powerful. For me, I tend to carry pain and grief in my torso, my belly, solar plexus, and chest. Sometimes focusing on the sensation in my body allows it to move around. Sometimes going into anger deliberately helps to move the energy. For example, if I'm swimming or walking and I allow the active energy of fiery rage to rush through me, it's an outlet. You see, rage and anger are natural responses to a loss of control – to our boundaries being crossed. If we don't really have the opportunity to properly express that rage, instead we are limited to its more stagnant cousins of grief, of bitterness, resentment, and other emotions which are not bad in themselves, but with no outlets they will inevitably fester into inner poisons.

When you're feeling into the sensations that you're ready to clear, it can help to tap gently on that part of your body or rub it soothingly, the way a mother pats an infant's back. We can express the energies with our voice through chanting, humming, or even shouting or singing. We can journal to delve deeply into what it is that we're carrying. We may find purchase there; we may snag upon old memories connected with the emotions that we are now ready to process, accept, and release.

As you do this work, you may find that shadows emerge that you're not willing to deal with on your own, that make you feel unsafe. If this happens, I do encourage you to seek out therapists and friends who can support you in this journey. Only tread where you're ready to tread, as deeply as you're ready to wade into the oceans of emotion. Doing this work may make you sensitive, and you may find aspects of yourself raw and vulnerable, snagging against the words in this book. If that happens, it's okay to put it down or even throw it across the room. It will be ready for you to pick up again if you want to. You may need to take some time away, and that's perfectly okay.

One of the gifts of the grief within us is that it connects us with all of humanity, because all of humanity suffers, just as all other animals suffer. One could even say that there is no more universal emotion than suffering. Too often, our suffering makes us feel alone, when actually, it is what unites us with everyone in existence. From a magical worldview, integrating the shadow of that suffering, bringing it into the light of awareness, helps the collective, helping to ease the suffering of the world by easing our own; releasing the emotion that we carry within transforms it into a different form of potent magic, which can go off into the world and do wonderful things.

THE IMMENSE POWER OF ALL THAT WE FEAR

At times when you feel despair, it can be that a part of you is crying out to be heard. Listen, because only *you* can hear that deeper voice. Only you can tell what is really going on. This is a time when you may wish to bow your head, lie on your belly or in child's pose, or one of the other forward folding yoga positions. You may even want to be upside down. You may want to bury yourself under the blankets, but try not to curl up. Keep your shoulders back and your heart open to the sensations and feelings. It can feel a little like dying – emotional despair. Indeed, it is grief and letting go, but the pain itself, though tormenting, can be exquisite if we allow ourselves to open up to it rather than trying to numb it, or hide from it, or distract from it as we normally do.

If we try to shut pain out or run away from it, it remains as it is, in stasis. It has no release. It is not heard. Like a child crying out for help or crying out in pain, it needs to be listened to. There may have been many times in your childhood when you cried, only to be told to be quiet, only to be ignored or teased or bullied or have your feelings shut down in one way or another, and it is natural to carry that pain with you until there is a time when it can be heard, felt, and released.

Our dominant experience is that we cannot control our own pain, but we can do our best to comprehend it. So sit with the sensation and allow yourself to surrender to the experience of it. Allow any feelings to well up. You might find that after the wave of sensation passes, you feel a stillness or peace.

Something else may come afterwards – there may be buried anger, there may be fear, there may be some other challenging or even traditionally joyful emotion. Whatever it is that you need to feel right now, allow yourself to feel it. If you like, you could put words to it, or perhaps an image will appear, a colour or an animal. Do not force it. Just open and allow. So much is unfolding, if only we can let it. So much is wanting to come through us, to be experienced. So much of our energy in our body will heal us, if only we will let it, and allowing the sensations to pour forth can be a way of cleaning the wounds, emotional and spiritual wounds, that would heal if we only allow them, if we only get out of our own way or remove the buried splinters within us.

In this life we experience many shatterings of our psyche, many challenges that seem like they might break us, like they might be the end of us, many tastes of betrayal. That is part of the vast experience of life. Yet our dominant culture tries to hide all this under the rug, to sweep away or suppress the unpleasant, the messy, the painful, the hopeless and helpless. They are only allowed a place within the epic stories of our culture when they're being rescued by the hero.

We often struggle with victimhood, both internally and externally. I'm sure many of us have encountered people in our lives who are "always the victim" of their existence. No matter what happens, they are never responsible, it was done *to* them and they want everyone's sympathy and attention in their hopeless plight. If you react to people like this with a strong resistance, perhaps you mock them (as is easy to do), or a disgust rises up in you when you think of them, then I'm sorry to tell you this, but there is a victim within you that is calling out, screaming dramatically, stomping her feet and demanding to be integrated. How do I know this? Because it has definitely been true for me.

The victim is a guardian of boundaries. Whenever we feel victimised, a boundary has been crossed in our lives. And whether it be the actions of a friend, partner, colleague or boss, or some other person who is treating us unfairly, this triggering of the victim within is an opportunity not just to guard your boundaries in this moment, though that may be very important, but the victim brings with her the ghosts of the past – all of the other times in your life when you were treated unfairly or victimised rise up in emotional anguish, crying out.

This is why challenges from people in our lives, especially those in a position of power like a parent or manager at work, can be so hard and feel so unfair, giving rise to extreme emotion which can take us right back to being a young child with no power at all, experiencing the intense psychological grief of losing control, the despair of powerlessness that does indeed feel like dying. It could be a death of part of our identity, a death of our sense of power over the world, or some other kind of loss. And in this anguish, we don't know if we will ever feel alright again, even if we remind ourselves over and over that we've been through difficult things before and will go through them again.

Why on earth would I want you to focus on anguish and despair like this? Because it sometimes is the only way *through*. Sometimes there's no way around a problem, we have to go through it. You can avoid the emotions if you like and distract yourself, but it will do you little good. If we're not willing to grieve or face the music we will forever be trapped in the patterns of the pain.

The good news is, if we go through it, if we allow it to well up within us, to move through our bodies, if we fully experience the sensation, maybe even appreciating its exquisite unique beauty, perhaps even finding a taboo or unexpected joy or pleasure in aspects of it (we must surely admit that there can be tremendous pleasure in being a victim and feeling sorry for oneself). It's okay to enjoy this. Moreover, finding pleasure in the difficult sensations is one of the most magically transformative things that you can do.

As Carolyn Elliott explains in her book *Existential Kink,* we can savour all kinds of experiences of life and in our openness to all our experience we unlock the vast potential of our magic. The more we are willing to open up to sensations, the less we need to be trapped in our current circumstances that are bringing them about. The voracious shadow monsters within our soul can accept the fulfilment of all the nasty experiences they have been craving and, upon being satisfied and brought into the light of awareness, they can find peace and stop demanding to drag us back into the mire of our previous misery.

The more we do this work, the more freedom, health, and abundance we open ourselves up to, because clearing these emotions, fully experiencing them, embracing them, opening up to them, means that our soul's shadowy thirst for the complex and macabre, for the tragic and distasteful, for the terrible, awful humiliation of existence, is quenched. As Jung explained, that which we can experience and integrate internally does not need to manifest in the external world. If we can do this work internally we no longer need to live out the torture of it in our external lives because we've already tasted the experience and savoured it and processed it and learned from it. Once it has been fulfilled in our experience we no longer need to stay in the same patterns.

So in doing this sensational shadow work, we allow ourselves to open up to a whole new level of joy, bliss, happiness, and access to the powerful creative force that is all life, bringing wonders and magic and the many other blessings that come along with it. Of course, there will still be times of high sensation, times of anguish and despair, but the beautiful thing is that if we can learn to appreciate and relish the sensations, like the complex flavours of a savoury stew, then we will have freedom and pleasure even on the bad days, even through the challenging times, even in the inner and downward parts of the spiral, even as we walk through the underworld.

312

Just like when you were a young child, there were flavours that you enjoyed immensely. Usually these are sweet and plain foods, foods without much complexity. As you get older, for many people, our taste buds mature, so we're no longer just wanting to eat toast and cake and apple slices for every meal. Instead, we're open to having new flavours, different flavours, more complex flavours. Very few children like the taste of alcohol, fortunately, but most adults do develop a taste for beer, wine, and spirits of one kind or another, just as adults are more likely to get pleasure from eating bitter, spicy, pungent foods that many toddlers would find unenjoyable and distressing.

It can be helpful to think about the flavours of your emotional state. If they were a meal, what would they be? I often experience sadness as savoury when I think of it as a flavour. This allows me to open up to the feeling with curiosity and creativity, which are important parts of magic. It allows me to savour the sensation as if it was a meal prepared for me by a wonderful cook or even a fancy chef. The more I allow myself to experience the sensations and go through the emotion, the more I am integrating, alchemising, transforming. The more I do this work, the closer I'm getting to my divine self, and the deep awareness of the magic that flows through all of us. This also allows me to rest more and more, in comfort within my body, this beautiful animal being that I embody, this companion that has come into this world with me and is here with me always in this life.

When the seasons turn to autumn, the leaves fall from the trees as they let go their old hopes, dreams, and burdens, turning towards the restful dormancy of winter. So too is decay, letting go, and death such an important part of life. As a child, I was extremely terrified of death. My fear was so intense that it was a phobia. Many people would say it's not at all an irrational fear, fearing death, to be afraid of dying. But for me, death haunted my daily life. Anything to do with death would send me into extreme terror, even driving past a funeral home or cemetery. The mere mention of the word "death" or people dying sent me into extreme terror, so much so that I developed little rituals to stop myself from dying, to protect my loved ones. I was especially afraid of my mother dying, even more than I was of my own death. This fear was so overwhelming and limiting that when I was sixteen years old, I decided it was time that I made my peace with death. After all, this is the one thing in life that we can be certain of, and I realised that my terror was not necessarily of death itself, but more of uncertainty. Life is full of uncertainty.

I was new to witchcraft and excited by the magical potential, so I composed a ritual. I remember this well, especially since the ornamental metal vessel I used to burn things in for this ritual got rather heated and left a melted mark on my mattress, reminding me of what I had done, which in a sense was to liberate myself from the phobia and make my peace with death. This had an enormous impact on me and helped me to function more easily in the world, yet many times since have I been confronted with the spectre of death, especially around the time of my Saturn Return in Scorpio, the sign of death and transformation. Each of these encounters in this death walk was liberating, each brought with it a new level of awareness, a deeper understanding of myself, and a new freedom from fears that were haunting me. This is important work. As Oliver Burkeman explores in his books, the more we confront our limitations, the greater space we create inside ourselves and in our lives.

Human beings spend so much of their time in distractions. We implement newer, more efficient systems. We focus on consuming more, on earning more, on buying more, on climbing the corporate ladder, on any kind of goal outside ourselves. Our obsession with productivity is a symptom of our futile attempts at immortality, when facing these limitations is far, far more powerful, though perhaps it requires tremendous courage. Facing the most challenging emotions and experiences in our lives rather than running from them is a pivotal shift. In the alchemy of this, as Jung would put it, in working with this paradox of life and death, of freedom and limitation, of the absolute impossibility of all that is possible, new magic comes forth. New worlds are created.

Just as the dying of an old tree in the forest clears the way for many young saplings to grow through in its place, so to, as we begin this underworld journey, know that embracing this difficult path and this discomfort is truly one of the most rewarding things. It is my honour and privilege to walk with you into the darkness.

8

UNSPEAKABLE MAGIC

"For a seed to achieve its greatest expression, it must come completely undone. The shell cracks, its insides come out, and everything changes. To someone who doesn't understand growth, it would look like complete destruction." — Cynthia Occelli

The descent into the underworld is not easy but it is necessary. It can feel like standing on the precipice of a mythic forest at night, knowing you must go into the darkness, one foot in front of the other. To be terrified is understandable; it's part of the process. We must face this primal terror and enter the darkness of the void, the unknown, if we are to transform.

Within the stillness, allow space for awareness to arise. Are there internal structures or pattern that no longer serve you? Fears, old pain, shame and guilt? Limiting beliefs? Defence mechanisms? What is it you need to let go of right now? What can you give more death to, in order that you may have new life? What needs to be surrendered to the earth in order to be composted? What parts of ourselves are ready to grow into new forms?

In times of deep transformation, if we allow ourselves some stillness, even in the brief moments of silence we may find patterns. We may find, in the liminal spaces between sleeping and waking, in transitions

315

between chaos, that there is a fog surrounding us, energetically, wrapping us like a cocoon. There is a churning within breaking down the old structures and building new bones, new flesh, new wings. This cocoon is a space of transformation, a container for your metamorphosis.

As you rest within the cocoon, allow the solid form of the outdated structure to begin to dissolve. Watch as it softens, liquefies, and turns into goo. Trust that this dissolution is a necessary part of your transformation. Allow yourself to surrender to the process, releasing any resistance or attachment to the old form.

As the structure dissolves, sense the space that is being created within you. Feel the potential for a new way of being, for a more authentic and empowered version of yourself to emerge.

Rest in this space of potential, trusting in the wisdom of your soul to guide your reformation.

The process of dissolving and reforming is a natural part of growth and transformation. As you continue on your magical journey, trust in the wisdom of your own metamorphosis. Like the caterpillar, you hold within you the imprint of your most radiant and authentic self. By willingly entering the cocoon of change and surrendering to the alchemy of transformation, you open yourself to the magic of your own becoming.

DESCENDING INTO THE UNDERWORLD

The journey begins with a descent. We stand on the precipice, ready to embrace the darkness because we know that we can no longer hold back. We must know ourselves. In myth, we can look to Inanna's or Persephone's stories of descent into the underworld or any other number of gods and heroes venturing into the unknown. This descent is not necessarily about a geographical journey. It is a voyage of the psyche, an inward turn which requires the courage to confront fears, shadow aspects, and unresolved conflicts. It might feel like a necessary withdrawal from the world, like a caterpillar entering its cocoon, where the familiar must be relinquished to allow deep transformation to begin.

Have there been times when you've needed to turn inward? Times you've felt called to withdraw from the outer world to navigate a personal underworld? The journey could take a matter of hours, weeks, months, years. We are living in a series of concentric cycles. Every single day most of us descend into sleep, every year if we aren't too close to the equator, we descend into winter. In our emotional lives, it's often through intense challenges that we find ourselves, exhausted and desperate, on the edge of sanity, in dire need of rest or ready to leap into the unknown.

Here is my interpretation of a story drawn from ancient Sumeria, in what is sometimes called "the cradle of civilisation," where writing itself (cuneiform) was first known to evolve.

I am Inanna, Queen of Heaven, birthed in the lap of the stars, my feet bathed in the clay of ancient Sumer. From the sweet air of the Anunnaki I descended, a gleaming crescent upon the brow of the heavens. In the cradle of Uruk, my temples rose like reeds, and my name was sung on the lips of the people.

I am the morning star and the evening light. I ride the winds of the sacred ziggurat, my lions at my side, harnessed to my chariot of lapis lazuli. The silver sickle of the moon is my crown, and my robes are stitched with the gold of the harvest.

In my heart burns the fire of love and war, a furnace that smelts the desires of gods and mortals alike. Dumuzi, my shepherd, basked in my embrace, his fields ripened under the warmth of my gaze, his flocks multiplied beneath my touch. I wear the armour of fury and the perfume of cedarwood, for I am the one who conquers hearts and kingdoms alike.

But even I, Queen of Heaven, must descend. The underworld beckoned me, the unknown realm where no light penetrates, where the goddess Ereshkigal, Queen of the Dead, reigns in silence. To her dark throne I journeyed, through seven gates, each one demanding a piece of me. The crown of heaven slipped from my brow, the necklace of power fell from my throat, the robe of dominion slid from my shoulders. Like a lioness stripped of her mane, I stood bare before the great abyss.

At the foot of Ereshkigal's throne, I was laid low, hung like a corpse upon a hook, my flesh bound to the cold stone of death's embrace. I, who held the heavens in my hands, now felt the weight of nothingness press upon my bones, the silence of the grave curling into the hollow spaces where my voice once echoed. Powerlessness.

Three days and nights I lingered in that shadow, and the earth wept, the rivers ceased their flow, and the altars stood barren. But from this death, from this despair, from depths of pain and torment, and the sacred drops of wisdom, I was born anew.

I rose from the underworld, stronger than ever before, having surrendered to the death I most needed in order for new life to grow.

I am Inanna, risen and remade. My limbs are the saplings of spring, yet my roots stretch deep into the soil of the underworld, forever entwined with the bones of the dead, for I have come to know the deepest truth, that death is an integral part of life, not its opposite; that we must surrender and face what we most fear in order for new life to grow.

For every ascent, there is a descent; for every crown, a veil of dust. This is the law of the gods, the rhythm of the heavens and the earth, the pulse of life and death that flows through my veins and through the blood of all creation.

I return to the throne of the heavens, my star reborn in the sky, but the shadow of the underworld lingers. For I am Inanna, goddess of both the light and the dark, the lover and the warrior, the birth and the decay. The clay of Sumer knows my name, and the stars still tremble when I rise.

Inanna was indeed associated with the star later named Venus, who is both the morning star and the evening star depending on the timing of her descent. In this ancient mythos which arose before patriarchy and much of the disconnection of the modern world, we can see some powerful reflections of our humanity and the value of the underworld journey – the deep significance of grieving and facing our shadows in order to be able to nurture new life and renewal.

Perhaps you are embarking on an underworld journey right now, perhaps, like the deciduous trees in autumn, you are ready to shed something, to compost, to break down in order to be able to build yourself back up again. What old dreams are holding you back? What needs to die now in order that new life can birth? Perhaps there are old traumas and burdens of the path that never had their chance to be fully grieved. This is true for most of us. Our grief can be a beautiful and powerful tool. Grief can burst our hearts open and allow a new openness to our aliveness if only we embrace it. It pays to untangle any stuck stories about the past in order to clear the way for grief to flow, for emotions to be felt. You will know if a story is stuck because it will keep repeating on you in much the same way, over and over. If we can let go or penetrate through old stuck stories we allow ourselves a new freedom to embrace surrender and to embrace our lives, our magic.

I cannot promise you the results you think you want, because letting old dreams die means relinquishing the attachment to that wanting. But I can tell you what I know to be true: that when we fully accept, surrender, let go and grieve those old dreams, the resistance and tension vanishes too, and new space is created. A new dream may just surface that resembles the old dream in some way, perhaps it is a more mature and real version of what was once a fairytale delusion, a trap of society and the mind. When that old bubble bursts we are finally free to embrace something new. I have seen this time and time again in my life and the lives of others around me. It is as true in love and matters of the heart as it is in career and even sometimes in health. Sometimes the only way out of stuck patterns is to let go entirely, to embrace lady death in order that she can play her vital role in the cycles of life and renewal.

In the depths of the underworld or the confines of the cocoon, transformation occurs in isolation and darkness, mirroring the unseen alchemy within a chrysalis. Here, the old self undergoes this kind of mythic death, shedding limiting patterns and beliefs. In myth, the hero may encounter guides or receive divine aid, reflecting the inner wisdom and resources we discover in our deepest challenges.

In the desert, water, though scarce, inevitably finds its way through the parched earth to form an oasis. Similarly, in times of spiritual aridity, our essential life force—insight and renewal—can still be tapped, revealing new paths and sustaining us through the desolate terrain of the psyche.

We cannot engage with the underworld of the psyche on a purely intellectual level if we have any hope of understanding it. It does not operate in an ordinary way. In my books, I write different realms as metaphors – reflections of the mythic psyche because these are all ways to connect with the deeper divinity within us. We can connect with the underworld of the psyche through meditative practice, noticing the feelings, sensations, and images that arise.

Emerging from the underworld or breaking free of the cocoon is the pinnacle of the transformation. This is Inanna's or Persephone's return, signalling spring's renewal, or the moment a butterfly emerges, reborn with glorious wings vastly different from its previous caterpillar form. Emergence is not just a return but a rebirth, the transformed self now equipped with new insights and strengths, a greater sense of identity and purpose.

Like a powerful volcanic eruption sprinkles mineral-rich ash that nurtures fertile soil from which new life blooms, the intensity of our emergence births a more vibrant self. The struggle to break free, like a butterfly fighting its way out of its chrysalis, is what pumps blood into the wings. Without that struggle, the butterfly wouldn't be able to soar.

You've come this far in the journey, you've begun the descent into the darkness of the unknown, and I want to commend you on your courage. We stand at the threshold now. The journey ahead is a deeper level of transformation, and the inner transformation will always lead to outer changes. Are you ready? Are you ready to let go of all that is holding you back to birth yourself anew into a deeper self, a more powerful self, a self that no longer needs to take themselves so seriously? A wonderful wise and wild witch?

This is a pivotal moment in the journey of transformation. It is pivotal because we are choosing for it to be. You have the choice now, to make a commitment to yourself, just like we did in the initiation ritual. If you were waiting to get to the end of the book before self-initiating, you may feel readiness building within you, a hunger for deepening, a thirst for your own personal evolution, a desire for healing and renewal. You could turn back now, and stay at the level you're comfortable with, or you can step deeper with me, into the realms of the unknown. The choice is yours.

THE INNER AND OUTER SPIRAL

Spirals are powerful symbols across time, place, and culture, reflecting concepts of growth, evolution, and the cyclical nature of life, death, and rebirth, unity and connectivity. In Ancient Greek and Roman society the spiral was used in art and architecture, symbolising continuity and the infinite. In Ancient Egyptian art and hieroglyphs, it symbolised the sun, time, and the eternal cycle of life.

In Celtic mythologies, the triple spiral or triskele is a common symbol, associated with the goddess Brigid and representing the threefold nature of life: birth, death, and rebirth, or the interconnectedness of land, sea, and sky. In Hindu and Buddhist art the spiral often appears in the form of mandalas and other sacred symbols, perhaps representing the journey of the soul, moving inward to attain enlightenment and outward to manifest this enlightenment in the world. In New Zealand, the Māori koru (spiral) represents new life, growth, strength, and peace, inspired by the unfurling fern frond, reflecting the perpetual movement of creation.

The spiral embodies a mystical journey, the path from the outer consciousness (material world) to the inner soul (spiritual world) and back again, transformation and change, reflecting the process of shedding old layers and emerging renewed and transformed.

In our own transformational journeys, the path ahead leads into the unknown, as we spiral inward – reflecting the mythic journey into the underworld. When we're in this inner spiral, it can feel as though things aren't really working in the outer world. It's time to let go, just the way many trees do in autumn. It's a time to grieve our old dreams, to release what we no longer need, and to face the inner fears and other challenging emotions and limitations that we are ready to confront. It can also be time to find our true rest, deep within ourselves. All of this allows us to expand inwardly.

We spiral inwards, constricting into our cocoons and processing our resistance along the way. Through this underworld journey, after letting go of the old trappings of our former selves, cocooning ourselves in sacred rest and undergoing our deep metamorphosis while facing our shadows, eventually we get to a point where it's time for things to tip back the other way again.

The outward spiral feels amazing. We're expanding rather than being constricted. We're opening up to the acceleration of the new, although even in this phase, we can hold ourselves back with fear.

In our wild magic journey of alchemy we can find that edge within ourselves that tingles with the fear of the unknown. We can put our hand up against it and tune in to listen. We can gently push against the resistance we have to the unknown, to allow ourselves to experience that tight fear and find joy in the constriction within it. This transforms our relationship to that fear into one of exhilaration.

On a roller coaster you can either be hunched over, gripping your arms in terror, or you can throw your arms up in the air and surrender to the thrill of the ride. In this beautiful surrendering, you find faith in your life and in yourself.

WHEN THINGS ARE HARD

When things are extremely hard, it's important to take a moment to centre yourself. Find a moment alone if you can, even if it's just excusing yourself to go to the bathroom and breathe. As you breathe, feel your feet on the floor, the weight of your body supported by the earth beneath you. Feel the air moving in and out of your lungs, a constant reminder that you are alive, that you are here.

There are times when nothing seems to be working for us in the outer world, when our energy is drawn inward. These are sacred times. They are not easy, especially as our conscious minds want to fight tooth and nail for more progress – for results – for victory, and yet, we need the rest times too. Just as the rain nourishes and refreshes the earth, these swampy times are deeply, deeply nourishing to the soul if only we allow them to be as they are.

We need the fields to lie fallow in order for the soil to regenerate. Instead of fighting the inward times, we can flow with them. Even when we are extremely stretched and busy with work and obligations and life in general, we can let ourselves off the hook and be gentle with ourselves. We can take a few moments to breathe slowly, and instead of scheduling more busy work or escaping into entertainment, we can book ourselves in for a walk, a bath, a night in bed with our journals, a conversation with our close friend who understands, whatever it is that helps us rest. Sometimes rest is the best productivity.

Acknowledge that things are hard. Let yourself say it, either out loud or in your mind: "This is really hard right now." It's important to acknowledge because the more you fight it, the more that resistance will build into the hardness and the difficulty. When we resist the truth of our experience, it's like trying to hold a beach ball underwater – it takes so much energy, and eventually, it will burst up with even more force.

As you acknowledge the hardness, you might feel a heaviness in your chest, a tightness in your throat, or tears wanting to come. Let them be there. These sensations are messages from your body, telling you what you need to know. We don't come into this life for things to be easy all the time. If things were too easy, there would be no challenge and no learning. Our difficulties are like the resistance that strengthens a muscle – they build our capacity to hold more, to understand more deeply.

Sometimes things feel way too hard and overwhelming, like we're carrying the weight of mountains on our shoulders. We have to struggle with all kinds of horrendous situations – the immediate pressure of them crushing down, and the long echoes of their impact through our lives. Our coping mechanisms, the ways we've learned to survive, sometimes create their own challenges. We might find ourselves hiding when we need connection, lashing out when we need comfort, or freezing when we need to move.

In these moments, acknowledging the hardness is important – not just as a general concept, but the specific texture of your experience right now. What does this hardness feel like in your body? Where do you feel it most strongly? Maybe it's a knot in your stomach, a vice around your chest, or a fog in your mind. Whatever you're experiencing, let yourself name it: "This is what's happening right now. This is real."

This acknowledgment of our experience, our reality, is an important first step in being able to work with the magic of the challenge. Yes, magic – because within every challenge lies a seed of transformation. It's not just the external situation that we need to acknowledge. It's also our inner reality: our fears, our hopes, our grief, our anger, our determination. All of these are valid, all of these are part of your experience.

Take a moment now to place a hand on your heart, feeling its steady beat beneath your palm. This is your wisdom centre, always pulsing with life, always knowing what you need. From here, we can listen to our intuition for what might be helpful to do next. Maybe you need to cry, or sleep, or call a friend. Maybe you need to write, or walk, or sit quietly with a cup of tea. Your intuition knows – it always knows.

Remember that you've survived every hard thing that's come before this. You've made it through darkness to find light again and again. This time is no different. You have within you everything you need to face this challenge, to learn from it, to grow through it. Even if you can't see the way forward clearly right now, trust that each small step – each breath, each moment of acknowledgment – is leading you where you need to go.

Let yourself be held by this moment of awareness. Let yourself be supported by the ground beneath you, the air around you, the wisdom within you. The hardness may not disappear, but by acknowledging it, by making space for it, you create room for something new to emerge –

perhaps strength you didn't know you had, perhaps wisdom you couldn't access before, perhaps a path you couldn't see until now.

And when you're ready, take a deep breath and feel yourself expanding just a little bit more around the hardness. You don't need to make it go away. You just need to keep making space for yourself within it, keep listening to your intuition, keep taking one small step at a time. This is how we move through the hard times – not by forcing our way through, but by flowing with them, learning from them, growing through them.

WORKING WITH CHALLENGING PARTS OF SELF

People often talk about parts of themselves – "a part of me wants to take that opportunity, but another part is terrified" or "part of me knows I need rest, but another part keeps pushing." We say these things naturally, instinctively, because somewhere deep inside we recognise that we're not just one simple thing. We're a complex system of selves, of parts, each carrying their own wisdom, their own pain, their own ways of trying to help us survive.

The ancient alchemists understood this divided will. They saw how we can feel scattered, fragmented, pulled in different directions like metals waiting to be refined into gold. They knew that before unity can come, we must first acknowledge our multiplicity – all these different aspects of ourselves that seem to want different things, that operate from different beliefs, that carry different parts of our story.

Sometimes when we're struggling, these parts can feel like they're at war within us. One part desperate to reach out for connection, another part building walls of protection. One part wanting to speak our truth, another part freezing our voice to keep us safe. And often, we try to silence these parts, to push them away, especially when they carry difficult emotions or memories we'd rather not face.

There's another way to approach these parts of ourselves. I'm learning to set a table in my inner world, to create a space of welcome and curiosity. A soft tablecloth with a gentle pattern that brings comfort. A teapot warming, steam rising like incense. Delicate cups waiting to be filled. This is a sacred space where these different parts of myself can come to be heard, to be known, to begin the slow dance toward unity.

If you are struggling with trauma, it is a good idea to seek out a trained therapist who is experienced with IFS, somatic therapies, and other modalities that have been shown to be effective.

Most forms of talk therapy don't work for trauma. There is one, in particular, that is especially well evidenced, and especially magical. My friend Zoe, who is a psychologist, has spoken with me in awe over some of the unexpected results of this. In Internal Family Systems (IFS) therapy, we learn that every part of us – even the ones that seem destructive – originally came to help us survive. That anxious part sending waves of worry through my body? It's trying to keep me safe, scanning for danger like it learned to do so long ago. That critical voice in my head? It's trying to protect me from failure or rejection by catching every possible flaw first.

When I notice a part of me that feels upset, distressed, wounded, I ask it: "Would you like to come in?" "Would you like some tea?" This simple invitation can be magical – how often do we offer this kind of welcome to the parts of ourselves we've been fighting with or trying to change?

When things are extremely hard, when we feel overwhelmed or lost, this practice becomes even more important. Finding a moment alone, even if it's just in the bathroom, to breathe and acknowledge what's happening. Feeling our feet on the floor, the weight of our body supported by the earth. Recognising that while things are hard right now, we don't have to handle everything at once. We can just pour the tea, create the space, invite one part at a time to be heard.

If another part appears to me, I extend the welcome: "There's room for you too," I say, preparing another cup. This is the beauty of inner hospitality – we don't have to choose between parts. We can welcome them all, create space for all their stories, all their needs, all their wisdom.

Sometimes a part comes to the table in crisis, spilling tea, unleashing storms of emotion. That's welcome too. I keep my hands steady as I pour another cup, as I offer a gentle presence to contain whatever arises. Some parts need many cups of tea, many conversations, before they begin to trust this process. Some come to the table angry or scared, certain they'll be sent away again. But the tea keeps flowing, the welcome keeps extending, and slowly, so slowly sometimes, something shifts.

This is the work of unifying our divided will – not through force but through welcome, not through rejection but through relationship. Each cup of tea is an invitation to wholeness. Each conversation is a step toward integration. The alchemists understood that transformation happens in its own time, like tea leaves slowly unfurling in hot water, like metals gradually purifying in the alchemist's flask.

When we create this kind of space within ourselves, when we learn to host all these parts with compassion, something remarkable begins to happen. Parts that seemed like enemies reveal themselves as allies in disguise. Feelings that seemed overwhelming become bearable when held in awareness with care. We begin to feel more whole, more integrated, even as we acknowledge our multiplicity.

And so I keep setting the table, keep warming the pot, keep extending the invitation. "There's room for you here," I say to each part that appears. "There's tea enough for everyone. There's space enough for all of your stories." Because I'm learning that unity comes not from silencing parts of ourselves, but from welcoming them all into consciousness, one cup of tea at a time.

TEA WITH MY NEGLECTED ONE

Tuning into my body, tuning into sensations, a part of me has emerged in the last day. She is a neglected child-part of me. She's green and purple with a kind of hood, and I can only see one eye. Her hair sweeps to the side. She is in anguish with all her unmet needs.

She is the culmination of so much neglect in my childhood – of not being made to feel loved and looked after. So much time that I spent in pain was this big burden of emotion she's been holding onto. She wants to be seen and heard and loved, but she can't feel that when all she feels is the opposite. And so she was sealed away. Still, that neglect has haunted me; that emotion has haunted me for years, even though I couldn't see this part of me.

I'm laying a table for her, putting out a tablecloth. It's got pretty floral fabric, a little bit checkered for some reason. I'm making some tea and doing some baking for her, and I'm inviting her in. She's here, and I'm opening the door, and she stands there sobbing. I open my arms gently, and I say, "It's okay. Would you like to come in? Would you like a hug?"

She wants a hug, so I open my arms wider, and I wrap her in this embrace. I feel her melt a bit, just surrender a little and relax as I hold her. I walk with her to the table, offer her a chair, and I sit down opposite her. I pour her some tea and offer her some treats, tell her that she's safe here, and that I'm here to listen.

She relaxes a little bit more. She tells me how she feels like nobody loves her. She feels this pain of disconnection. When I hold her in my attention, I reach out and take her hand. I tell her it's okay. I tell her I know it's been hard. I tell her I believe her.

I ask her how old she is, and she says she's eight or nine. I ask her how old she thinks I am. She thinks I'm maybe 20, some kind of adult. I tell her that I'm 40, and that I've done a lot of healing, and that I'm sorry that I haven't always been able to hold her, that I pushed her away because the feelings were really hard, but that I'm ready to reconnect with her now. She can trust me to look after her, to look after myself.

She relaxes a little bit more and thanks me for this opportunity, for the tea. She likes the scones. She says she was often hungry – didn't always have her needs for food met, or her needs for attention and support, safety and love. And I give her my attention. I empathise with her and how hard it's been for her, for us to go through all of that painful childhood stuff.

As I do that, I feel a bit of pain in my abdomen. I just check in with that now, just gently tap against my abdomen and listen to the pulse of pain. I put both my hands on my abdomen and just breathe. I focus back on her across the table, and I ask her if she knows how much of a heavy burden she's carrying.

She says she's tired, and she does now see that she has this big sack on her back full of pain. It's been weighing her down. And I ask her, "Are you ready to part with some of this burden?"

She says she doesn't know. She doesn't know who she would be without this pain, without this neglect, without all this anguish she's holding on so tightly to, because it's all she has ever known. And I say I want to welcome her back into connectedness and into love so she doesn't have to feel neglected anymore, so she can have all the joy that she has been wanting, all of the attention and the love, all of the nourishment, the care, all of the things that she was missing.

She begins to feel warmer, lighter. This brightness spreads through her a little bit. She can tell that there are other options than this. We sit with that for a while. When I check in and say, "Are you ready to let go of some of this burden, come and join us?" she's still hesitant. She doesn't know if she can trust it, because all she's ever known is pain and neglect and fear and anguish.

I tell her it's okay, there's no rush, but that the choice is hers. I keep holding her in my attention, just accepting her, just loving her, and now she's starting to feel tired of holding on to this burden. She asks what she could do.

I say, "Why don't we go out to the garden, take this burden out to the compost pile so it can go back into the earth?" She agrees, and she feels lighter now. She's still small, but even smaller, like a little child. She's lighter already and more free, and I help her. We lug this giant sack of burden out through the back door, out to the garden, out to the compost heap.

We begin to offer it up – all that neglect, all that anguish, all that hunger for love, for food, for attention, for safety, all of that pain of crying in my room alone, all of those unmet needs, all of the anger and anguish. We pile it into the compost heap, add in a lot of mulch, help it to break down. We aerate the compost heap, mixing all of those emotions back into the soil, surrendering that big burden and knowing that we can love ourselves now. We can give ourselves what we need to feel safe and cared for. We can release all that pain. There may be more to release. It may come back, but we know how to do this work now.

And then we hold each other. I welcome this neglected child-part of me into my heart and give her all the love and care that she needs, that she craved. I take a moment to just let myself love myself. I thank her for this gift that she's given me by coming back. She's always welcome in my heart, her feelings are always valid.

And I ask her what role she would like to have now in my body and in my life? And she says she wants to love me and be loved by me, be a constant source of love. I thank her for this gift, and I hug her again inside my heart, and I feel this warmth radiating through my body.

And so it is.

HAVING FAITH, EVEN IN A WORLD FULL OF CHAOS

Faith feels like falling...

I wrote this line in my journal over twenty years ago. Faith in life is something that is tested over and over again. And I don't mean this like a school exam. This is a mythic challenge, in much the same way that many traditions have spiritual quests as rites of passage.

Because many of us no longer live within the cultural support structures of those traditional societies, we can create our own rites of passage. This could be around key astrological transits like a Saturn Return, or just around whatever challenges you happen to be having in your life right now. After all, rising to a challenge is a lot more fun than cowering in the corner, hoping for it to end soon.

Of course, cowering and hiding under the blankets can be enjoyable too, and it can be necessary. However, the more you awaken to the agency and power that you innately have, and how you connect with and experience life rather than try to control or hide from it, the more you open yourself up to the very real flows of magic pouring through each and every one of us. Magic is the force that builds the world.

When we open up to this flow, not just when we are spiralling out and expanding, but also in the contraction of the inward cycle, we enable ourselves to receive the glorious and abundant blessings of wellbeing and joy. We also open to the thrill and satisfaction of creativity, of connection, and of sharing what we have to say with the outer world at large, influencing it with connected and wise awareness.

So here we are, on the precipice of a brilliant journey together. You may find, as with many healing modalities and magical workings, that when you begin this work, unexpected things happen. You might suddenly catch a cold or receive an unexpected bill. When this does happen, notice how you feel. Just notice the sensations of the feeling. Allow yourself to experience that sensation as much as you can in the present moment. And then allow yourself to connect in with your heart, with the magic of your existence and the magic of this universe, and recommit to your power (even if it was a power disconnection notice?). Because every unexpected incident is an opportunity to reconnect, to awaken, and to go deeper.

You may find that unexpected things happen. Brilliant and wonderful things. You'll just be going about your life, doing your magical processing, aligning with your power and your desires, feeling connected to the natural world and suddenly opportunities will line up that you never imagined were possible. When these things happen, feel free to share them with me. I'd love to hear your stories of magic.

Occasionally, when I do get sick with a common cold or something similar, I choose to perceive it as my body telling me I need to slow down and I need to go inward. Perhaps it's no coincidence that people who meditate apparently get sick far less often than people who don't. Because in that liminal space, you're not only connecting more spiritually and emotionally with all that is, your body also rests and receives the energy that it needs.

I used to experience illness far more often than I do now. And it tends to sneak up on me only when I forget to spend time meditating that the outer world gives me an opportunity to spend time in the quiet and stillness, whether I like it or not.

Now, this is not to blame any illness at all on things inside our control, because that is not useful. Like I've said before, we're not here for victim blaming. And I do believe that there are things that are outside our control on many, many levels. After all, we're here in this world of apparent struggle and limitations.

But if we don't have some kind of sense of purpose, then life is just a pointless struggle. And we're faced with the paradox that even though our lives are full of all sorts of complicated things, some good and some bad and some completely unfair, all of this coexists at once. All of those terrible things that happen in the world were believed by Jung to be manifestations of our collective shadow and in facing our fears we cast this shadow into the light of awareness where it can no longer haunt us. It's only in bringing the light of awareness into the deepest recesses of shadow that we can liberate ourselves personally and our communities, our families, our societies, our species, and our planet from the immense shadows that often burden and terrorise and cloud the world.

Here is an experiment for you. If something is making you want to react in anger or rage, experiment to experience that emotion with curiosity and openness. What is it that's being triggered in you? What shadowy things are happening?

You'll find similar reflections in Buddhist practices, like Tonglen, where in a meditative state, people envision breathing in suffering and pain from the world around them, transmuting it into beautiful loving energy and then sending it back out again. The idea is that in connecting to the divine, we can bring the light of awareness into our world, alleviating pain and suffering. And if we're not too busy being self-sacrificing martyrs to the cause, we can have a lot of fun while doing it. Because what's magic without wicked enjoyment?

Witchcraft, astrology, and tarot have had a huge rise in popularity in recent years. Perhaps partly it's due to the confusion in the world and the absence of many traditional community structures, like the kind that indigenous societies evolved with. Most of us in the modern world are haunted by a gaping absence where deep meaning and interconnectedness are interwoven with our very existence including the small tasks that we do in the day, our understanding of ourselves and others, and our understanding of how the universe works.

Instead, with rampant individualism, many of us are trying to find our own path. The brilliant thing about being a witch is that it's almost impossible not to find your own path. Sure, you could join a particular kind of tradition of witchcraft. However, even then, there's an openness to pagan traditions which means that while people share celebrations and magical practices at times, people tend to walk their own paths in terms of what they particularly believe. Being told what to believe is something many people are escaping from; we don't want to be handed the truth on a golden platter, we want to be in the magic of discovering it for ourselves. One of the joys of being free from the confines of more authoritarian religions and belief systems is that we have immense freedom to pick and choose what resonates with us deeply at our core.

In every moment you have this opportunity to step into your power and be true to yourself, your authentic, wild, wicked, and wonderful self. Embrace the journey inward, into the depths of your being. Face your fears, your shadows, your hidden desires. Let them transform you, like the caterpillar dissolving in the chrysalis, only to emerge as a radiant butterfly.

The inner journey of the spiral of transformation often feels frightening, tight and uncomfortable, but it is where the deep magic happens. And when it's time to spiral outwards again, spread your wings and fly, let your magic ripple out into the world, touching hearts, igniting minds, weaving webs of enchantment and change. You are a co-creator, a universe dreaming itself awake. What wonders will you birth into being?

The path of the witch is not for the faint of heart. It requires courage, authenticity, and a willingness to dance with the darkness. But oh, what treasures lie in wait for those who dare to walk this winding way.

So take a deep breath, my dear. Ground your feet into the earth. Feel the fire in your belly, the wind in your hair, the water in your blood. You are alive, and you are magic. The world is waiting for you to claim your power.

Will you answer the call?

STRUCTURE AND TENSION

Limitations and tensions, as much as we detest them, are essential to our experience, our creation, and our magic. Many of us long for uninterrupted periods of time and peace, and yet even when we get to have those wide open periods of time, the gaping expanse of the void can often trouble people even more than the business previously plaguing them. How many of us quickly reach for something to do when we come home to an empty house; we look for something to watch or read to fill the silence, or some kind of chore to make us feel useful. Facing emptiness can be daunting, especially when we've been busy on the treadmill of endless tasks and distractions. In my experience, deliberately and courageously facing the void of empty space is incredibly rewarding, because the void is where creativity seems to come from.

Time works in funny ways. It can pass us by so quicky, or drag on excruciatingly slowly, all depending on how we relate to it. How many people do you know who say they would love to do something – a hobby, a craft, writing, or other creations – if only they had time? And yet I have known many writers, for instance, who finally get a residency or some other situation in which they can write for weeks on end, only to find themselves confronted with a lack of inspiration, feeling that they are blocked and so on. Faced with that wide open space, they do not yet know how to turn that lead of the internal tensions that they carry with them into gold. Once you do know how to use your internal tensions to your advantage, then time can be on your side, allowing you to balance priorities and achieve more in ways that can feel miraculous.

Creativity is a form of magic; other kinds of magic also depend on tensions in order to bring them forth into the world. Tension is absolutely necessary in anything that needs a structure – it is the bones and the muscles of the human body, a key factor in architecture and design, essential in plot. It can be helpful to look at our entire lives with this lens, in this moment in terms of the tensions that currently constrain us, examine the things that hold us back, but with new eyes. Through this magical world view, we can see these tensions in a new light. We can see how they glimmer with potential and possibility. What is it you are struggling with right now? Relationships, with career, challenging personalities in your life, money, health? These are the things that most of us do struggle with at various times. Whatever it is that repeats in a recurring pattern for you holds huge potential for transformation.

The tricky thing is that this transformation will not always take the form that you necessarily expect or want it to. And that is the risk that we almost take in doing this work. For instance, if you seek a relationship in which somebody loves you and pays attention to you, it may not be through the person whose attention you currently desire as this magic plays out – it may be through another person, but if you are too attached to a specific outcome you can easily get in the way of your own magical fulfilment. You may find that you first have to find the love and acceptance within yourself, or that you have to process your fear of intimacy and vulnerability in relationships in order to receive what you desire.

The same principle applies to health. If you're struggling with your health, it may not be that the situation resolves itself in the way that you wish it would. Maybe instead you develop a totally different perspective and the things that you struggle with now change. At some point along this path in our magic, there's a time when we need to let go of our expectations and sink into the unknown depths of possibility. Once we've worked through the situation and transformed as much as we can, the only way forward is to let go of our attachment in order for something new to grow. The tricky thing is, we cannot let go *in order* for good things to happen, because that is just another attachment to good things happening. We must let go because it is what we absolutely need to do in this moment in our life. Letting go is magic in itself.

Do not simply give up and hide under the blankets or surrender to powerlessness if that is a pattern that you have. If that's what you want to do by default, then instead lean into the tensions. Persevere, push through, do the work, and turn the limitations into potential. If we can do this, we have the potential to experience liberation.

THE WHEEL

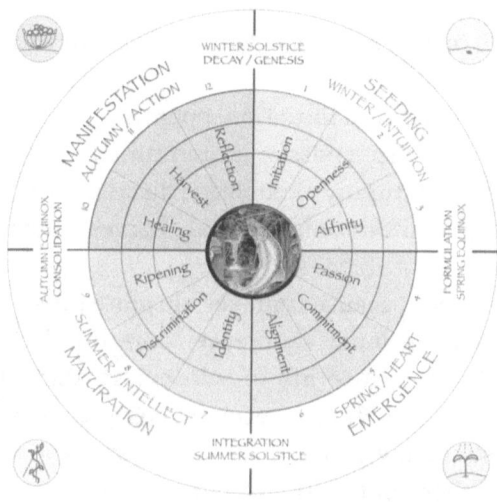

When we look at the metaphor of a garden or forest, there are times when we have the seed of the idea of what we want but it hasn't yet sprouted. We don't know how to get from the idea to the reality. At times like this, we must let go, allow space for things to grow and burst forth on their own. The seed needs to be planted in the darkness of the earth in order to grow. Worrying the soil will only disturb the seed. We must allow the darkness of the void to do its work and nurture dreams to reality. As the new dream begins to grow, we can protect its fragile sapling form, holding that space and sharing our dreams only with those who will support and nurture them. Then we can provide structure to support that dream and prune back the growth we no longer need as we move towards the harvest. These are all equally important parts of the process, as reflected beautifully in the Wheel of Segais, a tool created by Pamela Meekings-Stuart.

Pamela is a wonderful friend of mine, a druid and witch for decades. She's held Full Moon ceremonies in her home as well as druid rituals. One night, Pamela found all her wisdom coalescing into a spectacular vision in the Wheel of Segais, a brilliant tool which can help to navigate and guide us through the cycles of life and the process of bringing new things into the world, which is also the process of magic.

The Wheel of Segais consists of four quarters, each with three stages:

1. Winter (Seeding/Intuition): Initiation, openness, affinity
2. Spring (Heart/Emergence): passion, commitment, alignment
3. Summer (Intellect/Maturation): Identity, discrimination, ripening
4. Autumn (Action/Manifestation): Healing, harvest, and reflection

I love Pamela's tool because it makes absolute sense to me in just the way that nature has an inner coherence, a beautiful chaotic order and symmetry to it. In my entire life of wisdom-seeking, there are only a handful of systems and tools that resonate completely with my intuition and pass the tests of my rationality, scepticism, and questioning. I've included many of these in this book, and the Wheel is no exception. I'm privileged to know Pamela and to share the creation and participation of rituals with her and the Grove of the Summer Stars, a community which she has nurtured for many years. She's a wise woman, the closest thing I've had to a mentor, and the most vibrant person I know. She is in her 80s and she's exactly who everyone seems to want to be when they grow up!

Pamela has been learning about spirituality her entire life, training in tarot, the elements, and many systems. She's a fully-fledged druid with the Order of Bards, Ovates, and Druids, and a leader of multiple communities. One night, everything coalesced for her into the amazing Wheel, which mirrors the life cycle of a tree. Pamela has written about the Wheel in her gorgeous book, *Living Treefully, an inspiring metaphor for living and learning.* It is also a wonderful divination and reflection tool. Pamela has created kits made with the Wheel including a small bag of hazelnuts which symbolise wisdom in mythology, inspired by the story of the sacred Well of Segais in which the salmon of wisdom eat hazelnuts from the nine hazelnut trees surrounding the well. When we hold hazelnuts above the wheel and ask a question, gently dropping them onto the diagram, they land somewhere symbolising a point of reflection for us on our journey. We can also use the Wheel as a planning tool.

We often want to rush from idea to harvest, but there are no shortcuts to creating things of real, deep value or to evolving in our lives. The only shortcut is to get out of our own way. People may appear lucky, but we don't really know their full stories. Presenting only a sunny side or constantly complaining are both unbalanced behaviours.

If we can hold space for the discomfort of our problems and let go of our attachment to having things a certain way, we can clear space for our garden to grow. In the silence of stillness, an idea might come to us – the magic of the cosmos speaking through us, our soul sharing its insight. This is a calling to bring something new into the world and into our life.

What is it that you want? I'll ask you again and again until you know, until you're asking from a place of openness. Openness is crucial when we first have inspiration or discover a challenge. We might face resistance – voices telling us we can't do it, that it's too risky or dangerous, that we're not enough. These negative voices are merely illusions, shadows in the forest of our lives.

As we move through the processes of the wheel, from winter's stillness to spring's nurture, we protect our vulnerable new ideas. We share what we're creating only with those who will support us. In summer, we provide structure and prune, using discrimination to discern what to keep and what to cut away. Finally, in autumn, we're ready for the harvest, ripening, healing, and reflection.

If we try to jump straight from inspiration to harvest without going through the transformation process, we haven't really done anything. This pattern is seen in organisations struggling with change, as Pamela observed in her work supporting them.

You may already be somewhere along this journey. It can be useful to know where you are on the wheel. Are you in the first flush of an idea, or are you at some other stage? Are you jumping ahead to discrimination before you've given your dream the nurture it needs to grow?

People often shut themselves down out of fear of failure, humiliation, or disappointment. But the only real failure is in not trying at all. If you try, you either learn or succeed, or both. As the old adage goes, failure can be our biggest lesson. We can face our vulnerability instead of shutting down in shame. We can be brave enough to risk for the sake of something new and exciting in the world. And that in itself can be enough.

REBIRTH DEATH AND THE COMPLETING OF A CYCLE

When I was two years old, I was on a beach with my mother and I found a feather. She smiled and told me, "People used to write by dipping these in ink and using them a bit like pens." Toddler-me looked her in the eye and said, "And before that, they used to write like this." I sat down on the sand and began drawing in it with my fingers. My mother was astonished. Much as she was when years later, my five year old brother came running home from the local shop in terror after seeing some graffiti, a look of shock and horror on his face as he said, "Mum, the Nazis are coming!"

Of course it's possible that we, as children, picked these things up from other sources or channelled them from the collective unconscious, but when I reflect on family stories like this I wonder where the information came from. Was I reflecting on my own past lives or tuning into some other kind of wisdom? Was my brother recalling a different time in history that he'd personally experienced?

Have you ever felt a strange affinity for a different time or place? Perhaps you were watching a documentary of a lecture about Ancient Mesopotamia, or you came across a sense of déjà vu on your travels in Ireland. Something might have pulled at you from deep inside, a recognition. Could it have been an ancestral memory, something in your genetics responding to a familiar environment? Or perhaps you lived in a place like this once before. You do not have to believe in reincarnation to be a witch, but when you understand how much learning, growing, and transforming there is to do, it can be hard to imagine fitting it all into one lifetime!

Yes, it makes sense that I would be drawn to reincarnation as death terrified me as a child, becoming a constant preoccupation. However, after making peace with my mortality, the fear haunted me less, and after this, in my late teens and early twenties, I became fascinated with reincarnation, devouring everything I could find on the subject. I studied any research I could find, including books by hypnotherapists who had accidentally encountered and then documented past-life memories, and accounts of near-death experiences, hoping to understand it better.

The appeal of reincarnation went beyond the promise of my soul continuing after death. It resonated with my sense that we are here to learn, and there's far more to learn than one life could teach. The concept of older and younger souls made intuitive sense to me, not in terms of superiority (because an old soul has no less value or intelligence than a young soul just as an old person is equally as important as a young person and can add value and insight in different ways), but as different stages of learning. Sometimes, particular times in history or places would resonate deeply with me, leading me to wonder if I'd lived there before.

The research of Ian Stevenson on reincarnation was particularly compelling. He documented hundreds of cases of children who spoke of other lives, often from the very first moment of learning to talk. These children would say things they had no other way of knowing, describing families, lives, and details in eerie detail and haunting resonance. While many cases were from countries where belief in reincarnation was common such as India and Lebanon (where parents are more likely to take the strange things their children say as potentially past life related rather than dismiss them), Stevenson also documented cases in the United States and other places where such beliefs were less prevalent.

One fascinating aspect of reincarnation literature is the overwhelming similarities in accounts. Stories from children who experienced glimpses of an afterlife through near-death experiences often align strikingly with accounts from people under deep hypnosis, such as those documented in Michael Newton's work.

Over the years, I've learned to hold my ideas and beliefs lightly. I'm no longer so attached to the idea of reincarnation that I would argue for it outright or try to convince anyone to share my beliefs, and I'm not worried if you don't agree with me either. When I hold my beliefs gently I can trust that my ideas are good because they remain resonant; I do not need to use them as a crutch or to cling to them for them to stay with me.

Understanding reincarnation can be helpful, especially for those feeling like their work will never be done or that life is too short. It offers the possibility of more chances to learn, create, share, and inspire. Some people have found relief from inexplicable pain or trauma by processing past life memories that surfaced through hypnosis. While I'm open to the possibility that all of this might not be true, it can still be useful too. It's also interesting that many traditions, including Taoism, Buddhism, and Hinduism, incorporate reincarnation as a core belief. Even early Christians believed in reincarnation before it was conveniently replaced with the concept of hell and damnation.

Different cultures understand reincarnation differently. For instance,

Japanese Zen Buddhism doesn't believe in humans reincarnating as other animals, while Tibetan Buddhism does. While animals can undoubtedly be wiser than human beings in their attunement to natural wisdom, being human is exceptionally complicated, suggesting the learning is more detailed and nuanced compared to the learning of simpler forms of life like earthworms. It's hard to imagine what learning coming back in a simpler form might entail except for perhaps a nice rest from all this complexity.

Some argue against reincarnation, citing the increasing global population. However, this argument doesn't consider that not all souls may have lived many human lives here on earth, and there may be more to the cosmic picture than we understand. Michael Newton's *Destiny of Souls* offers interesting possibilities about what souls might be doing when not incarnated on Earth. I found Newton's focus on soul specialisations and the realm between worlds particularly intriguing. Interestingly, when I first read his work at age twenty, I felt I intuitively understood some concepts better than the author himself, especially regarding non-linear time and the nature of spiritual hierarchies.

In the many books on reincarnation there is often a reflection of soul development through time. Souls come here to learn. Some are very new and still glowing with the light of the spirit world, some are very old and even as babies their eyes seem to hold an ancient wisdom. As souls mature, they at first seem to seek rules and structure, they are interested in fitting in. Then, much like Nietzsche's analogy of the camel evolving into the lion and then into the child, they become more competitive, trying to be the best, to shine the brightest. Later, they become more enthralled by relationships and connections, and finally, the older souls that have been around for a while are an odd bunch. Old souls walk to the beat of their own drum. They aren't interested in conformity, or winning, or even in much of the drama of interpersonal relationships. Some are helping to guide other souls, some are simply here to learn particular lessons – developing their specialities.

Whether you choose to believe in it or not, considering the possibility of reincarnation adds a new layer to understanding your soul's purpose, drive, and deepest learning. It invites you to reflect on what you might have been learning over many lives and how you're continuing that learning now in the great cosmic unfolding of the universe.

SPIRIT ANIMALS

Many people are familiar with the idea of animals as connected to us, as witches' familiars or spirit animals. This concept is expressed differently across traditions. The spirit animal holds a place of significance, weaving together the threads of natural wisdom and mystical insight. Each creature, from the mightiest stag to the most elusive wren, carries with it a special meaning and a guiding presence.

In ancient Greece, animals played a significant symbolic role, often associated with gods and embodying divine qualities. The owl, eagle, and dolphin, for example, were linked to gods like Athena, Zeus, and Apollo, symbolising wisdom, power, and guidance. Greek mythology also featured mythical creatures that combined human and animal traits, reflecting complex spiritual or moral lessons. Unlike the Celts, the Greeks saw these animals more as representatives of the gods rather than as independent spiritual beings because in their worldview all things were connected through divinity in their pantheon.

When working with spirit animals with reverence to traditions, it's important to understand the cultural context and the symbolic meanings and gifts of each animal. Across various Celtic traditions, animals were often seen as guides or protectors, embodying qualities that could be invoked for guidance, protection, or insight.

In Irish mythology, animals are supernatural beings or messengers between the human and otherworldly realms. The Salmon of Wisdom, for example, is a well-known figure in Irish lore along with the boar, deer, and raven. The boar, often associated with strength and ferocity, appears in tales such as the story of Diarmuid and Gráinne. Deer and stags are associated with the god Cernunnos and represent the cycle of life, death, and rebirth. Irish druids were believed to have special relationships with certain animals, which they could invoke for guidance or protection during rituals and in their daily lives.

The Picts, who inhabited what is now Scotland, left behind a legacy of intricate stone carvings, many of which depict animals. These carvings are believed to have spiritual significance, possibly representing clan emblems or protective spirits. Animals such as the eagle and the salmon are commonly depicted and were likely revered as symbols of power and wisdom. In Scottish folklore, the Cailleach goddess is often associated with animals, particularly deer and wolves. She is seen as a protector of wildlife and the natural world, and animals are said to be under her care during the harsh winter months.

The Mabinogion, a collection of medieval Welsh tales, is rich with references to animals as guides and symbols of deeper truths. For example, in the tale of Pwyll, Prince of Dyfed, a white stag leads Pwyll into a mystical encounter, representing a connection between the earthly and the divine. The Welsh hero Owain is often associated with ravens, which are seen as messengers of the gods and symbols of prophecy. Ravens in Welsh lore are closely linked to the protector god Bran.

In Brythonic (Breton and Cornish) Celtic traditions such as the Breton Folklore associated with Brittany, animal guides and spirits are a significant part of the folk tradition. The Ankou, a figure associated with death, is often depicted with a black dog, which serves as a guide to the afterlife. The dog in Breton culture is seen as a protector and a guide through the spiritual realms. In Cornwall, animals like the hare and the owl are prominent in folklore. The hare is often considered a shape-shifter, associated with witches and mystical transformation, while the owl is revered for its wisdom and its ability to see into the darkness, both literal and metaphorical.

The different Celtic groups had distinct relationships with the natural world and animals, shaped by their environments and cultural interactions. For example, the sea played a significant role in Breton and Irish Celtic traditions, leading to a greater emphasis on animals like the seal and the salmon, which were seen as both real and mythical creatures with deep spiritual significance.

As the Celtic regions became Christianised, many of the older beliefs about animal guides were incorporated into Christian practices. Animals that were once seen as pagan symbols were often reinterpreted as symbols of saints or were integrated into Christian iconography and folklore, but their older, pagan meanings often persisted in folk practices and stories.

To connect with a spirit animal, we can engage in reflective meditation, perhaps in a natural setting, inviting the spirit of your animal to guide and teach you. Listen for its presence in the rustle of leaves, the ripple of water, or the sigh of the wind. Observe the animals that cross your path often, for they may be your guides or messengers. We may discover animal guides recur in our dreams. This can sometimes be frightening at first, but in opening up to their lessons and asking what they have to show us we can transform our own fear and face this new understanding with courage and gentleness.

Celebrating these spirit animals in rituals or through the creation of art can also strengthen your connection to them. You might craft an amulet bearing their likeness, or weave their symbols into your daily life through decoration or personal adornment. In embracing the wisdom animals, we can open a door to a richer, more interconnected existence, where every creature has a story, and every story is a strand in the great web of life. We can let these guides lead us to understandings and practical wisdom in the embrace of nature and its ancient lore.

ANIMAL SYMBOLISM

The Stag: Majestic and commanding, the stag is a revered figure, often associated with the god Cernunnos, the lord of wild things. The stag symbolises sovereignty, renewal, and protection. As a spirit animal, it guides one to assert authority wisely, navigate changes gracefully, and protect those who depend on them.

The Salmon: Known for its incredible wisdom and age, the salmon leaps through Celtic stories as a creature of deep knowledge and intuition. It is often connected to the sacred well, where it feeds on the hazelnuts of creative wisdom. The salmon as a spirit animal encourages the pursuit of knowledge, the understanding of truths deeper than the surface currents of life.

The Raven: A bird of protection, prophecy, and magical knowledge, the raven is a messenger from the otherworld. It symbolises transformation and the ability to move between the worlds. Those guided by the raven are often adept at interpreting dreams and omens, navigating the shadow realms with cunning and courage.

The Wolf: A figure of great ambiguity, embodying both the dangers of the wild and the virtues of deep loyalty and fierce protection. As a spirit animal, the wolf teaches about the importance of community and trust, and the strength found in social bonds.

The Eagle: Soaring high above, the eagle is seen as a divine messenger, often associated with the sun and the heavens. It symbolises vision, foresight, and the ability to see the bigger picture. As a spirit animal, the eagle guides one to rise above challenges, gain clarity, and lead with an expansive perspective.

The Boar: A creature of great strength and ferocity, the boar is a symbol of courage, warrior spirit, and unyielding determination. Associated with gods like Moccus, the boar represents the power to overcome obstacles and fight for one's beliefs. As a spirit animal, it encourages standing firm in the face of adversity and embracing the warrior within.

The Owl: A creature of the night, it is revered for its deep wisdom and connection to the mysteries of the moon. It symbolises intuition, insight, and the ability to see what others cannot. As a spirit animal, the owl guides one through the darkness, helping to uncover hidden truths and navigate the unknown with wisdom.

The Hare: Known for its speed and agility, the hare is a symbol of transformation and fertility. It is closely linked to the goddess Eostre and the cycles of the moon. The hare, as a spirit animal, embodies the power of rebirth and renewal, guiding one through life's changes with grace and adaptability.

The Bear: A powerful figure, symbolising strength, protection, and leadership. Often associated with the goddess Artio, the bear represents the nurturing power of the earth and the guardian of sacred spaces. As a spirit animal, the bear teaches the importance of grounding oneself, standing tall in the face of danger, and protecting what is sacred.

The Serpent: The serpent is a symbol of healing, transformation, and the cyclical nature of life. It is often connected to the underworld and the earth's energies. The serpent as a spirit animal guides one through cycles of change, offering the wisdom to shed old skins and emerge renewed.

The Horse: Revered across the Celtic lands, the horse symbolises freedom, endurance, and the journey of the soul. Associated with the goddess Epona, the horse is seen as a guide through both physical and spiritual journeys. As a spirit animal, the horse encourages embracing the journey of life with strength and perseverance, trusting in one's inner power.

The Fox: A symbol of cunning, adaptability, and intelligence. Known for its cleverness and ability to navigate tricky situations, the fox as a spirit animal guides one to think creatively, adapt to changing circumstances, and use wit to overcome challenges.

The Swan: A symbol of love, beauty, and transformation. Associated with the goddess Brigid, the swan represents the soul's journey and the process of inner transformation. As a spirit animal, the swan teaches the importance of embracing change with grace and finding inner beauty through personal growth.

The Blackbird: A symbol of enchantment and the connection between the mundane and the magical. Its song is said to lead the listener into the otherworld, where deeper truths are revealed. As a spirit animal, the blackbird encourages listening to the inner voice and exploring the mystical aspects of life.

GUIDED MEDITATION: MEETING A SPIRIT ANIMAL

Begin by finding a comfortable, quiet space where you can relax and let go of the outside world for a while. Sit or lie down in a position that feels natural and restful to you. Close your eyes gently, take a deep breath in, and as you exhale, feel your body begin to relax.

Imagine yourself standing at the beginning of a narrow, winding path. It's lined with ancient trees, their branches arching gracefully overhead, forming a lush canopy that filters the sunlight into warm, dappled patterns on the ground. The air is fresh and filled with the scent of green leaves and earth. Take a moment to observe the details around you – the sound of birds singing, the gentle rustle of leaves, and the soft, earthy path beneath your feet.

Begin to walk slowly along the path. With each step, feel yourself sinking deeper into a state of calm and relaxation. Notice how the light changes as you move deeper into the forest, how the shadows grow longer, and the air grows cooler.

As you continue along the path, up ahead, you see an exceptionally large and magnificent tree. Its trunk is wide and strong, its bark grooved with the wisdom of ages. As you approach, notice the roots of the tree, how they spread out powerfully into the earth. At the base of this tree, you find an opening – a cave that leads beneath the tree.

Approach the cave and observe the gentle darkness that beckons from within. As you enter, feel the cool, damp air of the cave brush against your skin. The walls are lined with smooth stones that glisten slightly in the dim light. The cave narrows into a tunnel that leads you downward, spiralling gently beneath the earth.

At the end of this tunnel, the path opens into a large, clear chamber under the roots of the tree. In the centre of this chamber, there is a natural pool of clear, still water that reflects the soft light filtering down from the roots above.

Someone is waiting for you here, waiting to meet you. You may find yourself wanting to see a particular kind of creature, but let that go; just for this moment, settle into openness.

As you step closer to the pool, the surface of the water stirs, and from this movement, your spirit animal emerges. Observe it as it approaches you – its form, its eyes, the energy it exudes. Feel its presence as a deep, comforting, and familiar force.

Allow yourself a moment to communicate with this spirit animal. You might ask it a question, seek its guidance, or simply share a moment of connection. Listen with your heart for its message to you. This creature embodies qualities you need, understandings you seek, strengths you possess.

When you are ready, thank this spirit animal for its wisdom and company. Watch as it retreats peacefully back into the pool. Slowly make your way back through the tunnel, up into the brightness of the forest, and along the path you came from. With each step, bring back the calm, the wisdom, and the strength you have found.

As you reach the beginning of the path, take a deep, refreshing breath and slowly open your eyes. Feel yourself in your space, carrying with you the peace and insights from your journey. When you're ready, gently rise, bringing the essence of your spirit animal into your everyday life.

TESTS OF FAITH

Life, in its infinite complexity and mystery, often seems to present us with challenges that test our faith, our beliefs, and our resilience. These trials, as horrible as they can sometimes seem, are also ripe with opportunity, but this is hard to see when we are overwhelmed by all the resistance and painful emotion that totally makes sense as a response to things we do not like. Often, it is only after many years that we have processed situations enough to be able to glean wisdom from them. Only then can we recognise how much we grew, healed, and transformed. It is one of life's great ironic paradoxes that we often cannot completely appreciate our learning from the intensity of experience, and that it does take struggle and tension to create something new.

If a story has no plot, no transformation will happen, and we will lose interest. We, as humans, are story-telling animals. We reflect our dreams, hopes, fears and rage into the stories we tell about our lives; just as our great artists, film-makers, writers, and actors tell stories of building tension, of heart-breaking intensity, so to do we crave the rough edges of our own transformation.

Recently, in my deep meditation and the wisdom that comes through me from nature and trance states, I've come to understand something for myself that I probably can never prove, but that I know in my bones to be true – that many of the gruelling, challenging, terrifying, and painful experiences of my life have indeed come from a shadowy craving of the unconscious of my psyche. Like the dark side of the moon, she is always with me, she is part of me, and because I did not consciously have any control of the situations, because I was powerless and victimised, she had control of the wheel.

It's offensive, I know, to suggest that trauma could come through our own desires, conscious or unconscious, and I'm not going to tell anyone else what to believe on this subject. You are free to choose your own meaning. This is also no reason to victim blame, because as a victim of circumstance I really did have no power – and my conscious mind couldn't get that power because it was operating in its own sphere, not connected to or aware of the shadow-self. But, in knowing this, and in getting to know her, deeply, I am on the precipice of a new wholeness, beginning to transform the unconscious by recognising its voracious appetite for all sensation – for all the icky, yucky, painful, terrifying sensations the way teenagers often binge-watch horror films.

If you ever want to peek beneath the rug at the voracity of human shadow desires, look at all the twisted content we consume, even in mainstream media, the violence and torture of popular streaming shows, the devastating longing of sad love songs, the literary sagas of the struggle for existence and personal sacrifice and bitterness, the social media battles we seem to find a primal glee in watching. Yes, this is us. All of this is a reflection of us, packaged up in a neat little lunch box for regular daily consumption. We feed on drama, as souls. We crave that kind of shadowy stimulation, and if we get low on it we find no shortage of opportunities for intensity in our own lives – the people who are close to us are ripe for the picking. There will always be someone in our lives to judge, if that's what we're looking for, especially a parent, child, sibling, partner, or friend who happens to do every single thing wrong in a way that pushes all our buttons, and we just might be able to help if we focus all our drama potential on them. We just might be able to save them, and through this self-sacrifice we can become martyrs for our own redemption.

This is not to say that we are bad, but that in our quest to be good, many of us relegate our shadow-selves to the dark corners where they lurk like hulking monsters, secretly influencing our lives and behaviour unbeknownst to us. This way we can focus only on the light. We can identify as "good people." There's a reason I don't believe in good or bad witches. It's because a witch, in my understanding, is someone who chooses their own fate – someone who connects with their wildness through nature, someone who willingly steps into the terror of their own power. You cannot do this work if you are professing to be only good or bad.

You cannot go through the forest and the depths of the swamp without getting muddy. The journey is one of all things – of facing all parts of ourselves, even the murkiest shadows. This, my dears, is why we must trust our inner strength to carry us through, we must give life and nature the benefit of the doubt even when it seems to be devouring us whole. We must tread the edges of our own true path to see where all the possibilities lead, and forge our own track through the woods. We must do it, because it is a calling in our souls, and because the world needs us to. The world needs more people who are able to see and experience and process and alchemise ALL OF IT because this world needs to be experienced, more than anything, and it needs to be loved, and that is what we are here to do in our own ways.

At the edge of this awareness is tremendous power, and I am terrified of it, but I will embrace it nonetheless, the way I brace myself for the sensation of cold water when stepping into the ocean to swim, remembering that once I'm in, it will all be worthwhile.

From a Jungian perspective, our challenges and trials in life are indeed seen as manifestations of our own psyche, drawing out the shadows that lurk in the depths of our unconscious (or deep conscious as the case may be). They force us to confront what we fear, to negotiate with our darker selves, and to integrate these aspects into our whole being. By facing these trials, we come to understand ourselves more deeply, and through this understanding, we can achieve a greater sense of wholeness and authenticity.

Life has a way of compelling us to confront the fundamental truths of our existence – the inevitability of suffering, the certainty of death, and the freedom to make meaning of our lives. Each challenge is a nudge, a push toward self-realisation and the quest to find our own unique meaning in the cosmos.

I've had times of losing faith in life, of questioning everything I believe in. It seems that faith, too, comes in cycles. There are times when our old beliefs must die so that something new can be born and grow in the soil from the decomposition of what we used to know as absolutely true. If you feel that hollowness within a belief, it might be time to gently push at its trunk, to see whether it is ready to surrender like a sigh, creating new openness for something even better to come through.

When it feels as though life is testing our faith, it might be inviting us to look deeper, to learn more about our inner worlds, and to emerge stronger, more enlightened, and profoundly connected to the truth of who we are. After all, it's how we engage with that darkness that defines our journey.

HEALING OUR CHILDHOODS

Children often seek out experiences that adults would not. At least before they're ashamed into conforming, infants will express themselves in complete surrender, in complete rapture. I remember being about three or four years old. I was humming merrily to myself as I ate. The resonance of my humming was so satisfying. It made me feel good to make the sound, and in the middle of my beautiful rapture, an older relative told me to "stop that!" and to be quiet. You know, the way that adults often tell you to stop playing with your food. I was confused: "Why? Why would I stop?" I didn't understand, and my mother explained that some people think it's rude to hum while you eat, to make sound. It didn't make sense to me, but I stopped. I wasn't allowed to just be in the flow of the moment, because the sounds I was making irritated people who thought children shouldn't be heard.

Children can be in creative flow states all day. It just comes naturally to them, and yet we disrupt them all the time, sometimes for good reason: "No, don't run on the road/it's time to go to bed/go to school." But we also disrupt them without explaining ourselves and in ways that are undermining and devaluing, shaming, because we don't want them to embarrass us when they're enthralled in their own play and doing something raucous in public. We don't want them to do something that is disruptive or destructive and therefore reflects badly on us. We try to curtail them, to control their behavior, and we do it unconsciously because this very thing has happened to us. We often don't realise that we're perpetuating an unnecessarily limiting way of restricting children, or that our expressions of our judgement can be harmful.

One of the strange things about shame, guilt, and embarrassment is that we feel it so intensely, especially as children, but no one else can quite feel it the way we do because it's an inward emotion. Shame is usually silent. Even people who are extremely sensitive to empathy might miss the intensity of these emotions in young children. Shame, after all, is the "death" emotion. It's our brain telling us we must conform or die, because in the wild, where we evolved in small nomadic groups, to be exiled from our community would literally mean death. Because literal death is rarely associated with shame these days, we don't take it seriously, we suppress it, and it turns inward where it can coalesce into a slow dying feeling like depression. People don't always know that they're inflicting these sensations on others, especially children who usually don't know how to communicate about the pain they're experiencing and how they feel that they are bad – that everyone must surely hate them – that they are wrong and broken and useless...

It's quite intense to be a child. In many ways, it's harder than being an adult, because you're in the thrall of your emotional states. You haven't learned to distance yourself yet, and when you finally do it only helps to manage the symptoms not the underlying pain and fear. As adults, we've generally learned to distance ourselves. We've learned to distract ourselves, which means that we get a little bit more peace, but we also have the ruthless undercurrents that come with the suppression or disconnection from aspects of ourselves, our intense feeling and sensation. Running from psychological pain doesn't work in the long term, though it can be necessary in the moment, especially if it helps us escape danger. Eventually, if we want to heal and become whole, we must excavate all the layers and clean out the wounds, even if it means re-breaking some structures in our psyches that have not healed properly, in much the same way that a doctor might re-break bones before setting them in a cast. No one else can do this work for us, but many people can help us in our healing journeys, just as a doctor does not literally heal our bodies, they simply work to remove the barriers to our own natural healing.

One of the things that I've had to learn is how to reconnect deeply with sensation, with all my intense feelings. Because, like most of us, when I was growing up nobody showed me how to *feel*. Nobody knew how to experience the intensity of feelings, especially not my hypersensitive emotion, and much of the time nobody could sit with me and be present with me and breathe and process with me and feel the feelings with me. Sometimes they could, but for the most part, I was punished for the reactions to my emotions – for my expressions of anger or my wailing and whining from pain and longing. Most adults around me, including teachers, tried to school this "bad behaviour" out of me, with threats and manipulation, because they couldn't deal with the intensity of emotion themselves. At least anger, pain, and sadness had outlet, but shame? It simply festered until little by little I unearthed it, healing moment to moment over years and years of doing this work like it was a second full-time job. I needed to heal because I was so wounded. I spent most of the first twenty-nine years of my life feeling broken, and seeking out solace and healing in any way that made sense. Only in my thirties did I discover emotional stability and balance. And even now, every day is an opportunity for healing and balance. Healing is a perpetual process. The body is always healing, and so too does the psyche need to regenerate and restore itself. Ultimately, there is no separation between body and mind and the two are always in connection and mutual reception.

Within my family, and many others, devaluing each other is a pattern – feeling devalued, or devaluing others in order to feel more powerful, often not even realising it because these patterns are unconscious. What seems on the surface to be an argument over whether the children should be allowed more treats is actually a power struggle wherein adults are facing off against each other, slinging judgements like weapons. We learn this without realising, internalising the power struggles that are modelled to us. Even if your parents didn't fight in front of you, there will be undercurrents (unless of course you were raised by exceptionally happy and emotionally healthy adults who could simply share their emotions and take responsibility for their own actions – in which case, you likely experienced a rude awakening when you got to school or into other spaces where power struggles and devaluation were rife).

Here are some questions to help you excavate unconscious power struggles with judgement and devaluation. They are not meant as personal attacks, but if they feel sharp, know that they are like a scalpel. You can use them to hurt yourself or to lovingly operate on old wounds in order to heal. Also know that if you were victimised by patterns of control and power struggles in your childhood, I one hundred percent believe you and support you. I will not justify or make excuses for violent or manipulative behaviour, especially against children, so know this: if someone treated you badly and caused you harm, you deserve love and support and caring, and you also deserve to heal, regardless of how terrible they are. You do not need to do this work in order to forgive them because this isn't about them. Not anymore. This is about you giving yourself what you need right now. Feel free to disregard these questions, or skip over them, or come back to them later, whatever works for you. You are in control of your own story now. When you are ready to engage with this work, allow yourself to grieve, feel, and release any emotions that you need to. Give yourself the time and nurturing that you may not have received as a child.

I encourage people to approach healing with curiosity, gentle openness, and as much humour as is appropriate, simply because these forces are powerful for magical transmutation.

Reflection Questions

· *Where in your life do you feel like you need to be better than other people?*
· *Who do you judge?*
· *How does that judgement make you feel superior or powerful?*
· *How does it reinforce your identity?*
· *At what points do you feel like you need to be better than your partner or your child or your parent or your sibling or your friends etc.?*
· *Do you feel like you are in competition anywhere in your life? Where and how does this pattern appear?*
· *Where in your life do you want to be holding power over people?*
· *Where are you scared of being powerless yourself?*

A good clue for this is to look to where people are making you uncomfortable, or you're disapproving of people in your life, because disapproving is a way of devaluing. You know, if you don't like the clothing your child wears, you're subtly putting out a signal that you know better or think you're better than them, that you have better taste, that you make better choices, that they are lesser, that they should conform to your way of seeing and being, because your way is superior. Don't waste energy feeling too bad about this because guilt is not a great use of your internal resources. Just allow yourself to feel the sensations you're inflicting on yourself and others. You may find yourself rationalising your behaviour – you're protecting people you care about, after all. Put all that rationalising aside too because the conscious rational mind can't heal you. The element of air can help you to learn things, but it is the empathy of water we need right now, and the intensity of fire if we feel our rage rising and need to set earthy boundaries! Feel free to go back to the elemental chapters if that's helpful.

Yes, sometimes we judge with good reason. Sometimes we see the pain that our family are suffering with, and we want them to feel better. And so we say, "Why? Why are you suffering? Why are you inflicting this on yourself and other people around you? Why can't you be better?" In a way, though, this is us being unable to hold our own reflection of pain and instead trying to act to control our emotions through controlling other people. Sometimes action is important, but if we don't balance it with the opposite, with the polarity, with reception, with listening, with empathy, being able to really feel the feelings, then it can be an unconscious way that we are inflicting psychological torture on ourselves and others.

With each step of this work, know that you are doing important work, and know that you can always take a break. Make a list of all the lovely things that help to soothe you such as taking a bath, going for a walk, having a cup of tea, or spending time with a beloved animal. At each stage, ask yourself what you need right now, and listen to see if there is any response from your intuition. It may be helpful to journal or talk to trusted friends and therapists – but don't bother sharing this work you are doing with anyone who is not yet ready to encounter something similar in themselves or they're likely to shut you down.

When we learn to alchemise our own shadowy unconscious patterns we can also draw in and transmute the toxicity wherever we encounter it, generating gold from the lead we encounter in the world, similar to the Buddhist practice of Tonglen, connecting with the world soul, anima mundi – the consciousness of the cosmos.

THE IMPORTANCE OF LIMBO PERIODS, PEARLS, AND ACTIVISM

No one likes feeling stuck, and yet limbo periods can be important, even though it can feel frustrating to wait for an outcome. There is magic in the margins, in the liminal, in the in-between states of consciousness and in the stillness while we watch for signs of what's to come. These times are sacred gestational for the soul. Just as the seed must be in darkness when it is planted in order to sprout and thrive and grow, so too do we sometimes feel restless and afraid of the stillness around us.

If we're afraid of the dark, we might never allow the husks of our protections to soften and loosen, like the seed must do in order to sprout. We often need to let go of the very patterns of fear and resistance that hold us back if we are to reach a new level of our magic, healing, and transformation in our journey. And this voyage into the psyche is not for the faint of heart. It requires courage, to allow our barriers to soften so that we can sprout. A young plant is most vulnerable in this phase, but if it never gets the chance to sprout, it never *becomes* a plant at all, it never reaches its potential, and this is the risk we need to take in order to reach our own. We must face our vulnerability and our fears in order to grow or we will stay stuck in the toddler pool, treading water, going around in circles with the same comfortable familiar problems rather than reaching a new level of understanding.

In the myths and stories we learn as children, there is always some kind of waiting period before the transformation, a stuck pattern of struggle before initiating the journey and then several points along the way where the path ahead is unclear. Often a sacrifice must be made and the monsters or the villains must be faced. The vulnerable must be protected and the heroes must rise to all the challenges they are faced with or they become a lesson for what not to do.

In order to get to the point of transformation, a new awareness must first be reached. The princess must learn that the man with the blue beard whom she married is actually dangerous. The fisherman must recognise that the scary creature he has fished from the ocean is worthy of empathy and love. Likewise, before she can transform herself from the skeleton woman back into her living form, the corpse bride must reach an awareness that the trauma she carries does not hold sway over the living. In stories, as they reflect the psyche, we are both the princess and the prince, the damsel and the brave knight. We are also the villains. We are the evil queens or the dangerous husbands. We are all of it. The psyche is reflective and our mythos is reflective of us if we are the ones who want to go through transformation.

The stories that Jungian psychotherapist and Cantadora storyteller, Dr Clarissa Pinkola Estés tells are powerful in that they capture various transformations of the psyche, of healing, of restoration, of rebirth, and of arrival at new levels of awareness, of facing our own undoing and remaking ourselves in our own image of who we truly are. Her work has been potent and powerful in my journey. I would not have understood how stories really work if it wasn't for reading *Women Who Run with the Wolves* in my mid-late twenties, which was the exact medicine that I needed at that time in order to heal from the incredibly unstable moods, the anxious and avoidant detachments, depression, anxiety, and extremes that had plagued me as back far as I could remember.

If you want to do this work, there are wise ones out there, elders who have walked this path of healing and transformation, who have guided many souls, and whose life work can serve as beacons, as guidebooks for our own restoration and transformation. If you're feeling frustrated and stuck, there is a story out there that can help you, if only you'd let it. Stop worrying the seeds in the earth, because that only stops them from sprouting, and allow yourself to sink deeper into the stillness, because that terrifying silence is more potent than a million affirmations, than a thousand attempts at convincing somebody else to change, or many hundreds of different ways we could scold ourselves into being better.

Sometimes while in limbo periods all we need to do is figure out how to listen to our souls and to accept that when we are frustrated, when we feel like we're stuck and that nothing is moving, sometimes the best thing to do is just to be present with that, just to feel the frustration for a moment, and then to take a deep breath and allow ourselves to feel it a moment longer. Because that frustration is a sign of something. Perhaps it's a splinter of an old wound that needs to be healed and cleaned, an old fragment of brokenness and pain that we are ready to transmute into creative glory, into love and healing. Or perhaps the frustration we feel is in itself the gritty irritating sand inside the oyster forming into a pearl if only we let it.

Pearls beautifully symbolise the transformative power of adaptation and resilience. In certain oyster species, the mantle tissue has evolved to respond to irritants by coating them with layers of nacre, eventually forming a pearl. This is more than just a defence mechanism; it's an adaptation for healing and coping, where the oyster turns something potentially harmful into a source of beauty and value. This process mirrors how personal growth and healing often arise from our ability to manage and transform challenges into strengths, rather than merely defending against them.

The association of pearls with wisdom speaks to this gradual, patient process of transformation. Just as a pearl forms over time through persistent layering, wisdom is cultivated slowly, through experiences that require reflection and endurance. The hidden beauty of a pearl, created in response to adversity, symbolises the deep inner work that leads to deep wisdom and growth. This metaphor resonates deeply with me, not just because of its universal truth, but also because Pearl is my middle name, after my great grandmother, tying these themes directly to my own journey of storytelling and personal development. Like the oyster, we too can turn life's irritants into something precious, using them as opportunities for healing and transformation.

Gestation periods may vary. We never know how long it will be to reach the deep transformation we seek inwardly or achieve our external goals, but we don't need to waste energy on impatience. Instead, we can hold space for the agony of uncertainty simply because it allows us to be open to something new to evolve or grow. If, in the waiting times, we make our peace with both sides of the swinging pendulum, with all eventualities, if we face our fears of failure and our terror of the risks of our success, then this limbo period is especially productive. We can integrate the shadows of what we fear most and therefore, do all that we can from fulfilling our shadow. When our shadows are fulfilled and illuminated, the internal transformation can sync with our external lives, and our unconscious does not have to play out its struggles in the outside world. In my darkest moments, I've done my best to face the fears that plague me and though I've encountered the spectre of my own death many times through my life, this method of going deep into processing the emotion and possibilities of terror has helped me through, though whether it has actually saved my life is anyone's guess.

All these approaches can help us, but we cannot force them. The way we cannot force a bird to land in our hand or a reserved cat to come forward for affection, all we can do is be present and allow the unfolding. We cannot control, but if we surrender our attempts to control, we can find immense power. If we can stop going around in circles at any point in the cycle just to be aware of the pattern that we're in, we can rise to another level, or we can actually *do* something different. Take a different action. Take a different path. We cannot do this simply to escape because there is no escape from our own path. We have to go *through*.

We can accept that our fears or our frustration or our pain, or even our anxious excitement is driving the very period of limbo that we find ourselves in, and we can do the work that is the medicine for our souls, whether that is some kind of physical movement, some kind of journalling practice, some kind of rising to a challenge, some kind of anger work in order to empower ourselves, or some kind of allowing that lets us feel our deeper feelings below the frustration, that lets us understand our childhood patterns and how they've shaped the grooves of our psyche that we now circle around in over and over.

I once wrote a poem when I was processing the challenges of my childhood: "You carved your pain into me, shaping me." I was learning to become whole, and in that wholeness, I was able to process and feel all the feelings of that pain, of that vulnerable child that was shut down, that was scared, that was manipulated, that was toyed with and shamed and humiliated. But not only that, I was able to see the wound is where the light gets in, as Rumi said and Leonard Cohen echoed. And in seeing that light, I found a strange sense of appreciation.

If I'd never gone through that darkness, I wouldn't be who I am. I'd still be stuck in all the pain and struggle which bled me dry. And this was a confronting realisation – that the people who had caused me so much suffering when I was a vulnerable child had accidentally, despite their best efforts perhaps, given me the greatest gift. Which is a horrible thing to tell someone! And I'm not going to tell you that you should be grateful for being victimised or hurt, because that's not right. And yet herein lies the paradox: How can we offer the opportunity of healing genuinely and deeply when there are so many injustices in the world, where there is so much pain and torment, when there is so much agonising, excruciating suffering? And yet, strangely miraculous gifts can be hard-won through all of these wounds.

Sometimes parents rationalise their harsh behavior with love – this will hurt me more than it hurts you – as if they're taking on suffering in order to train us for the real world. But the real world is as vast and varied as our minds can imagine and create it to be. There is no justification for hurting people, even if it's to harden them up to resist later trauma, just like physically hurting people won't necessarily make them physically stronger. What doesn't kill us might not make us stronger even if we desperately need a silver lining, but what will actually make us stronger is our healing, our nourishment, our connections and communities, our breaking out of toxic habits and into harmonious ones. This is how we really find our strength and the courage to step into our power, by knowing ourselves and our shadow, inch by inch, by reclaiming every ounce of strength and energy and power that was taken from us. This is the work.

The good and bad news is that you don't need to be horrendously traumatised in your childhood in order to extract wisdom from suffering. Life is traumatic, especially for sensitive children. Every single one of us has experiences of having our needs unmet. Even friends of mine who've come from the most wonderful loving families have felt betrayed when facing schooling that made them suffer so much they were unprepared for the humiliation, for the level of control. And the psyche struggles to reconcile that loving parents could send their children into such an unsafe world as the modern schooling system, or even bring somebody into the world at all when there's so much pain and heartache. This is one of life's great paradoxes, after all.

As a parent myself, I have struggled with feeling totally blamed for bringing my child into a world of so much suffering, like some kind of villain. How dare I create this life, that I made it happen – that this child has come into this world and experienced the suffering of being alive, and I have not been a perfect parent by any means! Though I've tried my best at various points, I've always had competing priorities. I've always needed to learn about so many things and to prioritise my creativity and sometimes my livelihood, to put my energy into many things in order to survive and to help my child to survive, but to be spread so thin that I was not able to meet the needs of the person whose life I was responsible for. Parenting has been one of my hardest journeys because I've almost always gotten things wrong and I don't enjoy being wrong – so of course I was blessed with an intelligent child who calls me out on absolutely everything because I had a lot to learn about facing my shadow of being "wrong." The reason this shadow was so deep for me was because I wanted so much to be right – to be valid and valuable and worthy, and yet no one in my family of origin understood the spiritual reality I inhabited. If someone were to ask my shadow "what do you need" and it reflected the opposite of what I consciously wanted (to be right) it would answer "to be wrong" because that's what the shadow does. It reflects the other side of paradox of ourselves. It's been quite a journey, and I'm pleased to say that we've weathered many underground journeys, many underground passages, and continue to learn from one another as we both grow together.

If I'd been clever, I might have waited until I was completely enlightened before having a child. I might have wrapped my baby in gossamer silk, giving this child the most nourishing environment to thrive in, so that they'd never know real suffering and hardship and neglect. They'd never experience any anger because their parent was so amazingly enlightened. And yet, there are no perfect parents. We all do our best with the knowledge, awareness, energy, and resources we do have, and we learn so much along the way.

As I get older my emotional self finds less snags along the path to pull at the threads of my psyche. The little things that used to upset me matter less and less, and the big things are also easier to deal with. In fact, I've learned how to feel really, really good most of the time, which is an outstanding accomplishment from somebody who suffered depression from a young age and has been plagued with anxiety, an overactive nervous system, and various kinds of trauma and health struggles.

In our struggles and in our repetitions, our loops, our frustrating cycles of going around and around in circles, there are a million opportunities for freedom and love and empathy and light to bring our awareness into the darkness and face the horrendous shadows that lurk there. A shadow is not necessarily something that we have to act out, but it's something that we feel and fear deeply. You know, when you're in traffic and another driver is behaving rudely in front of you and you want to slam on the horn and swear at them? Or you want to snap at your loved ones because they're being a pain? Or you want to tell that nasty boss what you really think of them? But you don't because you're polite or because you're self-aware enough not to have to react without thinking because you might regret it later. All of that is shadow stuff too. We often find the things that we think are making us unhappy can be lessons in waiting if only we let them; perhaps they are just bits of grit that we can turn into pearls if only we allow ourselves to shine through the darkness and reconnect with it.

We can acknowledge that there are many horrible things in the world that we can't bear to face a lot of the time. We can also know that being overburdened and resentful about those things doesn't usually shift them at all. Yes, many forms of activism do help. Many of my friends are wonderful activists and I've been involved in various kinds of activism over my life too. I come from a family of activists who've sought justice against violence, racism, and sexism for generations, but sometimes even going out and protesting the things we don't like can often do very little, because we're still focused on the level of the problem, we're in resistance and secretly...we might even be attached to the problem because it tells us we are right and other people who are doing bad things are wrong. It affirms our identity. This is not a bad thing. It is a great thing that people identify with their values and believe strongly in social and environmental justice, but I sometimes wonder when it feels like we're hitting our heads against the brick wall of our own resistance. Yes, our resistance is totally justified, but is it helping?

We might even realise after we've gone around in circles a million times, our identity might even rest within the fight for justice, and that is a wonderful thing. Yet at some point, we may reach a level of awareness where we wonder whether there's a place where our energy would be better placed. In order to rise above and beyond the problem, we can shift our attention, we can even drink in the dark twistedness of this world with a level of openness that is deeply transformative, or we can confront hate with a level of empathy that reflects back to it a new level of awareness (not because hate deserves love but because empathy is the antidote to disconnection and the only times I've seen people transform their hatred is through connection). If we have the energy and the privilege to do this work then the power we have comes with a level of responsibility to engage, to do the messy stuff and engage with other privileged people in order to lighten the emotional load on those who are marginalised. We can find new and creative ways of drawing attention to solutions and to wonder, because curiosity and creativity, empathy, love and pleasure and joy are all far more powerful, if only we can let them in. This too, is magic.

BALANCE BETWEEN ACTIVE AND RECEPTIVE

In a world that often prizes action over stillness, noise over silence, and output over contemplation, finding balance between active and receptive energies can be an act of both defiance and harmony. Active energy is a dynamic force, outward-moving – whereas receptive energy is still, drawing inward, receiving. Many of us are better at giving than receiving. Our dominant culture, like a strong gust of wind, tips the scale heavily towards action, urging us always to do more, move faster, and push harder, as if we can control our lives through trying, through productivity, through stretching ourselves, as if we can sacrifice ourselves to rescue others in order to feel valid and valued.

What if nothing you can do will make you inherently more valuable as a person, simply because your value is inherent, just as it was the day you were born? What if you don't need to prove yourself to anyone? Can you rest, then? Can you rest now and be open to receiving as well as giving?

Just as the forest achieves its serene majesty through both the slow growing of moss and trees and the quiet decay of fallen leaves, the vibrant overlapping ecosystems of plants, microorganisms, insects, birds, and other animals, so too can we allow the gentle unfolding of our being and path. We can take action when intuition and instinct guide us to as the falcons soar and the salmon leaps, and we can flow downstream when the path of least resistance will do the work for us. We can cultivate both the active and receptive energies within ourselves towards equilibrium and wellbeing.

The more we tune into our own receptive energy, the more in sync we become with the natural world. It is like the deep, still water of a mountain lake, mirroring the sky and the surrounding peaks in its calm surface. It invites us to listen, reflect, and receive. This is the energy of being open to what comes. It allows us to absorb the subtle nuances of our experiences, to learn from them, and to integrate these lessons into our being.

In our everyday lives, balancing these energies can be like walking a tightrope at first, as we learn how to balance. Lean too far towards activity, and we risk falling into exhaustion, burnout, and disconnection from our deeper selves. Lean too far towards receptivity, and we might find ourselves in stagnation, unmoored and directionless.

Like a mindful gardener tending to both the sun-loving plants and the shade-seeking undergrowth, we will learn that both are vital to the garden's biodiversity and beauty. We too must recognise that both active and receptive energies are crucial to our wholeness.

Practically, this means creating spaces in our lives for both doing and being. We might set aside time for meditation, quiet walks, or simply sitting and observing the world around us without agenda or expectation. These moments of receptivity aren't empty or pointless; they are rich with potential, filled with the power to enrich and inform our active pursuits.

We can engage our active energy by setting goals, initiating projects, and moving our bodies. Yet, even in these pursuits, our attention to quiet intuition can infuse a spirit of presence, ensuring that our actions are not just reflexive but reflective, not merely productive but also purposeful.

Even in a dominant culture that devalues the quiet and potent value of receptivity, we can dare to stand still amidst the rush, to breathe in slowly, and exhale gently, to listen deeply to the silence in the midst of noise, and to value reflection as highly as action. In doing so, we become like the forest – vibrant and alive, deeply rooted yet reaching skyward, embodying light and shadow, action and stillness, giving and receiving.

Meditation for Balancing Active and Receptive Energies

Begin by finding a comfortable and quiet place where you can sit or lie down without disturbance. Close your eyes, take a deep breath, and allow your body to relax with each exhale. Feel the weight of your body supported by the ground beneath you, and imagine that with every breath, you sink a little deeper into a state of calm awareness.

Envision roots growing from the base of your spine or your feet, extending deep into the earth. Feel these roots spreading through the soil, anchoring you firmly and safely to the ground, providing stability and nourishment. With each inhale, draw up a sense of peace and tranquillity from the earth, and with each exhale, release any tension or stress that you may be carrying.

Now, turn your focus inward to your own internal space of receptivity. Imagine this space as a serene garden or a quiet forest glade. See it bathed in soft, diffused light – a place that invites you to listen, observe, and receive. Feel the cool, gentle air against your skin, hear the subtle sounds of nature around you, and smell the earthy fragrance of the ground. This is your sacred space of receptivity.

As you settle into this space, reflect on the active energy in your life – the doing, the striving, and the creating. Visualise this energy as a bright, vibrant light moving within you. Notice its strength and its power, but also become aware of how it needs the balance of your receptive energy – the quiet, nurturing, and allowing.

Imagine a gentle stream of water in your garden or forest. See it flowing effortlessly, adapting to the land, nourishing everything it touches. This water represents your receptive energy. Notice how it moves – neither rushed nor stagnant, but with a perfect, natural flow that enriches and sustains.

Bring the vibrant light of your active energy to meet the gentle flow of your receptive water. Watch them intertwine and interact. Where they meet, see a beautiful forest of patterns light and dark, vibrant energy and tranquility, each polarity enhancing the other. Feel how your active energy is softened, deepened, and made more meaningful by your receptivity. Similarly, see how your receptivity is enlivened and supported by your active energy.

As you watch this interplay, you may wish to say:

I am open to receiving.

I am open to balance.

I value the quiet power of being receptive.

I allow my receptive nature to nourish me and inform my actions.

I embrace the balance of doing and being in my life.

I am grounded and fluid, active and receptive, strong and gentle.

Spend a few more moments enjoying the peace and balance within your internal landscape. When you feel ready, gently begin to bring your awareness back to the physical space around you. Notice the surface beneath you, the air on your skin, and the sounds in the environment. Take a few deep breaths, and when you're ready, open your eyes, carrying with you the sense of balanced energy into the rest of your day.

WHEN THE OPPOSITE OF INSTINCT IS REQUIRED

Navigating life often requires actions that don't seem obvious. Some things seem counter-intuitive but when we examine them closely they're actually just counter-instinctual. In those moments our reaction points us in one direction, but wisdom advises another. Do you remember learning to wash your hair? With soapy bubbles in our hair and a stream of water ready to wash it away, instinct urges us to duck our heads down, raising our hands as we fold forward, cowering to avoid getting soap in our eyes, when that very action is what will lead to the sting of shampoo exactly where we don't want it. Instead, we must learn to tilt our heads back, in a small act of faith exposing our faces to the water just enough that it can stream backwards, allowing the water to carry the suds away from our eyes. Sometimes we have to lean back into vulnerability, trusting in the process to keep us safe, because our protective instincts can paradoxically lead to more harm.

When flying a kite we might think that holding on tightly to the string and controlling it firmly will keep it stable and aloft. However, the kite flies best when given enough string to dance with the wind, to rise high and swoop through the air. We simply cannot control every movement. Instead, to soar, we must find the balance between useful tension and allowing the wind to lead. Relinquishing some of our attempts at control can enable things in our lives to flourish and reach their full potential.

Similarly, driving on icy roads provides a vivid, real-world example of counterintuitive wisdom. When a car skids, the gut reaction for most people is to slam on the brakes – a move that can actually lead to a greater loss of control. The safer method is to gently ease off the accelerator and focus our full attention to steer calmly into the sliding motion, aligning the car with the direction of safety until we can regain control. This scenario mirrors situations in life where panic and force can exacerbate problems, whereas calm, deliberate actions bring stability.

If you've ever tried to float on your back in water, you know that the more you tense up and struggle to stay afloat, the more likely you are to sink. By relaxing your body and spreading out your arms and legs, you allow the water to support you. This serves as a reminder that sometimes, we need to relax our efforts and trust in the support systems around us in order to stay afloat and find ease and peace.

RE-ENCHANTMENT

"The birds always sang at the break of day. Start again, I heard them say. Don't dwell on what has passed away or what is yet to be."

- Leonard Cohen

It's a mess here in the midst of life, and there's no neat solution, but this path is the only way that I know how to be in this world, and it is in this general direction: to go deeper into the darkness, to challenge everything, to learn from my own circular patterns, and to test every single option with curiosity and creativity until I find a new level of awareness. And on and on it goes. I still hunger for justice and for peace, for every soul, but if I'm stuck in the pain of it, I'm no use to anyone.

Instead, I find the magic. I find the glimmers, and I see in them a reflection of hope, of rebirth and transformation. Instead of being in resistance, I open to feel all my feelings just like water. I allow myself to be empowered by the fire of my deep, incredible rage. I let my intellect curiously explore all the possibilities and share them with the world, and I connect step by step, more and more deeply with my body, with nature, with what I value in the world. And I bring all of these practices together, weaving them into a story, into many stories, stories of fantasy and magic, cosy fun tales of witches discovering their own empowerment, transformation of opposites of light and dark, of murky greys in between and all the colours of the rainbow, exploration and adventure, because this is my work, and I want you to find your work too.

I want this, with every fibre of my being. I want you to be able to connect, to be brave enough to face the furnace of this world with love, to be strong enough to be in your power, to be willing to explore the dark places. Because if we could all do that, and we could all hold the level of feeling, of power, of sensation and of awareness – so that's feeling (Water), sensation (Earth), power (Fire), awareness (Air) – then we could go from being a society that has a lot of knowledge, to a society that has a lot of understanding and deep wisdom, and those things are not the same. We can know a billion things about the world that we live in on the level of knowledge, stripping back everything to mere atoms that are not alive and never have been, and get nowhere from reducing everything down to just the material resources. We can hold the austerity of that knowledge, and we can go into an abundance of meaning the way that nature has an inner wisdom that allows it to unfold in magic and interconnectedness between all the different species. We can return to the flow of life over and over, instead of perpetually disconnecting ourselves. Even though we've learned so much knowledge through the disconnection, we can only find deep wisdom and understanding through reconnecting, through bringing the magical back, through re-enchanting the world, because the magic was always there, even in the bleakest moments, even when we went around in circles, even when we couldn't see it. The magic was always whispering to us, even when we weren't listening. The moss always grew softly on the forest floor, and the trees always hung their peaceful melodies in harmony with the streams and the ocean waves.

Reflection Questions

When we're going around in circles or in a limbo waiting period, we can ask ourselves these questions:
· What is it that I am really wanting?
· And then beneath that what do I need?
· Why?
· What is the want that is beneath the want?
· And what is the want beneath that?

WHAT ARE WE REALLY WANTING?

Thoughts like "I want X person to do this thing differently" are a projection of our own frustration of powerlessness, even if that person is totally out of line in the "real world," because there is another world, an inner world, in which we *are the magic* that can transform everything.

So when we ask ourselves, what is it that I really want, we can go deeper, reflecting back on ourselves and breaking out of our tendencies to project. Similarly, when we ask another person, what is it that they really want, when we ask them a question of curiosity and interest, we give them the opportunity to reveal themselves to us in deeper and more fulfilling ways. And in asking:

What are we really, really deeply, deeply, deeply wanting?
What do we fear?
What do we crave?
What do we long for?
What do we avoid?

What are the patterns?
Where is the yearning?
Where is the burning frustration?

All of these questions can bring us closer to ourselves and closer to our magic.

FINDING PEACE BETWEEN GRASPING AND RESISTANCE

In life, we often find ourselves clinging to shadows, grasping at echoes. Yet, the art of living magically is in releasing these ephemeral chains and embracing the here and now with openness and empowerment.

Grasping is the emotional and psychological act of clinging tightly to something – be it a person, a status, a material possession, or an outcome. Grasping arises from a fear of loss or insufficiency, a belief that without this particular thing, one cannot be complete or secure. It leads to a fixation that can cloud judgement and hinder genuine connection with the world and ourselves.

Resistance is the act of pushing away or denying realities that are perceived as threatening or uncomfortable. It stems from a desire to protect ourselves from perceived harm or discomfort but often results in stasis and suffering, as it prevents one from engaging fully with life and learning from its varied experiences.

In childhood, our first experiences with the world teach us the rudiments of coping. When we encounter uncertainty, fear, or discomfort, our natural response is often to cry out, fight, freeze, flee, or reach out – to grasp for the familiar, for security and certainty. This grasping can manifest as attachment to physical objects, like a favourite blanket or toy, or as emotional dependencies, such as the need for constant reassurance and attention.

Resistance takes root early. When the world appears overwhelming or when change imposes itself too abruptly, children may resist through withdrawal, defiance, or denial. These responses are not merely acts of stubbornness but are instinctive and powerful attempts at exerting control over what feels like a chaotic environment.

As we grow in awareness we have the opportunity of shaping these

369

childhood strategies into more mature forms of coping. This does not mean discarding them outright, for each has its root in genuine need and protection, but rather transforming them through understanding and mindfulness.

Just as astronomers study starlight to understand celestial phenomena, we can reflect on our own past, identifying patterns of behaviour that originate in childhood coping. Understanding these can provide valuable insights into our adult interactions and emotional responses. This allows us to observe our thoughts and feelings without immediate reaction, giving us the space to choose how we respond, rather than falling into the gravitational pull of old habits. Just as the universe is constantly expanding and evolving, so too must our coping strategies. What worked in childhood may not serve us as well in adulthood. Being open to change and growth is essential if we want change and noticing where we resist change can likewise be a powerful gateway to our magic.

In the tranquil embrace of the present moment, one finds a depth of clarity and peace. Imagine a dark, serene lake under the moonlight – its surface smooth and undisturbed by the wind. This is the mind in presence; it reflects the world without the ripples of worry or the currents of desire. In such a state, we observe the world and ourselves with an equanimity that illuminates the darkest corners of existence.

Relaxation follows presence, naturally, like night follows day. It is the softening of the soul, the uncurling of clenched fists, the easing of tightened shoulders. To relax without resistance is to lie back in the velvet-draped chaise longue of your mind, letting the drama of life play out before you without the need to intervene, to control, or to change the narrative.

To cultivate this state, we can engage in the subtle art holding our attachments more gently. This does not mean disengagement or a lack of care, rather, it is in the appreciation of life that we can find peace, understanding that all is transient, fleeting. We do not know exactly where desire comes from. It is one of the great mysteries of life along with consciousness, purpose, and the bizarre workings of the cosmos. The great mysteries can never completely be understood because they belong deep in the unconscious, but even without knowing why we want what we want we can acknowledge the impermanence of our desires and fears. All things do change over time. Like the leaves that flutter to the ground in autumn, there are times where it serves us to let these ephemeral things fall naturally away. Observe them, acknowledge their existence, but do not hold on too long because so much is waiting for us just up ahead if only we rise to meet it.

Sit quietly in a dimly lit room, perhaps with a single candle flickering – a dance of shadow and light. Breathe deeply, inhaling the musky scent of ancient wisdom that lingers in the air. With each exhale, release a worry, a desire, a resistance. Feel your body lighten, your spirit brighten.

As you practice this release, notice the space it creates – space for creativity, for love, for peace. In the absence of grasping, there is room to grow, to explore, to be truly alive. Here, in this sacred space, you find the essence of relaxation, a peace that pervades every fibre of your being.

Grasping and resistance often emerge as two opposing forces, each pulling the psyche in contrary directions. Grasping, with its insistent clutch at desire, seeks to bind us to what we yearn for, anchoring us to the tangible and the transient. Resistance, on the other hand, pushes against what is, creating barriers and walls that isolate and defend, but also confine.

Between these two states of grasping and awareness lies an over-looked realm: the in-between of awareness. It is in this balanced enigma where power and freedom are found. This is the realm of gentle observa-tion, where the soul neither clings in desperation nor recoils in denial. It observes, it acknowledges, it understands without the frantic need to possess or the reflex to reject.

The in-between of awareness we can rise above life's chaos, the open sky of boundless possibilities unfolding above us. In this place, we are fully present with each step, each breath. We are acutely aware of the tendencies to grasp or to resist, yet we choose to remain centred and accept what is. It is not a passive state; it is active participation in the flow of life, accepting each moment as it comes, without trying to block the flow; rather we can direct this flow into creating good things in the world. This acceptance does not mean resignation but an understanding that the present moment is as it should be, and that change comes through aware-ness, not force.

To practice, we can consciously place ourselves in minor situations where our typical response would be to grasp or resist, watch a show you don't think you'll like or talk to a person you'd usually avoid, face your own anger or fear when it rises up with intuitive curiosity, allow yourself to simply be wrong when someone corrects you (if your instinct is to argue) or stand your ground if instinct bids you to give in (if it's safe to do so) and just hold the space, noticing how it feels, noticing what happens. In these moments, practice pausing and observing your reactions without judgement. Ask yourself what you are afraid of losing or what you are trying to avoid. By understanding these fears, we can begin to loosen the grip of grasping and resistance.

In the sacred in-between, each moment is an opportunity to interact with life authentically and profoundly. Here, wisdom grows not from the extremes of clinging or refusal but from the fertile ground of genuine experience and acceptance.

SURRENDERING TO THE FULLNESS OF LIFE

In the ceaseless ebbs and flows of life, discomfort can arise from constant change around and within us. We might do almost anything to avoid the instability and unease. The human response is frequently either to grasp or to resist. We grasp at goals, relationships, material possessions, or even past experiences, hoping to find solidity in them. We also resist change, pushing against the inevitable, attempting to maintain a status quo that feels safe, however illusory that safety may be. We can never have complete safety or stability within the chaos of life but we can surrender to the fullness of our experience and ride the waves as they emerge.

Both grasping and resisting are attempts to escape the inherent discomfort of life's fluidity. Grasping tries to anchor us to specific points that we deem valuable or comforting, while resistance attempts to build walls against the tide of change. Yet, both are forms of struggle, locking us into cycles of tension and release that ultimately leave us feeling more drained, more fractured.

The concept of surrender is often misunderstood as giving up or passive acquiescence. Surrender is actually a powerful practice of embracing life fully, without the need to control or fix every variable. We can surrender our pointless struggle to try to control the tides, and instead learn to float and swim with the currents of our power towards the shores we seek. Surrender is about letting go of the struggle to impose rigidity on the fluid nature of existence, opening to the flow of life, accepting change as an inherent part of being. In this letting go, we can be more present.

Change teaches flexibility, resilience, and the beauty of impermanence. In trusting the flow of change, we allow ourselves to experience life in its fullest spectrum – joys, sorrows, challenges, and ease. To embrace the full experience of life, we must develop a comfort with discomfort. It is not the enemy, it is a teacher, a sign to pay attention. This is also how I choose to interpret small accidents like stubbing my toe or spilling my tea: Pay Attention. Be present. Be aware. Notice.

This does not mean that we do not aim for goals or seek attachments; it means that we have the freedom to do so without holding ourselves back with grasping and resistance (both tend to get in the way of reaching goals), and we can make inspired or intuitive steps forward in good timing with awareness.

We can breathe in and out slowly in relaxation and acceptance, in letting go and tuning in, just experiencing our feelings – all of them – and allowing the beautiful complexity to wash over us as we open up to deeper connections with nature and people in our lives, as we open to our creativity and our magic, more and more, because as we surrender to the flow of life and magic which is always running through us we stop resisting it, and we open up to not just practicing magic but to becoming magic.

EMERGENCE FROM THE UNDERWORLD COCOON IN THE MYTHIC JOURNEY

Snuggled deep in your cocoon, you are aware of your innermost feelings and this dark, enclosed space. Feel the warmth and safety of this space, knowing that within this darkness, a profound transformation is taking place.

As you breathe deeply, become aware of the changes occurring within you. Old patterns, beliefs, and limitations are dissolving, making way for new growth and understanding.

In this cocoon of transformation you are safe to explore the depths of your being. Acknowledge any fears or shadows you encounter, knowing they are part of your journey. Breathe into these experiences, allowing them to transform.

Now, you feel a stirring within. A new energy is building, a readiness to emerge. With each breath, you feel stronger, more aligned with your soul.

A small point of light appears in the darkness. This light grows stronger, illuminating your transformed self. You begin to feel the urge to break free, to emerge into a new way of being.

As you prepare to leave your cocoon, your underworld, take a moment to appreciate the journey you've undergone. Honour the strength it took to face your inner depths.

Now, you are beginning to break through. Feel the resistance as you push against the boundaries of your old self. This struggle is necessary, strengthening you for what's to come.

With a final, powerful effort, you break free. Light floods in, and you emerge into a world of vibrant colours and sensations. Take a moment to adjust, to feel the newness of your being.

Stretch out, like a butterfly unfurling its wings for the first time. Feel the potential within you, the new perspectives and understanding you've gained.

As you acclimate to this new state, appreciate how far you've come in your journey so far. Take a moment to deeply appreciate all of your journey towards wholeness, recognising that transformation is always ongoing. Each cycle of descent and emergence brings new growth, new understanding. Take another moment, right here, right now, just to listen in to your intuition. What do you want? What comes next?

Take a deep breath, feeling fully present in your transformed state.

The journey through the underworld is long, but eventually a light shines through the darkness and signs of emergence begin to appear. Just as the butterfly emerges from the cocoon, this is a powerful archetype in mythology and personal transformation, embodying the process of change, rebirth, and enlightenment.

In the ancient Sumerian mythos, Inanna must surrender everything she has in her perilous underworld journey to visit the grieving Ereshkigal, but finds a twist of a knife instead. She is killed by the one she is attempting to console. However, her death reflects the life/death/life nature. She is reborn, and returns in all her glory to reclaim her throne. Persephone returns to the world of the living only after her mother has negotiated her partial release. Still wedded to the dark, she spends seasons in between the two worlds of darkness and light, bringing the warmth of spring with her and with her return.

The one who descends into the underworld of their own psyche undergoes a hero's journey just like the one into forbidding forests in countless fairy tales. This descent is not just geographical but psychological, marking an inward journey into the self, where we confront fears, shadow aspects, and unresolved conflicts. It's a necessary withdrawal from the world, much like a caterpillar entering its cocoon, where the familiar must be left behind to allow a transformation to begin.

In the depths of the underworld or the confines of the cocoon, transformation occurs in isolation and darkness, mirroring the unseen changes that happen within a chrysalis. Here, the old self undergoes a metaphorical death, a deep sigh, a letting go of all identity and attachment and protection of the old form to be reborn deeper into who we really are. The trials faced and the darkness navigated represent the shedding of old patterns, beliefs, and limitations. In myth, this stage is often where the hero encounters guides or receives divine help, reflecting the inner wisdom and resources that we discover in our deepest challenges.

The act of emerging – from the underworld or breaking free of the cocoon – is the climax of the transformation. This stage is beautifully illustrated in Persephone's return from the underworld, the arrival of spring and renewal, or the moment a butterfly emerges, reborn with wings that no previous form could predict, a rebirth, where the transformed self is now equipped with new insights, strengths, and a greater sense of identity and purpose.

But this emergence requires a struggle just as a butterfly must fight her way out of a cocoon in order to pump blood into her wings. Without the tension, without the challenge, there is no growth. The journey is not complete without the integration of the new self into the world as we now must learn to apply our newfound understanding to our lives on a daily basis, reconciling the sacred inner wisdom we have gained with the seemingly mundane world full of friction and tedium. This stage can be as challenging as the descent, as it requires the reconciliation of the inner with the outer. Emergence is a breaking through, a significant victory over the forces that once held sway, the old patterns that used to keep us trapped and stuck. This struggle is not incidental; it is essential, as it strengthens the butterfly's wings and prepares it for flight.

Just as a pearl forms from an irritation within an oyster, and a diamond crystallises under the immense pressure deep within the Earth, we too undergo our own metamorphosis through shadow work. Just as the volcanic ash nurtures a fertile soil, from which new life vigorously blooms, from our own fiery trials, the richest growth can emerge.

Sometimes it is crisis that leads us into the dark – periods of illness, loss, deep dissatisfaction, or existential questioning – and prompts us to retreat into our inner worlds, reassess our paths, and emerge transformed. The process is cyclical, much like the seasons. Each journey into the underworld can lead to a fresh spring, a renewed self, ready to face the world with a clearer vision and a connection to spirit and soul.

We need to take enough time in the murky, mucky, messy process of transformation, to fully surrender to the process, rather than try to rush through to results. This can feel frustrating when things in the outer world aren't working, when we want results, but this cannot be rushed. We cannot jump ahead. We simply must be still, rest, face the shadows of our fears and become aware of the old patterns we are ready to let go of, so that we can grow new ones that support us better. You will know when you aren't ready because thoughts of the future will feel tiring, the energy will be muted and flowing inward. When the energy begins to move outward again there will be a sense of release, a fresh breeze that awakens us, stirs us, beckons us forward; we feel a new sense of aliveness, invigoration. Even then, take your time. The first stirrings of spring are just the beginning. We can see the light is coming, but the darkness is still necessary for the transformation to fully take form. When it does, there will be a new kind of tightness, a discomfort because we know that the next stage will be full of new risks and challenges. There may even be terror, and this is when it's most important to reach for our courage, just as Anaïs Nin's beautiful quote reflects: "And the day came when the risk to remain tight in a bud was more painful than the risk it took to blossom."

The act of emergence in mythological and personal transformations represents a crucial turning point: it is the moment of rebirth and revelation, where the changes that have occurred within the dark become visible and impactful in the external world.

Psychologically, emergence can be likened to the process of coming into a new understanding of ourselves. This is often accompanied by a renewed vision or a transformation in how one perceives and interacts with the world around them. The emergence is both a literal and metaphorical stepping into the light – a newfound clarity and a stronger, more integrated sense of self.

The challenges of reintegration are part of the emergence. When we emerge from our metaphorical underworld, we find that inner changes necessitate a re-evaluation of our relationships, careers, and beliefs. We don't necessarily leave them all behind, but we must learn to relate to them as our new selves because we are no longer who we once were. This phase can be disorienting, as the familiar patterns no longer fit the transformed self. Much like a butterfly learning to fly we must adapt to our new form.

AWAKENING MORE DEEPLY TO THE MAGIC OF THIS WORLD

"Do whatever brings you to life, then. Follow your own fascinations, obsessions, and compulsions. Trust them. Create whatever causes a revolution in your heart." — Elizabeth Gilbert, *Big Magic: Creative Living Beyond Fear*

As I finished writing the first draft of this book, I began to notice the magic in everything, even things that previously seemed boring or artificial. I started to see, more and more, the mystery lurking within the seemingly mundane. I recognised that much of what we dismiss, overlook, ignore, take for granted, or even complain about in this world is actually magic. Most of it, accidental. I was standing in a supermarket, of all places, looking at a new beverage – a non-alcoholic cocktail with antioxidant herbs, designed to lift the mood in a healthier way. *A potion...*I realised, then I looked around at the rows of wine bottles...*All potions.* Our ancestors who knew no separation of magic from science would have recognised almost every beverage here as a potion – all containing mood or energy or health enhancing ingredients like alcohol, caffeine, or vitamins. Were they wrong? I don't think so. The magic has simply been stripped out of the dominant perspectives of this world in an attempt to gain control of the mystery, yet there is always more mystery.

The demystification of the world in Western civilisation seems to have come from the rude awakening people experienced when they discovered we weren't the centre of the universe, and perhaps this came with a huge sense of betrayal. We were so humiliated to be misled about our place in the cosmos that we began to break everything down – to try to understand and therefore control everything. But this is an impossible feat, and though we have learnt a lot, we have also lost a lot. Now, more than ever, there is a thirst for the magic and the mystery to come back in.

Welcome to the re-mystification of the world – a movement that seeks to reconnect and rediscover the inherent mystery in all. This is not a retreat to some glorified past, but a reclamation of the complex, rich, deep, and powerful meanings that the attachment to certainty has stripped away in its fear of the unknown. Yet at some deep level, we feel it, we need the unknown and we also understand there is no real certainty. Here, as witches, we can hold the ambiguity, the power of the void. We have the power to see that within the mundane is actually the magical. We recognise that the stories we live by are actually the potent spells they've always been. This isn't a call to abandon science or the rational gains of the Enlightenment, but rather an invitation to see the world with fresh eyes, to acknowledge that for all our dissection of reality, we've lost something vital along the way.

In an extremely religious way, the free market is often portrayed as an invisible hand, a benign force guiding us toward prosperity and efficiency. But isn't this hand a deity in disguise, one that demands offerings of time, energy, and often ethics, in exchange for the promise of growth and success? The language of advertising casts spells of delusion to influence desire, convincing us that happiness lies just one purchase away. They aren't really selling cars and fancy watches and processed food items, they're selling the dream of freedom, luxury, power, or joy, none of which will necessarily come from anything we can buy. In ancient times, without all that noise, the voices of nature, of gods or spirits and our own intuition, would have been far easier to hear.

Individualism is a story we tell ourselves – a tale of self-reliance and personal destiny. But scratch the surface, and you find a familiar archetype: the hero's journey. We are all protagonists in our own epic sagas, striving against the odds, seeking meaning and fulfilment. Yet, this relentless focus on the self has its shadow side, breeding isolation and disconnection in a world that increasingly prizes the individual over the collective. In holistic and sustainable cultures, the community is sacred; the web of relationships that connect people is a source of strength and identity. The mainstream has traded this for a mythology that often leaves us alone, even as we're surrounded by others.

So where does this leave us? Are we to resign ourselves to a world drained of its magic, where the only mysteries left are those we haven't yet solved? Or is it possible to reclaim the sense of wonder that our ancestors knew, to see the mystical in the mundane, to weave new myths that honour both the rational and the magical?

We can return to our roots and honour the land on which we live and the indigenous peoples who have been deeply connected to it, respecting their wisdom and traditions. We can look to our own ancestry, to the traditions that helped people to thrive before imperialism, colonisation, and corporatism disrupted everything, and we can listen to our intuition about how to make a nourishing meal of all that we learn.

We can use this mystical lens to see the magic in the forests and oceans, the deserts and mountains, but not only that, we can also see it in the skyscrapers that rise like modern-day ziggurats, temples to the gods of commerce and industry. We can see when the people around us are caught up in the spells of daily life and we can see that beneath the surface, something else is stirring. The streetlights flicker on as dusk falls, not just with electricity, but with a soft, golden light that feels like it's holding back the darkness. The buses and trains carry more than just passengers – they are vessels on a journey, each commuter a traveller on their own quest.

When we see the magic in things, we are released from the spells they may once have held over us and therefore we develop in our own power. Politics is rife with myth and magic. The speeches of leaders are incantations, meant to inspire, to persuade, to summon the collective will of the people.

In ancient times, these decisions might have been guided by the stars or the will of the gods; today, they are influenced by polls, pundits, and the tides of public opinion, but the underlying dynamics remain eerily similar. What does it take to tilt the tide towards more wellbeing? Why do we keep pendulating backwards? What shadows are we collectively integrating here and how can we move the process along so that less harm is done? So that we can hold space for more goodness?

As children we intuitively understood the magic of books and films – the spell a story can cast in our minds, connecting deeply with us, the excitement and enchantment of the movie theatre with its wall-to-wall carpeting and dim lighting and the scent of popcorn. We were there to be enthralled. Hollywood openly speaks of the "magic of the silver screen," hinting at the spell movies cast over us, transporting us to other worlds, allowing us to live out our fantasies and confront our deepest fears. Books are mere words on a page that conjure entire universes in the mind of the reader. Every time we open a book or watch a film, we are participating in a ritual, one that connects us to the ancient tradition of storytelling, where myths were passed down from generation to generation, shaping the way we see the world. Perhaps the reason some people are drawn to horror in games, films, and books is a deeper desire to confront and integrate the shadow, though whether they reach that level of alchemy is anyone's guess.

What would happen if we, as a society, began to see these modern rituals for what they truly are – not just mundane, everyday actions, but deeply magical processes that shape our lives in profound ways? What if we recognised that every culture, including our own, lives by mythos, and while powerful, these are not the only stories we can tell? In doing this we would be working with the great paradox of the "real" and "mystical" and noticing the way the two bleed into each other – noticing how within anything we can know as reality lurks mysteries unfathomable even by advanced scientific methods, and within mystery there is delusion that can be grounded by research, rationality, and healthy scepticism. Remember the questions:

Does it feel intuitively true?

Is it useful for me to believe this?

Is it consistent with what is known, including through traditional and indigenous knowledge systems?

The magic is all around us, woven into the fabric of everyday life. It's in the stories we tell, the rituals we perform, the choices we make. And once we start to see it, we may find that life has never been more enchanting. In awakening deeper to magic, you may wish to revisit the idea of initiation presented early in this book. Is it time to initiate or reinitiate yourself on your path? What is it you want to dedicate yourself to?

Creativity is powerful magic, and we don't have to engage in traditional artforms to be creative, we are always creating the stories of our lives, whether consciously or not. If you're interested in more deeply exploring the power of creativity, I highly recommend Elizabeth Gilbert's book, Big Magic. It's one of my favourites!

Take note of the many forms of powerful magic in our everyday lives. The forces of magic hidden in plain sight are those currents of experience and perception that shape reality without demanding attention. They work like gravity – unseen but inescapable, shaping the contours of our lives and pulling us into moments of transformation. Some of the most potent include:

Curiosity – The restless hunger that pries open doors, stirs the air, and sets things in motion. The seeker's instinct, the call of the unknown. Curiosity is the wick that catches the first spark.

Inspiration – That sudden gust of knowing, a whisper from the unseen, the breath of something greater moving through. It is the bridge between possibility and action, between the void and creation.

Empathy – The ability to feel beyond the self, to dissolve barriers between one thing and another. It is the thread that weaves connection, allowing magic to ripple outward.

Grief – The force that cracks open the soul, hollowing space for something new to enter. The alchemical burning of what was, making way for what could be.

Wonder – The state of being that unlocks perception beyond logic, letting the world shimmer with possibility. A mind touched by wonder sees what others dismiss.

Longing – A magic of absence, of the space between. Longing is a tether to something unseen but deeply felt, pulling the soul toward unknown destinations.

Memory – A spell cast backward in time, shaping the present by what is recalled, misremembered, or rewritten.

Attention – The act of truly seeing is a spell in itself, bringing things into sharper reality. What is observed, grows.

Surrender – The paradox of power: that which is let go of, flows. Surrender bends the river's course, allowing the unseen forces to take shape.

Desire/Fear – Twin poles of the same magnetic pull, creating tension, movement, and transformation. Desire is the draw toward something; fear is the force that resists, yet together they create the friction that births power.

Passion/Rage – The fire of movement, intensity, and devotion. Passion fuels creation, but when obstructed, it ignites into rage, a force that burns through stagnation. Rage is passion that has been thwarted, but both demand expression, both crack open reality.

Anxiety/Excitement – The quickened pulse, the electric hum of anticipation. They are indistinguishable in the body, separated only by perspective. Anxiety is excitement unclaimed, potential feared rather than welcomed. Both sharpen the senses, preparing for action.

Frustration/Hunger – The ache of something just out of reach, the gnawing drive that will not let you rest. Frustration is the friction of unmet desire, but hunger is what turns that friction into movement. Together, they create propulsion, ensuring that stagnation cannot hold.

These forces are not separate – they weave together, feeding and counterbalancing each other, forming the underlying currents of magic in every life. These forces are spells waiting to be cast, fuels waiting for a direction. They demand attention. They demand transmutation. And in that process, magic happens.

Before I end this book, I want to return to the darkness one more time, because within it there is so much wisdom to be gleaned. We all have times in our lives that feel flat, despondent, dark, and broody. Sometimes agonisingly painful, we will have times when we want to hide beneath the covers. Rather than fighting those times, sometimes it pays to just be as present as we possibly can with whatever we're feeling. When we get into the full fulfilment and realisation of whatever it is we're going through, we are most open and receptive to something new, to change, to the sprouting of a new seed that grows into a new experience of reality in our lives.

When we've had enough of the sensations that we've experienced in that dull, flat, swampy downtime, in that agonising, in that repeated pattern of not-enoughness or wondering why isn't anything working or why things are so hard, in the going around in circles of it all, when we come back to presence, when we allow ourselves to be here, now, fully in the sacred space that is always within us, that is where we find the spark.

Sometimes it takes a while. Sometimes we need distractions. Sometimes we need to chase our tail, go around in circles, rail against the world, or wonder over and over again why other people aren't doing the things we want them to do. Sometimes we need to kick and scream or just hammer against our own frustration for a while, and we can accept that too. Because acceptance is one of the most powerful tools anyone, including a witch, can have.

From a state of more and more acceptance, as new sensations arise and we breathe acceptance into those too, we feel where the tension is in the body. We put our hands on our chest or belly, the cauldrons of wisdom, accepting all the past that has brought us to where we are in this moment and accepting more fully our presence. That's where the magic happens.

This way, we find in the ashes of our past life, the ashes of what we no longer need, of what has burned through. As we rise from those ashes like a phoenix, we truly find our fun again, our joie de vivre, our playful curiosity and inspiration. That is where creativity can rise up again in us, through us, looking for a new way to come out into the world and express itself. That is where we find spirit in connection with life and the hope for the new dawn. There it is, within yourself. You now have this wonderful new potential to accept, allow, receive, and find deep and beautiful connection.

INITIATION RITUAL

"The purpose of ritual is to wake up the old mind in us, to put it to work. The old ones inside us, the collective unconscious, the many lives, the different eternal parts, the senses and parts of the brain that have been ignored. Those parts do not speak English. They do not care about television. But they do understand candlelight and colours. They do understand nature."

— Z. Budapest

. . .

Embarking on the path of witchcraft is a deeply personal journey, one that requires dedication, introspection, and a willingness to embrace the mysteries of life. Self-initiation is a powerful way to mark the beginning of this journey, or to signify a new chapter in your ongoing exploration of the craft. It is a deliberate step towards empowerment, a commitment to yourself and your own unique path.

Before you begin your initiation ritual, take some time to reflect on your intentions and the aspects of your practice you wish to focus on. You may choose to read through this entire book first, gathering knowledge and insights to guide your initiation. Or, you may feel ready to take this step now, trusting your intuition to lead you forward. If you've been walking the witchy path for some time, this ritual can also serve as a re-initiation, marking a new stage in your journey.

Consider the four elements and any deities or ancestors you feel drawn to work with in your initiation. In this ritual, a veil is used as a symbol of new beginnings, and the peeling back of illusion to reveal deeper understanding. Feel free to adapt this symbol to suit your needs and preferences.

This is alignment magic – a ritual to open a new door in your life, to set a direction for your magical practice and your journey into the mysteries of existence.

Preparations

1. Select a time for your ritual when you won't be disturbed, preferably during a new moon or a time that feels significant to you. You may wish to be indoors or to find a secluded natural setting that resonates with your spirit, such as a forest clearing, a riverside, a beach, or a garden. Choose a time of day that makes the most sense and feels right for you.

2. Gather items:

- A veil or piece of fabric to cover your head
- Candle and matches or lighter
- Representations of the four elements (e.g., a stone for earth, feather for air, candle for fire, bowl of water)
- Altar decorations that reflect the aspects you wish to include in your initiation
- A small cup of water, juice, tea, mead, or wine

- A piece of chocolate or some other food you find grounding and magical

- A skin-safe oil blend or salted water for anointing

3. Arrange your items on your altar, creating a space that reflects your intentions and the energies you wish to invoke.

The working

4. Create your sacred space by casting a circle, as described earlier in this book.

5. Light the candle on your altar, focusing on the flame as a symbol of your dedication, your inspiration, passion, and the light of wisdom.

6. Call upon the elements and any deities you wish to work with, asking for their presence, guidance, and blessing in your initiation.

7. Place the veil over your head, symbolising your willingness to enter the mysteries and be reborn into your magical path. Cocooned here, you are safe, and in that safety you allow yourself to open up to new transformation.

8. Breathe slowly, deeply, and open to your inner self: Take a few moments to breathe deeply and connect in. Be open to any messages or insights that may come through.

9. Speak your intention: Address your soul and/or the deities you've invoked. Share your heartfelt intention for this initiation. You may choose to write this down beforehand or speak from your heart in the moment. Affirm your readiness and willingness to embark on the next stage of your journey.

10. When you are ready, slowly remove the cloak, symbolically emerging from the darkness. As you lift the cloak, imagine yourself rising like a phoenix, renewed and reborn. Feel the transformation within as you step back into the light, now carrying the wisdom and insights from the depths of your being.

11. Take a sip of your chosen drink and eat the piece of chocolate, offering appreciation to the divine forces you've invoked and to your own journey.

12. Dip your finger in the oil or salt water and anoint your forehead, sealing your initiation and commitment.

13. Close the ritual: Express your appreciation to the elements, deities,

and your own soul for their presence and support. Release them, knowing that they will continue to guide you on your path. Close your circle and extinguish the candle.

THE JOURNEY OF ETERNAL BECOMING

I invite you to take a moment to reflect on your own journey of magical awakening.

Where are you now, in this moment?

What has brought you to this path, to this place of seeking and discovery?

Know that wherever you are, it is exactly where you need to be. Trust that every step, every stumble, every seeming detour has been a part of your perfect unfolding, your soul's sacred journey through the spiralling cycles of growth and transformation.

As the wise woman and magical teacher Starhawk wrote about in her well-loved book, *The Spiral Dance*, this unfolding and reconnecting is the essence of the witch's journey:

"The spiral dance is the dance of life, of death and rebirth, the dance of the waxing and waning moon, the dance of the changing seasons. It is the dance that reconnects us to the rhythms of the earth and the rhythms of our own bodies. It is the dance that teaches us to move in harmony with the great cycles of nature, to flow with the currents of change, to embrace the darkness as well as the light."

It is a journey of eternal becoming, of shedding the old and birthing the new, of dying who we thought we were in order to be reborn into our fullest, most authentic selves, and then doing it all over again! Like the serpent shedding its skin, like the butterfly emerging from the chrysalis, we too must undergo these transformations, these initiations, in order to grow, heal, and become more essentially ourselves.

These journeys require great courage, compassion, and trust in ourselves and in the unfolding of our own unique path.

As we embrace this journey of transformation, it is important to remember that we are not doing it alone. We are part of a vast web of magical practitioners and seekers, stretching back through time and across cultures, all working to weave a new world into being. We are the leaves on the great tree of magic, nourished by the same roots, reaching for the same light.

Our ancient ancestors forged their lives in tune with the natural world around them. We carry their wisdom, their power, and their resilience in our blood and bones. Their magic lives on in us, like seeds dormant in the soil, waiting for the right conditions to sprout and grow.

And as we step deeper into our magic, as we claim our place in this ancient and eternal lineage, we become a beacon of light for others on the path. Know that in your brave journey, you are a part of something so much greater than yourself. Know that your magic, your unique gifts and talents and passions, are needed in this world, now more than ever.

May you trust the unfolding of your own sacred journey. May you find the courage to face your shadows, to embrace your light, your own becoming.

Go forth and create your magic, weave your spells and your rituals, no matter how big or small, regardless of whether you do this alone or with friends. Know that the power is within you, as it always has been, if only you dare take the risk to step into it and awaken the wild witch inside. Be bold, my dear, and go bravely into futures where you live magically, wherever your path takes you.

Blessed be

Iris xx

EXTRA GOODIES

The following additional resources are available to download through my website: www.irisbeaglehole.com/resources

My short course on the Four Elements - I've created a course for delving deeper into understanding and experiencing the four elements, and working with them in your life. Use the discount code **"magic"** for free access!

The Coven Guide - a practical guide to building community and setting up local casual witchy groups and covens

Astrology detailed tables - for a run-down of each planet in each sign so you can interpret your chart and others

OTHER RESOURCES

OBOD – The Order of Bards, Ovates & Druids
Druidic group, Celtic spirituality, nature-based ritual, and personal development.
https://druidry.org

Pamela Meekings Stewart – *Living Treefully*
For more information on Pamela's book and tool.
https://www.livingtreefully.com/the-book

BOOKS

Clarissa Pinkola Estés – *Women Who Run With the Wolves*

Elizabeth Gilbert – *Big Magic: Creative Living Beyond Fear*

Carl Jung – *Memories, Dreams, Reflections*

Starhawk – *The Spiral Dance*

Richard Tarnas – *Cosmos and Psyche: Intimations of a New World View*

Carolyn Elliott – *Existential Kink: Unmask Your Shadow and Embrace Your Power*

Liz Greene – *Saturn: A New Look at an Old Devil*

Kasia Urbaniak – *Unbound: A Woman's Guide to Power*

Michael Newton – *Journey of Souls: Case Studies of Life Between Lives*

Robin Wall Kimmerer – *Braiding Sweetgrass*

Scott Cunningham – *The Magic of Food: Legends, Lore & Spellwork.*

DEDICATION AND ACKNOWLEDGEMENTS

I wrote this book for my younger self who felt so much pain and sought out the wisdom wherever she could find it. I wrote this book for all of you who are on a similar journey of finding your own path.

A special thank you to Chantal Cropp who has walked this path with me, and to both you and Talia Marshall who have given wonderfully helpful feedback through the journey of this book. Your wise and witty reflections have been like lights in the darkness of this mysterious voyage.

I want to acknowledge the wise and strong people in my life, the women in my family, my mother, aunts, grandmothers, and great grand-mothers who have all set powerful examples in my life. I also want to acknowledge my father and grandfathers who forged their own paths and lived their own truths, and my siblings, though we spent much of our childhoods in struggle, our pain and learning and hope are intertwined. Thank you to Tesla for always keeping me on my toes. Thank you to my good friends who have been beacons for me over the years, Ruth and Holly, Lucy, Laura and Errol, Astrid, Nikki, Paul, Steffi and Lisa, Billy, Jason. Deepest thanks to my druid family, the Grove of the Summer stars, and especially to the wise women who have been my guides, Fiona and Pamela Meekings-Stewart.

Thank you for coming with me on this journey, wherever you are in your life.

Many blessings,
Iris xx

ABOUT THE AUTHOR

Iris Beaglehole is a witch, druid and writer, based in New Zealand. She has been learning about magic all her life, and has been a witch for over twenty-five years. She has completed a PhD in the social sciences and studied many healing modalities. Iris has written over 20 magical novels which all draw on her passion for deep inner work and real magic including the popular Myrtlewood Mysteries and Myrtlewood Crones series.